Inequality, Crime, and Social Control

CRIME & SOCIETY

Series Editor
John Hagan, University of Toronto

EDITORIAL ADVISORY BOARD
John Braithwaite, Robert J. Bursik,
Kathleen Daly, Malcolm M. Feeley, Jack Katz,
Martha A. Myers, Robert J. Sampson,
and Wesley G. Skogan

Inequality, Crime, and Social Control, *edited by George S. Bridges and Martha A. Myers*

Alternatives to Imprisonment: Intentions and Reality, *Ulla V. Bondeson*

FORTHCOMING

Criminological Controversies, *John Hagan, A. R. Gillis, and David Brownfield*

Great Pretenders: A Study of Property Offenders, *Neal Shover*

Poverty, Ethnicity, and Violent Crime, *James F. Short*

Crime, Justice, and Public Opinion, *Julian Roberts and Loretta Stalens*

Crime, Justice, and Revolution in Eastern Europe, *Joachim J. Savelsberg*

Inequality, Crime, and Social Control

edited by
George S. Bridges
and Martha A. Myers

Westview Press
BOULDER • SAN FRANCISCO • OXFORD

To our mothers,
Helen C. Bridges and
Irene M. Myers

Crime & Society

All rights reserved. No part of this publication may be reproduced or transmitted in any form or by any means, electronic or mechanical, including photocopy, recording, or any information storage and retrieval system, without permission in writing from the publisher.

Copyright © 1994 by Westview Press, Inc.

Published in 1994 in the United States of America by Westview Press, Inc., 5500 Central Avenue, Boulder, Colorado 80301-2877, and in the United Kingdom by Westview Press, 36 Lonsdale Road, Summertown, Oxford OX2 7EW

Library of Congress Cataloging-in-Publication Data
Inequality, crime, and social control / [edited by] George S. Bridges and Martha A. Myers.
  p. cm.—(Crime & society)
Includes bibliographical references and index.
ISBN 0-8133-2004-6 (hard).—ISBN 0-8133-2005-4 (pbk.)
  1. Social control—Congresses. 2. Crime—Congresses.
3. Equality—Congresses. I. Bridges, George S. II. Myers, Martha A. III. Series: Crime & society (Boulder, Colo.)
HM291.I54 1994
303.3'3—dc20   93-38208
                                                                                                      CIP

Printed and bound in the United States of America

The paper used in this publication meets the requirements of the American National Standard for Permanence of Paper for Printed Library Materials Z39.48-1984.

10   9   8   7   6   5   4   3   2

Contents

List of Tables and Figures ix
Preface xi

PART ONE
Introduction

1 Problems and Prospects in the Study of Inequality, Crime, and Social Control, *George S. Bridges and Martha A. Myers*   3

PART TWO
Directions for Theory

2 The Theoretical Bases for Inequality in Formal Social Control, *Charles R. Tittle*   21

3 Modeling the Conflict Perspective of Social Control, *Allen E. Liska*   53

4 Rethinking and Unthinking "Social Control," *Anthony M. Platt*   72

5 The Police: Symbolic Capital, Class, and Control, *Peter K. Manning*   80

PART THREE
Dimensions of Inequality

6 Ethnicity: The Forgotten Dimension of American Social Control, *Darnell F. Hawkins*   99

7 Gender and Punishment Disparity, *Kathleen Daly*   117

8   Gender, Class, Racism, and Criminal Justice:
    Against Global and Gender-Centric Theories,
    For Poststructuralist Perspectives, *Pat Carlen* — 134

PART FOUR
Linkages Among Forms of Social Control

9   Labor Markets and the Relationships Among Forms of
    the Criminal Sanction, *James Inverarity* — 147

10 Gender, Race, and Social Control: Toward an
    Understanding of Sex Disparities in Imprisonment,
    George S. Bridges and Gina Beretta — 158

11 Lethal Social Control in the South: Lynchings and
    Executions Between 1880 and 1930, *Stewart E. Tolnay
    and E. M. Beck* — 176

12 Double Jeopardy: The Abuse and Punishment of Homeless
    Youth, *John Hagan and Bill McCarthy* — 195

PART FIVE
Human Agency

13 Eugenics, Class, and the Professionalization of
    Social Control, *Nicole Hahn Rafter* — 215

14 Children in the Therapeutic State: Lessons for the
    Sociology of Deviance and Social Control,
    John R. Sutton — 227

15 Crime and the Social Control of Blacks: Offender/Victim
    Race and the Sentencing of Violent Offenders,
    Cassia Spohn — 249

16 The Symbolic Punishment of White-Collar Offenders,
    Celesta A. Albonetti — 269

References — 283
About the Book — 323
About the Editors and Contributors — 325
Index — 327

Tables and Figures

Tables

10.1	Determinants of imprisonment rates, by gender	170
10.2	Determinants of imprisonment rates, by race and gender	172
11.1	Time-series regressions of number of black lynch victims, 1883–1930	184
11.2	Poisson regressions of number of black lynch victims, Deep South states, by decade	188
11.3	Poisson regressions of number of black lynch victims, Border South states, by decade	189
12.1	Coding and descriptive statistics for variables, by type of youth	204
15.1	Coding and descriptive statistics for variables	257
15.2	The effects of offender/victim race on sentence	258
15.3	The effects of offender/victim race on prison sentence, by type of crime and offender-victim relationship	260
15.4	The effects of offender/victim race on expected minimum sentence, by type of crime and offender-victim relationship	263
16.1	Coding and descriptive statistics for variables	274
16.2	Logistic estimates and odds predicting a suspended sentence	276
16.3	Logistic estimates and odds predicting a suspended sentence, by offense complexity	278

Figures

3.1 Modeling inconsistent causal processes 65
3.2 Modeling the causal structure underlying the conflict perspective 70

12.1 Revised model with standardized effects 207

Preface

In April 1992, twenty scholars met at the University of Georgia to discuss inequality, crime, and social control in society. Sponsored by the University of Georgia and the American Sociological Association, the meeting was designed to stimulate significant developments in theory and research. This edited volume is a compendium of papers developed from the meeting.

The meeting was held for three days at the Georgia Center for Continuing Education, with morning and afternoon sessions of three to four presenters. The sessions combined presentations and discussion periods into a working session format. Each session, focusing on a current concern in the field, addressed the linkages between inequality, crime, and social control. Opening sessions examined theoretical perspectives on inequality, crime, and social control. They were followed by sessions dealing with conceptual and organizational perspectives on class, race, ethnicity, and gender. The organization of this book emerged from critical issues, discussed in Chapter 1, that arose during the presentations and subsequent discussions.

We are indebted to the office of the vice president for academic affairs at the University of Georgia and to the American Sociological Association, whose grants enabled us to bring together distinguished scholars from North America and Europe. We also wish to thank the Departments of Sociology at the University of Georgia and the University of Washington for providing additional help in organizing the meeting and publishing this book. We are especially grateful for the encouragement and support given us by the chairs of our departments, Gary Alan Fine (University of Georgia) and Herbert L. Costner (University of Washington).

George S. Bridges
Martha A. Myers

PART ONE

Introduction

1

Problems and Prospects in the Study of Inequality, Crime, and Social Control

George S. Bridges and Martha A. Myers

Despite decades of social science research, the relationships among inequality, crime, and social control are poorly understood. Theorists from the disciplines of sociology, political science, and law agree that the mechanisms our society uses to control crime help preserve economic, political, and social order. Theorists disagree, however, in their assessment of whether and how inequality influences the use of these controls. Some theorists reason that formal social controls, primarily criminal law and the administration of criminal justice, are reactive: society punishes and controls individuals and groups commensurate with the importance of the norms they violate. The intellectual roots of this perspective extend to the ideas of Durkheim describing punishment as a "passionate reaction of graduated intensity that society exercises through the medium of a body acting upon those of its members who have violated certain rules of conduct" (Durkheim 1947: 96).

For these theorists, social control and punishment are little more than responses to crime and deviance. Inequality in society influences control and punishment indirectly, by creating conditions such as poverty or economic disadvantage in which criminality flourishes (Blumstein and Cohen 1973; Black 1976; Blumstein 1982; Langan 1985).

In contrast, other theorists assert that social control is often imposed as a direct function of inequality. Some adopt a Marxian perspective, arguing, for example, that the state and its agents impose social control disproportionately on poor and disadvantaged persons in an attempt to regulate and minimize their burden on society as a whole (Rusche and Kirchheimer 1939; Turk 1969a; Spitzer 1975, 1981; Cain and Hunt 1982). Reasoning that such groups are alienated and impoverished, these theorists maintain that the groups pose a significant threat of violence and of political mobilization against the state. According to Spitzer, the groups are "problem populations." And as societies shift toward capitalistic economies ruled by a small number of economic elites, "the implications for deviance production become twofold: (1) problem populations become gradually more problematic—both in their size and insensitivity to economic controls, and (2) the resources of the state need to be applied in greater proportion to protect capitalist relations of production" (Spitzer 1975: 647). In this same vein, oppressed racial minorities may be especially threatening to the political hegemony of whites. Thus, the legal process is used selectively in areas characterized by extreme racial inequality to control and incapacitate the most volatile segments of the minority population (Adamson 1984; Bridges and Crutchfield 1988). Courts and other control agencies, as arms of the state, promote and protect the interests of those with high political and economic standing by enforcing selectively laws and other norms that foster political and economic stability in society.

Neither the Durkheimian nor the Marxian perspectives, however, have escaped serious criticism and challenge. Critics of the former assert that Durkheimian studies of punishment are often predicated on unrealistic assumptions and tautological reasoning: that there exists within any modern society a "conscience collective"—a unitary moral order—and that punishments imposed by the society accurately reflect the values embodied in that order (see, for example, Garland and Young 1983). Critics of Marxian writing and research are no less charitable. They argue that Marxian or "conflict" studies typically reify the state as an instrument of economic and political elites and often ignore the collective moral bases of punishments and social controls (Ignatieff 1981; Garland and Young 1983; Young 1983; Garland 1990).

In recent years, these contrasting positions have led social scientists to grapple with at least four issues. The first is whether sociologists can reconcile theoretical perspectives on inequality, crime and social control. While debate over the role of inequality is often "mired in a swamp of 'either-or' arguments" (Bridges et al. 1987: 356), some scholars call for the integration of competing theoretical perspectives (Liska et al. 1989; Tittle 1989).

Proponents of theoretical integration in the study of crime (e.g., Liska et al. 1989) argue that sociologists must establish more effectively the linkages among different arguments that are common across theories of crime and social control. Scholars generally opposed to integration call instead for greater elaboration and specification of existing theories (Farnworth 1989; Hirschi 1989; Platt in this volume). Arguing that some theories are predicated upon fundamentally different underlying assumptions, these scholars assert that integration is an "unlikely solution to the 'crisis'" of reconciling competing theoretical perspectives and that knowledge about crime and its control will advance only if existing theories are extended as far as possible (Hirschi 1989).

A second issue involves the conceptualization of inequality in theory and research. Sociologists concerned with crime and its control have, at least historically, directed most of the attention on inequality to very few categories of subjugated persons or groups—primarily racial minorities and members of the lowest social class. For example, studies of inequality in the imposition of criminal punishments in the United States have focused almost entirely on racial differences in sentencing and on whether persons of color accused of crimes receive more severe penalties than comparable whites (see, e.g., Kleck 1981; Kempf and Austin 1989). Some scholars argue that sociologists have completely elided other, equally important dimensions of inequality such as ethnicity and gender. Very little writing, for example, has described or thoroughly documented differences among white ethnic groups or between men and women in the imposition of social controls. This elision has restricted the development and specification of theory, and the result has been a distorted treatment of control and punishment. In the preface to her history of women's prisons, Rafter recognizes this limitation in previous writing: "In recent years, historical research on crime and social control has grown rapidly and become an important field of inquiry in both the United States and Western Europe. Yet most of the new work ignores female criminals. . . . By paying little attention to institutions for women and girls, even recent prison histories present a skewed picture of the evolution and nature of incarceration" (Rafter 1985: xiii).

A related concern is that theories are based upon erroneous assumptions about the causal relationships between inequality, crime and social control. Most sociological theories offer monolithic explanations of control, assuming that dimensions of inequality such as race or class influence the forms and levels of control in manners that are unidirectional and consistent, regardless of the contexts or historical periods in which they occur. Donald Black's (1976) treatment of social stratification and law is illustrative. Arguing that social control varies with the quantity or level of stratification, Black (1976: 23) suggests that the law-stratification relationship is invariant across time and context: "To one degree or another, the same principle applies everywhere. It might be added that a judge or other official higher in rank than a litigant is less likely to find merit in his case. In a trial by jury, a party to a case has a disadvantage if the jury members are wealthier than he, but an advantage if they are beneath him. *At every stage, in every legal setting, a downward case is stronger than an upward case*" (emphasis added).

In contrast, many recent studies document the importance of historical periods and contexts in explaining variation in social controls

(Peterson and Hagan 1984; Myers and Talarico 1987; Myers 1990; Tolnay and Beck 1994). Their findings underscore the need to develop theories that accommodate and explain regional and temporal differences in the effects of inequality.

The third issue sociologists must examine is whether there exist important relationships among different forms of social control. Despite longstanding theoretical interest in these relationships (Durkheim 1947, 1978; Foucault 1977; Garland 1990), researchers have restricted empirical studies to examining one or two types of sanctions. Over the past two decades, for example, sociologists have restricted most of their research on social control to studies of criminal sentencing and imprisonment. While this emphasis has advanced knowledge about these particular types of sanctions, relationships among these and other forms of social control are poorly understood.

There is limited knowledge about relationships among social control mechanisms in at least two important areas. The first is the direction of these relationships. Some sociologists suggest that social controls imposed within society often lie in oppositional (i.e., inverse) relation with each other. Different forms of control may serve as substitutes for each other or may displace each other over time—that is, as one increases in frequency or use, others decrease (Spitzer 1975; Scull 1977, 1979; Black 1980). For example, as hospitalizations for mental illness increase in a particular area or region, imprisonments for crime within the same area may decrease (see Bridges and Beretta in this volume). However, other scholars argue that the imposition of one type of control reinforces or parallels the imposition of another type of control. In this case, controls increase or decrease parallel to or in conjunction with each other in relation to other social forces (Inverarity and Grattet 1989; Massey and Myers 1989; Liska 1992; Arvanites 1992). For example, Arvanites (1992: 148) argues that the linkages between mental health and criminal justice apparatuses of the state enable "them to complement each other in controlling socially unacceptable behavior."

The second area about which we have little knowledge is the mechanisms intervening between forms of control. Though many sociologists agree that forms of control are related, they often disagree about the process by which one form actually influences or is related to another. Some argue that the relationship is direct and that common social forces may influence different forms (Spitzer 1975; Bridges and Beretta, Tolnay and Beck in this volume). Others suggest that forms of social control, though driven by common factors, may be indirectly related through a complex causal sequence separating forms of control (Inverarity and Grattet 1989; Massey and Myers 1989; Liska 1992; Hagan and McCarthy, in this volume). One such possible sequence is through reciprocal causal effects between forms of social control and the threat created by social or economic inequality—that is, where social threat and social control influence each other (Liska, 1992). In this circumstance, Liska (1992: 181) argues that "as one form of social control expands, it reduces social threat, which reduces other forms of social control."

A fourth issue of sociological concern is the matter of "human agency," that is, the ways in which the values and beliefs of individuals and groups are transformed into the policies and practices of controlling institutions. Sociologists generally agree that the policies of institutions such as the police, courts, corrections, and child welfare and mental health agencies reflect the values and ideologies of groups in society. However, the mechanisms by which any one individual's or one group's beliefs and values are transformed into policies and programs of the society's institutions of social control are poorly understood (Turk 1969a, 1969b). Some scholars have examined this issue historically, focusing on the emergence of reformist movements in controlling institutions. For example, numerous studies of child welfare reform in the United States have documented the birth and evolution of the juvenile court (Platt 1969; Sutton 1988, 1990), stressing the important and related roles played by upper-middle-class "child savers" and expanding state governments at the turn of the twentieth century. Typically, these studies conclude that the values shared among reformist groups, in particular, their beliefs about the severity of specific social problems and needed reforms, are translated into law and governmental programs by state agencies or legislatures for the purpose of regulating threatening groups or classes within the larger population. A major limitation of these studies has been their reliance on simplistic assumptions about the relationships among reformist groups, governmental institutions, and other aspects of social structure (Ignatieff 1978, 1981; Rothman 1971, 1983; Sutton, in this volume). Further, relatively few studies have identified how these relationships vary over time and across societies.

Most sociologists, however, have approached the question of human agency quite differently. Over the past three decades, countless studies have examined the values and perceptions of justice officials as they influence inequality in the application of criminal sanctions. Of central interest in these studies is a determination of the relevance of the race, ethnicity, gender, and social class of the accused. For example, some scholars assert that racial differences in punishment are consequences, in part, of race itself. These consequences are variously manifested—as racial prejudice and discrimination by social control agents or as insufficient social and economic resources (e.g., effective counsel) to counter accusations of criminality successfully (Bridges et al. 1987).

More recently, researchers have shifted attention from the status characteristics of the individual to the contexts within which crimes are committed and social controls imposed (Peterson and Hagan 1984; Myers and Talarico 1986, 1987). To what extent does the importance of one's social standing depend on perceptions of justice officials or broader features of the community and the organization of its formal social control agencies? Of crucial significance is the assumption that the relationship between one's social standing and responses to one's behavior shifts significantly over time and space.

Scholars disagree about which contexts are relevant and precisely how or why they are linked with inequality, crime, and social control. Studies of urbanization and punishment, for example, have sought to determine whether courts in rural areas are more discriminatory than courts in urban areas. Some scholars argue that the political and legal cultures of rural areas favor an informal and arbitrary system of justice, in which prejudices and fears about minorities result in more severe treatment (Austin 1981; Hagan 1977a; Myers and Talarico 1987). Other scholars suggest that the informal justice of rural areas may in fact have the opposite effect. To the extent that rural officials are more paternalistic and view minorities as dependent and in greater need of rehabilitation, they may treat minority group members more leniently than whites (Bridges et al. 1987). In contrast, the large caseloads and bureaucratic procedures so characteristic of urban courts may militate against informality and the intrusion of personal prejudices. Race may recede in importance, and racial differences in punishment, if any, are attributable solely to racial differences in criminal behavior (Kleck 1981; Peterson and Hagan 1984; Myers and Talarico 1987).

This book is divided into four sections, which address each of the concerns specified above. Following this introductory first part, Part Two, Directions for Theory, examines the state of sociological theories of crime, inequality and social control, focusing on new directions for theoretical development. Part Three, Dimensions of Inequality, addresses the question of how inequality is conceptualized in theory and research. The fourth part, Linkages Among Forms of Social Control, explores the state of knowledge about relationships among forms of control and whether there exist common patterns in these relationships. The final part, Human Agency, examines how the values and beliefs of individuals and groups are transformed into laws and legal policies that produce inequality in the imposition of social control.

Directions for Theory

Concern over the state of sociological theory prompts the four authors in this section to examine problems and prospects for new developments in theory. The four chapters included in the section adopt quite different approaches in addressing this concern. Two chapters offer systematic overviews of sociological theories that examine the role of inequality in the study of crime and social control. Although both chapters identify important new avenues for the development of theory, one stresses the importance of theoretical integration, while the other calls for the elaboration of existing theories. Both chapters suggest specific directions for future empirical research. Another chapter reviews prospects for new developments in critical theory. It reveals how recent changes in the political order of socialist and communist states have influenced the study of crime and social control. The final chapter examines the ideas of Pierre Bourdieu, a French sociologist whose work has been only recently translated, on the role of symbolic capital in the regulation and control of social problems. The focus of this chapter is the application of Bourdieu's ideas to policing in the United States and whether contemporary policing actually reduces the symbolic capital of the lower class. The chapter uses these ideas as the framework for an innovative theoretical approach to the study of inequality and social control.

Charles Tittle, in "The Theoretical Bases for Inequality in Formal Social Control," argues that inequality in sanctioning and in the imposition of formal social controls is an inherent assumption of major sociological theories of crime and its control. Tittle reasons that among each of the most general theories, inequality in sanctioning is an inevitable result of important social forces. However, theories differ significantly in their explanations of why inequality emerges in sanctioning and how its patterns vary. For example, Tittle maintains that although conflict and consensus theories assume the existence of inequality in the sanctioning of crime and other deviant acts, the theories differ significantly in their explanations of how inequality emerges. Whereas consensus theory reasons that widely shared collective judgments about threats to social and political order give shape to sanctioning policies and practices that are directed at those threats, conflict theory reasons that the judgments of special interest groups and elites dictate which threats the larger society must regulate and sanction. Finally, arguing for theoretical integration, Tittle weaves themes from each of the major theories into a framework for a comprehensive and integrated theory of inequality, crime and social control.

In Chapter 3, "Modeling the Conflict Perspective of Social Control," Allen Liska offers an overview of contemporary theories of social control that, in contrast with Tittle's call for integration, stresses the need for theoretical elaboration of the conflict perspective. Liska asserts that this perspective has dominated all other theoretical perspectives over the past two decades in writing and research on social control. Nevertheless, he argues that contemporary specifications of conflict theory, despite their dominance, are vague and inconsistent. While conflict theory hypothesizes that inequality in the application of social controls is associated with threats to special interest groups and elites, Liska is concerned about ambiguity in the concept of threat. He asks, "What and who are threatening to whom?" Liska claims that conflict theorists have inadequately defined the nature of social threats and insufficiently specified the conditions under which threats translate into social control. His chapter ends with an approach to modeling the conflict perspective that clarifies and extends its logic. Further, the approach offers a framework for empirical inquiry that will facilitate elaboration of the theory.

Anthony Platt in "Rethinking and Unthinking 'Social Control'" offers a departure from the previous two chapters by examining recent changes in critical inquiry on social control. In reviewing major weaknesses in Marxist and conflict writings, he argues that the role of coercive institutions and the rationality of the state in maintaining social order have been overemphasized. For example, Platt stresses that recent work, which has been motivated in part by the political collapse of socialist and communist states, moves beyond the rigid economic determinism of traditional Marxist ideology. He draws from postmodernist and feminist writing to identify new directions for the study of social control. He calls for a multidisciplinary approach to the elaboration and extension of critical theory, the development of "inclusive" theoretical concepts that bridge different dimensions of social control within society, and a heavier reliance on studies of "human agency" to explain the relationships between the agents and subjects of controlling institutions.

The final chapter in Part Two, "The Police: Symbolic Capital, Class and Control" by Peter K. Manning, reviews the work and ideas of Pierre Bourdieu, a French structuralist, in developing a new theoretical framework for analyzing the linkages between inequality, crime and control. Manning's specific interest is the police and this chapter offers an illustrative application of Bourdieu's model to police practices in the United States. The beginning point of the analysis is the gap between knowledge about policing and the role police play in preserving and perpetuating an existing political or social order. A critical concept in Manning's (and Bourdieu's) perspective is symbolic capital, "the knowledge, background, skills and objective material" needed to preserve existing class relations. Manning argues that the police, like other legal institutions, protect the symbolic capital of the middle and upper classes by enforcing laws in ways that degrade and diminish the legal and social status of the working class. He also suggests that the ideology of contemporary law enforcement—egalitarian, neutral and objective—actually mystifies police practices to the working class and other subjugated groups.

Dimensions of Inequality

Too often sociologists have ignored dimensions of inequality that influence crime and its control. The three chapters included in Part Three examine problematic aspects of previous writing on inequality, focusing on race, gender and class. The authors discuss these different dimensions of inequality and suggest prospects for new developments in theory. One chapter offers a review of writing on race and ethnicity, suggesting that scholars have overlooked important ethnic differences in crime and its control. It offers new directions for both theory and research on ethnicity and social control. A second chapter examines the issue of gender, arguing that the methods used by sociologists and other social scientists to study gender differences in crime and social control often are insensitive to important qualitative differences in crimes and in the handling of individual cases by courts. The emphasis of this chapter is as much methodological as theoretical, and the call is for developing new methodological approaches to the study of gender inequality in writing and research on social control. The final chapter focuses primarily on the state of gender in "global" theories of social control, suggesting that these theories offer inadequate accounts of actual gender differences in punishment. By stressing the primacy of structural factors, most sociological theories ignore the role of social contexts and historical periods in the imposition of social controls. This chapter argues that poststructural theories, by according importance to the varied meaning of "gender" and other aspects of inequality across historical periods and social contexts, offer more useful explanations of social control.

Darnell Hawkins, in "Ethnicity: The Forgotten Dimension of American Social Control," examines the interconnections of race, ethnicity, crime and social control in American sociology. He argues that sociologists, preoccupied with the treatment of African-Americans in the southern United States, have ignored important ethnic cleavages among European Americans. And by ignoring these cleavages and their effects on crime and social control, scholars have become invested in race as a fundamental dimension of inequality in society. According to Hawkins, sociological theories of crime and social control have suffered; they may incorrectly specify the relationships between ethnicity, crime and social control. Hawkins argues for the development of theory and conceptualizations of social control that adequately explain differences in the control of ethnic subordinates/minorities in modern heterogeneous societies. To this end, he offers a series of questions and propositions linking ethnicity and race to levels of social control in society.

Kathleen Daly, in "Gender and Punishment Disparity," argues that few studies of crime and social control have incorporated or even considered gender as an important dimension of inequality. Of those studies that examine gender, most ignore important qualitative differences between men and women in the crimes they commit and how they are punished. Daly asserts that these problems are in part problems of measurement. Most empirical research on punishment misses the connection between (1) traditional legal and extralegal variables in research and (2) narrative and normative accounts of the workings of the legal process. In the case of gender and punishment, Daly reasons that most studies have gone no further than an "add-the-women-and-stir" approach, which implicitly assumes that gender inequality in the legal process is no different than other forms of inequality. Daly argues, quite forcefully, that this assumption is flawed. Drawing from her own empirical studies and the work of feminist scholars, she reasons that gender differences, like racial and ethnic differences, have their own, unique meaning to the legal process that cannot be accurately captured in traditional analyses of punishment disparity.

In "Gender, Class, Racism and Criminal Justice: Against Global and Gender-Centric Theories, For Poststructuralist Perspectives," Pat Carlen reviews dimensions of inequality—gender, class and race—in literature on criminal justice. Her focus, however, is on problematic aspects of theories of criminal justice, particularly "global" theories giving significant weight to the influence of inequality—as reflected in the race, ethnicity, class position and gender of persons processed through criminal justice agencies. Carlen calls for the development of "poststructural" explanations of crime and social control. According to Carlen, these explanations do not deny the importance of inequality in explaining mechanisms of social control. Rather, they recognize that aspects of social structure such as race, class and gender vary significantly in meaning and importance for the study of crime and social control across societies, historical periods and even across individuals. Therefore, Carlen argues against "global" theories of inequality and social control, reasoning that they ignore important variation in the influence of inequality on crime and social controls, across individuals and groups and over time.

Linkages Among Forms of Social Control

Although previous studies have focused limited attention on the linkages among forms of control, the chapters included in this part offer new empirical evidence and directions for research on this subject. The four chapters explore relationships among forms of social control, addressing quite different areas of concern. Three chapters report on empirical studies of whether there exist parallel or oppositional relationships among controls. While one of these observes a parallel relationship between lynchings and executions in the American South, another observes an inverse or oppositional relationship between aggregate levels of hospitalization of the mentally ill and rates of imprisonment. A third chapter points to the reinforcing effects of private sanctioning practices on the likelihood of public sanctioning. Further, two of the four chapters discuss in depth the mechanisms by which one form of social control may be related to another. One of these chapters identifies the concept of "human capital," which may serve as a unifying thread among many of the recent studies of economic production and social control. Another chapter explores how social controls imposed in families may, through a series of unintended consequences, result in the imposition of controls by the state.

James Inverarity, in "Labor Markets and the Relationships Among Forms of the Criminal Sanction," argues that the linkages between forms of social control are poorly understood. Few studies explain or even address major historical changes in these forms, the "transitions" among the types of sanctions imposed for deviant acts. Inverarity focuses on studies of economic production and criminal punishments, identifying two contrasting perspectives in the labor market literature related to transitions in punishment form. At the heart of Inverarity's argument is the idea that while each of the themes finds support in sociological theories of control, the concept of human capital—the size and quality of a society's investment in the labor force—may be particularly useful in reconciling these perspectives and in extending knowledge about economic production and forms of social control. According to Inverarity, "criminal sanction attenuates in form and duration as human capital increases." Further, group differences in sanctioning—for example, differential levels of punishment between racial or ethnic groups—may be linked to their differential positions in the labor force.

In Chapter 10, "Gender, Race and Social Control: Toward an Understanding of Sex Disparities in Imprisonment," George Bridges and Gina Beretta examine the pronounced disparities between men and women in punishment for crimes, contrasting different theoretical explanations of why these disparities occur. They also present the results of an empirical study of disparity, focusing on the influence of structural characteristics of states related to gender differences on state imprisonment rates. Their interpretation of theories argues that aspects of social structure—the laws and legal policies of states, the differential use of hospitalization in mental health facilities, differences in the economic standing of women relative to men, and racial differences among men and women—should assist in explaining disparities. Their empirical analysis reveals, however, that aspects of social structure have no differential effects on rates of imprisonment for men and women. Rather, gender-specific differences in rates of labor force participation and hospitalization for mental illness contribute to the disparities, above and beyond gender differences in involvement for serious and violent crimes. Bridges and Beretta call for revisions in contemporary theories of social control that more clearly specify the linkages between society's application of punishments and the application of other forms of social control.

Stewart Tolnay and E. M. Beck, in "Lethal Social Control in the South: Lynchings and Executions Between 1880 and 1930," contrast two theoretical perspectives on social control in examining the linkages between the mob lynching and legal execution of blacks in the American South. They argue that popular justice and conflict theories offer opposing predictions and explanations of the lynching-execution relationship. Whereas the former views lynchings as a substitute or alternative to executions and predicts an inverse relationship between the two forms over time, the latter views lynchings as a companion form of social control and predicts a positive relationship over time. Tolnay and Beck also present important historical evidence that is more consistent with the conflict interpretation of lynchings and executions. Their analyses reveal the forms of control as companion elements in the southern white community's effort to subjugate and control its black population. The analyses also lend support to the argument that developments in sociological theory are needed to explain the circumstances under which socially or politically dominant groups will use different forms of social control to regulate perceived threats to their social advantage.

John Hagan and Bill McCarthy, in "Double Jeopardy: The Abuse and Punishment of Homeless Youth," describe the linkages between private and public sanctioning, examining the relationship between social controls imposed by the family and those imposed by the state. Sociological perspectives suggest that under some circumstances family controls oppose state-imposed controls and under other circumstances they may actually reinforce controls imposed by the state. The primary focus of their chapter is juveniles and whether private sanctioning in the family increases the likelihood of sanctioning by police, the courts and other public agencies. Drawing from data on Toronto youth, Hagan and McCarthy show that severe family sanctioning in the form of abuse may have the unintended effect of driving children out of the home and actually increasing their involvement in behaviors (i.e., delinquency and homelessness) that elicit public sanction.

Human Agency

Studies of "human agency" examine the processes by which individuals or groups, as representatives of institutions or organizations, perpetuate those institutions through the imposition of social controls on others. The four chapters in this section address the issue of human agency in social control from two different perspectives. Two chapters discuss historical themes in social control, describing the emergence of reform movements in the nineteenth and early twentieth centuries. Their descriptions reveal the limitations of theories of social control that elide important historical and social contexts of reforms and the reformist groups involved. Two other chapters present the results of empirical studies of the imposition of criminal punishments. Both stress the importance of understanding the social and legal contexts of crime. While one chapter concludes that the severity of punishments imposed varies in relation to the context and judicial perceptions of crime, the other concludes that the severity of punishments varies in relation to the nature of the crime and the legal context in which the crime is prosecuted.

Nicole Hahn Rafter, in "Eugenics, Class, and the Professionalization of Social Control," describes the birth of the eugenics movement in the United States. Rafter maintains that eugenicists "biologized class relationships (and) imposed a form of social control rarely achieved, the prevention of reproduction." She argues that while shifts in the class structure and the increased popularity of hereditarian explanations of social problems contributed to the rise of eugenics, the professionalization of social work was critical to the movement's emergence at the end of the nineteenth century. Eugenics provided a coherent and popular explanation of social problems attributed to the lower classes and a program for solving the problems. It also reinforced the societal need for a class of professionals—social workers—who could manage the problems identified by eugenicists. Rafter's argument is that professional social work developed partly in response to this need and that its development reinforced the eugenics movement for a short period. However, her argument does not simply take an "instrumentalist" position. She concludes that the study of social control, particularly studies of movements such as eugenics, must examine the historical contexts in which movements emerge and the relationships between those contexts and the work and values of the individuals and groups involved.

John R. Sutton, in "Children in the Therapeutic State: Lessons for the Sociology of Deviance and Social Control," adopts a historical perspective, focusing on reformist movements in the control of children in the United States. He outlines theoretical concerns about the study of these movements and their implications for future research in the sociology of social control. Sutton argues that changes and reforms in the control of children have always been embedded in broader social and institutional trends, particularly in sweeping social reforms involving adult problem populations in the society. Further, he argues that the state plays a critical role in sponsoring and legitimating reformist movements. Accordingly, Sutton calls for a new "generic model of deviance and social control" that recognizes the importance of social and historical contexts in the imposition of punishments and controls by the state. This model must also be comparative, insofar as it considers the development and application of controls across institutional sectors of state control and across societies. Finally, the model must offer comprehensive explanations of control that integrate theories of behavior from cultural, organizational and individual-level perspectives.

In Chapter 15, "Crime and the Social Control of Blacks: Offender/Victim Race and the Sentencing of Violent Offenders," Cassia Spohn presents the results of an empirical study of racial disparities in criminal punishment. Spohn asserts that laws and punishments are applied differentially by race and by context, in relation to the degree of threat perceived by sentencing officials. Arguing from the perspective of conflict theory, she reasons that interracial violent crimes involving black defendants and white victims are more threatening to most sentencing judges and thus will be punished more severely than intraracial crimes or crimes involving white defendants. Spohn's results, based upon data collected from criminal cases in Detroit, support this reasoning, even following adjustments for differences in the severity of the crime, characteristics of the case, and background of the defendant. Further, they suggest that empirically minded sociologists who study punishment and social control may no longer content themselves by simply examining linear-additive models of the sentencing process. They must instead examine the relational contexts of crime and officials' perceptions and reactions to those contexts.

Finally, Celesta A. Albonetti's "The Symbolic Punishment of White-Collar Offenders" focuses on the social organization of the administration of criminal justice in explaining the punishment of white-collar offenders. Her focus is persons accused of white-collar crimes and how the administration of justice responds to these crimes. Albonetti argues that the severity and forms of punishments imposed in these cases vary by the complexity of each case and the degree of coordination across organizations in the administration of justice and that punishments are symbolic (i.e., least severe) in extremely complex cases where justice officials have worked collaboratively in prosecuting the crime. She presents the empirical results of a study of cases processed in seven U.S. District Courts. The study results support her argument, showing that white-collar offenders are more likely to receive lenient sentences when case complexity is high and when there is close coordination of case handling between prosecution and the courts. Thus, the social control of white-collar crimes is influenced mostly by the relationship between the type of case and the social and legal context in which the case is processed. Albonetti's chapter maintains that knowledge about the imposition of criminal punishments can be advanced only if sociologists direct greater attention to the "practical routines" in the daily work of courts and the perceptions of court officials as they carry out those routines.

Summary

This book examines the relationships among crime, inequality and social control, focusing on theoretical and conceptual inquiries of contemporary scholars. It explores four central themes. The first is the need for developments in theory and research that reconcile, or at least clarify, the contribution of competing theoretical perspectives. Quite certainly, scholars must identify and more fully develop the arguments that are common across theories of crime and social control. They must heed Tittle's admonition (in this volume) and resist being "so obsessed with their own themes that they omit essential parts of reality that are essential to achieve fuller explanations." At the same time, scholars must also accept the challenge proffered by Walker and Cohen (1985) to specify more effectively theories of crime and control by exploring the scope of individual theories—the conditions under which those theories are falsified. Thus, they must ensure that their theoretical formulations offer a clear and consistent model of social control, one that articulates fully how societies impose controls *and* why inequality persists.

A second theme is the need for analyses of inequality that extend beyond traditional conceptions of subjugated groups or classes. That studies of inequality in the imposition of controls have largely ignored major ethnic groups and women is extremely problematic: It has yielded distorted descriptions and explanations of inequality in the process of control. Similarly, there is need for research that moves beyond traditional analyses of inequality's effects on the imposition of controls. For example, scholars must more effectively examine the role of historical influences and contextual effects in explaining variation in controls. Along these lines, we must heed Carlen's suggestion (in this volume) and ascertain how aspects of inequality, like gender and ethnic differences, have unique meaning to the processes of control during specific historical periods and in specific geographic or cultural contexts.

A third theme identified in the volume emerges from work on the linkages among different forms of social control. Because sociologists have restricted much of their research to studies of formal legal controls, knowledge about the relationships between these controls and other forms of control is severely limited (Liska 1992, this volume). In the absence of such knowledge, disagreement over many aspects of these relationships abounds. At a minimum, however, research is needed that identifies the circumstances under which forms of control serve as substitutes for each other and those circumstances under which they displace each other over time. Similarly, research is needed that examines the circumstances under which controls increase or decrease in conjunction with each other. Research such as Tolnay and Beck's (this volume) analysis of lynching is particularly useful because it reveals specific historical and political contexts in which companion forms of control are used to maintain a particular moral order.

Finally, there is compelling need for theory and research that explain how the beliefs of individuals and groups become the policies and practices of controlling institutions. While previous studies suggest that beliefs are translated into law and governmental programs by the actions of officials, agencies or entire legislatures, many of the studies have inadequately specified how individual beliefs are actually transformed into decisions to punish or policies of control.

Most apparent in the present work is the very clear need for greater understanding of officials' perceptions and reactions to crime and the social contexts in which crimes occur. These perceptions shape the routine policies and practices of officials, which, in turn, determine who is subjected to punishments or other social controls and under what circumstances punishments and other controls are imposed.

PART TWO
Directions for Theory

2

The Theoretical Bases for Inequality in Formal Social Control

Charles R. Tittle

This paper concerns inequality in formal social control implemented through legal processes and agencies. One of the most important issues about criminal sanctioning concerns unequal treatment of those who are objects of such efforts at social control. But research on processing and/or sanctioning by criminal justice agencies has been undertaken, to a large extent, with only limited theoretical guidance, and such studies have been culture bound. Most of these studies have focused on the United States, have typically dealt with public issues about possible injustice or unfairness, and generally have contrasted "legal" and extralegal factors implicated in decision making (Garber et al. 1983; Hagan and Bumiller 1983). Such an approach, however, is meaningful only in democratic societies with legal guarantees of civil rights, and even there, it discourages systematic theoretical explanation in favor of documentation and attribution of racial, sexual, and class discrimination.

Although some research and interpretation have been driven by theory, and data showing unfairness have allowed some assessments of theoretical arguments, most "social scientific" work on formal negative social control has had little linkage with theory. Instead, philosophical questions about justice that involve latent, atheoretical assumptions that equality is both possible and likely unless perverted by intentional evil have been central. Moreover, even when explanation has been paramount, the spectrum of theories brought into play or tested has been narrow. Thus, scientific knowledge of criminal sanctioning is limited, and the body of work about legal processing cannot be used to help explain social processes and organization outside that context. In the following pages I describe four broadly based general orientations that provide explanations of patterns of formal social control. This exposition reveals little theoretical reason ever to expect equality in formal social control.

Indeed, contrary to the assumptions of a public issues orientation, major theories suggest that inequality is perverse only in a comprehensive moral sense. In addition, even though all four of the theoretical orientations to be discussed predict inequality in social control, they differ markedly in the specific patterns of inequality they anticipate, and they offer divergent explanations for those patterns. Therefore, narrow focus on one or another of them yields limited and incomplete prediction, explanation, and/or understanding of inequality. Fortunately, there are points of convergence around which efforts to merge the four theoretical orientations can be focused in developing a more comprehensive, integrated theory of formal social control.

The orientations to be discussed are consensus (or functional), conflict, social-psychological, and bureaucratic (or organizational). Since the consensus and conflict perspectives have broader sweep than the other two, I regard them as foundational. Nevertheless, the social-psychological and bureaucratic approaches, although portrayed as supplemental, are also quite general. Moreover, as conceived, all are generic. Each orientation encompasses numerous specific formulations with different foci. I do not describe these permutations, nor attribute the broad arguments in the general orientations to any particular theorist or theorists. Indeed, in many cases there has been no systematic statement of the premises underlying even the specific focused formulations, much less their generic forms. Therefore, I will take liberties in spelling out the transcendent arguments that unify diverse versions of the particular general theories, or orientations.

My objective is to go behind specific theoretical statements within each "orientation" to get to the foundational premises expressed by them and then to explicate the implications of these generic arguments for the connection between inequality and social control. So, in answer to the question "What specific theorist said that?" that may arise, I will say: "Perhaps none; the important issue is not who may or may not have said it, but rather, whether it could be said logically, given the collective arguments and implied assumptions of theorists who work within the theoretical tradition being discussed."

Foundational Perspectives

The Consensus Orientation

The consensus (sometimes referred to as functional) perspective begins with an image of society as a collection of people organized for mutual benefit. Most members of any society are thought to share some basic values and to recognize their common interdependencies for survival as well as the realization of shared values. From this perspective, society is an organic unit of cooperating persons who agree upon common collective goals. These common goals are (1) survival and continuity of the society and (2) preservation of the basic values that are thought to epitomize the essence of the group and to be essential to its maintenance (see Davis 1976; Davis and Moore 1945; Durkheim 1947; Parsons 1951; Bernard 1983). From this collectivist point of view, forms of behavior, individuals, subgroups, and categories of people that most members of a society perceive as contributing to the survival and maintenance of the group as a whole, or that are perceived as promoting its basic values, will be rewarded, encouraged, and protected. Forms of behavior, individuals, subgroups, and categories of people that most members of a society believe contribute little or nothing to the survival and maintenance of the collectivity will be discouraged and discredited. Those behaviors, individuals, subgroups, and categories of people that are thought actually to threaten the survival or continuity of society or that are believed by most societal members to undermine the group's basic values will be regarded as dangerous and bad and will be prohibited, punished, and blocked. The extent to which a given behavior, individual, subgroup, or category of people is subject to formal social control, and whether the sanctions being used will be positive or negative, depends upon the extent to which it is perceived by most members of society as contributing to, being neutral toward, or threatening central goals and values. Positive sanctions will be granted to encourage behaviors, individuals, subgroups, or categories of people believed by most to have functional import for the total social group. Mild negative sanctions will be used against behaviors, individuals, subgroups, or categories of people who do little or nothing for the group. And strong, suppressive, negative sanctions will be imposed on those social behaviors or entities perceived as threatening to the interests of the whole.

From this theoretical perspective, inequality in the administration of criminal justice is inevitable and can be predicted from a knowledge of two things: (1) public perceptions about what and who are either dangerous, neutral, or useful to the long-range survival of the group and (2) what and who are supportive, neutral, or threatening to the fundamental shared values of the group. Hence, if one can accurately delineate the shared societal values of a group and can assess the extent to which social entities are perceived as likely to jeopardize those values, or can tap public opinion about who or what is helpful to the survival and continuity of the group, he/she can anticipate patterns of differential criminal processing and sanctioning. That is, regardless of the form of government or legislative process or of legal guarantees of civil rights, the content of the criminal law and the patterns of its administration will, in the main and in the long range, embody the spirit of societal protection and promotion of fundamental values.

The consensus perspective, then, suggests that the criminal law and its administration inevitably will be discriminatory, particularly in the way it manages different kinds of behavior. What is prohibited or subject to punishment will not be "fair"; it will, however, be "useful" to the preservation of the group (in the minds of most of the people) or consistent with underlying values shared by the collectivity. Moreover, processing of individuals through the system of formal social control, in the particular instance, and processing of members of subgroups or categories, in the general case, will be "just" or "equal" only under unusual circumstances. Instead it will be patterned to achieve societal survival (again, as perceived by the majority) and continuity of shared values. Those individuals or groupings of individuals that are actually punished will not necessarily "deserve" it; their punishment, however, will be perceived as necessary for the benefit of the society.

According to this theory, patterns of inequality in legal sanctioning will reflect the fundamental nature of society, and they will follow logically from public perceptions about the usefulness of different behaviors and people and from the extent to which basic collective values are perceived as being reinforced by particular behaviors, individuals, social entities, or groups. Specifically, these patterns are as follows: (1) acts that are publicly regarded as "useful" will rarely result in criminal sanction; (2) those who do "useful" things for society, or whose personal styles and subgroup or category memberships suggest general proneness toward doing useful things, will rarely be subject to the likelihood of criminal sanctions—and when they are processed with that possibility as an end product, they will be advantaged; (3) acts that are neither "useful" nor "dangerous" to society will sometimes result in modest criminal sanctions; (4) those who do neutral things, or whose life patterns suggest such likelihood, will sometimes be subject to modest criminal sanctions, and those whose group memberships and personal characteristics suggest proneness toward neutral acts will enjoy no advantages and only slight disadvantages in being processed through the system of criminal justice; (5) acts that are threatening or dangerous (or generally perceived to be so) to society will be severely and frequently sanctioned; and (6) those who do things generally regarded as dangerous or threatening to society will often feel the weight of criminal sanctions, and those whose characteristics suggest proneness toward dangerous or threatening acts (again in the opinion of most people) will be distinctly disadvantaged in criminal justice processing.

To apply, or test, this general theory, it is necessary to translate its abstract premises into specific empirical implications, or hypotheses. To do that, one must recognize, first, the survival themes of a given society. Every society is presumably concerned with regulation and control of social interaction and individual behaviors in order to channel activities toward collective continuity. Societal survival is thought to be linked especially with successful control of acts of violence against its own members either by other members of the society or by outside enemies and to be linked with successful encouragement of activities that aid basic institutions such as the reproductive/socialization mechanisms, the economy, the government, the military, and religion that allow the society to do the things necessary for its own survival.

In pursuit of these goals, any society will presumably prohibit and severely sanction acts that (1) most people in that society think endanger the collectivity (such as treason), (2) eliminate needed members of the society (such as murder or careless use of chemicals on a massive scale) or inhibit victims' ability to contribute to the society's goals (such as assault or rape, which might physically or psychologically reduce a person's capability of performing sustenance or reproductive activities and which might undermine mutual trust on which human interaction and commercial exchange are based), or (3) threaten the basic institutions (such as, in modern societies, sexual behavior involving people of widely differing ages that affects the family or bribery and fraud, which affect confidence in business or governmental activities).

Furthermore, because society cannot effectively sanction all specific instances of these threatening behaviors, it will attempt to reduce the likelihood of their occurrence by focusing especially on those individuals whose personal or group-linked characteristics suggest greater proneness toward the dangerous conduct. In practice, this means that there will be differential sanctioning of individuals who commit similar forms of behavior, and those individuals whose life-styles, past histories, or personalities suggest greater threat to the group as a whole will be more severely sanctioned regardless of the current offense of which they are accused. Furthermore, in order to help control social entities perceived to be dangerous, those individuals who are members of groups or categories whose life-styles, past histories, and current political orientations portend potential threat to the collectivity and its values will be more often the objects of control and more often the recipients of severe sanctions than other social entities.

Consider physical violence and sexual expression in the United States. Street fighting is illegal, typically prompting police action to prevent it and court-administered punishments to incapacitate, at least for a time, those who have done it as well as to deter those who are likely to do it. Observation by any witnesses of aggressive activities, as well as physical evidence of injuries to participants, are taken as evidence in courts of law to help convict street fighters of criminal assault. In addition, most citizens, as well as the police and court officials, believe (on the basis of experience or prejudice) that the most likely individuals or segments of the population to be fighting in the street are minorities, males, and young people. Therefore, young male members of minority groups are most likely to be arrested, jailed, convicted, and incarcerated for street fighting, even though in any specific incident others (non-minority, female, older, or some cross combination) might be more culpable.

On the other hand, prize fighting, which involves the same kind of behavior—physical contact intended to inflict pain and injury—is not criminal, is not harassed by the police, nor does it bring unusual attention by criminal justice agents to those similar to participants. Indeed, prize fighting is a popular form of entertainment in which participants are highly rewarded, sometimes lionized and held up as exceptions to the usually assumed dangerousness of members of the categories they typically represent. Furthermore, witnesses (fans) to the acts of physical aggression (actual hitting) do not feel compelled to activate the police. Injuries, rather than being used as evidence of criminal assault in courts of law, are taken as signs of effective boxing talent—an ultimate manifestation of manhood and successful achievement in a competitive society.

What accounts for this discrepancy in the social control of violence? According to the consensus perspective, street fighting is criminally sanctioned while prize fighting isn't because street fighting cannot be regulated to serve societal interests or to prevent dangerous consequences, such as injury or death to innocent bystanders. By contrast, organized contact sports, like prize fighting, are regulated by legal rules and institutional procedures, thereby limiting their potential destructive consequences while allowing them to serve societal interests by epitomizing the restrained competitive spirit that undergirds the American value system and by contributing to a consumption-oriented economic system.

Thus, as this example illustrates, American society skews its processes of formal social control in an effort to control street fighting, as well as those most likely to do it, because this behavior is generally perceived as having little value for societal survival—in fact it threatens that continuity. However, the contrast between prize fighting and street fighting also illustrates that total prohibition of all classes of behaviors that might endanger a society or its institutions would be counterproductive (and, no doubt, impossible). Potentially dangerous acts can often serve larger societal goals. Even though an individual is not allowed to kill another to promote his/her own interests, an executioner, a police officer, or a soldier can kill, if authorized by the societal authorities, because such killing is thought by most to serve collective interests.

In addition, there are hierarchies of values and institutions that collective opinion mandates as worthy of protection from particular acts or social entities. The more important the value or the institution, the more likely are concerns about it to take precedence in instances where there is potential contradiction. For example, although the family is regarded as an exceptionally important institution in many societies, immediate national security always takes precedence over long-range protection of the family when the two are in conflict. Thus, societies will often negatively sanction prostitution in peacetime, when major concern is focused on long-range population maintenance, but will permit it in wartime, when the nurturance of fighting personnel is paramount.

Furthermore, the degree of threat posed by a particular behavior determines the extent to which it is sanctioned. For example, every society presumably has an interest in regulated reproduction—that which produces new societal members in an orderly way so that they can be appropriately socialized and supported (Davis 1976). In many societies the family, officially recognized through marriage, is the designated institution through which orderly reproduction and socialization are expected to occur. In such societies, there is strong collective interest in motivating people to make and maintain marriages and to become responsible parents. One often-used method of producing that motivation is to try to restrict sexual expression to marital partners by sanctioning its occurrence in all nonmarital contexts (at the moment I am ignoring the additional interest society has in preventing the spread of disease that is enhanced by open sexuality). But some forms of nonmarital sex pose more of a danger to the family (and thereby to society) than others. Consider comparisons among bestiality, homosexuality, adultery, and premarital sex. Sexual expression between people and animals logically poses the greatest threat to marriage and responsible parenthood because it constitutes an alternative sexual outlet that can reduce the general motive for marriage, and under no circumstances can it ever lead to marriage with the sex partner or to reproduction. The second greatest danger inheres in homosexual expression. It provides an alternative libidinal outlet that diminishes the general motive for opposite-sex marriage, which might produce children. However, homosexual activity is less threatening to the family than bestiality because homosexual liaisons can at least lead to supportive alliances that sustain partners' participation in other essential institutions. Following the same logic, extramarital sex is prohibited because it may lead to marital breakup in preference for a lover or because it loosens the sexually motivated bond to maintain marriages. But it is less dangerous to society than animal or homosexual contacts because, unlike those forms of sexual expression, extramarital sex may lead to another marriage or at least to reproduction. Finally, premarital sex is somewhat disadvantageous to society because it provides an alternative to marriage and because it may lead to irresponsible parenthood. However, premarital sex is far less threatening than bestiality, homosexuality, or adultery because premarital sex does not jeopardize an already existing marriage or family, it actually often leads to marriage, and at the very least it may result in reproduction.

If the consensus argument is correct, formal social control is most likely to be imposed on these four forms of non-conventional sexual expression in the order of their danger—the most likely for bestiality, the second most likely for homosexuality, the third most likely for adultery, and the least likely for premarital sex. The severity of the sanctions imposed will follow the same patterns. The most severely sanctioned will be bestiality and the least serious will be premarital sex. Furthermore, those individuals, subgroups, or categories of individuals who are thought by most people to be prone toward the various forms of unconventional sex will be most subject to social control. For example, males, more than females, are thought more prone toward bestiality and homosexuality, perhaps because their physiology may make such sexual expression easier. This contributes to an overall pool of potential dangerousness attributed to males—a pool composed of a large number of such potentialities in many realms (not just the sexual) that lead societal members to perceive males as more threatening than females. As a result, males will be the objects of formal social control more often than females.

The logic of the consensus theory also suggests that patterns of social control will change as societal circumstances and survival requirements change. Sexual expression can again serve as an example. According to the theory, encouraging marriage and responsible reproduction will be of great importance to societies with high mortality rates and of less import to those with low mortalities. As the technology of food production and distribution, and that of public health and medical treatment, improve, as it has historically in modern Western societies, mortality declines (Weeks 1981). Therefore, the likelihood and severity of social control exercised against all forms of non-conventional sexual expression should decline with demographic improvements. Tolerance for bestiality, homosexuality, adultery, and premarital sex should have increased in Western societies over the past century or two (Lipton 1966), and such tolerance should increase in developing countries over the next few decades as their mortality decreases. A clear indication of such liberalization in the United States was the growing popularity of swinging—consensual sharing of sexual partners among married couples and singles—among middle-class segments of the population in the 1960s and 1970s before the AIDS epidemic hit in the 1980s (Symonds 1971; Davis 1976). Interestingly enough, however, the sustaining rationale was that it provided sexual variety in a context that did not threaten marriage (Walshok 1971). Given the social arrangements in the United States during the time period in question, swinging was perceived by some as a necessity because the roles of males and females had changed so much that the possibility of sexual encounters outside marriage had begun to pose a threat to marriage itself. Tolerance for swinging, then, presumably reflected reduced societal need for reproduction, but the predominance of collective interest is illustrated by the justification of swinging as a method for preserving marriage and the family in the face of external eroding influences.

According to the logic of the consensus perspective, if most people could be persuaded to recognize that benefit, then swinging would gradually become less disapproved, perhaps it might even become normative. Still, the inherent disease-spreading potential of swinging makes it less desirable than monogamous sexual exclusivity for most people and for the collectivity, as has become so clear with the rise of the AIDS epidemic and the proliferation of numerous other sexually transmitted diseases. The popularity of, and tolerance for, swinging declined quickly when the threat these diseases pose for individuals and society became apparent. Reactivation of modes of formal social control directed toward confining sexual expression to marital partners should not be far behind, if the consensus theory is correct, unless, of course, medical advances provide increased protection from sexually transmitted diseases. In this fashion, then, as other perceived societal "needs" change, so should patterns of formal social control.

In addition to the nurturance of institutions and activities aimed at societal survival, all societies are also presumably preoccupied with preserving core values that represent the essence of the groups. Some core values will, of course, be nearly universal because they embody the principles necessary for any group's continuity and survival. Such would be the case with the value of life as it applies to the society's own members and/or the value of loyalty to the group. In addition, however, core values may vary somewhat from one society to another. For instance, people in the United States presumably share a core value for controlled competition whereas contemporary Chinese people presumably embrace a core value for cooperation. Consensus theorists provide no guidelines for empirically identifying core values, but the logic suggests that if they can be identified, a great deal about patterns in formal social control can be predicted. Consider the putative shared value in the United States endorsing the worth of controlled competition.

American citizens believe that competition, as long as it is not cutthroat, is good and essential (Williams 1952; Kluegel and Smith 1986). Everything in the United States seems to be oriented around competition. People are trained to compete, but to do so *within rules*. Most believe that competition, up to a certain point, is necessary for achieving personal and societal goals but that unrestrained competition is dangerous to the survival of all and a threat to the general welfare. Hence, business people presumably contribute to productivity and overall societal welfare by competing for customers. This benefit is lost, however, if the competition involves extortion, intimidation, or "dirty tricks" because productive participants are eliminated and the individual benefit of one player in the economic game rises above the general welfare that is supposedly promoted when all compete to provide the best product or service at the lowest price. Similarly, athletes are thought to reinforce basic societal values of competition when they struggle to win a game, but they undermine basic values when they break the rules to win. In a comparable way the basic value of restrained competition infuses courtship, politics, personal status seeking, scholarship, recreation, and every other walk of American life.

Following the logic of the theory, then, legal procedures and institutions will differentially sanction behaviors and social entities thought by most to be inclined toward those behaviors that undermine the principle of regulated competition. The earlier example of street fighting and prize fighting can also be used to illustrate this point. Prize fighting is subject only to the formal social control aimed at making it fair. Conspiracies to fix fights, coercion to force individuals to fight, allowing fights when one or both fighters have health problems, etc., are sometimes the subject of control. From the consensus perspective, prize fighting is permitted because it serves the societal objective of reinforcing the basic value of regulated competition so essential to our social fabric. On the other hand, because street fighting transpires without benefit of regulation, it undermines the central social value of controlled competition that undergirds almost all institutions.

Conditions of Equality. Contrary to the assumptions of some (Quinney 1970; Chambliss and Seidman 1971), consensus theory predicts great inequality in the process of formal social control. In fact, according to its logic, there are only three circumstances where anything close to equality in formal social control might prevail. One of those conditions would be extreme homogeneity. If everybody were alike, it would be difficult for collective judgments to coalesce around particular individuals or categories of individuals as more or less likely to do things that threaten the group as a whole or that undermine core values. But even in relatively homogeneous societies there are still age and gender differences, so the conditions for total equality in formal social control are unrealistic. Moreover, all societies, even those relatively homogeneous, always perceive some actions as more dangerous to the survival of the group, or contrary to collective values, than others.

A second condition of near equality might prevail where the vast majority of a society actually share a basic belief in equality. There the very practice of differentiating individuals, groups, or categories would threaten a fundamental value and as a result might be discouraged. Yet, it would seem inevitable that in such societies, especially if they were somewhat heterogeneous, perceptions of differential propensity for dangerous behavior would emerge to challenge commitments to equality. Ambivalence generated by conflict between a core value and collective concerns for survival and continuity of the group would seem likely to produce at least some sporadic and inconsistent deviation from the principles of equality even if most people were fully committed to equality. More relevant, however, is the extreme rarity of genuine societal commitment to equality, especially in modern complex societies. Even utopian groups founded explicitly to promote equality rarely achieve it, and then only for short periods of time (Kephardt 1991). The evidence is clear that the American population does not really value equality in formal social control, despite constitutional guarantees and occasional lip service by public figures to the ideal. Numerous surveys show that most citizens endorse inequality in concrete situations, if not in the abstract (Kluegel and Smith 1986). And even the founding fathers explicitly built discrimination into the Constitution when they differentiated between slaves and other people in counting the population for apportionment of representatives to the Congress and between freemen, landholders, and females in specifying entitlement to vote.

A third condition of near equality might prevail in tight-knit societies that are so secure that very little poses a danger to their cohesion or continuity and where fear of diverse individuals, groups, or categories is minimal. Such societies might be able to treat all as equally valued contributors to the group and might practice what Braithwaite (1989) calls shaming and reintegration on an equal footing. Such social self-confidence is, of course, quite unusual, and to the extent that it exists, it probably characterizes only simple societies. Again, extending from the Alien and Sedition Acts through McCarthyism to the contemporary scene, history provides dramatic testimony that the United States lacks this sense of security (Turk 1982).

In summary, expecting equality, as is implied by analyses of formal social control designed to expose perverse discrimination, is contrary to consensus theory. If the theoretical argument is correct, it would be most unusual to find equality in formal social control. An alternative to the exposé, and certainly one that is more useful, would be research and analysis that apply the theoretical premises contained in consensus (and other theories to be discussed) to try to spell out the conditions for various patterns and degrees of inequality in processing and to try to understand why these phenomena take particular forms. Not only would this alternative be more scientifically defensible, but for those with a policy agenda for promoting greater justice (however it might be defined), it would provide the knowledge necessary for the task. Moreover, this approach would save us from appearing naive in constantly uncovering "discrimination."

Limitations. Despite the superiority of employing the consensus perspective rather than an atheoretical public policy approach to the study of formal social control, this perspective alone cannot account for the patterns that are likely to be found. First, as numerous critics have noted, consensus theory pays no attention to how public opinions about threats to society are formed and expressed in the immediate context. Second, it does not satisfactorily explain the content of core values. Concerns about societal welfare cannot take shape mystically and cultural variability in values challenges the evolutionary argument so often put forward. There is very good reason to think that public perceptions are malleable, affected by mass media, social movements, influential leadership, content of school curricula, and ordinary political processes, all of which are to some extent servants of private interest and reflections of differential power. Third, the theory completely ignores potential effects of social-psychological processes of identification and fear (which will be discussed later) on the implementation of social control. Finally, consensus theory takes no account of organizational processes or constraints that might distort the public's will, even if there is one, in controlling dangerous behavior or people.

Consequently, although consensus theory is more astute and accurate than its current discredited status implies, some of its predictions and explanations concerning patterns of formal social control are probably wrong or at least less accurate than they could be. To more effectively do its job, then, this theory must be modified and expanded to take into account the overlooked elements noted above. Since there are already other theories dealing with those elements, elaboration of consensus theory actually implies integration with them. But all theories bearing on formal social control are individually incomplete because each leaves out something that one or another of the remaining ones, including consensus theory, features. Hence it is necessary to integrate the four theories discussed in this paper to achieve an efficient and comprehensive formulation that permits full understanding of patterns in formal social control.

The Conflict Perspective

Because they address micro as well as macro patterns in social control, conflict theories are somewhat more complex than consensus theories. The two perspectives agree, however, in predicting much inequality in the practice of formal social control. But because conflict theories view society in an entirely different light than do consensus theories, their explanations diverge sharply from those implied by the consensus perspective. Conflict theorists conceive of society as a collection of individuals and groups with separate and distinct interests struggling among themselves for power to protect and promote things beneficial to themselves rather than a mutual benefit association composed of individual members or segments sharing core values and working together to preserve society and promote the collective welfare. Success in competition for power creates the capability of manipulating social and physical arrangements for the winner's own benefit, including the marshalling of material rewards. In addition, power allows its holders to maximize the chances of remaining in positions to promote their own interests over a long period of time.

The point of conflict theory is that power determines everything, and since power is distributed unequally, formal social control will be applied differentially (Dahrendorf 1959; Bonger 1969; Chambliss 1973; Collins 1975; Turk 1969a; Quinney 1970). However, since the exercise of power is constrained by continuous competition for its acquisition and retention, these inequalities are not necessarily straightforward nor totally obvious (Turk 1969a) because power holders often employ strategic ploys rather than raw coercion to achieve their ends. This may involve concessions to challengers that are expressed in greater semblance of equality in everyday practice of formal social control, mitigating what otherwise might be great differentials. Thus despite ongoing struggle, much stability may characterize any social and political system because, at any given point in time, those on top can formulate and persuade others to embrace normative rules that actually serve elite interests, and they can institutionalize and win legitimacy for coercive processes that force conformity among non-believers. Moreover, institutionalized apparatuses of formal social control can be fashioned to help keep at bay potential threats to the positions and interests of elites. Hence, behaviors, individuals, subgroups, and categories of individuals that are useful to power holders, or at least that do not threaten them or their interests, will end up advantaged in formal social control. At the same time, those behaviors, individuals, subgroups, and categories of people that are not useful for elites, especially those that elites perceive as actually endangering their interests, will be disadvantaged in the practice of formal social control.

This implies that the police, the courts, the probation agencies, and the prisons will focus mainly on acts and social entities that threaten elite interests. However, it is not likely that this will be obvious or gross, except in the most blatant instances of challenge from a contender for power, because it is to the advantage of elites to minimize opposition and garner legitimacy. Thus, elites are said to use their power to influence the content of mass media messages, school curricula, and other sources of information to persuade most non-elite members of society to regard actions that are taken on behalf of elites as also for public welfare (creation of "false consciousness"). Furthermore, having control of the means for dispersing information presumably enables power holders to create favorable moral sensitivities in the general population concerning actions and categories of people that are, in reality, mainly of expedient concern to elites. The result is inequality in the everyday operation of social control, although the patterns of its expression may be subtle. The exact nature these subtle patterns can be expected to take, however, depends at least partly upon which version of macro-level conflict theory one consults.

One macro-level conflict approach, deriving from the ideas of Karl Marx, is dualistic (Bonger 1969; Quinney 1970; Chambliss 1973). It assumes that societies, particularly capitalistic ones, are divided into two major classes. The elites, or bourgeoisie, constitute one class, the members of which are united in promoting the interests of those with wealth, land, or capital resources (the means of production). The other major class is less united, composed of non-elites, or the proletariat, who have little wealth, land, or capital resources but who work for and are dependent upon the bourgeoisie. According to dualistic conflict theories, although different segments of the elite class ostensibly may hold power at different times, laws that relate to the interests of the elite class as a whole will be made and implemented through the mechanisms of formal social control.

A second type of conflict theory views society as composed of multiple power groups, organized around many foci in addition to economic interests, that vie for influence about particular issues and within different domains (Clark 1975). For example, competition for power concerning religion in schools will involve different participants than will the struggle for influence over immigration issues. And even those with mainly economic interests will not necessarily be united but may be contending among themselves to realize idiosyncratic interests. Thus, what is good for General Motors may not be good for the insurance industry. The auto industry has low regard for safety devices because they add to manufacturing costs, thereby potentially reducing profits, but companies selling insurance to motorists favor safety devices because they reduce the number and costliness of accidents, thereby potentially increasing profits. As another example, things beneficial to the financial industry, such as high interest rates, will often be devastating for the construction or real estate industries. Therefore, at any given point in time, and concerning specific issues, any one of a multitude of contenders may temporarily dominate the scene, promoting social arrangements and legal procedures that serve their own interests with as little regard as possible for how it might affect others.

According to the pluralistic conception of society, then, rather than a unified system of norms and formal control procedures consistent with some supposed general interest of all elites, any society will reflect a hodgepodge and changing system of norms and processes of formal social control representing the collective residue of arrangements instituted at one time or another by a number of different power groups with divergent concerns. For example, the prohibitionist amendment to the U.S. Constitution represents the triumph of one kind of interest group over another (Gusfield 1963). It came about because of organized political activity by a group with moral and religious concerns—the Women's Christian Temperance Union—in opposition to the desires and interests of the liquor and entertainment industries, which are usually quite powerful and in fact regained the upper hand with the repeal of the prohibitionist amendment.

Regardless of which macro-level version of conflict theory we focus on, the main implication is the same. Patterns of formal social control in general will reflect the focused interests of previous and continuing elite groups in using sanctions to protect themselves and their interests, and the result will be inequality. To test this idea and to predict outcomes of formal social control, one must be able to differentiate people by the amount of power they possess in various domains and to identify what those with the most power perceive as being in their interests. Specifically, explaining outcomes of formal social control requires an appreciation of the way in which particular behaviors, individuals, subgroups, or categories of individuals might threaten the positions or well-being of power holders.

Recall the differences between street fighting and prize fighting discussed earlier. According to the conflict perspective, street fighting is criminalized and those individuals, subgroups of individuals, and categories of individuals most likely to engage in street fighting are subject to greater formal social control than others, particularly more so than those who engage in, or who are likely to engage in, prize fighting for two reasons. First, elites fear that the hostility and aggression being expressed in street fighting will get out of hand and spill over into organized violence against power holders, who may come to be perceived as the real enemies of the class of people likely to be street fighters. And, elites may think street fighting potentially threatens the survival, health, and strength of members of the labor force that many power holders depend upon for economic well-being. This second factor is said to be particularly important in a capitalist society like the United States because the generally most influential elites are economically oriented owners and managers. Since capitalist success depends on a readily available, plentiful, and easily exploited labor force, elites will try to discourage activities that might reduce the ability of members of that labor force to work or which might reduce the overall size of the labor force, as street fighting and other forms of assault hold the potential for doing.

Prize fighting and other body contact sports, on the other hand, are not criminalized nor are their participants subjected to greater formal social control because (1) such activities produce huge profits for certain economic interests that promote and market them as mass entertainment and (2) elites in general recognize that violent sports allow safe, vicarious release of hostility and aggressiveness that might otherwise be directed against power holders. Hence, owners, advertisers, and the broadcast industry all share an economic interest in making sure that violent sports are promoted as useful and good things and in guaranteeing that this view is adopted by the general population, while other elites without direct economic interests in these activities are likely to acquiesce to placate the general population of exploited workers (the main consumers of violent sports entertainment). Consequently, all economic elites end up endorsing the acceptability of contact sports and assisting the direct interest groups in making sure they are adopted as part of the American way of life.

There are also micro-level conflict theories that apply to formal social control. Whereas macro versions are concerned with the larger institutional processes by which power holders make and implement rules, micro versions concern themselves with the ability of individuals, subgroups, and categories of individuals to escape social control when they transgress the rules or threaten social arrangements that are already in place. Labelling theory (Gove 1980; Schur 1971), the best-known micro conflict formulation, as well as Black's theory (1989) of sociological justice take the legal rules as given but explain variations in the application of those rules as reflections of the ability of potential objects of social control to resist. Labelling theory goes beyond this by attempting to spell out the social and psychological consequences for the individual of unsuccessful resistance to being processed as an object of formal social control, but here I am interested only in its bearing on inequality in the process of social control.

Micro conflict theory implies that the probability of a social entity's (an individual, subgroup, or category of individuals) being subject to social control (being processed and ultimately sanctioned) varies inversely with the ability to resist. The capability of resistance is regarded as a product of the general level of power in society held by the social entity, the entity's capacity for marshalling resources, or by the entity's skill in manipulating the circumstances (interpersonal power in the case of individuals). Consider the likelihood that a person will be arrested, prosecuted, and punished for having fought in the streets. Since street fighters are usually young people, and are less able to counter official control, the chances of their being the objects of attempted social control are greater than for many other adult violators. Moreover, though both lower- and upper-status youth sometimes engage in street fights, upper-status youth have more ability to manipulate social arrangements in their own favor. Their greater financial resources make effective defense lawyers possible, and they usually possess greater interpersonal skills, which enable them to influence social control personnel. As a result, the chances of higher-status youth being arrested, prosecuted, and punished for street fighting are less than for lower-status youth. But despite the greater general probability of lower-status youth being the objects of control (being labeled), some lower-status youth fare better than others because their charm, demeanor, or good looks allow them to escape the full brunt of control efforts.

According to conflict theory, then, social control will usually reflect inequality. To predict exact patterns of inequality one must measure capacities for exercising and countering power, taking appropriate account of the subtle interplay of coercion and resistance as well as the general strategies used by elites to promote their interests and preserve their positions.

Conditions of Equality. According to conflict theory, social control must always be exercised unequally, at least as far as some acts and some categories of people are concerned. If the theory is correct, one could never imagine social control agencies, which are presumably the handmaidens of elites, dealing with revolutionary behavior aimed at an alteration in the distribution of wealth in the same way they deal with minor theft, and it would be impossible to conceive of the members of an ethnic or occupational group regarded as potentially threatening by elites, particularly if similar in social characteristics to those publicly committed to revolution, being treated generally in the same manner as members of an acquiescent group. However, within limited realms and under some circumstances, there might be some similarity in the way social control is applied across individuals, subgroups, organizations, and categories. This might occur if a dominant elite has succeeded in creating a thorough sense of false consciousness in its favor or when power is distributed in a social system such that strategic gamesmanship requires elites to accommodate by guaranteeing more or less equal processing of all segments of the population. Such circumstances are unlikely to occur often or to last long; nonetheless, it is worth noting that the conditions of equality suggested by this theory have little to do with moral principles, the central focus of public policy orientations. In fact, equality might emerge strictly in response to oppositional power. Hence equality or near-equality in social control might prevail in the presence of widespread prejudice and in the face of cultural ideologies supporting privilege.

Limitations. Conflict theory self-consciously denies what consensus theory asserts—that people with different amounts of power can be united around a sense of collective responsibility or genuinely share a set of values underlying cultural and social processes. Yet, despite their expression sometimes being autocratically suppressed or spuriously invented, nationalism, patriotism, and communitarianism are common human feelings often persevering beyond political regimes based on self-interested coercion and often showing themselves to be easily provoked. In addition, much evidence suggests that cultural values sometimes transcend momentary structural arrangements, frequently prevailing despite the efforts of temporary power holders to change or ignore them. Thus, there is usually substantial agreement about what behaviors, individuals, subgroups, or organizations pose a danger to a collectivity (Rossi 1974; Tittle 1980), even among those most likely to do the behavior. Lawbreakers rarely contend that the criminal behavior for which they are the objects of attempted control should not be prevented if possible, especially if they or their loved ones are potential victims. Typical criminals grant the legitimacy of the social system, even while attempting to manipulate it for personal benefit.

Contending that all such expressions of consensus stem from effective intellectual hegemony resulting in false consciousness is a large stretch. In fact, the main technique elites use to try to enlist others in supporting arrangements that mainly benefit elites is to argue that those arrangements are, after all, in the public interest. From this it would appear that collective sentiments are taken for granted, even by manipulative elites. But, where do taken-for-granted collective sentiments come from, if they do not grow from something fundamental in society? Moreover, it is a good bet that most processes of formal social control aimed at curbing serious offenses would not change much even with a complete reshuffling of arrangements by which decisions are made. Most people, rich and poor alike, fear violence, and no matter how meager their property, most people want it protected, perhaps even in inverse order to the amount owned. Would lower-class murderers necessarily be any differently handled than they are now if lower-class people could make the decisions about whether and how to deal with them? Would male robbers be any more or less disadvantaged if all police, court, and correctional personnel were females? Would minority rapists be any better off if all the police, court and correctional personnel who dealt with them were also minorities? I suspect that the differences would be small. This is because the possibility of being murdered affects those of lower socioeconomic standing as well as those of higher standing, the fear of robbery is as real for females as for males, and rape is no less a concern for minorities than for others. For these reasons the conflict argument would seem to have most force when applied to those acts, and their likely perpetrators, that are less serious and less direct or that bear less immediately on personal safety and well-being.

Hence, one limitation of conflict theory in providing a satisfactory account of processes of formal social control is its neglect of collective sentiment and unifying values, the elements featured by consensus theory. There are others. For one thing, conflict theory ignores the inherent tendencies of bureaucratic organizations to subordinate official goals to the struggle to survive and promote their own organizational agendas (Gouldner 1959, 1973). Bureaucracy can foil even the best-laid plans of power holders. In addition, there appear to be some more or less universal social-psychological principles concerning fear and identification that must be juxtaposed against the backdrop of political and social conflict to get an accurate picture of social control.

Conflict theory by itself cannot provide full explanation of formal social control any more than consensus theory can. A more adequate theory for understanding social control will have to incorporate some of the principles of the consensus and conflict theories, and in addition it will have to include bureaucratic and social-psychological principles.

Supplemental General Theories

The social-psychological and organizational theories to be presented are far less comprehensive than the conflict and consensus theories. They are general in the sense that their principles apply in a wide variety of situations and appear to be inherent to social life. However, they serve best as adjuncts to the two main theories discussed before because they apply to specific operational outcomes rather than to larger structural processes. Since they take for granted the overarching processes that conflict and consensus theories attempt to explain, they are best thought of as supplemental general theories.

The Social-Psychological Perspective

A social-psychological perspective has not often been used to explain aspects of social control and, in fact, my own use of it to account for sentencing anomalies in Florida's juvenile courts (Tittle and Curran 1988) may be the only time it has been applied at the macro level. Therefore, I will take this opportunity to elaborate and expand the underlying argument that Debra Curran and I developed.

A social-psychological approach basically contends that aggregated emotions of dominants in a given society, as well as individual emotions of the proximate agents of formal social control, affect, if not determine, patterns of sanctioning. It predicts that social control will be differentially employed against those who commit acts that have emotional significance for dominants and against individuals whose group memberships or personal characteristics constitute an ever-present symbolic threat with emotional overtones.

Unlike conflict theory, which assumes that dominants are concerned only with promoting political or economic interests and protecting their positions, and unlike consensus theory, which assumes that people act to promote the general welfare and preserve essential community values, this approach points to emotional concerns that often take precedence. Thus, the actions of dominants and proximate control agents, as they bear on formal social control, may be influenced by numerous social-psychological factors. In court or sentencing decisions, for example, an irritable, impatient judge may lean in ways disadvantageous for those slow of thought and expression. Or if a judge is personally prejudiced against minorities, it might show up in patterns of disadvantage for minorities in his/her court. However, because such effects must be expressed against the backdrop of norms about judicial restraint, they are probably not large. Similarly on the aggregate level, particularistic, personal social-psychological attributes are of minimal import because they vary so much from person to person and situation to situation.

When particular emotions are nearly universal, however, they are likely to find collective expression in all social institutions, including those concerned with formal social control (Rachman 1974; Tuan 1979; Scruton 1986). Two such emotions are particularly important. One is identification. People tend to assess events and persons from an internal comparative framework, at least initially. They try to imagine whether they could do the things that were done, whether they would derive pleasure or benefit from it, whether its expression implies admired qualities such as courage, and whether it deviates from their own standards of right and wrong. They also try to imagine whether the persons doing the prohibited acts, or likely to do them, are similar to themselves. The extent to which an individual can imagine him/her self doing an act, can admire the qualities necessary to accomplish the act, or imagine him/her self as like the one committing, or likely to commit, the act, the greater is the degree of "identification." In general, the greater the degree of identification, the less one is prone to exercise or favor negative social control.

The second is fear. Other individuals, groups of individuals, or events may pose an imminent danger to anybody's property and life, and when they do, fear is stimulated. But fear is also evoked by what people imag-

The Theoretical Bases for Inequality

ine might jeopardize their social positions or general welfare. Thus, everybody responds emotionally to individuals or groups who seem to be competitors, direct or indirect, for economic goods, jobs, lovers, or prestige. This is because a competitor's success not only directly threatens a valued entity but it also poses a danger to the person's public image and self-image; competitive success may result in the humiliation of the loser (Katz 1988). Being robbed may cause financial hardship, and being beaten is painful, but it is doubly distressing to have one's autonomy removed by being forced to surrender one's money or submit to another's will. Moreover, losing out in a real or symbolic contest, whether it be for a job, a business deal, a lover, or a status position, is embarrassing, a fundamental blow to one's self-esteem and public image. Even being reminded of one's likely inadequacies for such contests can have a similar effect.

Fear, then, gives birth to other emotions like jealousy, resentment, and envy. Jealousy springs from the fear that a valued relationship with a member of the opposite sex will be lost. And the anticipated unpleasantness of that potential loss includes the humiliation of having one's competence as a lover or spouse challenged. Similarly, practically everybody develops resentment toward, or envy for, those who have what they don't or who are more successful in whatever kinds of contests they might imagine. Such emotions are sometimes specifically focused on an actual person or event, but usually they are diffuse, symbolically directed toward categories of people or actions that might challenge various competencies or threaten beneficial arrangements. Hence, everybody possesses generalized images of potential threats; the extent to which they become particularized depends on the proximity of the provocative acts, persons, or threatening groups.

Symbolically driven emotions rooted in identification and fear heavily influence the way individuals react to people and events. The less the identification and the greater the fear, the more likely is social control to be attempted. For example, a person will be more or less outraged by an act of rape, and willing to impose sanctions, depending upon whether rapes like the one in question pose a symbolic threat to him/her, either directly or indirectly. All rapes will symbolically threaten females more than males, unless it is the rare case where the victim is male. A particular rape of a female, and others like it that might occur, will pose more of a symbolic threat to married males than to unmarried ones and to fathers more than non-fathers because husbands and fathers can imagine that their wives or daughters might be a target of such rapes. And, it will symbolically affect married males whose wives have life-styles similar to that of the victim more than it does husbands whose wives follow different patterns.

In a similar way, identification and fear lie behind generalized prejudicial or stereotypical judgments about individuals and categories of individuals, and they energize tendencies toward social control. Specifically, people will be more willing to use sanctions against those who represent symbolic threats than against others. Thus, blue-collar workers are more likely to want to exercise social control against other blue-collar workers and laborers than against white-collar workers or professionals because they regard similarly skilled or potentially skilled workers as symbolic competitors for their jobs. Average white males may want to exercise negative social control against black males more than against other white males because they may perceive, based on traditional stereotypes, that black males are more manly than they, as well as more attractive to females, both of which threaten their masculine self-concepts.

For individuals, then, all else equal, we would expect desires for, and attempts at, social control to follow patterns of identification and fear. Usually these two converge, but sometimes they conflict. When the two clash, fear takes precedence. For example, a female will be more inclined to exercise negative social control against male prostitutes than female ones because women can more easily identify with females than males. However, if a female prostitute, by her pattern of soliciting men like this woman's husband or lover, poses more of a symbolic threat than do male prostitutes, the woman in question will more readily exercise negative social control against the female prostitute. And even though a white, male police officer may identify with a young, white, male assaulter, he may nevertheless impose harsh sanctions through rough handling in arrest because he fears such offenders may physically defeat or verbally humiliate him or because he envies the offender's strength and courage, which may be beyond the officer's capacity.

Through the daily actions of control agents, these univeralistic personal proclivities intrude directly into formal social control. Police officers, court personnel (including probation and parole officers), and prison officials, to the extent that they can do so within the constraints of their jobs, therefore, can be hypothesized to administer sanctions in ways consistent with their own identification and fear emotions. Consequently, controlling for structural constraints, one should find more advantageous treatment for clients with whom functionaries can identify; that is, who are like the functionaries themselves. Specific acts should evoke different kinds of response depending upon whether functionaries can imagine themselves doing those acts, admire the skills necessary for their performance, and regard themselves as essentially similar to those who usually do them. Furthermore, patterns in sanctioning should reflect the general fears, resentments, jealousies, and envies of agents and functionaries. To understand and predict patterns of formal social control, therefore, one must be able to pinpoint the main foci of identity and fear among control personnel.

Yet, there is more to the social psychology of formal social control than individual functionaries acting on the basis of identification and personal threat in judging who and/or what should be sanctioned. There are also macro, transcendent effects. To understand macro-level social-psychological effects, one must consider how individual proclivities are translated into organizational or societal processes. First, this approach assumes that any social system is stratified and that the emotions of individual members of the dominant strata will be expressed as aggregate cultural patterns embedded in all institutions and institutional processes. Because controllers, including legislators and interpreters of law, will attempt to implement the feelings of those they believe are most important and relevant, formal social control in education, government, religion, organized recreation, the economy, and law will be exercised in a manner consistent with the patterns of identification and fear among dominant groups or categories.

Before the implications of this can be appreciated, one must recognize that there is rarely one dominant group or category for all domains of human activity or with respect to all behaviors. Dominance is fluid; what and who dominates changes with the focus and image. An individual may be part of a prevailing influence in one context and with respect to some things while being in the non-prevailing position in another context or with respect to another type of behavior. Dominants, therefore, are not a concrete, stationary body of people. For example, adults dominate youths, but whites, including white youth, dominate blacks. Males dominate females, but adult females dominate male children. Among males, strong men dominate weak ones in areas requiring physical strength, although weak males may dominate strong ones in the intellectual domain. Moreover, within a category that is dominant, the degree of that dominance may vary with the particular issue. While men may generally dominate women, women may dominate when it comes to the domain of child issues. Hence, the idea that societal institutions encompass the emotions of the dominant groups or categories is not as simple as it might seem, and spelling out the exact empirical expressions of identification and fear in the social control process is complicated.

Using these principles to predict patterns in social control is less complicated if domination is clear, as it is in juvenile court processing, where adults are always dealing with subordinate youth (Tittle and Curran 1988) or where it is achieved by raw coercion, as it might be with an occupying army or where one racial group thoroughly prevails, as whites did during the early 1800's in the U.S. South. But dominance is not always clear-cut or based strictly on coercion. In such instances, dominants' fears and identifications are translated into patterns of inequality in somewhat subtle ways, their effects usually being supplementary to main-line outcomes oriented around routine cases.

When dominance is not obvious or coercive, relative population numbers come into play. Under such circumstances control agents will attempt to implement the feelings of those they assume are most relevant and important. This means they will favor those who embody traits allowing for the widest possible identification and who pose the least overall threat to the largest number with respect to the domain of concern. For example, whites outnumber blacks, Hispanics, and Native Americans in the contemporary United States. Because of this, controllers will assume that whites garner the greatest total degree of identification and pose the least total amount of threat. As a result, their actions will embody the emotions of whites. Of course, this is tempered by the race of the controllers themselves, who, if non-white, may have difficulty personally identifying with particular suspects or perceiving them as non-threatening.

Another example where dominance is neither obvious nor coercive involves male-female differences in the United States. According to the social-psychological theory, females should be the prime pivot for identification and should be most often perceived as non-threatening because they outnumber males. Therefore, if the argument is correct, one would expect contemporary control agents to act in ways that reflect the emotions and social-psychological concerns of females; that is, females should be differentially advantaged in the process of formal social control. However, when some females engage in behaviors that threaten the status of females generally or challenge the public images characteristic of most females, those individual females should be more subject to social control even than males. Thus in general, females should less often be the objects of formal social control than males, but females whose behavior contradicts traditional female roles and status should more often be the object of social control. Following this theory, extraordinary efforts at control of unconventional females flow from the threat that unfeminine behavior poses for conventional females, not from male fear of such behavior. This application is especially interesting because it contradicts conflict-oriented theories, including some feminist ones, that suggest that males ought to be advantaged in the processes of formal social control because they have more control of resources and more overt power.

Although the influence of emotions is straightforward where domination is clear or based solely on coercion, it becomes complicated under conditions of social change. Sometimes coercive power arrangements change without immediately affecting preexisting patterns of inequality in formal social control. This is because identities and fears are passed from one generation to the next through socialization. People are not born with specific content to their emotional tendencies; they must learn to identify with some particular categories and things and to regard some specific things or people as threatening. Such learning is consistent with social dominance, provided the social system is stable. But since adults impart their own proclivities to children, who in turn train their young along the same line, it is a long time before changes in social structure get translated into large-scale alterations of patterns of identification and fear.

As a result, cognitive and affectional placement of objects, events, and people in social space is inherently quite conservative. If some group has been dominant, its influence on emotional development will continue for a time, even when the reality of numbers or actual power has changed. Thus, in modern postindustrial societies males can still project their identifications and fears into many domains even though they can no longer dominate females coercively and even though females currently outnumber males. This is because the political power of females as well as their numerical dominance is a fairly recent product of historical trends wherein advanced technology has freed women from traditional constraints and has generated mortality advantages for them that exceed male sex ratio advantages that prevail from birth through the first third of the life cycle (Guttentag and Secord 1983). Yet children are still taught to regard males as most relevant because of the generational lags built into the socialization process. Therefore despite female numerical superiority, males still have the most power and dominate in many domains, which implies that they garner much identification and represent less total threat than they might otherwise and as a result have their emotional concerns attended in some aspects of formal social control.

Conditions of Equality. Like the theories discussed before, this one also suggests that equality in formal social control is practically impossible. In fact, the only conditions where even a semblance of equality in the practice of formal social control might prevail would be in unstratified societies characterized by almost complete homogeneity of social characteristics and behavior. There the processes of identification would not cause inequality of social control. But a sexless, ageless society would soon become extinct. Moreover, even homogeneity would not be enough to produce complete equality of formal social control because the psychological processes of fear would still operate. That everybody is similar does not preclude their being competitors for lovers and resources nor does it relieve the symbolic humiliation of their potential success, whether undertaken by hook, crook, or natural talent. If the social-psychological arguments can be believed, imagining inequality to be perverse, as public issue–oriented analyses seem to imply, is simple minded because it assumes that the human emotions of identification and fear can be suppressed.

Limitations. The social-psychological perspective begins where consensus and conflict theories leave off. It takes for granted whatever system of stratification happens to exist and it simply contends that human emotions are interwoven with, and give meaning to, processes of social control that are structured by power distributions or patterns of dominance. Except for instances where dominance is not obvious or founded on coercion, this approach does not indicate exactly how and when particular emotions will be translated into inequality of processing. Furthermore, the theory does not take into account, or explain, structural constraints on expression of emotions, among which may be legal norms rooted in collective values of justice as well as bureaucratic procedures that minimize their manifestation. It is clear, therefore, that social-psychological theory must be integrated with larger structural theories if it is to be of maximum usefulness.

The Bureaucratic Perspective

Because most aspects of formal social control are carried out within formal organizations, at least in modern societies, procedures and outcomes reflect the principles of organizational operation and survival. A bureaucratic perspective assumes that any formal organization operates with three main objectives, each contingent on success of the previous. The most important objective is survival; the second is to meet its own needs as easily as possible; and assuming that these two are fulfilled, the third is to grow and expand (Gouldner 1959). Regardless of the ostensible goals organizations are established to achieve, they will "adapt and accommodate," do whatever they do in the easiest way possible in light of the resources available, and struggle to grow in size and influence. In adapting for survival or growth (accommodating to the external environment), organizations must be concerned with sources of financial and political support, particularly with the distributions of power in the social context in which they operate. Hence, an organization (1) will provide advantages for those who can help or hurt it, which incidentally means that in a comparative sense (2) their operations will disadvantage those with no influence over the organization's survival or mode of operation.

The bureaucratic perspective makes no attempt to explain why power and influence are distributed as they are or why resources are distributed in particular ways. Rather it takes those as given in a specific organizational context. Hence, if a particular class of people in a given jurisdiction has influence and power, regardless of how it came to have them, then the operations of formal agencies of control will reflect that reality by handling its business in ways advantageous to the powerful. If some segments of the population are so highly visible that their processing can bring unwanted attention to the organization, then such cases will be processed in a manner designed to reflect best on the organization, often implying more or less advantage for the person, the kind of case, or the category of people represented by a case or client in question. If particular groups, or categories of individuals, can mobilize moral responses that might help or hurt an organization, cases involving members of those groups or categories will be handled in a manner advantageous to the organization.

In addition, organizations respond to the constraints of their internal environments. They manage their everyday affairs with an eye to ease of operation and available resources. Organizations will always attempt to expand their resources, but failing that, they adapt to whatever they have. For example, given fixed resources, an organization will mold its operation to meet the work load. If the load is large, the organization will try to perform more efficiently by simplifying, categorizing, and routinizing. In agencies of formal social control, individualized information will be ignored, cases will be stereotyped, and standard procedures for handling "normal" (typical, routine) cases will be implemented (Sudnow 1965; Emerson 1969, 1992; Cloyd 1977). This, of course, advantages some and disadvantages others, but not always in conformity with social or demographic structures in the external environment. For instance, a "normal" burglary (one done in the typical manner that functionaries have come to expect, by the types of individuals typically expected) can be handled by routine arrest, a plea bargain, and standard penalty, while an "abnormal" one might require extraordinary police work, a trial, and an unusual sentence. As a result, some defendants with little power and few resources may actually come out better than others with more power and many resources because their stereotypical characteristics provoke "normalization."

On the other hand, given the same fixed resources and a small or declining caseload, an organization will respond differently. Since the object is to use all of the resources available to avoid losing them in future budget allocations as well as to establish a need for more, the organization will expand its procedures to absorb all available resources. One way is to complicate and individualize, avoid categorization and routinization, and instead scrutinize cases one by one and manage them as if they were unique. Again, this can advantage some while disadvantaging others. Individualization may mean that one person is punished more severely than another despite similar external characteristics because the minute details of the situation, previously ignored but now examined, indicate more or less culpability or more or less potential dangerousness of the accused.

Accommodations to the external and internal environments often converge, but sometimes they come into conflict. When internal and external accommodations contradict each other, the goal of survival takes precedence. Whether internal or external forces are more immediately crucial to survival depends on the social and political context, but external accommodation usually prevails.

Thus, the bureaucratic perspective suggests that to explain and predict patterns of formal social control one must understand the social, political, and physical environments within which agencies of formal control operate, as they bear on the organizational concerns of survival, ease of operation, and growth. Accommodations that organizations make in response to these concerns create inequalities, but not inevitably in one direction or another. Usually there emerges a complex interaction of accommodations that produce patterns of inequality that might not be obvious from ordinary social arrangements.

Conditions of Equality. The bureaucratic perspective suggests that formal social control in modern societies is highly unlikely to be administered with equality. It is perhaps conceivable that a utopian society might be so fundamentally committed to social equality that agencies of social control would have to accommodate to the external environment in ways that reflect such equality. That is, they might have to justify themselves by showing that all cases are processed with no significant deviations from patterns justified by the law, which if it were a utopian, egalitarian society, would itself permit variations only on the basis of some objective measure of benefit or harm. But it would be inconceivable that formal control agencies, even in a utopian, egalitarian society, might accommodate to their internal environments in ways that produced equality.

Imagine, for instance, that a social control agency could correctly anticipate handling a particular number of cases, of various types, within a given time period. How many resources should it ask for, be given, or somehow obtain? From the organization's point of view, the answer will be "all it can get." But nonpartisans prevail and the hypothetical egalitarian society allocates resources that decision makers think is adequate to process the cases and preserve equality in the doing. But, if organizational theory is correct, that agency will adapt its processing in order to use all of the allocated resources and be in a position to "need" more next time (objective 3: grow if possible). Hence, even if in the beginning allocated resources are "just the right amount" (whatever that might mean) to avoid too much categorization (that might lead to inequality) as well as too much individualization (which might also lead to inequality), the organization will nevertheless "over-individualize" so as to produce a shortage of resources that will justify a larger allocation. If the external society responds with increased resources, further "over-individualization" (and its accompanying inequality) will occur. If, on the other hand, the external society sees what is happening and restricts resources to avoid over-individualization, the organization will respond with categorization, which leads to another kind of inequality. And so it goes.

The bureaucratic perspective, then, predicts that inequality in the practice of formal social control in modern societies is to be expected. It does not deny that equality might happen in some ways and for restricted periods of time, but it would view these as more or less coincidental consequences of the unanticipated convergence of organizational processes operating in their own orbits and with their own principles. Thus, investigating formal social control as if equality were the standard of judgment misplaces the emphasis and reflects a lack of understanding of organizational phenomena.

Limitations. While bureaucratic theory offers an important counterbalance to consensus, conflict, and social-psychological theories, it is far more limited than they are because it takes for granted much of what they attempt to explain. No bureaucracy operates in a vacuum: all must have a reason for being, which is a reflection of the societal context in which they operate, and all must depend upon a social environment for resources. In addition, bureaucracies must at least ostensibly service the goals of their creators, no matter how distorted those goals may become in the process. And despite the principles of bureaucratic operation, human emotions necessarily intrude to color what happens. Therefore bureaucratic theory can only explain deviations from the general patterns suggested by the broader theories of conflict, consensus, and social psychology; it cannot explain the main effects. Yet the phenomena it deals with are so vital that adequate explanation of patterns of formal social control will require the other theories to incorporate principles of the bureaucratic perspective.

Foci for Integration

Each of the theories bearing on processes of formal social control has limitations that make it less effective or comprehensive than it could be. Moreover, some flaws in each of the theories is a strength of one or another of the others. Therefore, it would seem sensible to try to formulate a more effective general theory by merging elements from the separate perspectives.

Recall that a major weakness of consensus theory is its failure to recognize that perceptions of what or who poses a danger or threat to the society as a whole must also be explained. The theory implies that they are somehow transcendent, rooted in a mystical, inherent sense of collective consciousness. This oversight can be corrected by bringing in the conflict notion that general perceptions of collective danger are influenced by powerful interest groups who can use their resources to affect indirectly the content of mass media messages, school curricula, and legislative activity as well as to affect directly the actions of agents of formal social control. Similarly the arguments of conflict theory can be used to explain the content of the collective values around which societies are supposedly organized.

On the other hand, a major weakness of conflict theory is its failure to incorporate the underlying collectivist concerns shared by members of a society whether they have power or not. If there were no common values built around concerns for societal welfare that are fundamental to societal organization, why would it be necessary for elites to create false consciousness? Moreover, elites can only rarely maintain themselves with raw power; they almost always find it necessary to create some sense in others that the elites deserve to be in powerful positions because they do, or have done, something good for the collectivity. In other words, while powerful people can influence ideas of who or what is valuable, it is also true that preexisting ideas of what is valuable or important for the society, perhaps rooted in unique historical processes or maybe inherent to particular structural forms, may influence who comes to hold and exercise power.

Therefore, an effective integrated theory will show when, how, and why collective concerns emerge and prevail, despite oppositional private concerns, as well as when, how, and why private concerns dominate public interests. No doubt such an integration will also identify zones of overlap where collective and special interests converge. I suspect that such confluence will be greatest for serious and obviously predatory behavior that potentially endangers all, without redeeming virtue, and for individuals or categories of people who seem to jeopardize just about everybody by what they have done, or might do, to damage the collective organizational apparatus or spirit (Hagan et al. 1977). Confluence probably will be least for less serious and less obviously predatory behavior that may have redeeming virtue or for individuals or categories of people whose potential behavior has ambiguous consequences for the collective organizational apparatus or spirit.

But any integrated formulation along the lines suggested here will not be enough unless it also incorporates the effects of widespread emotional concerns centered around identification and fear. An effective theory will spell out the conditions under which those emotions are intertwined with collectivist notions in contrast to elite interests as well as the conditions under which they parallel, or can be manipulated to parallel, vested group interests. In addition it will point to circumstances where emotions spill over the boundaries of either collectivist or private group guidelines to "run wild" as it were or to serve only the whims of individual functionaries.

Finally, a fully integrated theory must have a place for the operation of bureaucratic tendencies. Even if a formulation shows how and when private or public interests come to the fore, and specifies the interlinkages among those conditions and social-psychological concerns, it will fall short unless it recognizes that formal social control, at least in modern societies, is exercised ultimately through bureaucratic organizations that have their own inherent tendencies toward survival and growth that influence how their declared missions are carried out. But this recognition must take the form of specific propositions about the conditions under which one or another organizational outcome will be likely, propositions that are interwoven with an integrated formulation merging consensus, conflict, and social-psychological theories.

Conclusion

Three conclusions follow from this consideration of theories about formal social control. First, none of the four perspectives leads one to expect equality in the practice of formal social control, except under very narrow and unusual circumstances. Judging by the logic of these theories, the commonly used policy-oriented rationale for discussion and research, that of discovering or documenting discrimination as if it would expose a well-hidden secret, is naive and of little scientific value. The important task is not to find out if there is inequality but rather to explain *why* there is inequality. In answering this question, theory must also specify the patterns through which inequality is expressed and the conditions under which one pattern rather than another is likely.

Considered in isolation, each of the theoretical perspectives bearing on formal social control is too narrow or incomplete to provide the kind of efficient explanation and prediction needed. They all seem to be so obsessed with their own themes that they omit essential parts of reality that are necessary to achieve fuller explanation. Thus, each one of them deals only with a fragment of a larger, yet-to-be-specified general theory.

It appears, however, that the four theories can, and should, be integrated. There are three main points of convergence around which an integration might be focused. The first is the intersection of private and collective concerns. The second involves the infusion of the social-psychological elements of identification and fear into the abstract collectivist stream as well as the day-to-day operational level. The third concerns inherent tendencies for bureaucratic agencies through which formal social control, at least in modern societies, is exercised to give precedence to their own survival and growth.

It will not be easy to work out all of the interconnections and permutations of a general integrated theory of formal social control. Moreover, such a theory will have to come to terms with empirical research, some of which challenges the overweening import of each of the four perspectives discussed in this essay. Ironically, the anomaly of actual equality in formal social control, snatches of which have been reported by researchers, may someday stimulate theorists to modify whatever integrated general theory might emerge from the limited perspectives looked at here. Nevertheless, it behooves us to formulate a more inclusive theory, even if it also ultimately proves deficient.

3

Modeling the Conflict Perspective of Social Control

Allen E. Liska

Although always an integral part of sociology, the study of social control has waxed and waned. Originally, the concept was defined broadly as any structure, process, relationship, or act that contributes to the social order; indeed, the concepts of social order and social control were indistinguishable (Meier 1982). Only recently have researchers defined social control independently and examined it as the focus of study.

These studies can be categorized as either micro or macro. Using individuals as the units of analysis, micro studies examine how various control activities, such as arresting, prosecuting, and sentencing, are affected by the legal, psychological, and social characteristics of people and their behavior. These studies are reasonably well organized and synthesized, constituting a clearly defined body of literature. Using collectives such as organizations and communities as the units of analysis, macro studies examine how social control patterns are affected by culture and social structure.

Numerous studies examine the structure and functions of the criminal justice system as the major social control bureaucracy, including studies of prison size and admission rates, prosecution rates, arrest rates, and police contact rates. More recently studies have also examined the structure and functions of the mental health system, focusing on factors that influence its size and social composition, and the structure and functions of the social welfare system, focusing on factors that influence its size and scope (such as eligibility restrictions and payments). Additionally, studies examine informal community control patterns and collective forms of social control, such as the historical emergence of the Ku Klux Klan, historical patterns of lynching, and the recent emergence of the Guardian Angels.

Most macro research takes the form of case studies, which only weakly test sociological perspectives on deviance and crime control (Erikson 1966; Harring 1983). Most of this research focuses on only one organization, program, or policy of control either within the criminal justice, mental health, or welfare systems, and most of these studies, isolated from each other, do not constitute a recognized body of research, "a literature," and their implications for a general macro theory of deviance and crime control are not fully exploited. The general purpose of this paper is to organize this research into a theoretical literature.

Theoretical Perspectives

Many of these studies can be organized within one of three general theoretical perspectives: rational choice or economic, structural-functionalism, and conflict.

Rational Choice or Economic Perspective

Within this perspective social control research focuses on crime control. It is generally macro, comparative, and theory testing, and it constitutes a recognized body of research that bears on general economic theory. Hence, it cannot and should not be ignored by other social scientists. The perspective (Becker 1968; Ehrlich 1973; Schmidt and Witte 1984) assumes that people have relatively stable preferences or interests, that they weigh the benefits and costs of behavior alternatives, and that they behave so as to maximize the ratio of benefits to costs. The study of crime control is always considered with regard to its impact on crime, particularly with developing policies and programs to control crime. Crime control and crime are thus part of one general model composed of three equations that predict (1) criminal behavior (crime generation equation); (2) crime control activities, such as arrests and convictions, which affect the cost of criminal behavior (production function equation); and (3) crime control resources, such as capital and labor, which affect the production of crime control activities (demand equation).

Criminal behavior is thought to be just like any other behavior. People engage in crime when the ratio of benefits to costs is higher for engaging in it than non-criminal alternatives. Effective crime control policies should decrease the benefits and increase the costs of crime and/or increase the benefits and decrease the costs of alternatives to crime (Becker 1968; Ehrlich 1973). One major cost of crime is punishment. Crime rates (equation 1) are thought to be a negative function of the level of punishment, especially the severity and certainty of punishment (Cook 1977; Blumstein et al. 1978). The level of crime control activity, e.g., the relative certainty of punishment, is conceptualized as a production function. It is assumed to be negatively affected by workload (crime rates) and positively affected by resources (capital and labor). Given constant resources, as the crime rate increases, the proportion of crimes cleared by arrests, prosecutions, or convictions should decrease, and given constant crime rates, as resources increase, the proportion of crimes cleared by arrests, prosecutions, and convictions should increase. Crime control resources (capital and labor) are viewed as a positive function of fiscal capacity and workload, such as crime rates. Resources allocated to crime control are thought to be constrained by a community's fiscal capacity, in the sense that a rich community can afford more crime control per capita (as it can afford more social services in general) than can a poor community (Phillips and Votey 1981).

Research has focused on the effect of a community's mean income, tax rate, and intergovernmental transfers, on crime control resources (Weicher 1970), and on the effect of crime rates (workload) on resources. As crime increases, citizens are thought to demand more crime control services. They are willing to increase revenues for crime control and to support political candidates who advocate strong crime control (McPheters and Stronge 1974; Carr-Hill and Stern 1979; Phillips and Votey 1981). In sum, crime control is approached as part of a clearly specified model, linking crime rates and crime control, which can be derived from a general rational choice theory of behavior. This has led to some very rigorous theory testing research that bears not only on the crime control model but on the general theory itself. Sociologists could learn much from the logical and empirical rigor of this work. Yet, the theory—particularly the three-equation model of crime and crime control—is built on some very questionable assumptions (Loftin and McDowall 1982), which direct research away from some fundamental questions.

Two assumptions, regarding interests and power, are particularly relevant to the study of crime control. First, crime is assumed to be more or less costly to all citizens, and thus all are assumed to be motivated and interested in controlling it. The power to influence crime control policy is equated with the vote, and elections are equated with a free market where information on candidates' crime control policies is fully available (Becker 1968; Ehrlich 1973; Phillips and Votey 1981). In effect, people are thought to have similar and enlightened self-interests regarding crime control and equal power to influence crime control policy. These assumptions depoliticize crime control and direct attention to the aggregate demand for crime control and to the objective social conditions that influence demand, such as crime rates and community resources.

These two assumptions should be considered very carefully. Interests and motivations to control crime are not self-evident. Indeed, they seem to be quite variable—varying over time, among societies, and among social statuses within societies. Rational choice theorists appear to be generally unconcerned either in explaining the distribution of interests in crime control and the distribution of power to influence crime control policy or in taking these distributions into account in explaining variation in crime control among social units.

Structural-Functional Perspective

The classical structural functional perspective conceives of society as integrated and orderly. It assumes that there is a general consensus on goals and values, that general needs for survival can be identified, that social structures (persistent patterns of behavior) function to maintain society's values, goals, and needs, and that social structures can be explained by these functions. While "modern or neo" structural-functionalism (Alexander 1985) may not make many of these assumptions, much contemporary social control theory and research is guided by them. Social control is thought to maintain society's values-goals-needs and to be explained by them. To the extent that the structure of social control is effective—functional—it is assumed to persist and remain stable.

This perspective has some general similarities to the rational choice (economic) perspective. Both assume that there is a consensus and stability of values and goals (in economic terms, preferences and interests) and that persistent patterns of social control come into existence and are maintained because they contribute to society's values and goals. While economists explicate the underlying processes in terms of enlightened self-interests and market mechanisms, structural functionalists talk more vaguely about social values and hidden feedback mechanisms, frequently couched in teleological and evolutionary terms.

From the general structural functional perspective three propositions can be identified regarding consequences, change, and stability in punishment as a form of social control.

Consequences. Durkheim (1938) noted various consequences of punishment, including the maintenance of social solidarity, social identity, social boundaries, as well as the control of crime. Social systems are assumed to sustain the level of punishment required to maintain necessary social states, such as social solidarity and social boundaries. Whether punishment controls crime is of secondary importance to its other functions. Crime enters into the analysis not as a negative social state to be controlled but as a stimulant to crime control (punishment). Thus, crime is frequently thought of as making positive contributions to society.

The "consequences" proposition has generated a loosely organized body of research composed of historical (Erikson 1966; Currie 1968; Connor 1972; Ben-Yehuda 1980), field observational (Dentler and Erikson 1959; Scott 1976), and laboratory-experimental studies (Lauderdale 1976;

Lauderdale et al. 1984). For example, Erikson (1966) describes in fascinating detail three crises in Puritan society initiated by the immigration of culturally dissimilar groups. He argues that these crises (Quaker persecution, Antinomian controversy, and witchcraft hysteria) stimulated crime control, which in turn functioned to redefine moral boundaries and sustain social solidarity.

Change in Punishment. Within the structural-functional perspective on crime control, social change tends to be treated as an extraordinary event. Yet, from time to time social systems, even those that are predominantly stable, experience events (e.g., political movements, immigration, economic inflation/depression, and war) that threaten the social order. According to the perspective, people respond to these threats with acts that reaffirm and strengthen their collective values and identity. In times of social stress, simple norm infractions are magnified and take on great symbolic significance, whereas in normal times they may just be ignored. Hence, during times of stress we might expect little tolerance and considerable punishment for norm violations.

Some support for this proposition can be found in historical studies, especially in studies on witchcraft. Erikson (1966), Currie (1968), and Ben-Yehuda (1980) interpret changes in the punishment of witchcraft as a response to boundary crises precipitated by socially disruptive events, such as an influx of culturally different people or a technological revolution. Yet most of these studies illustrate, rather than test, the theory. They are steeped in the contextual detail of a particular time and place, making comparisons across times and places difficult. Pivotal concepts, such as "boundary crisis," are not clearly defined so that they can be operationalized across historical contexts.

Stability of Punishment. Within the structural-functional perspective, patterns of behavior that are functional are assumed to persist (remain stable); since punishment is assumed to be functional, it too is assumed to be stable. This reasoning leads to interesting corollaries. Assuming that the overall level of punishment is stable, then as the crime rate increases, only the most serious crimes can be punished and the less serious ones must be ignored. Indeed, Durkheim (1938) argued that even the social definition of crime expands and contracts in relationship to the general volume of undesirable behavior. He described this in what has come to be known as the society of saints parable (Durkheim 1938: 68–69): "Imagine a society of saints, a perfect cloister of exemplary individuals. Crimes, properly so called, will there be unknown; but faults which appear venial to the layman will create there the same scandal that the ordinary offense does in ordinary consciousness. If, then, this society has the power to judge and punish, it will define these acts as criminal and treat them as such."

Considerable research, stimulated by the work of Blumstein and his colleagues, has addressed this issue. Their work has two interrelated thrusts: documenting the stability of punishment and identifying the causal processes that underlie it. Blumstein and associates (Blumstein and Cohen 1973; Blumstein et al. 1976; Blumstein and Moitra 1979) use time series techniques to examine the stability of imprisonment rates in the United States from 1926 to 1974, in Canada from 1880 to 1959, and in Norway from 1880 to 1964. They argue that imprisonment rates in these countries are generated by a stationary process, that is, the observed statistical variation in punishment over time can be modelled as statistical variation around a constant mean. In a reanalysis of these data, Rauma (1981a) argues that while a stationary process may indeed generate these observations, there is just as much evidence that a nonstationary process generates them. Furthermore, he argues that a univariate time series analysis can tell us very little about the causal processes, as specified by Durkheim and others, that underlie whatever level of stability is observed (Rauma 1981b).

In a second related research thrust, Blumstein tries to show how stability in punishment is maintained by continual adjustments in the type of behavior punished. In one study, Blumstein and Cohen (1973) examine the relationship between crime and arrest rates for serious and nonserious crimes in the United States. Their findings suggest that as the general crime rate increases, the arrest rate of nonserious crimes increases, thereby maintaining a stable general arrest rate (see also Tremblay 1986). In short, Blumstein and his associates have attempted to model the social process that underlies the stability of punishment. The model, however, is underidentified. They circumvent this problem by studying either the outcomes of the process (univariate times series) or by providing "guesstimates" of some of the parameters. What is needed now is research measuring more of the model variables and empirically estimating more of the model parameters.

Continuing in the Blumstein tradition, Berk et al. (1981) have also attempted to identify the equilibrating mechanism that underlies the stability of punishment. Assuming that the punishment rate varies somewhat around a specific level that is functional for a given society—the system target—then the growth rate of punishment is a simple function of the growth rate of the population. If for some reason punishment rates exceed the target, responding to changes in the external environment, future growth rates in punishment should decrease. And if rates fall below the target, future growth rates should increase. Growth rates of punishment are then the "mechanism" by which societies adjust the punishment rate to system targets. Berk et al. (1981), using a time series of imprisonment rates in California from 1851 to 1970, find no empirical support for this equilibrium hypothesis.

Generally, research leaves considerable doubt that the punishment rate in social systems is stable over time and that this stability is sustained because it is somehow functional. Moreover, research suffers from theoretical ambiguity in conceptualizing the social process underlying stability—an ambiguity that can be traced to Durkheim. Theorists and researchers alike assume that societies have certain requisites for survival, such as solidarity and boundary maintenance, and that a level of punishment persists because it functions to maintain these needs. But neither Durkheim nor recent researchers, such as Erikson, Blumstein, Rauma, or Berk, clearly specify the social process by which a level of punishment persists that maintains a system's requisites for survival. Instead, research examines the logical consequences of the punishment stability assumption. Assuming that punishment is stable, Blumstein and Cohen (1973) suggest that if the crime rate is high, then only the most serious crimes can be punished. Berk et al. (1981) imply that if the punishment rate is high, then the punishment growth rate will be low. These relationships are construed as the dynamic mechanisms by which stability is sustained. This is correct, but only in a logical or definitional sense. If the relationship between the rate of punishment and the growth of that rate is negative, then of course the punishment rate will tend toward stability. Yet, the study of such relationships does not shed light on the substantive causal processes by which this stability is sustained, that is, on those causal processes by which the consequences of punishment, such as solidarity or boundary maintenance, influence punishment so as to sustain a stable level of punishment.

Some researchers (Erikson 1966; Berk et al. 1983), and to a lesser extent even Blumstein and Cohen (1973), argue that the observed stability of punishment may simply reflect stability in the processing capacity of control systems. For example, stability in the prison population may simply reflect stability in prison size. Berk et al. (1983) argue that the constraints of prison capacity operate through the many daily admission and release decisions of criminal justice administrators. While interesting, this explanation of punishment stability is unrelated to the logic of structural functionalism. That is, if the capacity of a control system is stable, thereby limiting and stabilizing the level of punishment, then the postulation of unobservable goals, targets, and needs to explain stability is quite unnecessary. Blumstein et al. (1976:319–20), apparently unsatisfied with an explanation in terms of system capacity, argue "that social forces accounting for stability include more than simple prison-cell capacity.... More fundamental considerations of social structure are probably at work. If too large a portion of society is declared deviant, then the fundamental stability of society will be disrupted. Likewise, if too few are punished, the identifying values of society will not be adequately articulated and reinforced, again leading to social instability."

It is interesting that Erikson, Blumstein, and Berk make references both to unobservable targets, goals, and needs and to the capacity of the social control system in explaining the stability of punishment. Emphasis on the latter links their research to an explicit causal mechanism missing in the former, and emphasis on the former links their work to a general theoretical framework missing in the latter.

Conflict Perspective

While both the economic and structural perspectives have been important for studying and understanding social control, since the mid-1960s the conflict perspective has been the dominant perspective for organizing and stimulating macro research on social control. Contemporary conflict approaches to the study of social control can be traced to the work of Karl Marx and more recently to the work of Ralf Dahrendorf. Observing nineteenth-century Europe, Marx argued that class conflict is the basic social process—it is key to understanding other social processes and structures. In industrial societies there are two major classes: those who own the means of production (capitalists) and those who are employed by the owners (laborers). Their interests are diametrically opposed. As labor is an element or resource in the process of production, it is in the interest of capitalists to maintain low wages, which makes them more competitive on national and international markets. On the other hand, as the cost of labor to capitalists is income to laborers, it is in the interest of labor to increase the cost of labor. Thus, in accordance with the laws of competition the ranks of labor swell with unsuccessful capitalists, artisans, and farmers; laborers' standard of living decreases; and, thus, social conflict prevails. Marx also argued that the system of economic relationships affects the political, cultural, and religious institutions of society. Capitalistic societies, for example, develop laws, religions, and science that protect the interests of capitalists.

Ralf Dahrendorf's work (1959, 1968) is sometimes described as an adaptation of Marx to twentieth-century industrial societies. Dahrendorf argues that in contemporary industrial societies power is divorced from ownership and is based on institutional authority and that authority relationships in one institution (economic) do not necessarily overlap with authority relationships in other institutions (education, religion, government). Social conflict is fractured. Economic structures are important but not necessarily central.

Drawing on Marx and Dahrendorf, contemporary social conflict theorists conceptualize the study of social control in terms of the following questions: Why are the norms of some social groups transformed into law, thus criminalizing conflicting groups? Why are some laws enforced but not others, thus criminalizing those who violate some laws but not others? Why are laws enforced against certain groups but not others, thus criminalizing some law violators but not others? In answering these questions, conflict theorists argue that social power determines what norms become laws and what laws are enforced against what classes of people. During the late 1960s and early 1970s various pluralistic conflict theories of social control emerged, such as the work of Turk (1969a) on authority-subject conflict and the work of Blalock (1967) on racial conflict. During the mid-to-late 1970s much of the work on conflict reemphasized the importance of economic conflict in capitalist societies, such as the work of Quinney (1974, 1977) and Spitzer (1975).

Pluralistic Conflict Theories. Austin T. Turk's (1969a) book, *Criminality and Legal Order*, was one of the first efforts to formulate a general conflict theory of crime control. Following Dahrendorf, Turk focuses on conflict between those who have power to control behavior (authorities) and those who do not (subjects) in coordinated relationships (institutions). Like Dahrendorf, he does not link authority to ownership of the means of production or even to positions in the economic order, and he examines situational authority-subject relationships within institutions rather than overarching authority-subject relationships across institutions. Specifically, Turk asks two questions: Under what conditions are cultural and behavioral differences between authorities and subjects transformed into legal conflict? Under what conditions do those who violate laws (norms of authorities) become criminalized? Concerning the first question, Turk argues that authorities and subjects are most prone to struggle when their behavioral differences also reflect cultural differences; when subjects are organized enough to resist; and when subjects are unsophisticated, that is, violating laws in ways that bring public attention to their violation. Concerning the second question, Turk argues that the probability of law enforcement increases as the congruence between cultural and behavioral norms of authorities decreases, as the power of subjects to resist decreases, and as the sophistication of law violators decreases.

In one of the first general works on majority-minority relations, Blalock (1967) examines the social processes that underlie minority discrimination, which functions as a major mechanism by which majorities control minorities. Minority discrimination is hypothesized to be a function of threat to majorities, which in turn is related to minority size (proportion of the population); resources (such as money, property, prestige, authority, education, voting rights); and mobilization (proportion of resources that is utilized or expended). Blalock distinguishes two types of majority interests (economic and political), thus also distinguishing between economic and political threat. Concerning the former, he argues that discrimination (social control) is an additive function of economic competition (threat), which in turn is a function of minority size, mobilization, and resources. As any one of the three increases, threat to the majority increases. And as the latter increases, discrimination increases (in the form of geographical segregation, political disenfranchisement, blocked educational opportunities), which in turn reduces minority resources. Lacking the resources to mobilize (compete), minority size is no longer threatening to the majority. This causal process yields a curvilinear relationship between minority size and economic threat: as minority size increases, economic threat increases at a decreasing rate. Concerning politics, Blalock argues that political discrimination (social control) is a function of political threat, which is a simple multiplicative function of minority size, mobilization, and resources. Therefore, as any one of these increases, threat increases at an increasing rate. Any level of minority size is more threatening at higher than lower levels of minority resources and mobilization.

Economic Conflict Theories. By the mid-1970s Marxist conflict theory reemerged, reflected in the work of Richard Quinney (1974, 1977) and Steven Spitzer (1975). Drawing on general Marxism, Quinney argues that much of the Western world is entering an advanced stage of capitalism in which inherent contradictions become severe. Competition culminates in the failure of many capitalists, thereby increasing the ranks of the proletarian class, and the economic order becomes more technological and cyclical, thereby increasing the ranks of the surplus labor (the unemployed). Both the proletarian and the unemployed populations are threatening to established elites. Drawing on the work of O'Connor (1973), Quinney argues that the ruling class controls the threatening classes through both social welfare and coercive bureaucracies. Therefore, he argues that as capitalism matures, the proletarian and surplus labor increase, which increases the threat to ruling elites, which in turn increases welfare and coercive control bureaucracies.

While Quinney's theory provides a general analysis of social (crime) control in a capitalist society, various other Marxian conflict theorists have addressed specific issues of control, outlining in detail the social processes by which a capitalist economic structure affects the nature of social (crime) control. In an influential paper, Steve Spitzer (1975) discusses the classes of people that constitute problems for a capitalist society, how these classes of people are created, and how they are controlled (criminalized). Those people constitute a problem in a capitalist society who impede or hinder any of the following: the mode of production (e.g., people who refuse or are unable to work); the mode of distribution (e.g., the poor who steal from the rich); the processes of socialization into the modes of production and distribution (e.g., youth who do not attend or do poorly in school); and the ideology that supports the modes of production and distribution (e.g., vocal advocates of economic reform or revolution).

Problematic people are created by two inherent contradictions in the capitalist system. First, in advanced capitalism, competition culminates in the failure of many capitalists, thereby increasing the ranks of the proletariat. The economic order becomes increasingly technological and cyclical, thereby increasing the surplus population. Both the large proletarian class and the surplus population hinder the modes of production and distribution. Second, mass education, which is needed in a technologically advanced capitalist society, sharpens the critical abilities of working-class children, creating a population potentially critical of the capitalist ideology.

Problematic people are criminalized or controlled as the size of problematic populations increases; as the political organization of problematic populations decreases; and as other forms of social control become less effective, such as informal social control (e.g., the family and the church), military conscription of the poor, and private social control agencies (e.g., private police and vigilantes). In sum, Spitzer states that criminalization of problematic populations depends on the extent to which these populations are perceived as threatening, which in turn is related to their size, their political organization, and the effectiveness of other forms of social control.

Synthesizing Conflict Theories of Control

While concerned with group conflict, these theories focus on different social processes and describe them in very different terms. Turk talks of authority-subject conflicts and criminalization; Blalock talks about racial conflict and discrimination; Quinney talks about capitalist-proletarian conflicts and social control; and Spitzer talks about problematic populations and criminalization. These differences are not just differences of terminology for similar concepts, although there is some of that; they are real differences among these theories regarding who and what are threatening to whom. As to who is threatening, the Marxists (Quinney and Spitzer) refer to economic elites, and the pluralists refer to various powerful social categories, including institutional authorities (Turk) and majorities (Blalock). As to what is threatened, the Marxists refer to economic positions, Turk refers to authority positions, and Blalock refers to social positions. As to who and what are threatening, Quinney refers to proletarian and surplus labor; Turk refers to cultural and behavioral differences between authorities and subjects and to the organization and sophistication of subjects; Blalock refers to the relative size, resources, and mobilization of subjects; and Spitzer refers to the relative size and organization of problematic populations.

Despite the bewildering array of concepts (problematic populations, surplus populations, minority populations, culturally dissimilar populations), there is common logic that underlies these theories. Social control is a response of a ruling social category (economic elites, organizational authorities, majorities) to threaten, which itself is a function of the relative size, power, organization, and mobilization of a subjected social category, the threatening population. Among these theories there is perhaps one common and relatively consistent proposition: as the relative size of the subjected population increases, threat to the ruling category increases. Quinney refers to the size of the proletarian and surplus population; Turk refers to the size of the culturally dissimilar population; Blalock refers to the size of the minority population; and Spitzer refers to the size of the problematic population.

There are, however, also critical inconsistencies among the four theories. For example, Blalock argues that resources, which are the bases for power, lead to an increase in threat among the majority, which leads to an increase in social control; whereas Turk argues that the power of subjects leads to a decrease in social control. Also both Blalock and Spitzer argue that the organization of minorities and problematic populations leads to an increase in social control, whereas Turk argues that organization of subjects leads to a decrease in social control. Are subjects substantially different than minorities or problematic populations? I do not think so.

These theorists postulate different mediating causal processes. Blalock and Spitzer assume that threat to the ruling category mediates the effect of resources/organization on social control, thus the effect is positive. Turk postulates that the ability of subjects to resist control mediates the effect of resources/organization on social control, thus the effect is negative. Hence, if research shows a positive relationship, then the organization of the subjected is assumed to threaten the ruling categories, thereby supporting conflict theory, and if research shows a negative relationship, then the organization of the subjected is assumed to increase their ability to resist, thereby supporting conflict theory. Conflict theory explains everything and predicts nothing. Yet, both effects could exist. The organization of threatening populations could well increase their threat to the ruling category, which increases social control and could well increase their ability to resist, which decreases social control. To estimate the effect of one process, the effects of the other must be controlled. In so modeling these causal processes, theoretical inconsistencies become research problems (see model 1A, Figure 3.1).

There is also an apparent critical ambiguity concerning the relationship between forms of social control. Quinney explicitly states that threat

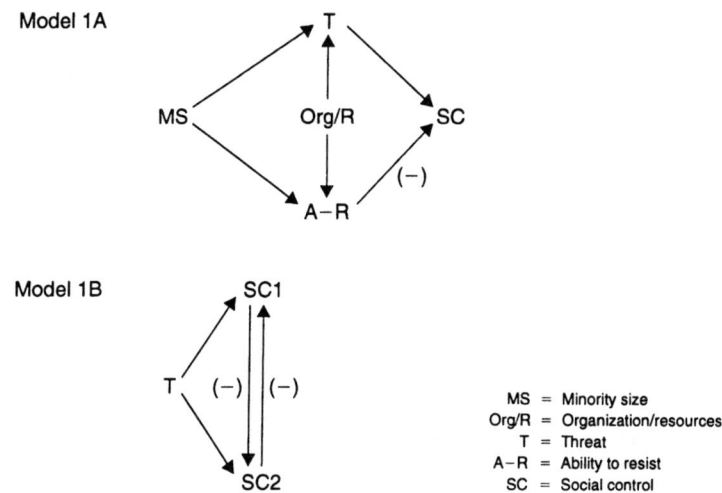

FIGURE 3.1 Modeling inconsistent causal processes

positively affects all forms of social control, thereby implying a positive relationship between them. Spitzer argues that if alternative forms of social control are effective, coercive forms (such as the criminal justice system) decrease, thereby implying a negative relationship between them. Hence, if research shows a positive relationship between forms of social control, it is taken to reflect the positive effect of threat on all forms of social control, thereby supporting conflict theory. And if research shows a negative relationship between some forms of social control, it is taken to reflect the suppressing effect of an effective form of control on the development of other forms, thereby supporting conflict theory. Again, conflict theory explains everything and predicts nothing.

Yet, both processes could be true. Threat can affect all forms of social control, yielding a positive relationship between them, and one effective form could retard the development of another, yielding a negative relationship between them (model 1B, Figure 3.1). To estimate the effects of one causal process, we must control those of the others. We can examine the negative effect of one form of social control on another by controlling for the positive effect of threat, and we can examine the positive effect of threat by controlling for the negative effect of one form on another.

In both of the above cases, different theorists suggest seemingly inconsistent social processes. This does not mean that conflict theory is contradictory; it only means that the theory is complex and thus that the implications of both processes must be considered simultaneously in a multivariate causal model.

In sum, drawing on traditional and general theories of social conflict

(Marx and Dahrendorf), scholars during the 1960s and 1970s explored the implications of social conflict for social control. Although all theorists seem to emphasize the importance of threat to a ruling social category, they disagree as to what and who are threatening to whom, yielding inconsistent and ambiguous propositions. Hence, research conducted in the 1980s always seems to support conflict theory without testing it. Yet, without testing it, the theory has not developed, and today after a decade of research, it remains about the same as originally formulated twenty years ago: it explains everything and predicts nothing.

Organization of Research Since the 1980s

While the 1960s and 1970s were a period of theorizing, the 1980s and 1990s have been a period of research,[1] much of it stimulated by the conflict perspective. I now turn to this work.

Because the critical causal variables of the perspective are not well defined, theoretically and operationally, and are not clearly linked to each other in the form of propositions or a causal model, the relevant research literature is also not well defined and integrated. Consequently, while research mushrooms, studies are organized and categorized by substantive forms of control (lynching, imprisonment, arrests, hospitalization, welfare) rather than by theoretical propositions. Researchers studying imprisonment are criminologists interested in prisons; researchers studying lynching are specialists in race relations or collective behavior; researchers studying mental hospital admissions are interested in mental health; and researchers studying welfare are experts in social services. Causal variables are selected that are important to a substantive form of control, that are readily accessible, and that are generally amenable to a conflict interpretation. Conflict theory and the threat hypothesis in particular are employed to loosely guide research and to interpret findings.

This body of research does not provide critical tests of conflict theory. Theoretical variables, such as "cultural dissimilarity between authorities and subjects" and the "mobilization/resources/power of subjugated populations" are not directly operationalized and studied. Indeed, they are not even treated as variables; rather they are used to "interpret" why one social category is threatening to another. Whites, for example, are thought to be threatened by blacks because they are culturally dissimilar; therefore, as the relative size of the black population increases, the threat to whites increases.

Moreover, while some studies do focus on theoretical issues and variables, these studies are so isolated in distinct literatures that it is difficult to grasp their cumulative implications for conflict theory. For example, one crucial issue is the relationship among forms of social control. One version of conflict theory posits a positive relationship among them and another version posits a negative relationship. Three research literatures have developed: lynching and executions, prison and psychiatric admissions, and criminal justice and welfare expenditures. While these literatures deal with similar theoretical issues, they are completely isolated from each other, rarely even citing each other. Those studying the relationship between lynching and executions in the South are specialists in race relations and historical demography (Beck et al. 1989). They have little interest in contemporary mental health and social welfare bureaucracies. Those studying the relationship between prison and mental hospital admissions seem to be primarily interested in exploring the consequences of the recent deinstitutionalization of mental hospitals (Steadman et al. 1984). They have little interest in historical race relations or the social welfare system. Those studying the relationship between criminal justice and social welfare expenditures seem to be primarily interested in welfare as a means of controlling the poor (Inverarity and McCarthy 1988). They have little interest in mental health and historical race relations. While all three literatures have loosely developed within the conflict perspective, research issues are not conceptualized that cut across these specific literatures, and no one has taken stock of findings that are common among the literatures.

Consider a second example. As previously mentioned, the relative size of a subjected population is perhaps the one variable that is common among conflict theories and the one theoretical variable that is easily measured. Thus, it is a crucial variable. There have been numerous studies (e.g., Isaac and Kelly 1981; Liska et al. 1981) of the effect of the relative size of subjected economic and racial populations (measured as the percent poor, below poverty, unemployed, nonwhite, and black) on various components of the criminal justice system (police size, use of deadly force, arrests, prison admissions), the mental health system (admissions, headcounts, expenditures), the welfare system (eligibility restrictions, payments, and number of recipients), and collective actions (lynchings). Yet, no one has taken stock of this work across these many forms of control, across just the bureaucratic forms, or even across just the many components of one bureaucratic form.

Again, the problem lies in the organization of knowledge. Those who study the effect of the percentage of nonwhites on welfare are primarily interested in welfare and those who study its effect on the criminal justice system are primarily interested in criminal justice. Even among those who study the latter, those who study its effect on arrests are primarily interested in police, and those who study its effect on prison admission are primarily interested in prisons. Very few researchers are primarily interested in studying the consequences of minority size on social control as a crucial test of conflict theory. A review of this relationship across literature might yield some interesting conclusions. My cursory review suggests that the relative size of racial minorities may be more important than the relative size of the economically disadvantaged for the criminal justice system but that the reverse may be true for the welfare system. What are the implications for conflict theory?

In sum, perhaps, because conflict theory is so vague and inconsistent it is difficult to know what research constitutes a crucial test of it. Perhaps because of this and for various other reasons, most macro research on social control is organized around forms of control. While conflict theory has been used to stimulate and interpret much of this research, for the most part this research has not been synthesized across forms of control and has not been used to critically test conflict theory. Conflict theory and conflict research remain worlds apart.

Modeling the Conflict Perspective

The primary task of this paper is to formulate a conflict theory of social control that generates research problems that cut across specific forms of social control. The theory need not be complex or complicated, just clear. What then are the fundamental implications of social conflict for social control? Whereas most perspectives focus on threats to the common interests of all or most social groups and categories, reflecting assumptions of social consensus, the conflict perspective focuses on threats to interests unique to powerful groups and social categories, reflecting its assumptions about social conflict. A first step in this undertaking, then, is conceptual organization. What and who are threatening to whom?

Theory and research include a bewildering array of sources of threat. They can, however, be conceptualized into three general categories: acts, people, and social distributions. The first refers to voluntary acts, such as crime, riots, and labor strikes, that are perceived by the powerful to threaten their interests. The second refers to categories of people who are perceived by the powerful to threaten their interests depending on their relative size, organization, mobilization, and resources. The third refers to distributions of people across social space (income equality and racial segregation) that are perceived by the powerful to threaten their interests.

It is also important to distinguish among various threatened and ruling social categories. In postindustrial societies there are many sources of power: economic elites, institutional authorities, and majorities. What is threatening to one is not to another and the response of one may be different from that of another. For example, economic elites may be less threatened by street crime, which they can easily avoid, than by economic disorder (strikes), which may affect their position in the social order, and they may respond through political processes by strengthening the capacity for social control (e.g., police size), which is then available, if needed, to preserve the social order. Institutional authorities such as upper- and lower-level criminal justice managers may be very threatened by street crime and the categories of people whom they associate with it. Attempting to control their working environment, they may respond by increasing arrests and imprisonments. Majorities, on the other hand, may feel very threatened by minorities who compete for housing and jobs, and they may respond by various forms of market discrimination that control minorities. The point is that in most postindustrial societies there are various power sources. While threat to the interests of powerful social categories may well increase social control, the level and form of social control may well depend on what and who are threatened.

When bringing together ideas from loosely related theories, in addition to developing a set of overarching concepts, it is necessary to develop a set of integrated (consistent) propositions and to explore their implications taken together (Liska et al. 1989). One method of doing this is through causal modeling. Representing ideas in a causal model (and corresponding equations) explicates the underlying logic that links the propositions, which is vital to locating inconsistencies among them and to exploring their net implications.

Consider a simple causal model (model 2A, Figure 3.2) in which social control is a function of the level of threatening acts, people, social distributions. The shape of the function is left undefined and its strength depends on what social category is threatening. The model does nothing more than formalize the logic of the threat hypothesis in terms of conceptual categories that apply to most forms of social control. It can be complicated systematically by adding multiple forms of social control and other social processes.

By studying more than one form of social control, we can estimate the relative effects of threatening acts, people, and social distributions on different forms of control and examine how the size and change in one form influences another (see model 2B, Figure 3.2). Consider other social processes. While threat may generally affect social control, various forms of social control may require resources as well as threat. Elites, for example, may be motivated to expand the capacity of the criminal justice system (police size and prison size); yet, this may be difficult to do in a fiscal crisis. Indeed, some social conditions that simulate threat (e.g., percent unemployed) may be related to social conditions (declining economy) that decrease resources. Hence, resources may both independently affect social control and interact with threat to affect social control (see model

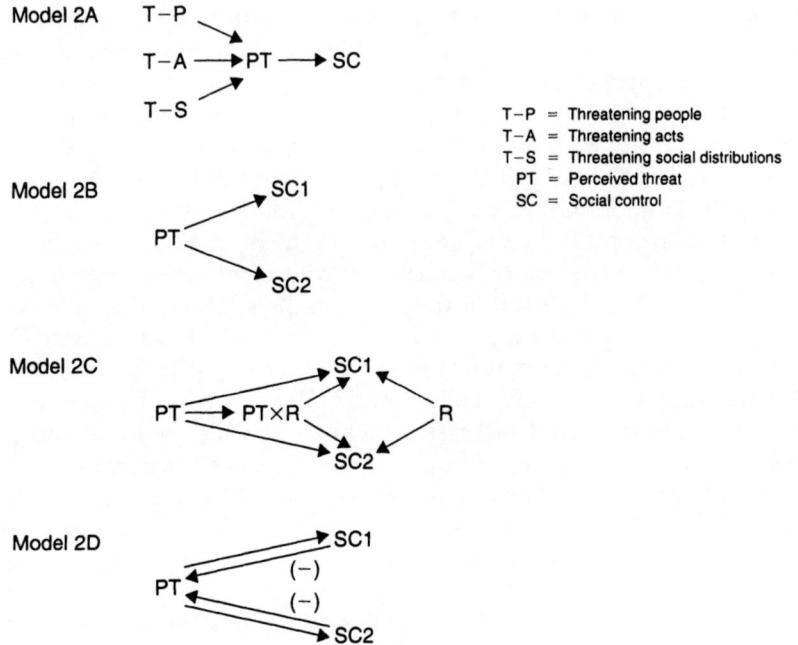

FIGURE 3.2 Modeling the causal structure underlying the conflict perspective

2C, Figure 3.2). Also, while threat is infinite, resources are finite. Resources use to finance one form of control are simply not available to finance others. This constraint may lead to a negative relationship between some forms of social control.

As another social process, consider the effect of social control on the perceived threat of the powerful. Forms of control that are perceived as effective may reduce the perceived threat, which in turn may reduce other forms of social control. Explicitly postulating negative feedback loops from social control to perceived threat (see model 2D, Figure 3.2) leads to the study of equilibrating processes and their implications for relationships between sources of threat and forms of control and for relationships among forms of control.

In sum, we need to extract the implications of social conflict for social control, formulate these implications in a clear and consistent model, and generate research problems that cut across forms of control, thereby organizing research on different forms of control in terms of a unified theory.

Conclusion

This paper has examined the implications of social conflict for social control. Compared to traditional perspectives of social control, the conflict perspective directs research to the social conditions that threaten the powerful. Specific conflict theories have not explicated the implications of this and other assumptions, yielding inconsistent propositions. Lacking a clear theoretical framework, research has been organized around specific forms of control, yielding little research accumulation and theoretical feedback. This paper has used causal modeling to clarify the underlying logic of the perspective, to extricate its empirical implications, and to identify issues that cut across forms of control.

Notes

1. During the 1980s, conflict theory developed in the work of feminists who focus on gender conflict and social control. Much of this work is a critique and uncovering of forms of gender discrimination and control; much of it is written by humanist and literary scholars who are not very concerned with rigorous theory testing; and much of it focuses on informal controls (e.g., family controls) rather than on formal or bureaucratic forms of control. Thus, as might be expected, much of the theory and research on gender conflict and social control are not well integrated with the theory and research on class/race/ethnicity and social control, which is the focus of this paper. Nonetheless, there is much among feminist theory and research that is relevant to this body of work, such as the role of the social welfare system in controlling the behavior of women—a topic I discuss elsewhere.

4

Rethinking and Unthinking "Social Control"

Anthony M. Platt

Optimism of the heart and pessimism of the mind, as the leftist adage goes, is reversed for me these days. The political defeat and self-destruction of revolutionary social movements and parties, the military hegemony of the United States, and the staying power of the capitalist world economy have quickly sapped the spirit of even the most enthusiastic leftist. The models for achieving human equality that seemed so promising only twenty years ago—whether the state socialism of the former USSR and Eastern Europe, the decolonization and national liberation struggles in the Third World, or Keynesian-style social democracy in the West—are in crisis and disarray (Wallerstein 1991a). However, in this moment of paralysis in practice and strategy, new critiques of taken-for-granted paradigms and new developments in theory are quickly liberating our minds, if not our souls. As Immanuel Wallerstein (1991b) has noted, we need to not only *rethink* our strategies and analyses but also to *unthink* much of the intellectual baggage that we inherited from nineteenth-century social science (Marxism included). In this paper, I will sketch out for discussion some aspects of this theoretical moment in the U.S.

Critique

It is a healthy sign that many of us who positioned ourselves in the sociological left and focused on issues of "social control"—whether from the starting point of praxis in radical criminology or the Marxist wing of the sociology of deviancy or a more general interest in political economy—are undertaking a reconsideration of our past theoretical journeys. The work, for example, of David Garland (1990) and Dario Melossi (1990) is enormously helpful in guiding us, once again, through the trajectory from Durkheim to Foucault. Using radical criminology and social control theory as a lens, let me examine some central points of the critique.

First, social control theory in the 1960s and 1970s broke with both the "legal syllogism" of the Durkheimian tradition and the technocratic managerialism of policy research (Melossi 1989, 1990). Classless depictions of "society" and efforts to construct a disinterested science by leading intellectuals were ruthlessly debunked (Platt 1991). Our theoretical constructs were typically eclectic and derivative. We borrowed heavily from political polemics, interwoven with civil libertarian critiques of the state, revisionist history, and ethnomethodology.

Both labeling theory and conflict theory, which had traditionally been used apolitically or to justify social control, were now used by humanists and leftists to examine the repressive, discriminatory, and arbitrary practices of the state, its managers and professional surrogates. And it was not so much Marx, Engels and Lenin who guided this development as it was Erving Goffman (1961), Howard Becker (1963) and Thomas Szasz (1965). The Old Left did not exactly share the New Left's affinity for Goffman's rebels subverting the authority of total institutions, Becker's cool bohemians smoking grass in jazz clubs, or Ned Polsky's (1967) hustlers hanging out in pool halls. And our critiques of the "caretakers" of social control and petty officialdom, as Alvin Gouldner (1968) noted in his well-known essay that challenged the radical pretensions of labeling theory, were hardly the stuff of political economy.

When we looked for grander theoretical models, there was a tendency to import mostly non-Marxist or unorthodox Marxist work—Taylor, Walton and Young's *The New Criminology* (1973), anarchist-oriented writings from Scandinavia (such as Mathiesen's *The Politics of Abolition* [1974]), the 1968 reissued version of Rusche and Kirchheimer's *Punishment and Social Structure* (a 1939 product of the Frankfurt School), Fanon's *The Wretched of the Earth* (first published in the U.S. in 1965), and, later, Michel Foucault's *Discipline and Punish* (published in the U.S. in 1977 and popularized here via French Canadian intellectuals), and the work of the Birmingham school in England (Hall et al. 1978). One positive result of this eclecticism was that social control theorists in the U.S. did not adopt some of the more dogmatic and reductionist tendencies within Marxism.

The second critique argues that social control theory of the 1960s and early 1970s drew heavily upon instrumentalist theories of the capitalist state and functionalist interpretations of power. My own work *The Child Savers* (1977) was very much in this tradition. So too was Piven and Cloward's *Regulating the Poor* (1971) and Rusche and Kirchheimer's *Punishment and Social Structure* (1939), which argued for a direct relationship between welfare policy and modes of penal punishment on the one hand

and fluctuations in the capitalist labor market on the other. As we now know—from post-Foucault, post-gender studies, post-cultural studies—there are some major weaknesses and omissions in this approach.

The first weakness was an overemphasis on the centrality of punitive and coercive institutions in the maintenance of social order. When we take into account the continuum of discipline from parents to school, the technologies of self-discipline, and the power of ideological representations, then prisons and police seem to occupy a more marginal, or at least more modest, place in the maintenance of social order. What could be more totalitarian, for example, than Barrett and McIntosh's (1991) "antisocial family" or Takaki's (1979) Republican, corporate and demonic "iron cages"? Second, as Melossi has noted, there was a tendency to reify and depersonalize the state as well as to imbue it with an exaggerated degree of concerted rationality. Third, like Durkheim, social control theorists typically focused on the reactive and power-maintaining role of the police, courts and other legal-penal institutions, and in doing so minimized their creative and innovative aspects. As Foucault observed, "Prison is an organization that is too complex to be reduced to purely negative functions of exclusion; its cost, its importance, the care that one takes in administering it, the justifications that one tries to give for it seem to indicate that it possesses positive functions" (Simon 1991: 28). The Foucauldian perspective encourages us to explore the "eliminative process" of the prison and the symbolic meaning of its procedures of exclusion. Fourth, the targets of social control were often characterized as robotic victims or, worse, romantic rebels.[1] Accounts of socialist experiments in criminal justice, such as the Ricketts' *Prisoners of Liberation* (1973), were often mechanically imported without serious discussion of what was applicable from a China or a Cuba to this country (Horton and Platt 1986). As I shall discuss later, cultural studies, postmodernism and feminism have quickly changed all that.

New Directions

New developments in theory that emerged in the 1980s were given a boost by the collapse of the Soviet Union and East European communism. Those of us who had reluctantly supported or refrained from publicly criticizing states that violated socialist norms were freed from an obligation to defend our enemies' enemies.[2] Let me briefly identify some important theoretical developments over the past decade.

First, we are beginning to move beyond overly determined, overly economic, and essentialist conceptions of class—and with it mechanical distinctions between base and superstructure. We are much more wary of "privileging" class over ethnicity/race and gender/sexuality and of universal, transcendental, and ahistorical theories that rank oppressions and advocate absolutist solutions. There is a new richness and complexity to our understanding of power and social control when it is informed by a class analysis in which race and gender are *constitutive* of the material relations of production and reproduction, when racism and sexism are reciprocally determining processes, not simply a social *by-product* of exploitation (McCaughan 1991; Wallerstein 1988). The work, for example, of Takaki (1979), Hooks and West (1991) and Andersen and Collins (1992) in the U.S. and of Hall (1988a, 1988b, 1990), Bhabha (1990), Gilroy (1987) and others in England exemplifies this fruitful reworking of class analysis. Similarly, studies of race and racism are being enriched by reconstructing the concept of ethnicity, and the study of gender has benefitted enormously from the application of social constructionism to the history of sexuality (Boswell 1990; Hall 1990).

Second, Left theories of social control have always been concerned about the ideological means through which relations of domination are enforced, contested, and received: the cultural space between the formal institutions of power and people's daily lived reality. Postmodernism and deconstruction and gender and cultural studies have enriched and enlarged this field of inquiry, especially given the political defeat of Leninism. Gramscian notions of hegemony have taken on a new complexity that befits a world of globalized culture (Eagleton 1991). No longer can we characterize ideology as only a reactive instrument of power or culture as simply another important site of investigation to be added to economic analysis. The challenge, as Wolff (1991: 171) has observed, is "the integral place of culture *in* social processes and in social change: the cultural formation and identity of social groups, as well as of ideologies, discourses, and practices." Recent work on nationalism and patriotism perhaps best exemplifies Wolff's call for a cultural materialism that integrates texts and representations into economic and political processes (Hall et al. 1978; Samuel 1989; Bhabha 1990; Anderson 1991; Parker et al. 1992).

Third, human agency once again reinvigorates theories of social control, giving us instruments of social control who have been humanized and made into flesh-and-blood actors. Women's and gender studies, for example, have given us qualitatively new insights into the "first wave" of feminism and the contradictory role played by female child savers, social workers, educators and political reformers from the 1870s through the 1920s. The new petty bourgeois women were not only surrogates of the rising managerial class nor simply "symbolic crusaders" filled with "status anxiety." Now we can variously understand them as entering politics through voluntary work and public space, as forging a "female dominion" in state bureaucracies, as making a professional self-identity at the expense of working-class women and women of color, and as active participants in the gendered construction of social policy (Baker 1984; Mink 1990; Ryan 1990; Walkowitz 1990; Frankel and Dye 1991; Muncy 1991).

Moreover, historians and sociologists have also begun to pay attention not only to "the voices which the past has left, but also the silences" (Cunningham 1991: 232). Some contributions within cultural studies in particular have enabled us to explore the Gramscian approach to ideology from the bottom up and thus to appreciate how hegemony is constructed, shaped and contested in the shifting, unstable terrain of everyday "common sense" (Clarke 1991). When we return, for example, to the child-saving movement through the experiences of working-class families, we find that the juvenile court was not only an imposed instrument of class rule and bourgeois morality, but also an institution to which many single mothers turned in a search to reinforce their declining authority over rebellious daughters (Odem 1991). "What some historians have labeled social control," notes Boris (1991: 82), "can therefore be more accurately interpreted as an intervention into families on the part of the state and professional experts, mediated by the gender, class, race, and ethnicity of both family members and interveners. This process was more interactive than the concept of social control suggests." This emphasis on the *resonance* of social control within working-class communities and popular culture is a common theme in the new social history and cultural studies. Hall's (1988) analysis of Thatcherism's appeal to an "authoritarian populism" is perhaps the best-known example of this genre.

Occasionally we can find studies in which the two worlds of human agency so engage each other in all their dynamic complexity that we are able to understand the actual processes through which "social control" is contested and imposed. In Gutierrez's (1991: xvii–xviii) social history of New Mexico through three centuries of Spanish, Mexican and Indian relations between 1500 and 1846, we learn about both the "visions of the victors" and the "voice of the mute and silent," not as separate, disconnected monologues, but as

> a dialogue between cultures, each of which had many voices that often spoke in unison, but just as often were diverse and divisive. . . . [T]he historical process that unfolds here is a story of contestation, of mediation and negotiation between cultures and between social groups. This is not the history of Spanish men or of Indian men, or of their battles, triumphs, and defeats. It is a history of the complex web of interactions between men and women, young and old, rich and poor, slave and free, Spanish and Indian, all of whom fundamentally depended on the other for their own self-definition.

A similar multidimensional perspective informs Deutsch's (1987) analysis of the cultural and economic contests between Anglos and Hispanics in the Southwest from 1880 to 1940.

Fourth, new work on ethnicity, racism and culture has opened up some exciting new theoretical and strategic possibilities. In the past, most writings on racism and social control focused on exposing victimization and documenting the dynamics of racial oppression. Moreover, most work was not only race specific but also tended to emphasize only one ethnicity, typically African-Americans, typically framed in gender-neutral terms (Carmichael and Hamilton 1967; Blauner 1972). This was a necessary building block and corrective to racism in the social sciences but it was also a limitation.

In recent years there has been a qualitative break with this kind of linear interpretation. As Hall (1988b) has observed, we are at the end of a certain innocence in cultural politics. Many intellectuals seem to be following West's admonition that a "race-transcending prophet is someone who never forgets about the significance of race but refuses to be confined by race" (Hooks and West 1991: 49). Takaki's (1979) ground-breaking work on race and culture in the nineteenth century, published over a decade ago, gave us some important insights, which we have been slow to develop. "Where scholars have examined separately the oppression of blacks, Indians, Mexicans, and Asians," wrote Takaki (1979: xiii, 136), "I have tried to analyze the ways the experiences of these different groups related to each other.... While studies ... have advanced our understanding of the subordination of blacks and women respectively, they have tended to analyze the two groups separately."

This dynamic, relational and dialectical approach to race and gender, in which cultural attitudes and representations are located in their material contexts, sets the stage for further studies that are gradually challenging the theoretical ghettoization of race. "Whiteness" is no longer seen as an unproblematized given, but, like "blackness" and other racial categories, is a matter of political, cultural and social construction (Gilroy 1987; Saxton 1990; Roediger 1991). Similarly, it is not enough to add gender and sexuality to class and gender, but, as in the films of Marlon Riggs ("Ethnic Notions" and "Tongues Untied") and the writings of Hooks, Hall and others, one must understand their constitutive interdependence.

Conclusion

I would like to conclude with some tentative suggestions for the future direction of social control theory. First, we need to move beyond the constraints that are imposed on theory by established canons and territorial professionalism. The kind of imaginative work that is under way demonstrates the importance of moving back and forth between academic disciplines and different levels of theory. Davis (1990: 265–322), for example, draws upon urban sociology, architecture, race relations, and criminology to make sense of the "war on drugs" in Los Angeles's ghettos and barrios. "Sociology," "criminology" and "law," the traditional homes of social control theory, need to quickly learn from and incorporate the new insights coming from history, philosophy, literary criticism, gender and cultural studies, and ethnic studies. Moreover, it is not accidental that most new, ground-breaking work is coming from the marginalized others of academia, notably women and intellectuals of color who are challenging the established gatekeepers of knowledge (including Marxist orthodoxy).

Second, we need to move beyond the "separate spheres" approach to social control. We have sufficient case studies of specific sites of domination and power—prison, family, law, ideology, racism, heterosexism, corporate economy, and so on—to begin to understand the dynamic interplay between formal and informal, direct and indirect, coercive and persuasive institutions. Moreover, it does not make analytical or political sense to pit class against race, or race against gender, or gender and race against class analysis. If human equality is to be neither negotiable nor ranked, then we need theoretical constructs that are inclusive and expansive.

Third, we should not abandon the insights accumulated from the many studies of the political economy of social control. I still think that we live in a world capitalist economy and that the "stamp" of its class-conscious leadership shapes the contours, ideologies, assumptions, and prerogatives of institutions of power. It is understandable that recent work in radical and critical criminology has become more local and decentered in its focus, partly in reaction to the dogmatism of earlier theories of the state and partly in the search for mid-range policy options that are necessitated by the crisis in revolutionary strategies (Matthews and Young 1986, 1992; Pepinsky and Quinney 1991). But in a world that is becoming increasingly interdependent and increasingly at the mercy of transnational corporations, we should not abandon the study of capitalist states (Barak 1991) or the political-economic dynamics of social control (*Social Justice* 1991). However, we also need to pay close attention to the studies of human agency that give us a richer, more complex and contradictory view of both the agents and subjects of social control. The Left in particular needs to be armed with a much more sophisticated body of theory in order to understand the resiliency of capitalism and the failures of seemingly revolutionary movements and states (McCaughan 1991).

Finally, the new developments in theory should be welcomed. In revitalizing and reconstructing the field of "social control," they help us to break out of dogmas and compartments that gave us a false sense of security and put blinders on our imagination. Of course there is a danger that the search for complexity will degenerate into an amoral relativism and what Hall (1988b: 28) calls an "endlessly sliding discursive liberal-pluralism." We need to take that risk. The structures of domination are more resourceful than we thought, the struggles for equality more difficult. We need the kind of interdisciplinary and comparative theory that not only gives us a better grasp of the dynamics of social control but also enables us to construct a political vision of equality that resonates in the public imagination. There is much to both rethink and unthink.

Notes

1. Let us not forget the characterization of "street crime" as a form of "primitive rebellion" (to abuse Hobsbawm's concept), or Eldridge Cleaver's characterization of rape as an act of liberation, or "Tear Down The Walls" as the slogan of the 1970s prison movement.

2. My thanks to Gregory Shank for this point.

5

The Police: Symbolic Capital, Class, and Control

Peter K. Manning

Social control, the response to behavior defined as deviant, including both over-conformity and norm violation, which is closely linked to the authoritative or political process of ordering groups (Clark and Gibbs 1965), should be studied contextually.[1] Studied "contextually" means that an analysis should take into account the dualistic meaning of structures of social control. They enable subjective responses and are dependent upon them; they both shape and are shaped by social practices (Giddens 1981). Social control takes place within the constraints of structures (rules for patterning and patterns of allocation of the valued) and schema that serve to maintain structures (Bourdieu 1977; Giddens 1984; Sewell 1992). The links between conceptions of social control and the practices of agencies of control remain underdeveloped (Lemert 1967b).

Police studies are no exception to this general rule. Analysis of the police role in maintaining social control, vertical and horizontal stratification, is especially underdeveloped (see Cooper and Platt 1968; Westley 1970; Center for Research on Criminal Justice 1977; Harring 1983; Marx 1989). Their role in authoritative ordering is little explored.[2] However, in order to understand authoritative ordering one requires a theoretically grounded conception of the social order and its reproduction, the nature of the differential access of groups to goods and services, and of how classes, or structures of interests and life chances, are shaped by policing. Only by examining the practices that sustain control can one understand patterns of formal social control in the courts, prisons, police, and social welfare. Following Pierre Bourdieu, a French sociologist whose work links mental schemata, objective constraints and social structures, this chapter outlines the role of the American police in sustaining the distribution of the valued, or symbolic, capital in policing domestic conflicts. The police apply violence, reducing the capital of the working classes and the poor, and mystify their own strategies and tactics.

Production and Reproduction of Social Order

Bourdieu has written widely on academic life (1988), peasant economies (1962, 1977), ideology (1990a), education (Bourdieu and Passeron 1977), art and photography (1990b), and language (1991). An overview of his work, a collaborative effort with Loic J.D. Wacquant, was recently published (Bourdieu and Wacquant 1992). He combines an elegant structural/linguistic model with a sophisticated, dynamic analysis of agency and choice.

Bourdieu argues that a linguistic model of structure can be combined with a mentalistic schema or mode of perception to demonstrate stability in the distribution of valued resources or what he calls "capital" (DiMaggio 1979:1460). He assumes that classes seek a monopoly of symbolic violence in order to maintain their position and to reduce others' resources. Symbolic violence is the cost of inequality—it is violence done without the recognition of individuals. Belief, for example, in equality of access to law may serve to destroy motivation to uncover or correct extant inequalities. In the modern state, the police hold the legitimate monopoly on violence and in theory apply it in the interests of the state. Thus, virtually any application of official violence is a window into the operation of social control and to the ordering of class relations.

An analysis of the police role requires an overview of the relationships between social units, that is, social segments with a given set of resources, including beliefs, technologies, skills, especially language skills (Bourdieu 1990a) and material goods, in vertically and horizontally ordered systems. These systems rank various forms of capital or resources mobilized by schema (Sewell 1992). The systems are governed by deep principles, something like a code or set of rules for translating surface features of social life into enduring order. Bourdieu's theory is not primarily social psychological although meanings and action choices play an important role. It links "mental structures" and the "world of objects" (Bourdieu 1977:91). Bourdieu's analyses explore both the dynamic and static aspects of social control: how are classes ordered and how is that order produced and reproduced?

Bourdieu assumes a system governed by normative rules and underlying codes, of which surface features, or social life, are illustrations. Classes are clusters of material and ideal interests, animated by people with shared experiences and collective representations striving to control markets in goods and services. Classes occupy social spaces characterized by objective conditions as well as subjective responses and definitions of those conditions. Classes possess symbolic capital, the knowledge, background, skills and objective material that may be passed on to future generations. Unlike the Marxian emphasis on the material, Bourdieu sees objects as coming under the control of mental schema and as being reflexively interrelated. Schema enable material resources and material resources enable the realization of schema. Classes remain in conflict over control of these forms of capital with other classes. Crosscutting classes are fields (of struggle), objective sets of organized normative structures such as science, the arts, and literature that are differentially organized within institutional structures (e.g., universities, research organizations, the police). Classes struggle on institutionally ordered fields.

Actors employ the schema or habitus validated within their class, consistent with the symbolic control of the dominant classes (Bourdieu 1991). The habitus links structure and choice "unknowingly," for there is no person or "subject" in this decentered theory. The habitus is the internalized structure or modes of perception, conception and action common to members of the same group or class (Bourdieu 1977). The habitus links by predisposition mental schema and resources, both enabling and providing choices and constraining them. Much like an English speaker articulates unreflectively a sentence using the grammatical style, vocabulary, and codes typical of his or her class, Bourdieu's actor enacts social choices (Thompson, in Bourdieu 1991).

The habitus is linked to classes because choices are produced that mark, define and reproduce particular forms of capital. Bourdieu's interest is in structures of distinction and education (in both secondary and university settings) and aesthetics. Bourdieu's conception of capital includes several types (e.g., economic, cultural, symbolic, artistic) and metaphorically depicts the distribution of resources. The habitus, like language itself, is unconscious and governed by unrecognized principles of deference and legitimation, actions and conduct, that reproduce the vertical structure of society. Clusters of value and class do not entirely cohere, and thus tensions and anomalies exist in the ranking of groups with regard to capital. Classes differentially value and accumulate cultural and economic capital, but the power of the dominant classes maintains the vertical organization of society, reproduced on the whole in the many distributions of different kinds of capital. The types of capital controlled by the higher classes are viewed as superior. Class-based positions are seen as "natural" and not arbitrary. Their arbitrary vertically ordering dimensions go unrecognized, obscured by ideology and insured by socialized principles of (mis)recognition and complicity.

The habitus creates paradoxes and anomalies because practices arise in different work groups and organizations (subfields) that may contradict the dominant habitus. The habitus gives only partial guidance in the complex matter of deciding how to apply a given strategy to new and to changing situations. The complex meaning of any set of resources and the conflict of structures create the potential for change and contradiction (Sewell 1992).

Classes seek a monopoly of symbolic violence or control over forms of symbolic capital and to impose arbitrary constraints using instruments of knowledge and experience to insure their standing (Bourdieu 1977). The horizontally ordering forms, social institutions, retain their internal shape because a "natural adjustment" to the principles of order is insured by patterns of institutional misrecognition. The role of active complicity in dominance is maintained and ignorance of the associated costs is maintained. Further, the surplus value that accrues through exchange to the more powerful (individual or groups) is masked by notions such as fealty, loyalty, and honor. These notions tie dependent groups, who see their domination through these status-conferring terms, firmly to more powerful groups.

Although individuals are socialized into the habitus perpetuated by a hierarchical system, conflict between and within groups remains. Patterns of symbolic exchange are driven by control and domination interests. The dominant classes are split internally into segments with material wealth and those with cultural capital (resources of taste, knowledge, and skill), just as the class hierarchy is divided (roughly along the white- and blue-collar line). Social integration is maintained by shared beliefs about the differential evaluation of capital and control over modes of capital transformation. Vertical hierarchies in institutional fields, such as science, literature and art (see Bourdieu 1981), are mapped back onto the class structure. Bourdieu and others (Bernstein 1971, 1973, 1979; Karabel and Halsey 1977) have demonstrated the differential accumulation of cultural capital by education. In this way, the social reproduction of vertical hierarchies, such as educational achievement, involves constant symbolic transformation of one kind of exchange (educational capital or symbolic capital) into another (material resources).

Bourdieu's theory sees the maintenance of order both as a conscious matter of strategies designed to sustain capital and to transform many kinds of capital into self-sustaining resources and as ideological preconditioning or predisposition to deference and compliance. But actors must make sense of and organize responses when differential pressures and forces within a field arise or when several schemata are relevant to a decision. In Bourdieu's work, formal agencies of control have no apparent role, and one must extrapolate and infer their domain of influence. Active social control, the selective, active, systematic application of sanctions by legally mandated organizations, dramatizes the loose boundaries between classes and institutions. In effect, the police mediate the symbolic claims of groups and stand between claims and honor.

The Study of the Police and Social Control

Police studies in America are predominantly atheoretical. One indication of this atheoretical heritage is that no generally accepted definition of police or policing exists. American police research has focused relatively narrowly on street-level interactions, lower segments of the organization, the occupational and organizational culture, and organizational reform. Very few new ethnographies have appeared. Police researchers have not confronted the dramatic changes in policing and the condition of the cities in the past ten years, nor have they explored the consequences of twelve years of ultra-conservative federal rule. With some exceptions, quantitative police research focuses on correlates of selected officially generated outcome measures, e.g., arrests, without analyses of the context, structural or interactional, within which those outcomes are produced (see Langworthy 1986; Slovak 1986). Policing studies, even when critical of police practice, corruption, violence and brutality, adopt the police perspective, often unreflectively borrowing police problem definitions and ideology. Many recent works take a direct, ameliorative and policy-oriented approach to police administration and strategy.[3] Like most textbooks in criminal justice, the tacit purpose of the research is to elevate the dramatic dilemmas of the police, the costs and risks of crime, and to at least implicitly validate police ideology.[4] In many of these works, the questions of what policing is about, why police do what they do and what their moral and political mandate ought to be are implicit or defined by default by studying a narrowly defined range of the consequences of policing.[5]

No systematic study exists detailing the strategies and tactics by which the American police maintain the vertical and horizontal distribution of groups in social space. Works on Anglo-American policing place it in a broader socioeconomic context (Banton 1964; Black 1976, 1980, 1989; Ericson 1981, 1982, 1989, 1991; Reiner 1991, 1992). It is assumed by most studies that the mandate of the police for reproducing social order, both ritualistically and instrumentally, is revealed primarily in police patrol decision-making. This is only one type of police decision and does not reveal patterns of resource allocation (budgeting and equipment purchase, for example), police management and the high politics of policing (Reiner 1991). The explicit role of policing within the political economy of symbolic capital and how it affects the distribution of forms of capital should be further examined.

Bourdieu and the Police

Bourdieu provides a logical structure for the analysis of police actions. From this framework, one can discern how police maintain social hierarchies. Bourdieu sees the objective structure of society as translated in action choices guided by disposition and predisposition. The habitus, or mental set, tends to reproduce the objective conditions that initially shaped the habitus. The interventions of control agencies would be presumed to sustain the vertical array of classes but also to illuminate the sources of societal contradiction and change. A conception of policing would require a definition of the police consistent with a theoretical analysis of social control.

The Police: A Definition

The work of Egon Bittner is phenomenologically grounded and consistent with the conception of society outlined above. Bittner (1970:39) defines the police as "a mechanism for the distribution of situationally justified force in society." The police, he asserts, are required to stand ready to respond to complex human problems when it is imagined that the application of force may be necessary (Bittner 1970: 44).

Bittner's definition features a situational emphasis, a focus on violence, and an "intuitive grasp of situational exigencies" (Bittner 1970:46). It omits an explicit a priori legal dimension. The exercise of force, in Bittner's scheme, is grounded in the authority of the state and the deference of citizens to the legal order.[6]

Bittner emphasizes the technique or craft of policing. Policing requires the management of intense, situated, authority-based, phenomenologically defined encounters by negotiation, persuasion, violence or local knowledge to achieve the purposes, often emergent, of the controller. Such a technique works superbly when and insofar as an officer commands the necessary self-confidence, skill, competence, patience and local knowledge to accomplish the necessary. It is the absence of violence, not its presence, that defines the craft of policing.

All definitions contain multiple facets and ambiguities that reveal social attitudes and institutional contradictions. This definition of the core of policing, like all definitions, provides useful "strategic ambiguities" or "terms that clearly reveal the strategic spots where ambiguities necessarily arise" (Burke 1969:xv). The essential or fundamental ambiguity is that while police are known to be violent, they mystify their role as violent protectors of the status quo, preferring to refer to their mandate as "law enforcement," "peacekeeping," or preserving "public safety." From a dramaturgical perspective, this definition reveals the central paradoxes of modern policing: the core of the role is denied. The police control and coerce groups regardless of the degree of citizen compliance and represent the essential need for violence in a democratic society. Yet, both police and public publicly eschew violence and claim Victorian standards as measures of civility (Bittner 1970). The primary function of the police is to mark and sustain the moral boundaries of the society. Police mark these boundaries and rules dramaturgically by selective amplification of the reality of certain types of crime and delicts. They thus reaffirm rankings in the multiple moral hierarchies of an industrialized society (Manning 1988). Unlike the Kabyle, a peasant people in Algeria (Bourdieu 1962, 1977), where individuals developed personal and familial strategies to produce, enhance, and exchange capital and avoid its loss, complex institutions mediate these risks in industrialized societies. Among these mediating institutions are the police.

Several inferences, required for the following analysis, can be drawn. Police work is best viewed within a theoretic perspective sensitizing the observer to how the differential application of violence and the threat of violence sustains social order. Debate about the role of the police in symbolic marking of order is well illustrated by legal moves constraining the police and criminalizing domestic conflict. The police response to domestic conflict well illustrates also the vagaries of the police mandate. Police arrests in domestic conflict situations are seen by some as enhancing symbolic capital by "empowering women," reducing the capital of other groups (men) and taking steps to set more humane standards (Stark 1993). For other observers, it creates yet another intrusion of the state into private relations, an enforcement of class-biased notions about disputing, and a source of exacerbation of conflict and increased costs to lower-class domestic units (Manning 1992). Perhaps all are a part of the police actions. The problem of police response to domestic violence has general theoretic potential.

Domestic Conflict

The meaning of domestic conflict has evolved over the past twenty-five years and entails changes in policing, the law, and public perceptions and toleration of violence. Family disturbances, arguments, fights, "domestics," and the like are among the most common, repetitive and vexing police problems (Antunes and Scott 1981). They reveal the borderland between civil and criminal law and between patterns of morality and the law. Several interrelated features of such incidents make them problematic for officers. First, legal remedies have been scarce for private disturbances. They were seen as private matters to be regulated by tradition, convention, local customs, and common and civil law. Second, such disputes often become risky tests of officers' personal authority (Manning 1982) and contain unstable coalitions and triads (an officer and two feuding parties). Third, they have violence potential and force may be required, they often involve repeat players, and they result in injuries to officers. Fourth, they are not easily and efficiently solved or managed. In the past, when arrest was rarely used, interpersonal persuasion, tactics, and threats were the only resources. Although the threat of arrest was often used, few arrests were made unless an officer was assaulted. Fifth, whatever the officers' skills, it is difficult to intervene successfully. The purpose of the intervention is not to solve the dispute or even to mediate it but simply to tactically separate the parties and leave the scene (Davis 1983). Sixth, disputes are often sources of complaints about officers' behavior. Seventh, they raise contradictions between officers' own feelings and values, which may resemble the parties', and the behavior of the parties they seek to manage. Officers frequently identify with one of the combatants. Finally, recent political debate about the proper handling of domestic conflicts has raised questions about control of officers' discretion, the most valued feature of the role. Fetters on discretion are always resisted in principle.

The U.S. Crime Commission Report (1967) urged that specialized units in domestic dispute resolution or conflict management be trained and used, noting the lack of training and skills and that many police injuries had resulted from interventions in domestics. In the 1980s, increasing concern about the problem arose, fueled by the rise of feminism as a political ideology and organized force, media attention to the issues of spouse, child and domestic abuse, and broader trends toward reducing gender bias in hiring and recruiting, pay, promotion and benefits. Other trends in society such as increasing mobility, the decline in inner city social services, the deterioration of effective kin networks and neighborhoods and the apparent lowered threshold at which violence occurs, and the increase in the number of households with guns all contribute to rates of domestic violence. Many politically active groups and the media (cf. Loseke 1992), viewing females generally as the victims of patriarchy and correlate violence, argued that rape (and related crimes) were violent crimes, whether in or out of marriage. Legal changes made it possible to prosecute spouses for rape and/or assault. The literature on aspects of domestic sexual violence is vast and is only summarized here (see Denzin 1984; Buzawa and Buzawa 1990, 1992).

Research also affected the public perception of domestic violence. Sherman and Berk (1984), in an experimental study based on research in Minneapolis, reported that arrests of spouses in "domestics" reduced the likelihood of rearrest in subsequent months. This study was widely reported as reducing spouse abuse. Many states enacted mandatory arrest legislation that enabled officers to arrest spouses on the basis of credible verbal evidence or reasonable suspicion that assault had taken place rather than requiring a signed affidavit from the spouse for a bench warrant (Buzawa and Buzawa 1990: Table 9.1). Police departments altered their policies as well (Sherman and Cohn 1989). Critics debated the experimental design, the sample, inferences drawn, and the claims made by Sherman and others (Buzawa and Buzawa 1990: 72–73ff). Additional research in six cities, sponsored by the National Institute of Justice, and a study published by Dunford et al. (1990) have raised serious doubts about the extrapolation of the conclusions of this study. So too has a recent article by Sherman et al. (1991), based on data gathered on the effects of arrests on subsequent rearrest in Milwaukee.

Research that focuses on arrests without examining the context of the conflict exaggerates their importance and impact. Arrest or rearrest are surrogate measures for the existence of violence or domestic chaos. The class bias of police actions was little discussed until the Sherman et al. (1991) article. They argue that arrest only deters married, employed men from rearrest. For others (namely, the unemployed and unmarried), arrest increases the likelihood of rearrest. Why this occurs is only speculated about. The authors suggest that frustration causes the resurfacing of violence leading to arrest. The ways in which policing sustains, or in Bourdieu's terms "reproduces," the social order is not explicated. Since the study sample was from an inner city area, little is actually known about the distribution of the generic effects of arrest on domestic violence. Does policing domestic conflict reflect Bourdieu's ideas? Some general propositions concerning the transformation of capital derived from Bourdieu guide the following analysis.

Policing Domestic Conflict

Service Distribution

An overview of the functioning of policing in the class order generally reveals their potential. The police distribute services, including traffic control and mass disturbance control, random patrol, recovery of lost and stolen property, coordination of information, transportation, and emergency medical services, among others (Cumming et al. 1962; Shearing 1984). Police affirm the distribution of services in the society. Whereas middle class and above segments employ private services, ambulances, counseling, and medical care, the police provide the same services, ambulances, medical care, transportation, counseling and marital therapies to the working classes. In addition, policing is a collective good (Feeley 1970) to which all are expected to contribute, sustaining police authority. The public are differentially served by them. The police serve the middle classes in crime control functions in connection with property crimes in which they are victims or witnesses and in incidents related to traffic and traffic accidents (Wilson 1968). The police are involved with the working classes in crime-related and other service relationships as well as in adversarial contexts, such as when individuals are suspects, villains, or nuisance sources because of public drunkenness, fighting, or noisy parties. The order-maintaining activities of the police are focused on the working classes.

The police differentially serve family-like units in conflict. Violence (defined contextually) is found in all classes and is generally used by men to control women (Strauss and Gelles 1986). Police response to "domestics" disproportionately involves members of the lower middle class, especially blacks. This results in part because of differential reporting. While not all such incidents are reported, those who call the police are from these groups. The absence of other forms of control means that neighbors are more likely to call the police about family fights in lower-class neighborhoods than elsewhere (cf. Black 1983). Officers resist making arrests generally, but the arrest sanction is most likely to be applied (usually to men) among these same lower-class groups (Buzawa and Buzawa 1990: chs. 1–4). Other forms of social control—therapy, education, or restitution (Black 1976)—are used by middle classes and above in analogous situations. Even in cases where police departments mandate arrest, or are under consent decrees, police practices seem little changed (Ferraro 1989). As mentioned above, officers' aims in "domestics" are not to protect the weaker party or solve an underlying or even immediate problem. They aim to separate and calm the adversaries sufficiently to "restore the semblance of order" and leave (Davis 1983).

In this sense, then, the police affirm the patriarchal order and the class-biased character of policing. Interventions in domestic conflicts also maintain the dependency of the urban lower-classes on police "service." Police intervention is an objective material condition of lower class domestic life. Governmental social control is directed "down," whereas self-help, the violence of women toward men, is directed "up" (Black 1983). Whether arrest reduces risks to women is now unknown (cf. Sherman and Berk 1984; Dunford et al. 1990; Sherman et al. 1991). It certainly has little or no capacity to "deter" violence and is a form of violence itself. There is every likelihood, as Skolnick and Fyfe (1993) reason, that violence escalates and produces violence in return rather than reducing or quelling it.

Tension Production and Amplification

While the police routinely apply violence or coercion, it is applied to those groups most distrusted and seen as likely to be violent. Bittner

(1970) argues convincingly that violence is applied based upon a "reading" of a situation when it is thought that (1) the situation has potential to worsen or expand in ways that create additional troubles for the police; (2) other remedies seem unlikely to work or have failed previously; and (3) the underlying ordering of the situation (the field) may change and produce additional conflicts. However, the police favor benign neglect unless serious injury or weapons are present or the parties are drunk, belligerent, or non-deferential to the officers (Buzawa and Buzawa 1990: ch. 4). Overt physical violence is disproportionately directed to those who represent "trouble." These are, in the eyes of the police, the urban lower classes.

Crime Control

Not only do they differentially supply service and violence, the police also distribute differentially crime control functions. Police actions reify class relations. Active intervention on the street, in public places, and in private has always been the practice of the police. The police, when applying formal social control or refusing to do so, enact the class hierarchy (Black 1976, 1983). Police inactivity in other sorts of crime—those associated with the cultural capital of the higher classes such as fraud, embezzlement, political crime, and other governmental corruption—also sustains the status quo ante. A possible consequence of the expansion of police arrest powers in domestic conflict is an increase in the lower-class arrest and crime rate. As Bittner (1970) correctly notes, the police increase class tensions and alter differential life chances because that is precisely their historic role.

Capital Gained and Lost

Police actions, it is likely, reduce the cultural capital of the lower classes. No analysis has yet explored how sanctioning-oriented formal social control such as policing reduces the cultural capital of the dominated classes and valorizes the cultural capital of the dominant classes. There are some suggestions, however.

The process works as follows. The police are record-keepers of the accumulated "marks" (stops, tickets, arrests, previous record of convictions, jail and prison time) of the working classes. These "marks" are carefully recorded and reproduced at various critical points such as in court, at job interviews, in subsequent encounters with the police, and on applications for education or training. They serve important symbolic functions. "Marks" disqualify people for positions, reduce competition with the middle classes for skilled and professional positions, and often produce "tipping" points at which people are jailed or permanently dispossessed.[7] This process of accumulating "black marks" not only reduces competition but also helps maintain low wages, a large surplus labor pool, and a floating demimonde of petty criminals (Chiricos and DeLone 1992).

Patterns of differential sanctioning of symbolic violence and the accumulation of symbolic capital tacitly tolerated in the society are accentuated by policing practices in at least two quite different ways. The first is that any given institution maintains its own complex definition and social construction of the meaning of the "external world" and the effects of the institution upon it. The police have elaborate recipe knowledge, moral beliefs, and an occupational culture that maintains work control, setting the acceptable level of effort and response to events. Police act to control, at every critical turning point within the police communications system (PCS), the level and kind of response made to "domestics" (Manning 1988, 1992). Police responses are determined by the wish to control work load generally, the negative view of non-crime work, the repeated and understandably frustrating character of such calls and the danger they are seen to represent. The generally sexist lower-middle-class morality of the police favors male dominance and female compliance in a cohabiting or married relationship (Hunt 1984). Thus, the interests of the police filter and pattern response to domestics (Manning 1982). The second is that the police absence in middle-class neighborhoods and their presence in poorer neighborhoods dramatize the social location of problematic violence. The police produce few negative marks for the middle classes, nor the potential for arrest, violence, and injury. These are associated with frequent police visits to lower-class residences. Since assignments to the same address may result in a reputation among the officers for family fights at that address, a lower threshold of tolerance at these addresses may result. Police, in effect, micro-manage the conflict to reduce calls back (Lempert 1989).

The Police and Institutional Misrecognition

The dominant police ideology, their institutional bias, is that they are a neutral, objective, democratic, "law enforcement" agency that dispenses "services" without prejudice. This partially reveals and partially conceals police practices. The failure to see the differential allocation of service and violence is an instance of institutional misrecognition. Police ideology blinds both the police and the public to the consequences of police practices. Police actions, like the habitus that maintains class domination, are in fact largely unreflective and tacit rather than systematic attempts at direct domination.

This mental activity works in three ways to obscure public knowledge of policing. First, the systematic ideology of the institution supports and facilitates police efforts to control the types of crime that maintain the present social hierarchies. These include vice and morals violations, public drug trafficking, and most public order violations. They ignore, cannot skillfully investigate, or de-emphasize others such as "white-collar crime," fraud, embezzlement, computer crime, organizational crimes generally, and crimes involving trust (violation of which is symbolic violence directed to societal victims) rather than direct violence. This is in part a result of consciously chosen police tactics employed differentially in social spaces and in part a function of the reactive nature of much of police work. Most work arises in response to processed telephone calls to the police. This selective attention makes visible certain crimes and violations and suppresses and makes invisible others.

Second, a belief in the democratic ideology of the police produces compliance and deference from those to whom it is directed. The working classes are among the strongest supporters of the police. Third, victims of crime are frequently also the perpetrators. Although crime and the fear of crime affect all class sectors, most crime is local and directed against other lower-class people of the same race. Crime, unreported or reported, is yet another mode of reducing the symbolic capital of the working class. Although crime has some positive economic consequences, on balance it is destructive of social relations.

Innovative forms of symbolic distortion have been developed by the police, perhaps in a dialectic with the decline of police legitimacy. Recently, the police have adapted the "community policing" rhetoric that claims among other things that the citizens should shoulder more responsibility for their own policing. This shifts the burden of policing to citizens through such schemes as neighborhood watch and equates policing to other services governed by market forces. The economic rhetoric that sees policing as a service to "clients," the reference to police command personnel as "managers," the calls for "efficiency in police management," and the conception of the police officer as a community-based "demand manager" all echo the stilted language of business and economics. By seeing policing as a service something like education, which can be purchased in one of several markets, this metaphor obscures the quite different markets that operate.

This "service strategy" is used to co-opt the poor into their own defense while selling the respectable middle class on "crime control," the "war on drugs," and "zero tolerance." This "split" or segregated audience strategy aims to sell crime control and community crime watch to the middle classes and self-policing to the lower classes. Urban neighborhoods of lower middle class people organize self-help and vigilante groups to patrol their neighborhoods. This suggests that the political economy of policing generates some indigenous forms of justice. Overall, because the community policing strategy valorizes middle-class capital and reduces the symbolic capital of others, it maintains the status quo.

The police act to maintain the symbolic capital of the dominant classes in unrecognized fashion is mystified by a democratic ideology. The allocation and distribution of the "service" shapes class habitus by retaining deference and dependency and reducing their symbolic capital. Police ideology maintains the myth of full enforcement as a self-protective theme. It is argued publicly that officers have no discretion when faced with an infraction and must act if they are. This ideological theme denies the selective role police have in responding to domestic conflict. They act through passive and generally inactive "interviews" and threats. The community policing ideology urges close contact between the police and the public and an informal problem-solving approach to incidents that previously might have produced a call to the police. Informal settlements are most likely to reproduce the extant distribution of power in families and neighborhoods, while use of the arrest sanction asserts authority that may counter the balance in private relations. The irony is that informal practices emphasize even more than arrests the authority of dominant groups.

Conclusion

It has been argued that Bourdieu's perspective illuminates the police role in social control of domestic conflict. A number of inferences consistent with the perspective show the impact of policing domestic violence. This discussion of the class structure and role of the police has not considered the role of individual strategies and tactics and their effect on capital accumulation. The controversy about the efficacy of arrest in reported incidents of domestic conflict, touched off by societal trends and research, is an example of the limits of a case focus. The failure to examine how such policies affect the fate of women as a group, that is, how policies might increase or decrease their symbolic capital or alter the life chances of groups within classes, reveals an acceptance of the police overvaluation of arrest. It is likely, although this inference is not analyzed here, that within classes, women more than men lose capital by the affirmation of the dominance of men and selective response to domestic violence calls. Police use of violence to control a situation is an option that follows the absence of deference to the police authority. This is often precipitated by drinking. Evidence gathered on citizen-police encounters in domestic situations suggests that police defer to the habitus of the middle classes and are less likely to arrest in domestics when the conventional ties between the couples are "stronger," that is, the couples are married rather than estranged, cohabiting rather than unrelated couples (Black 1976).

In short, the debate about domestic violence and its control is a very fine example of the obfuscation of the reality of control by ideologically driven posturing and thinly disguised self-serving presented as analysis. The police have very little capacity to control or regulate domestic violence, and arrest, used for such diverse ends, is a very crude and inadequate proximal surrogate for control of violence. The consequence of police intervention, whether arrest or not, is erosion of the capital of the working classes, men and women alike.

Notes

1. I am grateful to George Bridges and Kathleen Daly for comments on earlier drafts and to Betsy Cullum-Swan and Eva Buzawa for discussions about the meaning and impact of policing domestic violence.

2. American urban police have been studied well in these terms. Among the most relevant historical works are Lane (1967), Richardson (1970), Johnson (1979), Miller (1977), and Monkkonen (1981, 1992). Comparative works include Bayley (1985); organizational research, Wilson (1968), Reiss (1971, 1992) and Manning (1977); ethnographies, Skolnick (1966), Rubinstein (1973), van Maanen (1974, 1988) and Muir (1977).

3. Consider as examples Trojanowicz and Bucqueroux (1989), Goldstein (1990), Sparrow et al. (1990), (Kleiman (1992), the Harvard University Department of Justice Policy papers, and others directly associated with the Police Foundation and/or PERF. Ironically, one of the latest reformist volumes (Sparrow et al. 1990) praises the accomplishments of a series of now-resigned police chiefs, including Daryl Gates of Los Angeles. It also uncritically elevates and dramatizes the role of the chief in reform and makes prescriptive statements with dubious evidence. The rhetorical vehicle, "community policing," when linked with police problem-solving, is advanced as a solution to the current complex burdens of policing.

4. Ironically, a police idea that originated in the grand and elevating notions of restraint and deterrence was developed in the late eighteenth century by Jeremy Bentham, Edward Chadwick and John Stuart Mill in the posturing of potential. It finds its fundamental grounding in the to-be-avoided violence. Given its essential violence, the claim that policing is "law enforcement" is a misleading synecdoche. Rarely does policing require the direct use of the law. Appeals to the law often mystify a situation of violence application because the law provides no prospective guidance about when it can be applied. Nor is the law in fact the principal constraint on police actions (Bittner 1970; Manning 1977). Similarly, the term "peace officer" is a created and misleading oxymoron, suggesting that the officer is peaceful and the task peacemaking. The euphemisms of economics and business connoted by the concept of "police management," currently used in

police-training institutes, firmly deny or at least obscure the concrete and often primitive nature of the tasks to be "managed." These strategic ambiguities suggest that symbolic work goes on in society to sustain precisely this nuanced edge between violence, control and order, and that much of this work of selectively maintaining such a working construction of the mandate occurs backstage.

5. Some British works (e.g., Hall et al. 1978) critically approach policing. These English neo-Marxian analyses criticize the police for (1) failing to fulfill their legal obligation to control crime, thus increasing the burden of the working class and (2) the absence of accountability, especially on the part of chief constables, to the public and the law (Reiner 1991, 1992). One recent theoretical paper (Henry and Milovanovic 1991) wrestles with the question of the focus of criminal justice research but contains no systematic empirical data.

6. Both Black and Bittner owe a considerable debt to Weber's sociology of law (1967: 5). Weber defines law in this way: "An order will be called a law if it is externally guaranteed by the probability that coercion (physical or psychological) to bring about conformity or avenge violation will be applied by a staff holding themselves ready for that purpose." The Weberian definition must be elaborated as well. Police violence is not simply applied without authority and is legitimated ("authorized") and sanctioned ultimately by the state. It serves in that sense the state's interests, regardless of the intuitive bases for the situational application of coercive violence. The interests of the state are thus not easily identified in advance or inferred directly from the power of any social group. The police are not simply local, so a definition must include other variations on policing. "Police" include numerous agencies such as private security companies, detectives and reserve constables, regardless of their precise linkage to the state or the criminal law. Thus, the contemporary connection between police use of force and legal grounds for justification is a fairly recent innovation. The grounding norm that permits police use of force is the state's legitimacy. Deference to the law is a feature of that legitimacy. Inevitably, this connection means that the powerful interests that sustain the state provide tacit "authorization" for policing, and the thrust of police objectivity is in the direction of the elites (Manning 1977: 40–41, 101–102). Policing with force is an oxymoron in a modern welfare state, because it means, metaphorically at least, that the state will act toward itself, in the form of the citizens who constitute it, in a violent and punitive fashion. This definition does not place policing within the political economy that shapes its organizational mandate nor within the internal question of compliance as a central question in the mobilization of action.

7. In the broad sense, the idea of disqualifying certain people temporarily or permanently is elaborated by Marx (1989) and others (e.g., Rusche and Kirchheimer 1939; Thompson 1964; Ericson 1981, 1982, 1989). In policing, for example, Cicourel (1968) demonstrates how juvenile policing works on several rather mundane principles. The first aim is harassment and increasing the transaction costs to those stopped or investigated. The second is control and maintaining deference to police authority. The third aim is the construction of a file or record that semiotically indexes a "moral career." Over time, accumulated stops, questionings, arrests and investigations become evidence of the troublesome and

suspicious nature of the person. This evidence is used as a basis for arrest or conviction in court. The fact that the stops and arrests are not independent measures of juvenile behavior or of crime is irrelevant to police purposes. Each "mark" is part of an overall pattern that increases police willingness to act rather than overlook a given delict and displays in official language the flawed character of those stopped.

PART THREE
Dimensions of Inequality

6

Ethnicity: The Forgotten Dimension of American Social Control

Darnell F. Hawkins

The study of racial inequality has been a routine and ubiquitous part of the social scientific investigation of all aspects of life in American society for much of this century (e.g., Pettigrew 1980; Jaynes and Williams 1989). During the past half-century, guided most often by the principles of the conflict perspective, numerous researchers have examined the relationship between race and social control in the United States. They have noted the control and subordination of nonwhites by those of European ancestry and have shown that indices of crime and punishment are a direct reflection of such subordination. However, a review of the literature on social control reveals that in comparison to race, researchers have been relatively inattentive to concerns of ethnicity. For example, they have provided limited discussion of the social control of the nation's white or nonwhite ethnics or of the extent to which interethnic differences exist.

The major argument advanced in this chapter is that the experiences of ethnic groups, both white and nonwhite, represent a forgotten or ignored dimension of the relationship among crime, inequality and social control in the United States.[1] I contend that the failure of researchers to examine these experiences has important implications for the making of both social theory and public policy. A series of questions and propositions are used to illustrate the importance of considering ethnicity when analyzing patterns of social control in the United States. I suggest that through the study of ethnic differences researchers will be able to further specify and test the conflict perspective and other theories of social control. Such an analysis may also inform contemporary debate regarding the comparative significance of race versus social class in

American society. Let us begin by considering America's white ethnics, whose experiences now represent a largely forgotten saga of crime and punishment in the United States.

Early Crime and Punishment Among America's White Ethnics

The incidence of officially reported crime and punishment among white ethnic Americans during the latter decades of the nineteenth century and continuing into the first decades of the twentieth century has received considerable notice (Taft 1936; Ross 1937; Handlin 1941; Hobbs 1943; Powell 1966; Ferdinand 1967; Greeley 1972; Alexander 1973; Lane 1979; Steinberg 1989). Public discourse about the disproportionate rate of involvement in crime for some white ethnics during this period closely resembles contemporary discussion of the racial and ethnic distribution of crime in the United States. While the foreign-born from all of Europe were a frequent target of such public concern, the crimes of the Irish and Italians received perhaps the most scrutiny (Hobbs 1943:202; Greeley 1972:225). A common query was why rates of crime for these two groups appeared to be higher than those of other white ethnic groupings, most notably the English, Scottish and German immigrants who preceded them.

As early as 1796, a French observer of the newly liberated United States noted:

> In the latter state (Pennsylvania) out of ten convicts, seven at least are in general strangers, and in particular natives of Ireland, who bring with them from their own country little besides poverty, ignorance and habits of indolence, the seeds of every kind of vice. . . . (Hobbs 1943: 202).

With the increase in Irish immigration during the middle of the nineteenth century came renewed scrutiny of their criminal conduct. An 1860s account of Irish crime in *Harper's Magazine* read:

> (the Irish) have so behaved themselves that nearly 75% of our criminals are Irish, that fully 75% of the crimes of violence committed against us are the work of Irishmen (Greeley 1972: 225).

Disproportionate involvement of the Irish in the criminal justice system has been noted by other, more scholarly analysts. Alexander (1973: 19–20) reported that between 1794 and 1800, the Irish accounted for 37 percent of all convictions in Philadelphia, a rate more than four times their share of the city's population during the period. The Irish and a small free black population were said to make up more than 68 percent of all convictions. Other studies of Philadelphia between 1790 and 1810

(Hobbs 1943) and of Boston between 1790 and 1865 report similar findings (Handlin 1941). Some analysts have found that during certain decades of the nineteenth century the rates of serious crime for the Irish and other groups in selected cities may have equaled or exceeded those of African-Americans (Powell 1966; Lane 1986). During the middle to late nineteenth-century heyday of European immigration to the United States, Italians joined the ranks of those ethnic/nationality groups whose criminal behavior was widely noted (Ferdinand 1967:98). In discussing crime in Boston between 1849 and 1951, Ferdinand (1967:98) observed that

> Boston was inundated in the nineteenth century, first, by the starving yeoman of Ireland and, then, by the impoverished peasants of Sicily and southern Italy. These immigrants were eventually assimilated by the city, but both the immigrants and the city suffered grievously in the process. There can be little doubt that the gradual adjustment of the descendants of the Irish and Italian immigrants to the urban patterns of Boston has resulted in a gradual reduction in the city's crime rate.

Petty property crimes, public order offenses and vice were most frequently associated with the Irish, Italians, blacks and other members of the "dangerous classes" during this period and earlier (Monkkonen 1975; Hindus 1980). Various ethnic groups also came to be associated with violence and organized criminal activity. The Irish played a crucial role during the late nineteenth century in organizing gambling and arranging political protections, but by the twentieth century Jews and Italians had begun to share the control of these activities (Haller 1973: 285). Nelli (1970:125) noted that Americans reacted to crime among Italians with a frenzy of emotion aroused by no other ethnic group. Official reports, books, pamphlets, and magazine and newspaper articles decried "Southern" (i.e., Sicilian) criminality, a code word for the Mafia.

As Steinberg (1989) notes, by the turn of the century crime among the country's white ethnics/nationalities had become something of a national obsession. In 1911 the United States Immigration Commission issued a report on crime among the nation's newest immigrants. After collecting crime data in New York, Chicago, and Massachusetts, the Commission concluded that the various "races and nationalities" exhibited "clearly defined criminal characteristics" (U.S. Immigration Commission 1911:2; Steinberg 1989:116). Public concern for such crime differences continued for the next several decades, and in 1931 the National Commission on Law Observance and Enforcement (1931) reached conclusions similar to those reported in 1911. By the time the latter report appeared, the crime rates found among the Irish had been reduced substantially and a host of newer immigrants, primarily from eastern and southern Europe, were shown to be disproportionately involved in crime. Cahalan (1974) has documented the extensive imprisonment of white ethnics during the decades between 1880 and World War II.[2] In sum, both governmental documents and many analysts of the nineteenth-century social order in the United States have reported a comparatively high rate of officially sanctioned crime among a diverse array of white ethnic or national groupings.

Explaining White Ethnic Crime Patterns

How do we explain the high rates of crime and punishment among America's white ethnics during this period? The considerable public attention paid to the criminality of the foreign-born and specific nationalities reflected an obvious concern for the causes of crime among these groups. Many popular perceptions of reasons for elevated rates of crime among various nationalities were products of the xenophobia and ethnocentrism that permeated much of American life during the peak of the "new" immigration. Other explanations represented attempts by social scientists to counter such perceptions.

Sutherland (1924, 1934) and Sellin (1938) were among early criminologists whose work was aimed at responding to reported evidence of high rates of crime among recently arrived European immigrants in the United States. The criminality of white, urban immigrants in the United States was also a prominent theme in the work of the Chicago School of sociology (Park et al. 1928; Shaw and McKay 1969). Bonger (1943) examined ethnic and racial crime rates across several western societies. Like other social theorists of the period, the work of these analysts was designed to counter explanations for ethnic and racial group differences and social policies that emerged from the writings of biological determinists.

These alternative social scientific explanations have generally flowed from positivistic notions of the etiology of criminal behavior. Two major themes are evident. One, a now traditional etiological perspective in the study of crime, emphasizes the effects of economic deprivation and inequality. The crime of nineteenth-century immigrants is linked to the pauper-like conditions under which they often lived. Shaw and McKay (1969) suggested that a group's economic condition, and not cultural traits unique to the group, determined its rate of crime and delinquency. The gradual movement of these groups into the middle class or other more advantaged statuses was said to account for a reduction in their level of involvement in crime (Steinberg 1989; Hawkins 1993).

A competing perspective linked high rates of white ethnic crime during the past to conflicts between their cultures and the culture they found in the United States. Sellin's (1938) notion of a "conflict of conduct norms" provides an early statement of this position, although the general notion can be found in the earlier work of Sutherland (1924, 1934). Sellin argued that when peoples from distinctly different cultures come into contact with each other, there is often conflict. These normative conflicts were said by Sellin to weaken primary social institutions, such as the family, thus leading to a rise in rates of antisocial and criminal conduct. His account of the conflict of conduct norms lacks detail in some regards, but it offers, as he intended, an alternative to various theories of the period that explained criminality as a product of biological differences (1938:57–116).

But a close examination of the work of researchers in these traditions reveals that neither of the two orientations fully reflects a concern for the effects of intergroup conflict and bias on ethnic or racial differences in the rate of crime and punishment. When these are considered, they are generally considered to be more relevant for analyzing the crime and punishment of black Americans than of white ethnics (Hawkins 1993). With few exceptions, disparities in rates of punishment across white ethnic groups or between foreign-born and native whites are attributed primarily to differences in conduct. This is true even when such conduct differences are seen to result from the lack of opportunity and socioeconomic deprivation. Missing, therefore, from these accounts are the basic themes of the conflict perspective and similar models of social control.[3] This same approach to the study of crime and punishment is also evident in contemporary analyses of crime and punishment among whites as compared to nonwhites and in the less frequent comparisons among groups of nonwhites.

Further, in contrast to the governmental reports cited above, social scientists of the past and today have shown relatively little interest in exploring interethnic differences in rates of crime and punishment among European Americans. Many of the scholarly treatments of foreign-born versus native crime rates have tended to de-emphasize the extent to which ethnic and nationality differences exist among both immigrant and native groupings. While social scientists must be careful to reject methodologically and conceptually flawed ethnic comparisons (e.g., Sutherland 1934; Sellin 1938), as I suggest below, the study of differences in crime and punishment among white ethnics can contribute much to our knowledge of American social control.

Ethnicity and Contemporary Crime

Like those of their white counterparts, ethnic differences in social control *within* America's nonwhite populations have been largely ignored or underinvestigated. Indeed, researchers have sometimes seemed unaware of the considerable ethnic diversity found among those varied groups labeled as nonwhites in the United States. For example, the considerable cultural mix among those groups labeled as "Asian" or "Hispanic" is seldom acknowledged or studied by analysts of crime and justice. Researchers have also shown only minimal interest in comparing nonwhite groupings to each other such as Asians versus Hispanics. As in other areas of social research, the study of crime, punishment and social control has largely involved white-nonwhite comparisons. In those rare instances when nonwhite groups are compared to each other, questions have been raised that are similar to those posed by analysts of white ethnics. Since few intra-group, ethnic comparisons among nonwhites have been made, I use intergroup differences to illustrate the potential value of ethnic studies for exploring these questions.

Among these is the question of why some groups among those that appear to be similarly situated socioeconomically are more represented among those punished for crime than others. To the extent that nonwhites differ substantially in their experiences with social control, theories that emphasize the hegemonic effects of race, and frequently social class, in America are brought into question. For example, the now frequent labeling of some Asian-American populations, notably the Japanese and Chinese, as "model minorities" is based partly on their comparatively low level of involvement in crime. Bonger (1943:30–32) noted low rates of crime for both Chinese and Japanese Americans during the 1930s, with especially low rates observed for those of Japanese ancestry. More recent crime statistics show a continuation of this pattern. By comparison, African-Americans, some Hispanic populations and Native Americans have been observed to have disproportionately high rates of criminal involvement and punishment for crime. Native Americans during the 1980s had the second-highest rate (after blacks) of imprisonment among all racial and ethnic groups in the United States. Hispanics are imprisoned in federal and state institutions at a rate higher than non-Hispanic whites and Asians (Flowers 1988:165).

What explains such differences in indices of social control among American nonwhites? As in the case of white ethnic groups during the past, explanations for these differences have centered around notions of either culture conflict or economic deprivation. Though nonwhite crime rate differences have been noted, few explanations have been offered. Flowers (1988: 99) suggests that high rates of Hispanic involvement in crime result from their low socioeconomic status and the unfamiliarity of living in a foreign culture. He uses a similar combination of culture conflict (Sellin 1938) and deprivation perspectives to explain high rates of crime found among Native Americans (Flowers 1988: 113–117), noting that Native Americans are perhaps the most economically disadvantaged American minority group. On the other hand, Flowers (1988: 75, 116), like researchers before him, has difficulty accounting for the low rate of reported crime found among Asians who, like Native Americans, experienced significant racial discrimination and economic deprivation. He suggests that to the extent that racial bigotry is associated with high levels of crime and/or social control, Asian-Americans should exhibit higher rates of punishment for crime than official data reveal. In fact, recent work by Farley (1990) raises questions regarding whether blacks are uniquely economically disadvantaged in comparison to the increasingly diverse ethnic and racial groups that have immigrated to the United States in recent decades.

While Flowers was largely concerned with explaining differences across nonwhite racial groups, increasing ethnic diversity will likely lead to comparisons *within* groups of racial minorities. For example, in many urban areas the criminal activities of blacks born in the United States are contrasted with the seemingly lower rates found among blacks born in Africa or the Caribbean. Dominicans, Cubans, Salvadorans, and others are compared to Hispanic groups of longer residence, such as Mexicans and Puerto Ricans. Similarly, in those areas where they have settled, the involvement in crime found among the Vietnamese, Laotians, Cambodians, Koreans, Thais, and other Asian immigrants is sometimes compared to the rates found among American-born Japanese and Chinese residents in the United States. These within-race comparisons have led to many conclusions, not all of which are grounded in social fact.[4]

Inattention to Ethnicity: Causes and Effects

To what can we attribute the relative inattention by social scientists to the study of ethnicity and social control? As in other areas of social research, the study of social control relies heavily on the use of data collected by the state. Both today and during the past, a major limitation of these data has been the lack of reliable measures of ethnicity. Neither the decennial censuses nor governmental crime and punishment statistics/ documents have traditionally identified the ethnicity of those persons enumerated. This lack of data has significantly affected the analysis of both contemporary and historical patterns of social control (Inciardi 1977; Pisciotta 1981).

Inattention to ethnic group differences in social control may also partly reflect biases and themes inherent in extant theories of social control in the United States. Such bias has to do with conceptualizations of the nature and determinants of subordination and dominance. For example, proponents of the conflict perspective have sought to identify universal principles or laws of social control. Like all such principles, they have been designed to apply ideally to a diverse array of social groups and settings, including racially and ethnically diverse populations. While obviously cognizant of ethnic/racial cleavages within American society and differences in social control across these groups, the seminal accounts of the conflict perspective have tended to view the social control of members of various groups as a function of their social class standing rather than their ethnicity or race (Turk 1969a; Quinney 1970; Chambliss and Seidman 1971; Black 1976). Much of this same theoretical tendency is seen in the work of Sutherland (1924, 1934) and Sellin (1938), despite their greater attention to the effects of culture differences.

In these accounts, the greater social control of some ethnic/racial groups as compared to others is attributed to their lack of power and influence rather than their skin color, ethnic heritage, or the sometimes unique experiences that individual groups encounter. Race and ethnic differences are seen as important determinants of group differences in social control, but only to the extent that they are coterminous with dimensions of power and privilege. This attempt to ground social control in class divisions rather than on considerations of race and ethnicity has obvious ideological and heuristic appeal. But it may also conceal or ignore significant differences in the treatment of ethnic/racial groups and de-emphasize the need to study them. For example, Sellin (1938:78) noted the relative inattention of social scientists to the high rates of crime among some white ethnic Americans as compared to the study of the crime rates of Mexicans or Oriental groups.[5]

At odds with this view of ethnic and racial differences in social control is the work of scholars who have examined the effects of racism and racial stratification on American society. Among them are historians, legal scholars, and social scientists who have stressed the uniqueness of the treatment of blacks and other nonwhites as compared to white powerless groups in the United States (e.g., Blauner 1972; Takaki 1979, 1982; Bell 1980). They argue that nonwhites in the United States have been subjected to greater deprivations and more intense social control than similarly situated groups of whites. In that sense they echo the themes of early analysts of African-American life who stressed the "peculiar" conditions of subordination experienced by blacks (e.g., DuBois 1899).[6]

The debate that arose in response to William Wilson's (1978) notion of the declining significance of race highlighted the views of both these scholarly camps. Explicit in the race/class debate is skepticism regarding whether subordinate whites and nonwhites experience similar rates and types of social control, as conflict models often appear to propose. In an earlier work (Hawkins 1987), I suggested that the race versus social class debate has important implications for efforts to rethink conflict models of social control as they have been used to explain black-white differences in punishment for crime. It is also evident that such rethinking requires a careful examination of the relationships among ethnicity, social class, and social control.

Whether viewed from the perspective of positivistic criminology or a conflict model, two etiological puzzles emerge from research on ethnicity, crime and punishment. The first of these is the question of what accounts for apparent differences across American ethnic and nationality groups of seemingly similar social status in their levels of social control. For example, both governmental documents and social scientific studies of the past have suggested that some nationalities show considerably higher rates of contact with the criminal justice system than others. A second puzzle involves the attempt to account for change over time in the rate of social control for various ethnic groups. Why do some ethnic groups show greater change than others? These topics are discussed below.

Ethnicity and Social Control: Directions for Future Research

The observations and group comparisons above have obvious importance for our understanding of crime and punishment in American society. The discussion also reveals that many questions regarding the relationship between ethnicity, and indeed race, and social control remain unanswered and frequently unexplored. I offer the following questions and research propositions as heuristic devices for examining the potential lessons to be learned from studies of ethnic differences in crime and social control.

Ethnic Bias and Social Control

Question 1: To what extent were disproportionate rates of reported crime among pre–twentieth century Irish, Italians and other white ethnic groups in the United States the result of bias in the administration of justice?

For nearly a century, this rather straightforward query, as applied to the study of African-Americans, has been the mainstay of criminological and social control research. Yet, despite evidence of high rates of reported crime among nineteenth and early twentieth-century Irish, Italians, and other white ethnics in the United States, only a small number of researchers have posed the question above in response to this observation and explored it systematically. This is true despite evidence that suggests that bias in the administration of justice cannot be discounted as a factor that may have contributed to the social control of white ethnics.

Extant histories of the Irish and Italians in the United States reveal that the dynamics of their social interactions with more privileged ethnic groups were similar to the experiences of subordinate nonwhites (Nelli 1970; Duff 1971; Greeley 1972; Steinberg 1989). Those studies also reveal that like the interactions of nonwhites, the interactions of the Irish and Italians with privileged groups were characterized by ethnic/racial tensions as well as the conflict that accompanies class cleavages. Steinberg (1989) provides evidence of such in arguing that late twentieth century images of American ethnic pluralism and tolerance are products of myth and ideology rather than historical fact. To what extent did these tensions contribute to the disproportionate presence of Irish and Italian Americans in the nation's criminal justice system?

Ironically, the recent histories of the Irish and Italians in the United States pay relatively little attention to rates of criminal conduct or punishment for crime. While stressing the importance of ethnicity in American life and avoiding the kind of "melting pot" view of American intergroup relations that once permeated popular thought, these historical analyses nevertheless appear to underemphasize the past experiences of these groups within the nation's criminal justice system. Hence, they give little insight into the kinds of issues raised in this chapter.[7]

On the other hand, many historical accounts of crime and justice, such as Johnson's (1973) study of crime patterns in Philadelphia between 1840 and 1870, discuss crime and punishment rates without any mention of ethnic group differences. Similarly, Friedman's (1981) account of crime and punishment in Alameda County, California, between 1870 and 1910 does not note the extent to which ethnicity and nationality differences may have accounted for some of the patterns he observed. Consistent with the theoretical frameworks discussed above, ethnic distinctions are ignored and immigrant populations are treated as undifferentiated masses of the poor and downtrodden.

The recent work of Brown and Warner (1992) offers an illustration of the application of the conflict perspective to the study of white ethnic crime patterns in the United States. They suggest that by the turn of the last century the ever-increasing numbers of immigrants represented political, economic and cultural threats to native middle- and upper-class Americans. In many of the largest cities during this period, indigenous Americans used the police to attempt to control various undesirable aspects of the "foreign" community's lifestyle. Their observations may be helpful for beginning to understand why the criminal conduct of some ethnic groups has been more widely noted than that of others. They note that the political machines that controlled policing in America's cities at the turn of the century directed their actions toward those clearly defined groups with little standing (particularly political power) in the community. As various groups gained such standing, they were able to redirect policing activities toward other communities.

On the other hand, Brown and Warner (citing Blalock 1967) suggest that whether an ethnic population was targeted by the police depended also on the level of their threat to the existing political, social and cultural order. For example, the greater attention to the crime of the Irish and Italians in the United States during the past may reflect the perception of dominant ethnic groups that they posed a greater threat than other recently arrived groups. As Blalock (1967) has noted, this perception of threat is often tied to the population size of the subordinate group. Both the Irish (post–potato famine) and Italians arrived in relatively large numbers over a relatively brief period of American history. This may explain why they, rather than other recent immigrants, received the brunt of the public outcry over law and order during the late 1800s.

Brown and Warner offer valuable insights, but they rely heavily on traditional conflict theory with its emphasis on class-based notions of group threat. Do considerations of ethnicity apart from class status explain any of the trends in social control observed in their study? What factors apart from population size contribute to the level of social control that an ethnic group experiences? The following propositions derived partly from the work of earlier analysts, notably Sellin (1938) and Blalock (1956, 1957, 1967), are offered as guides for exploring this and other questions posed above.

Insularity and Social Control

Proposition 1a: The nature and extent of the social control of an ethnic or racial group is partly a function of its relative insularity vis-à-vis dominant groups or their agents.

Proposition 1b: Given similar levels of insularity, those ethnic/racial groups that are characterized as the greatest "social distance" from the dominant group will be subject to the greatest social control.

Blalock (1967) made a valuable contribution to the study of social control among racial and ethnic groups through the development of his "power threat" hypothesis. He argued that social control is not an all-or-none game and that it is not solely dependent on the "will" to control of the dominant group. Rather, even under the greatest oppression, subordinate groups are not completely powerless to affect the nature and extent of the social control that they experience. He suggests that researchers must seek to identify those social factors that determine the success of efforts at social control.

Past research and theory support the idea that the level of social control that a group experiences may be partly a function of the extent to which members of the group can isolate themselves from the dominant group and its agents of control. To the extent that this ability varies across racial/ethnic lines, it may explain both historical and contemporary ethnic/racial differences in rates of social control among similarly disadvantaged groups. I suggest that within multi-ethnic and multi-racial societies, those subordinate racial/ethnic groups that are able to erect barriers between themselves and dominant groups/agents of social control are less likely than other groups to be "controlled" (e.g., Sellin 1938).

In some instances relative insularity may be accomplished through the exertion of a subordinate group's limited power and influence. As Blalock notes, subordinate groups often mobilize politically to protect themselves from the social control of dominant groups. But this kind of political power is not always a necessary prerequisite to achieve the kind of insularity that might reduce a group's contact with agents of social control. Some forms of group insularity may be tied to the degree of geographic and/or residential isolation a group is able to achieve. Such insularity may be associated with regional separation, rural or urban enclaves, and similar forms of voluntary (or involuntary) segregation.

Other groups may be able to achieve relative insularity despite geographic proximity to dominant groups. For example, those groups that are able to carve out unique and specialized occupational niches, that is, occupations that do not bring them into direct conflict with the existing economic interests of the dominant group, may be subject to less social control than groups that are not able to do so. This lack of competitiveness may constitute a form of insularity that results in reduced levels of the kinds of interactions that lead to social control. In complex multi-ethnic societies, reduced social control will likely result only when groups have achieved a degree of isolation from both the elites who control the larger society and their brokers, other lower-status ethnic groups that provide personnel for agencies of social control such as the police.

The reportedly high rates of social control found among nineteenth-century Irish and Italians may reflect in part their concentration in occupations and geographic sites that afforded them minimal protection from the social control of the dominant group. Urban areas, in contrast to smaller towns and rural sites, have historically displayed higher levels of social control. Cities, due to their greater economic resources, can afford to support the mechanisms (jails, prisons, and the like) and agents (police, courts) of social control. Both population density and the structuring of urban life may reduce the degree of insularity that potentially conflicting groups can achieve.

Golab (1973) noted that Poles and other Eastern Europeans in Pennsylvania between 1870 and 1920 tended to settle in smaller towns and regions of the state away from the intense interethnic conflicts experienced by the Irish and Italians in that state. Only the most highly skilled Poles settled in Philadelphia. Unlike the Irish and Italians, the crime and punishment of many groups of Eastern Europeans have not been so widely noted. Similarly, the social control of Germans, Scandinavians and other major ethnic groupings in America has been less evident than that of the Irish and Italians. The greater social insularity afforded ethnic/racial groups outside of major urban areas (sometimes within them) during the past may explain some of the differences in levels of social control. The ability of Asian-Americans to achieve similar isolation from mainstream society may partly account for their lower rates of social control (e.g., Pogrebin and Poole 1988–89). It may be that rates of social control for Native Americans would be even greater were it not for the relative insularity provided by reservations and other forms of segregation. The relative lack of insularity may also contribute to the high rate of official social control experienced by African-Americans, both today and in the past.

Social Distance and Group Differences in Social Control

The social control of ethnic and racial groups also raises the question of the role played by perceptions of social distance. Bogardus (1928, 1933, 1959) and recent investigators (Smith and Dempsey 1983) have measured the extent of the perceived social distance between members of America's ethnic and racial groups. These researchers have suggested that such perceptions may underlie earlier Social Darwinist–inspired attempts to restrict the immigration of white ethnics and limit the rights of nonwhite Americans. I suggest that these perceptions of group differences as measured in surveys of social distance have had a direct effect on the social control of both ethnic and racial groups in the United States.

Proposition 1b suggests that once other significant influences are considered, perceptions by the dominant racial/ethnic groups of cultural and/or physical dissimilarity will explain differences in levels of social control across subordinate groups. As previously noted, Sellin (1938:73) also believed that social distance was a factor affecting the "artificially raised" rates of crime that he observed among ethnic groups in the United States. Bogardus (1959) has shown that Americans have varying valuative judgements of the distance between their own racial/ethnic group and others and of the relative "goodness" of these groups. Most nonwhites are generally negatively evaluated by whites, but substantial difference is also shown in the evaluation of white ethnic groups. I propose that during the past and today these perceptions/evaluations largely parallel the experiences of these groups as targets of social control. The hostility directed against Eastern and Southern European immigrants by dominant-group Americans of Western European ancestry has been well documented. It is not implausible that such sentiments resulted in heightened social control.

In examining social distance in the United States, future researchers must also consider its role in accounting for black-white differences as well as the effects of race on perceptions of ethnic group interactions. Among relevant questions are the following: (1) How did the increasing post–Civil War and post–World War I presence of African-Americans in non-southern cities affect the social control of the white ethnic underclass? (2) Given the greater social distance between blacks and whites than among white ethnics, did blacks replace white ethnic outgroups as targets of social control with a resulting decrease in the overrepresentation of those groups?

Social Change and Social Control

Question 2: What explains the gradual reduction over time in the rate of reported crime and punishment among various white ethnic groups in the United States? Does this change have relevance for our understanding of crime patterns currently found among African-Americans, Latinos and other nonwhite populations?

In the view of many observers, America's white ethnics have been transformed during the past century from a lawbreaking underclass to a law-abiding bourgeoisie. Their seeming "success" is compared to the plight of contemporary African-Americans and some groups of Latinos. An "immigrant analogy" in response to the crime patterns of nonwhites has been unavoidable. Given the absence of sound research on the social control of white ethnics, the appropriateness of that analogy remains in question. But, the mere fact that some white ethnic groups are no longer as disproportionately represented among those punished for crime as they were in the past suggests that much may be learned through the study of that social change.

An understanding of the change over time in levels and forms of social control may be gained through not only the study of whites ethnics but Asian Americans as well. As many commentators have noted, the idea that Japanese and Chinese in the United States are "model minorities" tends to obscure both the racial bigotry they experienced and the dismal social conditions under which they lived during the past (Takaki 1979, 1982). One manifestation of these experiences was the disproportionate crime and imprisonment among Chinese Americans during the late 1800s. Like their European counterparts in the eastern United States, Chinese laborers in the west were confined at very high rates. In 1890 their rate of confinement was second only to that of Native Americans and exceeded those of African-Americans (DuBois 1904: 11). Although the past criminality of Asian Americans has not been a topic of interest among social scientists, explanations for the decrease over time in their rates of reported crime have tended to mirror those used for white ethnics. That is, it would likely be attributed to a lessening of economic deprivation and increasing acculturation.

The seeming "success" stories vis-à-vis social control of white ethnics and Asians have led to questions regarding the lack of "success" for other groups. For example, Lane (1986) observed that while both African-American and white ethnic crime rates were elevated during the middle to late 1800s in Philadelphia, only African-American rates have remained high. Explanations for the continuing high rate of crime among some nonwhites have ranged from notions of biological/genetic predispositions (Wilson and Herrnstein 1985) to the kinds of sociologically oriented explanations discussed earlier in this paper.

The lack of appreciation for the role of differential social control on the disproportionate presence of some white ethnics among those punished for crime during the past has implications for perceptions of contemporary racial and ethnic differences. The belief that white ethnics achieved economic success and "abandoned" their criminal ways has shaped public response to the persistence of high rates of crime and punishment among nonwhites in the United States today. During the past two decades, many analysts have de-emphasized the significance of racial bias as a factor that contributes to the disproportionate representation of minorities among those processed through the American criminal justice system (Hawkins 1990). Given the societal changes that have occurred in response to the "Civil Rights Revolution" of the past half-century, some have suggested that no systemic discrimination exists in the contemporary American criminal justice system (Wilbanks 1987).

Regardless of the accuracy or inaccuracy of these views, they highlight the need for studies of ethnicity and social control. Researchers must attempt to account for change over time in the representation of ethnic and racial groups among those arrested, convicted and punished for crime. An informed social change perspective would have to account not only for behavioral change on the part of those targets of social control but also change in the actions of social control agents. The next proposition explores this latter concern.

Changing Agents of Social Control

Proposition 2: Because they are recruited from among economically marginal groups, including those populations characterized by high rates of social control, the police and other lower-level agents of social control play a pivotal role in determining the extent of ethnic/racial differences. As marginal ethnic/racial groups become represented as lower-level agents of social control, the disproportionate representation of members of their group will gradually be reduced.

One of the presumptions underlying the traditional conflict perspectives is the idea that change in the comparative social status of a given ethnic/racial group will lead to a concomitant reduction in the level of social control experienced by that group. Proposition 2 suggests that one of the earliest manifestations of change in social status is the employment of members of ethnic outgroups as lower-level agents of social control. The entry of once-marginal white ethnic groups into police departments once dominated by members of other groups has been documented in the United States. Within a relatively short period in many American cities, members of these groups came to be seen as the "typical" policeman. The Irish in many areas of the northeastern and midwestern U.S. provide a classic example of this transition.

A possible precursor to such a change in employment practice may be change in group perceptions of social distance and/or the emergence of shifts in political power. Their hiring may simply reflect an acknowledgement of the threat to dominant interests posed by members of the ethnic group from which they come. For example, much of the impetus for the hiring of African-American law enforcement officers in the United States came after the civil disturbances of the late 1960s. It was not a direct response to the equal employment requests of civil rights leaders of the period. It was believed by many that black policemen could do a more effective job than white officers of preventing future disturbances (e.g., National Advisory Commission on Civil Disorders 1968). Similarly, the hiring of the Irish and other once-despised ethnic groups as urban policemen may have been in response to the perceived threat posed by the continuing immigration of whites from Eastern and Southern Europe and the migration of blacks from the rural South.

Whatever underlies this change, I propose that one result of the presence within law enforcement of once-excluded white ethnics was a gradual reduction of the rate of arrests and convictions for members of their own ethnic groups. Their continued presence and actions served to counteract those perceptions of social distance and threat that shaped earlier policies directed at members of their ethnic groups. Given the relative recency of significant numbers of African-Americans in the ranks of law enforcement, it is too early to know if similar reductions in the rate of black social control will follow. But to the extent that the experiences of white ethnics provide a model, it is likely that such a reduction will occur.

Conclusion

The discussion in this chapter illustrates the relevance of the conflict perspective for explaining ethnic variations in social control. Ethnic and racial differences in social control are less a reflection of primordial urges than the kinds of social inequalities described by advocates of the conflict perspective. However, the discussion also points to the need for the development of a more reflexive theory of social control. It is clear that conflict theorists and other analysts must begin to examine the extent to which social control reflects not only racial but also ethnic stratification and inequality. Social inequality in modern, multi-racial, multi-ethnic societies is not unidimensional. Along with race, conflict surrounding ethnic differences has shaped much of the history of humankind. The accuracy and validity of models of social control for multi-ethnic societies will be diminished to the extent that such conflict remains a neglected area of investigation.

Notes

1. I argue that ethnicity has been a largely unexamined dimension of American social control during both the past and today. However, the term "forgotten" is also used to indicate evidence of a greater awareness of the relevance of ethnicity among analysts of the past than among those writing today. Social science obviously reflects the social concerns of the times in which it is written. The era of Sutherland and Sellin was marked by greater public interest in white ethnic differences than is found today. Yet, given the well-documented preoccupation of American society with the crime of the foreign-born during the past century, many historians and other analysts of the period show little interest in retrospectively examining the phenomenon. I do not suggest that the differential involvement in crime and punishment of various ethnic groups in the United States has gone completely without notice. I do suggest that what are today considered to be conceptions of social control derived from conflict orientations are virtually absent in discussions of such ethnic differences. I also suggest that in comparison to racial differences these ethnic differences are "underinvestigated" by researchers.

2. The 1911 report described Italians as prominently involved in crimes of personal violence. The Irish were reported to have high rates of drunkenness and vagrancy, while the French and Jews had disproportionate rates of arrest for prostitution. American-born whites were reported to be heavily involved in burglary, larceny, and receiving stolen goods. Among those groups cited for disproportionate violations of city ordinances that regulated peddling and trade were Greeks, Italians and Jews (Steinberg 1989:116).

3. In response to the reportedly high rates of crime among the foreign-born, Sellin (1938:73) observed that "there is ample evidence to show that the immigrant suffers from differential treatment in the process of law administration." His notion of "artificially raised crime rates" reflects aspects of a conflict orientation, but it was never fully explored or developed in his work on white ethnics. He considered such evidence of bias to be more important in explaining crime and punishment among African-Americans (Sellin 1928, 1935).

4. For example, Jamaicans and other Caribbean blacks are frequently said to have lower rates of crime than native American blacks. The high crime rates of Puerto Ricans is compared to the somewhat more moderate rates of Mexican-Americans and the lower rates of Cuban Americans. The comparatively high rates of crime for Koreans and Vietnamese, including involvement in gang activities, have been recently noted by some law enforcement officials.

5. While this orientation toward subordination and social control may in some instances lead to an effort to document similarities in the treatment of various racial and ethnic groups, it may also lead to a tendency to use one subordinate group as a proxy for another. That is, group differences are not fully investigated.

6. Advocates of both the conflict perspective and those who stress the significance of race provide sound arguments and evidence in support of their views of ethnicity, race and social control. For example, although they differ in many respects, historical patterns of social control for the Irish, Italians and other white ethnic groups appear to have many features in common with those observed for blacks and other nonwhites. On the other hand, white ethnics cannot be said to have experienced the same level of prejudice, discrimination, or legal restriction of rights as nonwhites. The point of the present discussion is that only systematic, comparative study of the experiences of both ethnic and racial groups will help determine which of these competing views is more accurate.

7. The tendency to overlook or ignore differential rates of crime, imprisonment, and other criminal justice–related indices of social control is also evident in historical studies of African-Americans.

7

Gender and Punishment Disparity

Kathleen Daly

Studies of punishment have been the stock-in-trade of socio-legal scholars for over half a century.[1] Research normally addresses these areas: How are "normal" or "typical" cases handled? How does punishment vary by defendant attributes? How do organizational, professional, legal, and ideological constraints and contexts shape the process? These questions invite theoretical work on the patterns of discretionary power to punish. Another tack is taken by philosophers and legal scholars who raise normative questions about the character and qualities of justice: How should punishment be justified? Should defendants be punished "equally" for the same offense? What criteria should be used in deciding if decisions are just?

One aim of this essay is to bring the empirical and philosophical more closely together. I would like to see social scientists grapple with normative questions about the character and quality of justice and to have philosophers ground their prescriptive claims in the world of justice system practices. A second aim for the essay is feminist. All justice scholars must appreciate that crime and punishment are sexed and gendered[2] and that measures of the punishment process should reflect those qualities. There has been much conjecture on gender and punishment, but research to date has not answered a simple question: Are men and women punished differently for "like crimes"[3] and for reasons we find unacceptable?

My aims of bringing the empirical and philosophical closer and of raising feminist questions are inspired by several developments that trouble me. These are (1) how punishment disparity is measured and explained by social scientists; (2) how gender disparity is measured and explained; (3) the utilization of disparity research by policy-makers; and (4) the reluctance of feminist scholars to explore the disparity question. I shall review these developments, highlight findings from my research in the New Haven felony court, and propose alternative methods of measuring the punishment process.

Problems with Research on Disparity

One of the earliest social science studies of punishment in the United States was Martin's (1934) research on Texas criminal courts. Unlike studies after his, Martin's was exceptional in analyzing many defendant attributes; he devoted separate chapters to race, sex, family, nativity, residence, age, occupation, and education.[4] Unlike social science research to follow, Martin chose not to make any interpretations: "Opinion need have no place in such a study as this . . . explanatory observations therefore have been scrupulously avoided" (Martin 1934: 244). Like all social science studies in the 1940s and 1950s, Martin's results were restricted to bivariate tabular comparisons, with perhaps one "control variable."[5]

During the next three decades, research centered on race differences in sentencing. Attention was given to variation in the treatment of men; gender differences or the intersection of race and gender is a recent development.[6] Then, as today, disparity was measured by determining if there were statistically significant differences in punishments imposed on selected subgroups. A caricature of a disparity study helps to show how social scientists all too frequently frame this type of research. It begins by asking, Are members of some subgroups (i.e., black, young, poor) more likely to be convicted and to receive more serious punishment than others? Available data are sparse and incomplete: little is known about the offense, measures of the outcome or punishment are crude, and information on the defendant is limited. Analyses are conducted in different ways, but the bottom line is to see if there are statistically significant subgroup differences. If there are, the author concludes that disparity or discrimination[7] exists in the punishment process. Or, as is more frequent, when there are no differences, the author concludes (often with reluctance or surprise) that disparity is apparently absent. In studies of racial disparity, scholars commonly found no difference in non-capital sentencing. This conclusion seemed to go against conventional and sociological wisdom.[8]

There are three problems with disparity research. The first is a lack of congruence between the adjudication process and its modeling by social science variables; the second is minimal attention to *who* and *what* are punished; and the third is using statistical significance as moral authority.

The Dataset Mentality

I have come away from reading sentencing studies wondering if authors had ever been in a courtroom to see how cases are handled, discussed, or disposed. And in broaching this question to researchers, I have discovered that, indeed, they have never been in a courtroom. Instead, they had access to a dataset, from which they constructed variables that previous researchers had used or that made sense to them. A good deal of social science research is done this way, and understandably so because our questions may not permit observation. For research on contemporary criminal court practices, such a position is untenable.

It behooves researchers to go to courthouses and related locales and appreciate what they are trying to measure, assess, or compare. Other researchers have called attention to the misfit between court routines and statistical representations of outcomes (e.g., Maynard 1982; Emerson 1983; Hawkins 1986). The challenge is to find a way to move between the studies of interaction and process (narrative) and research on outcomes and disparity (numbers) in making accurate claims about justice system practices.

Formless Crimes and Faceless Defendants

Qualitative research on the courts has centered on how officials or juries respond to defendants, organizational process, and bureaucratic constraints and how justice is constructed (e.g., Heumann 1977; Feeley 1979; Mather 1979; Maynard 1982, 1984; Nardulli et al. 1988; LaFree 1989). Less attention has been directed to *who* and especially *what* is subject to punishment. A Vera Institute of Justice (1977) study, *Felony Arrests*, was one of the first in the United States to describe the character of cases using a systematic methodology. One important finding was an "obvious but often overlooked reality: criminal conduct is often the explosive spillover from ruptured personal relations among neighbors, friends, and former spouses" (Vera Institute of Justice 1977: 135). A second finding was the impact of a defendant's prior record on conviction and sentencing, and a third was the combination of prior relations and prior record, which created "unexpected complexities" in how cases were disposed. *Felony Arrests* showed readers what a "robbery" or an "aggravated assault" or a "rape" prosecuted in criminal court was.

Looking back on my first statistical study of sentencing (Daly 1987a), I am chagrined with my failure to consider the qualities of an offense and a defendant's prior record in greater detail. Instead, I simply "controlled" for these "legal variables," with measures of the severity of the offense, the type of offense, and two measures of the defendant's prior record. Such an approach is standard practice in disparity research, but it contributes to a false sense that offense variability and seriousness has been controlled for. This problem of effective controls is central to research on gender and sentencing.

As to who is punished, researchers normally have information on a defendant's gender, race, age, perhaps employment status or welfare status, and educational attainment. What is missing is a connection between these variables and the lives of those accused of crime. Bureaucratic or assembly-line court practices, which researchers criticize, are recapitulated in the ways in which court practices are described and assessed by researchers.

Statistical and Moral Significance

Determining whether subgroups are treated "differently" in the courts is as much an art as a science. Statistically significant "sex effects" can be achieved with a large number of cases, and they can be attenuated by introducing variables such as pretrial status (Kruttschnitt and Green 1984) or probation officers' recommendations (Frazier et al. 1983). My concerns here are not technical but conceptual. How do we "know" when a subgroup difference in punishment is significantly different in a moral sense? Are we troubled when 10 percent of black men are more likely jailed than white men (holding other variables constant if you like), but not when the difference is five percentage points? Would our criteria be different were we to compare gender groups or age groups? Researchers might try to wean themselves from the teat of statistical significance by addressing the normative questions raised from their research.

To sum up my criticism with disparity research, I am not taking aim simply at the "garbage in–garbage out" problem created by limited datasets and knowledge of the adjudication process, though that could surely be raised. Instead, I wish to take a positive tack: social scientists have been unduly constrained by their methods of inquiry.

Compared with social science findings of no racial difference in noncapital punishment, *stories* of disparity were more frequent. These accounts emerged from individuals making comparisons with others in the punishments they received. Legal scholars, judges, and advocates for prisoners may have been in a better position than social scientists to see and to document such comparisons (e.g., American Friends Service Committee 1971; Frankel 1972). Or perhaps, like journalists seeking a good story, they felt less constrained by social science methods in their reports. I would argue that it has been the compelling stories of disparity, not social science research, that spawned the sentencing reform movement in the United States in the mid-1970s. The available evidence from social science research suggested little reason for change.[9]

Legal scholars or advocates raised moral and political questions about punishment that were elided in the traditional statistical disparity study. They listened to individual stories of justice and asked deceptively simple questions: Why did person A receive jail while person B received probation for apparently like crimes? Or, why *was* jail imposed on person A in the first place?

Social scientists do have something to contribute. There are standard procedures for collecting and analyzing materials and a methodological self-consciousness about the limitations of samples for making generalizations. Foremost, there is concern to map variability and identify typicality. I suspect most researchers would wince at the cases illustrating "discretion in sentencing" in the American Friends Service Committee's *Struggle for Justice* (1971: 126–128). The authors give no information for how the cases were selected or their typicalness. But the cases should alert researchers to a key element in judgments of justice: they reveal the power of narrative in describing crime and punishment.

Adding Women to Penality

Compared to racial disparity studies, which often yield no "race effects" in non-capital sentencing, "sex effects" are common. Gary Kleck's (1981) review suggests that of 23 studies of non-capital sentencing with a control for prior record, only 2 (or 9 percent) show race effects favoring white defendants. Using the same criteria as Kleck's, a colleague and I conducted a review of all published statistical studies of gender and sentencing (Daly and Bordt 1991).[10]

We determined that of thirty-eight studies with a control for prior record, 45 percent showed sex effects, apparently favoring women defendants. Contrary to what one might expect, the high-quality studies were as likely to find sex effects as the low-quality studies (75 percent and 73 percent, respectively); studies in the mid-range were less likely to show sex effects (33 percent). We also found that studies in felony courts and urban jurisdictions were more likely to find sex effects than those in other jurisdictions or areas. In a weighted analysis by study quality, of the 249 total *outcomes* analyzed in the studies, 58 percent showed effects favoring women; 5 percent, effects favoring men; and 37 percent, no effects.

Statistical studies of punishment therefore raise puzzling problems. Why, in light of court defendants' stories of racism and classism in the criminal justice system, do disparity studies typically find little support for racial differences? And why, in light of women's subordinate status in comparison to men, would about half of statistical studies suggest that women are favored?[11] The question arises: Is there reason to be skeptical of these studies?

We should query the logic and findings of gender disparity studies. Women defendants or the "sex variable" have simply been inserted in the analysis without considering how gender relations shape variability in lawbreaking—the "seriousness" of the current offense and previous lawbreaking—or variability in markers of conventionality such as family, work, or community ties. Most disparity studies have adopted the "add-women-and-stir" posture, endemic to social research (see Stacey and

Thorne 1985). This means that the particular histories and practices of gender and sexuality—modes of domination, resistance, and bases of inequality—are not in the frame. Nor have most scholars understood that constructs of masculinity and femininity shape what people think of themselves and others, how they act, and how they explain their own and others' behavior. Instead, using "add-women-and-stir," the nonfeminist researcher posits gender as if it were the same relation as class or race or age: women are merely "added" to the analysis as non-gendered beings or as if they were men.[12]

The "Holding Constant" Fallacy

We should also be skeptical of multivariate studies in which authors claim to be holding constant the severity of the offense charged. Can we assume that variability in the organization and contexts of men's and women's homicides, assaults, robberies, or larcenies is held constant? Are the measures of men's and women's previous arrests and convictions sufficient in holding constant prior record?

My research in the New Haven felony court sheds light on these questions. For this study (Daly forthcoming), I collected data from the Clerk's docket books on 189 women and 208 men, whose cases were disposed of by conviction in the court. With these cases, which I term the "wide sample," I carried out a regression analysis with the standard statistical controls. I found that men were 20 percent more likely to receive an incarceration sentence and that the average length of sentence was thirteen months longer for men.[13] From the wide sample, I selected 40 women and 40 men, whose charges at arraignment and conviction were the same.[14] For this group, which I term the "deep sample," the gender gap in the proportions jailed narrowed from 20 to 10 percentage points.

I analyzed the content of the deep sample offenses and discovered that while the statutory categories were the same, some men's offenses were more serious. Specifically, I judged 40 percent of men's offenses to be more serious than women's and 12 percent of women's to be more serious than men's; about half were comparably serious.[15] I also learned that for each major offense type (interpersonal violence, robbery, larceny, drugs), different analytic problems emerged in attempting to make gender comparisons. For example, in coding elements from the robbery narratives, men's and women's robberies appeared to be "the same" in that similar proportions used a weapon, caused injury, and took active or equal roles. But when I *read* the narratives, a portion of the men's robberies registered greater seriousness. How could that be? I realized that my list of coded elements was not sufficient to describe the overall seriousness of the robbery or what I term the "gestalt of the harm."[16] For the larcenies, different problems arose. The larcenies contained a heterogenous set of harms, including burglaries and robberies for which the state's evidence was weak, many acts consolidated in one case, and offenses involving organizational and individual victims.

In sum, the seriousness of a case was constructed by varied combinations of offense elements, the defendant's previous lawbreaking, and some bits of the defendant's social history.[17] What researchers term "legal variables" such as statutory severity or type of offense do not effectively control for variation in seriousness of men's and women's offenses, nor are researchers' methods of coding variables for previous lawbreaking sufficiently finetuned.

The failures of an "add-women-and stir" approach are theoretical and methodological. Theoretically, gender is simply incorporated onto the punishment matrix as if it were the same social relation as class, race, or age. Methodologically, scholars have not addressed gender-based variation in the social organization of the offense, including measures of "seriousness" or "culpability" and how these are related to the defendant's previous lawbreaking and social history.

The Uses of Disparity Research for Policy

Merely "adding women" to disparity research has profound consequences for policy. If, as my review of the statistical literature suggests, most high-quality studies show that women receive less severe sentences than men (Daly and Bordt 1991), then policy-makers and legislators may move to rectify the problem by punishing women more harshly in the name of equality with men. Blumstein and his colleagues (1983: 114) have considered the impact of gender disparity studies for policy by outlining three "solutions" to disparity if the policy objective is to "equalize sentences": "If there is discrimination in sentence outcomes by sex (or by race or class), a range of "solutions" is available for eliminating discrimination. If the objective is to equalize sentences, one can shift the outcomes of the disadvantaged group to equal those of the advantaged group, or vice versa, or one can shift both groups to achieve some average of past sentencing practices." By "disadvantaged" group, Blumstein presumably refers to the group whose average sentence is greater or longer than the "advantaged" group. Note, though, that the terminology of "advantaged" and "disadvantaged" cannot be applied in the same way for gender as it can for race and class. We may assume that disadvantaged groups in the wider society are also disadvantaged when accused of crime. That assumption may hold for members of race and class groups, but not necessarily for gender. I make this point to emphasize the different structural relations of class and race in comparison to those of gender and to underscore the difficulty of extrapolating from these relations in theorizing about gender disparity.

Blumstein and his colleagues draw from research on California's

Determinate Sentencing Law (DSL) to show what can happen when a "split-the-difference" approach is taken to reduce an apparent gender gap in punishment. In a split-the-difference approach, men's and women's average sentences are averaged together, and this new average is applied to both groups at sentencing. Blumstein et al. (1983: 114) suggest that one consequence of the "averaging approach ... was to markedly increase the sentences of women—especially for violent offenses." The DSL example is a chilling reminder of what can occur when sentencing reformers are bent on achieving punishment equality for men and women. Their stance of closing the "gender gap" seems guided almost entirely by what the numbers show and nothing else.

In the Blumstein et al. passage above, there are three contingencies, all of which are central to the gender and punishment puzzle. First, "*if* there is discrimination"; second, "*if* the objective is to equalize sentences"; and third, there are "a range of 'solutions' ... for eliminating discrimination." For the first, while about half of statistical studies show statistical effects favoring women, we cannot be sure if women are treated more leniently or even if men and women are punished differently for "like" offenses. For the second, it is arguable that the objective of sentencing reform should be "equal sentencing," whatever one means by this phrase. Few challenge the bedrock value of equality in the criminal justice system.[18] But it is not hard to imagine that equal sentencing may be unjust, or the reverse: that unequal sentencing is just. My point—equality of punishment does not necessarily mean justice—may not seem new (see Morris 1981), but it is novel to raise this issue for gender and punishment. For example, so-called gender-neutral sentencing guidelines have an adverse effect on women (Raeder 1993), and some suggest that because conditions of incarceration are worse for women than men, the "same" length of sentence imposed on men and women is a harsher sentence for women (Rafter 1990: 206).

For the third, the existence of a "range of 'solutions,'" the word "solutions" is put in quotes to signal the authors' skepticism of a policy fix to the punishment puzzle. Although "solutions" may be found in philosophical principles, they are less identifiable (or clear) in practices. For the sake of argument, let us assume that equal sentencing is the aim of punishment. What approach should be taken to achieve this objective? Do we treat women more "like men"? Do we treat men more "like women"? Or do we split the difference? It is instructive to see that sentencing reformers have only been able to imagine two of these "solutions": punish women more like men (more severely) or find an average between them. No one has yet contemplated (at least in print) using women as the standard. In general, men's lives and behavior are the standard in virtually all social contexts and in law. But for punishment, men and women may be better off if women, not men, were the standard. Some may resist this idea; for example, feminists may recoil because some men would not be "punished enough" for certain offenses (see Finstad 1990). Because replacing a male standard with a female standard may be (arguably) no better, I would suggest that we take an initial step of rethinking the aims and purposes of punishment by imagining women in the frame as lawbreakers.[19]

The Disparity Question for Feminists

The stakes are high in the punishment game: gender disparity research matters in forming policy, and this research is being used in ways we should find worrisome. Thus I am concerned that some feminist colleagues seem reluctant to study disparity or see such research as mired in androcentrism. I shall consider the ideas of Maureen Cain, Carol Smart, and Alison Young. Before doing so, I want to say that we agree on these fundamentals: that the legal framing of gender "equality" and "difference" is restrictive for feminist purposes; that with men as the standard in law, equality and justice are largely determined by changing women to accord to the male standard; and that the law is a limited tool to achieve feminist objectives (for reviews, see Smart 1989; Daly 1990; Young 1990; Bartlett and Kennedy 1991). For some time, feminist law scholars have recognized that legal remedies for discrimination or methods of legal redress are limited. As MacKinnon (1987: 32–45) argues, the law's emphasis on group comparisons ("difference") ignores power relationships that structure gender and sexuality ("dominance").[20] Some suggest that the law is "male"; others, that it is "gendered" (Smart 1992).

I think it is possible to embrace a feminist critique of law and of equality discourse in law and to engage in feminist research on disparity. In a recent essay, however, Cain (1990: 2) sees the two as incompatible, since "a concern with equity leaves the substance of what is being equalized un-analyzed." I think Cain has thrown out the disparity "baby" with the equality "bath water." She rightly points out the limits of equal treatment studies ("the substance of what is being equalized [is] unanalyzed"), but she seems to suggest that there is no reason to compare men and women. Smart (1990: 79) and Young (1992: 42–43) also take issue with how disparity research has been framed. Smart suggests that the "equality paradigm always reaffirms the centrality of men." Young argues that "the form taken by anti-discrimination critics is highly problematic ... for its reliance on the identification of bias and omission in criminological accounts and practices ... and second, for the manner of approach to the question of discrimination itself, which leaves Woman to be measured in relation to the master-category, Man." In pointing out the deficiencies and assumptions in work to date, Cain, Smart, and Young imply that any type of disparity research is problematic. I agree that the social and legal construction of gender situates women in a subordinate position to men and that extant equality legal discourse cannot remedy this power relationship. However, feminist research need not situate women as "other" or men as "central" or "master-category" in order to compare the treatment of or the response to men and women accused of lawbreaking.

A useful analog is jobs and wages. We know that an equality focus leaves unanalyzed why some types of jobs are paid more than others. Yet, feminist analyses of jobs of comparable worth are carried out, and they have been critical for raising the consciousness and the pay of women workers (Remick 1984). Group comparisons by gender are relevant in paid employment, and they are appropriate to a feminist project. From them we identified the androcentric assumptions of the "normal worker" and the systematic devaluation of women's paid work. Why, then, can't we make the same comparisons in the penal context? Perhaps the initial findings do not look good for women, that is, the findings do not support the idea that a more subordinated group is a more likely object of penality or that women are punished more severely than men. For penality, we do not have the metaphor of "59 cents" that has defined and politicized pay disparities.

With over a decade of sentencing reform in many states (and now in the federal system), based on guideline systems aimed at closing "gaps" in sentencing, the implications of disparity studies are enormous for women. Scholars must take gender disparity research seriously; we do not have the luxury of ignoring this work because it may be easily stuck in androcentric assumptions. It is possible, I think, to construct a method for studying punishment that does not presume men as the standard and which problematizes gender, along with raced and classed gender constructions.

Beyond the Disparity "Baby" and Equality "Bath Water"

We need to fashion a method to measure punishment practices that moves comfortably and reliably between the narratives and numbers, that attends closely to the multiple bases of inequality, and that contains a normative component. By normative I wish to include researchers' concepts of justice. When do we think a decision is just or unjust? Space precludes a complete presentation of my proposed method; it is described elsewhere (Daly forthcoming).

I begin by taking seriously the views of narrative scholars such as Laurel Richardson (1990: 117), who suggest that narrative in sociology is "used as human 'filler' to 'flesh out' statistical findings" but should be seen as "quintessential to the understanding and communication of the sociological." Drawing from Bruner (1986), Richardson suggests that there are two modes of reasoning that "are irreducible to each other and complementary": logico-scientific and narrative (Richardson 1990: 118).[21] These modes provide a distinctive way of ordering experience and constructing reality. Each has its own operating principles and criteria of "well-formedness." Causality plays a central role in both modes, but each defines it differently. The logico-scientific mode looks for universal truth conditions, whereas the narrative mode looks for particular connections between events. Explanation in the narrative mode is contextually embedded, whereas logico-scientific explanation is abstracted from special and temporal contexts. Both modes are "rational" ways of making meaning.

Richardson's contrast[22] identifies the strengths and limitations of logico-science (numbers) and narrative and acknowledges their "irreducible" qualities. Perhaps I am too optimistic, but I think it is possible to find a truce between those whose representations of the social world are numerical and logico-scientific and those whose representations take a more narrative form. Such a truce will assume some bilingualism in the strengths of statistics and storytelling in the creation of plausible truth claims. It will also take some faith by knowledge-producers in the possibility of oscillating between their familiar, or home, pole and another pole. The work of oscillation means a commitment to a non-adversarial, non-hierarchical stance about the superiority of logico-science or narrative,[23] although participants will no doubt feel one pole is home, more familiar. I am proposing that a measure of justice can be found in that oscillation.

Toward a Measure of Justice

I use the term "measure of justice" metaphorically because I can imagine a variety of measuring tools and normative meanings of justice. My measure builds on previous efforts in analyzing punishment practices; problematizes concepts such as disparity and justice; and is open ended empirically and normatively.

Building on Past Research

Culpability and Outcome. Baldus et al. (1986) offer detailed protocols for addressing proportionality and racial discrimination in the imposition of the death penalty. They identify several methods of assessing punishment for cases of similar culpability: a priori–normative, qualitative-empirical, and quantitative-empirical approaches. From Baldus we learn that (1) cases can be compared once a culpability scoring device is established; (2) reading crime narratives is essential in gauging seriousness and establishing culpability levels; and (3) culpability includes the defendant's actions as well as his or her previous lawbreaking.

It is instructive to see that the authors' assessments of culpability are gender marked: race, but not gender, is omitted (Baldus et al. 1986: 178–179). In an appended set of crime narratives, the defendant's and victim's gender are given only if the person is a woman. Similarly, from a regression analysis, "female victim" was one of eighteen case elements significantly associated with the imposition of the death penalty. Again, the defendant is presumed to be a man, not unreasonable in light of the low numbers of women subject to the death penalty.[24] My point is that greater culpability was not described as "a man killing a woman," but rather it was simply "a female victim."[25] Baldus and his colleagues' work has been important and pathbreaking, but we can see that measures of culpability will become more complex when the gendered and sexed dimensions of harm are fully in the frame.

How might we apply Baldus's methods to non-capital sentencing? Three areas of revision would be required. First, researchers and jurists would have to devise culpability elements from a more diverse set of crime narratives, ranging from selling small amounts of illegal drugs, to embezzling large sums of money, to sexual abuse of a child. This may best be accomplished initially by an a priori–normative method, although such judgments must include gender. Drawing from my experience in coding crime narratives in New Haven (discussed earlier), it is essential that coded elements reflect an overall sense of the gestalt of the harm. Second, a measure of punishment would need to be more complex than the dichotomous death penalty outcome. Centuries of discussion suggest no agreement on what the relationship ought to be between crime and punishment; even desert-based scholars admit that their theories do not offer much guidance in where to "anchor the penalty scale: . . . the cardinal limits will necessarily be imprecise" (von Hirsch 1985: 45). As scholars consider these questions, they cannot assume that men are the only targets of penality. Moreover, we should investigate whether the deprivations of time in prison are comparable for men and women. Third, crime narratives and punishment outcomes must have both men and women in the frame. Because research shows that the concept of "culpability" is deeply enmeshed in presuppositions that men transgress,[26] we must begin by reading crime narratives across diverse harms committed by both men and women. The development of a meaningful notion of "crime seriousness" that reflects the gendered and sexed character of lawbreaking will be a major achievement of scholars and jurists committed to numerical-narrative oscillation. The development of a punishment scale that reflects the gendered character of punishment will be much tougher and more contentious. In both instances, a presumptive male standard will be made visible and perhaps challenged.

Pair-wise Comparisons from a Larger Sample. Baldus and his colleagues approach the study of punishment by identifying a set of cases, measuring culpability, and determining whether outcomes vary by levels of culpability or other criteria. Another approach would be to compare pairs of cases, the method I took in my research in the New Haven felony court. I developed a comparative justice metric to judge the punishment outcomes of the forty deep sample pairs. Fifteen raised a question of disparity in my mind: for nine, women received a more lenient sentence, and in six, men did. In probing these cases further, I was satisfied that the disparity could be explained fully for all but three.[27] For these remaining pairs, there were two in which the disparity could be explained, though it still troubled me. There was only *one* pair out of the 40 where I felt the disparity could not be explained at all. I concluded that the regression analysis gave the misleading impression of substantial "sex effects" favoring women, when a comparison of cases at closer range showed the differences to be almost negligible.

An important element in pair-wise comparisons is that one must know the larger population from which cases are selected. A drawback is that unless one has access to the crime narratives and information on the defendant's previous lawbreaking, selecting cases will be based on legal statutory categories of presumptive "culpability," which is not optimal unless one wishes to demonstrate gender-based variation in these categories.

"Out-Group" Subjectivities. I have assumed a particular narrative perspective thus far: the state's account of what the defendant did—what was said in state-sponsored ceremonies (like sentencing) or state-produced documents (like police or court reports). Another approach would be to examine justice system processes from defendants' points of view. In taking this tack, "out-group" subjectivities (Delgado 1989) or "the collective story [of] silenced people" (Richardson 1990) is brought forward. Research on out-group subjectivities is crucial for understanding the meanings of a variety of "isms" (sexism, racism, etc.) in the criminal justice system. Much feminist scholarship has centered on out-group subjectivities of women crime victims, particularly those raped and assaulted (e.g., Russell 1978; Holmstrom and Burgess 1978; Browne 1987; Chaudhuri and Daly 1992). This research challenges a homogenous referent for "out-group" in justice system processes in that several out-groups exit, often in adversarial relation to each other.

Problematizing Concepts

Although scholars must define the terms they aspire to measure, we cannot expect uniformity in definitions. Nettler (1979: 28) observes that "justice, like crime, is an idea. It is not an entity. It is a concept whose referents move with the morality that underwrites its conception."

Although several tensions are evident in justice systems, one that appears most intractable is the "demand that the criminal law be applied both uniformly and individually." The concept of uniformity, where justice means equality of treatment, pushes up against the concept of individuality, where justice means responding to the specifics of the person and the case.

There are several meanings of equality as well (Nettler 1979: 30–31): numerical ("one person, one vote"), proportional ("distributing burdens and benefits [on the basis] of some measure of need or desert"), and subjective (distributing burdens and benefits "according to a shifting standard of need, merit, or ability"). In justice systems, the proportional meaning is expressed in a desert-based model, while the subjective meaning is found in an individualized model.

Some scholars argue for a decoupling of equality from justice (Morris 1981), and others argue for justice as equality (von Hirsch 1985). From my New Haven research, I would argue for conceptualizing equality (or the disparity problem) and justice (or the right response) as separate criteria of punishment practices, even if they may overlap in many decisions.

Open and Normative

Matza (1964: 105) suggests that "the precise point at which justice ends and injustice begins cannot be definitively stated. It is in some measure a matter of perspective and opinion and thus eternally problematic." An important dimension of punishment is its public and normative character. Thus, a crucial research component should be presenting and discussing decisions (or outcomes) in a manner that allows researchers and readers the chance to reflect on crime, punishment, and justice. In so doing, social scientists can be more than technical analysts of punishment practices or reporters of statistical significance. We can initiate a discussion within the scholarly ranks and to wider publics about the qualities and meanings of justice.

Notes

1. My thanks to Marie-Andree Bertrand, Lisa Maher, and David Baldus for their comments on earlier drafts. I am indebted to Rebecca Bordt and Molly Chaudhuri for research assistance and to members of the Connecticut Judicial Department for their cooperation. Support for this research came from the Russell Sage and Rockefeller Foundations.

2. I refer here to the ways in which relations of gender and sexuality inscribe history, structure, and meaning on social life and social institutions. In giving attention to gender and sexuality, I am not suggesting that other relations such as class or race are eclipsed. Rather, I focus on gender as an axis of punishment.

3. The meaning of "like crimes," disparity," "differently," and other comparative dimensions of criminal court cases is problematized in this essay. I put these words in quotes only for their first appearance in the text.

4. Martin's study was limited in analyzing each attribute separately. Although the limits of bivariate analysis are well known, few researchers have considered the interactional (Crenshaw 1989) or multiple (King 1988) influences of defendants' social locations. The latter line of work has been developed by feminist scholars, but it has been applied largely to employment discrimination and, to some degree, rape.

5. Measuring tools such as "control variables" are also problematized in this essay. As suggested below, it is unclear what is being "held constant" or whether important sources of variability are "controlled" in statistical analyses of punishment disparity.

6. The first statistical study in the U.S. to compare sentencing by race and gender was published in 1984 (Gruhl et al. 1984); the few quantitative studies since then include Spohn (1985), Daly (1989a), and Bickle and Peterson (1991). Kruttschnitt (1980–81, 1982a, 1982b) and Mann (1984) have analyzed racial differences in the response to women. With the exception of conflicting results reported in Krutschnitt (1980–81, 1982), no study shows race effects during the sentencing of women.

7. Until recently, social scientists tended to use the terms "disparity" and "discrimination" interchangeably and, perhaps, too loosely. See Blumstein et al. (1983: 72–77) for defining disparity and discrimination in sentencing and Hagan (1977b) on finding discrimination.

8. For reviews, see Hagan (1974), Kleck (1981), Hagan and Bumiller (1983) and Wilbanks (1987), who show that race-based variability in punishment that favors whites is rare. In contrast, some commentators (Morris 1981; Nagel 1989) say that disparity is common but cite no research evidence. I assume that the latter are drawing from compelling stories rather than statistics of disparity, as discussed below.

9. The politics of state legitimation loom large, of course, and what radical and liberal reformers hoped to see change did not materialize (Greenberg and Humphries 1980). A troubling consequence of sentencing reform is that mandatory minimum sentences for drug law violations have widened the "race gaps" at the same time that federal guideline policies were designed to close them.

10. We analyzed the findings from fifty unique datasets that included a "sex" variable, that were subjected to analyses, and that were available in published form. Most, though not all, studies were of sentencing practices in the United States.

11. The few studies of race and gender show that gender differences hold across race and ethnic groups. From my research (Daly 1989a) and that of others (Gruhl et al. 1984; Spohn et al. 1985), the "gender gap" may be widest for black defendants.

12. The phenomenon of "add-race-and-stir" occurs as well. The linkages of race and class are often made by seeing the former as theoretically derived from the latter.

13. The incarceration "gap" is like that found in other studies of criminal courts, which show a range of 8 percent to 25 percent (Daly and Bordt 1991). These results exclude the fraction of defendants who were found guilty at trial. The "gender gap" was evident for both black and white defendants.

14. Readers may recognize the terms "wide" and "deep samples" from the Vera Institute of Justice (1977) research design. The deep sample of cases has several forms of interpersonal violence (e.g., homicide, assault), robbery, larceny and drug offenses. Men convicted of rape are analyzed separately.

15. For more information on how these judgments were reached, see Daly (forthcoming). I drew from research on interpersonal violence, robbery, larceny and drug offenses in making the judgments, and I present the narratives to readers, inviting them to reflect as well on what makes one act "more serious" than another.

16. The elements in the "gestalt of the harm" were taken from Katz's (1988) discussion of "doing stickup." I learned that the gender composition of men's robbery groups (all male) and the somewhat greater numbers of women who knew their victims were important in constructing some men's robberies as "more serious" than women's.

17. Like Wheeler (1988), I found that court officials focussed on notions of harm (e.g., the nature of the offense) and defendant blameworthiness (e.g., going backward and forward in time, using information about prior record, work and family ties) in constructing a notion of the seriousness of "the case."

18. Feminist scholars are an important "exception" in challenging the meaning of equality and equal treatment when men are the norm in law and in social institutions (see Wisconsin Women's Law Review 1987; Young 1990). As I suggest elsewhere (Daly 1989b), the state's emphasis on "equality of punishment" may serve largely to legitimate the state's power to punish.

19. There is precedent for thinking along racial lines in proposing penal benchmarks or standards. For race and death penalty jurisprudence, Baldus et al. (1986: 206) draw on the employment discrimination framework and argue that the treatment of defendants with black victims could provide "a benchmark for determining liability and a remedy for defendants with white victims."

20. I am referring to MacKinnon's critique of Gilligan's (1982) "different voice" construct, not to poststructuralist and linguistic questions about difference. See Marcus et al. (1985) for an early exchange.

21. Richardson (1990: 119) notes, of course, that "both modes are framed in meta-narratives such as 'science' ... or 'religion.' [Thus] narrative structures are pre-operative, regardless of whether one is writing primarily in a 'narrative' or a 'logico-scientific' code."

22. This contrast puts each "side" into relief, but it may not be clear which reasoning prevails in some sociological studies. For example, what are termed "qualitative" methods in the social sciences draw on interviews, observations or documentary material but may gather and order that material in a logico-scientific frame.

23. Because narrative scholars usually claim a subordinate status, the presumptive superiority of the logico-scientific scholars may need to be addressed.

24. Of over 180 cases, only 5 involved women defendants.

25. The most serious forms of death-eligible murders involved sexual abuse, rape and mutilation. It is not clear from the narratives whether women victims were subjected to these additional forms of violence more often than the men or whether perceived "heinousness" is intensified when violence is etched on women's bodies.

26. Rossi et al.'s (1985: 77) vignette study showed that citizens regarded cases involving female defendants "with less severity" than cases involving males. Wolfgang et al.'s (1985) crime severity scale genders some offenses, but the "unmarked" lawbreaker is a man.

27. The disparities were largely explained by differences in prior record and, to a lesser degree, by the offense, evidence, interest of justice, age and mental competency. I expected gender-based family responsibilities to affect disparity, but they did not.

8

Gender, Class, Racism, and Criminal Justice: Against Global and Gender-Centric Theories, For Poststructuralist Perspectives

Pat Carlen

The title and contents of this paper were provoked by two questions: (1) How important is gender in the theorization of the penal control of lawbreaking women? and (2) How best can the other (non-gendered or more-than-gendered) constituents of unequal power relationships (especially class and racism) be theorized in relation to the gendered constituents? To structure and deconstruct discussion of these two questions, the paper is divided into three parts. The first briefly outlines the main empirical findings, the dominant substantive concepts and the major modes of formal theorizing that have informed recent work on the control of women by the criminal justice and penal systems. The second suggests that poststructuralist perspectives might productively inform new analyses of the relationships between lawbreaking, class, gender, racism and criminal justice in different societies and at different historical conjunctures, and the third addresses some criticisms that feminists have made of poststructuralisms.

Women and Criminal Justice

During the past fifteen years there has been a much more sustained focus upon the control of women by the criminal justice system than there had been prior to the mid-1970s.[1] Study after study has argued, first, that women's crimes are committed in different circumstances to men's and that women's crimes are usually the crimes of the powerless, and second, that the response to women's lawbreaking is constituted within typifications of femininity and womanhood, which further add to women's oppression. In other words, the emphasis has been upon lawbreaking, women's economic and political powerlessness and their ideological and physical coercion. Dominant constructs informing the analyses of the control of women, therefore, have been those relating to (1) control via ideologies of femininity; (2) control via the economic systems and ideological structures of patriarchy; and (3) control via the politico-economic institutions of family, marriage and welfare. A fourth type of "control theory" (Hirschi 1969) has been invoked to explain not only women's regulation but also the relatively low rates of women's lawbreaking (Heidensohn 1985) as well as the actual conditioning of their crimes and punishments (Carlen 1988).

Control via Ideologies of Femininity

Much of the work that has privileged ideologies of femininity (and masculinity) in explaining the differential social controls imposed on women and men has been of an empirical exposé kind. In unravelling the discourses within which women are controlled as such, ethnographers and deconstructive analysts have also contended that ideologies of femininity are dominant in shaping the regulatory discourses and practices constitutive of the informal control of women in general (Hutter and Williams 1981); the disciplinary regulation of female adolescents in particular (Hudson 1984; Cain 1989); and the discourses and practices of psychiatry (Chesler 1972); the courts (Edwards 1984; Allen 1987); probation (Worrall 1990); and the women's prisons (Carlen 1983).

Most theorists have employed more than one theory to inform analysis of empirical data relating to the social control of women, though it has been a criticism of gender-centric theories that they underplay (or cannot explain) the relationships between gender, class and racism as empirical factors constitutive (albeit in different combinations) of women's experiences and women's consciousness (see, e.g., Rice 1990). Such a criticism, however, involves a realism that assumes that all theories should have a one-to-one relationship, or at least a verisimilitude, with the empirical object. This is not a theoretical tenet that I hold (see Lacan 1977: 171; Ulmer 1985: 88; and below).

Control via Economic Systems and the Ideology of Patriarchy

Although several feminist writers on the social control of women have argued that the values and logic of law (both criminal and civil) operate in the interests of men (Smart 1976, 1984; MacKinnon 1983; Dahl 1987; Fineman and Thomadsen 1991), only Messerschmidt (1986) has attempted to develop a theory that posits both the class and the sexual divisions of labor as being equally important factors in lawbreaking. But

Messerschmidt's analysis relates only to crime *causation*, not crime *control*, and based upon Hartmann's (1981) definition of patriarchy as "a set of social relations of power in which the male gender appropriates the labor power of women and controls their sexuality (Messerschmidt 1986:*x*)," Messerschmidt employs the term patriarchy merely as a descriptive category rather than an explanatory concept. Nonetheless, Messerschmidt's book does have the virtue of insisting upon the mutuality of patriarchal and class relations in *crime* production, though it is unlikely that useful knowledge of the political effects of class and gender phenomena can be gained via their conflation in the process of theoretical production (see Cousins 1978).

My own reluctance to invoke a universalizable concept of patriarchy as providing more than part explanation of the official response to lawbreaking women is that, unmodified by regional analysis, it would imply that the effects of gender relations on criminal law are homogeneous, global and always-already in the interests of men (cf., Cousins 1980). Apart from the fact that such a position would imply that the (male) state has an omniscient feedback mechanism that functions in the interests of all men regardless of race and class, such a position would preempt any possibilities for penal politics and change. It would also be a barrier to the development of regional theories that might wish to privilege (or problematize) either class relations or racism as explanatory (or as yet untheorized) formulations in analyzing the operations of the criminal law.

One substantive area of study, in which analyses of specific instances of patriarchal domination have been productive, is in the deconstruction of judicial logic in cases of female rape victims and domestic homicides by women. For when in these cases the meanings of women's actions have to be judged in order that "consent" (in the case of rape) or guilty intent (in the case of homicide) can be imputed, there is considerable evidence that English courts tend to render women's experience null and void as they compute culpability according to what they think the normal male would do in similar circumstances (see, e.g., Adler 1987). Likewise, women who fetch a knife in order to protect themselves against violent husbands are seen as acting with guilty premeditation. Yet it could be argued that they are merely acting as *reasonable women* (with prior experience of their powerlessness to confront male violence effectively without a weapon) might be expected to act. However, though these specific instances of patriarchal judicial reasoning provide useful evidence of one system of gender discrimination in the administration of criminal law, it cannot be argued from them that the logic of the criminal courts is essentially and universally predicated on *all* men's experience, equally in the interests of *all* men, or even that it uniformly disadvantages female defendants (see, e.g., Allen 1987). Moreover, in the cases of black women, a white man's judicial reasoning may well be more influenced by racial stereotypes about "black promiscuity" or "black violence" than by patriarchal stereotypes about how "normal" (i.e., moral) women could be expected to behave if only they were to behave like reasonable men!

Control via Family and Welfare Institutions

The strength of the best studies that analyze the social control of women within the interrelationships of the politico-economic institutions of family, marriage and welfare lies firstly in their historical specificity. Secondly, it inheres in a thoroughgoing materialism that, in prioritizing analysis of the political, ideological and economic conditions in which women's physical and economic control is accomplished, at the same time is also able to facilitate explanation of the modes of control wherein their *subjective* coercion is achieved. A good example of this type of study is that of Ehrenreich and English, which was published in 1978 and entitled *For Her Own Good*. Subtitled "159 Years of the Experts' Advice to Women," the book shows how nineteenth- and early twentieth-century experts controlled women (and taught middle-class "ladies" how to control working-class "housewives") via an attractive mix of rationalist and romanticist discourses that both objectified women's sexuality in the service of men and denied them their independence for the "good of the family." Thus, although Ehrenreich and English do indeed use the term "patriarchy" to refer to the historical phenomenon of male domination in every area of economic, cultural and political life, they do not invoke it as a teleology. Instead, they analyze changing historical discourses to explain just why patriarchy took the form it did in the nineteenth and early twentieth centuries.

Explaining Control via Control Theory

In 1985, when I began the research project that was eventually published as *Women, Crime and Poverty* (Carlen 1988), I set out to investigate why contemporary English women's criminal careers take the form that they do take within (1) a society characterized by increasing inequalities of wealth and income (Bull and Wilding 1983) and (2) a criminal justice system that systematically employs a differential sentencing logic based on class, gender and racial stereotypes (Box 1987). The major problem with which I had to contend at the outset of the research was a recognition that on the whole British women are a law-abiding lot, accounting in 1985 for approximately only 13 percent of all serious crime (Central Statistical Office 1987) and constituting a mere 3 to 4 percent of the total daily prison population (Home Office 1985). So, whatever experiences I was likely to posit as being part cause of some women's crimes were likely to have been shared by many more women who had never been convicted of lawbreaking. It seemed, therefore, that as far as gender differences in lawbreaking were concerned I should be posing questions more about women's *conformity* than about their relatively rare criminal activities, and it was at this point that I decided to employ "control theory" (Hirschi 1969; Kornhauser 1978; Rosenbaum 1981) in my analyses of the ethnographic data.

Instead of posing the question "Why do people break the law?" control theory asks, "Why do people conform?" It replies that people are more likely to conform when they perceive that they have a vested interest in so doing, when they have more to gain than lose by lawbreaking. This perspective has the capacity to explain the lawbreaking of both rich and poor, though economic factors are not posited as being the only determinants of how people calculate the rewards expected from either lawbreaking or conformity. Nor need positive calculation be a prerequisite to lawbreaking. A drift into crime, accompanied by the concomitant rewards of friendship, financial gain and excitement, can engender the alternative "controls" that gradually commit the woman lawbreaker to a way of life more satisfying (initially, at least) than that offered by conventional labor and marriage markets and/or meager, and often uncertain, welfare payments.

The relative rarity of women's (detected) crime led me to use control theory as a formal orientation to research about women's careers. However, empirical evidence of relationships between class, gender, race and criminal justice suggested an urgent need to develop alternative conceptualizations, ones that explain the form of *some* women's lawbreaking and judicial and penal regulation while at the same time denying that women's experiences of crime, courts and custody have a necessary and unitary existence. Denial of *"women's* lawbreaking" as a unitary object necessitated a denial that *women's* lawbreaking could possibly be in a symmetrical relationship with any posited (but impossible) *"women's* conformity." In other words, an inversion of a control theory explaining why the majority of women appear to be law abiding would only partly explain why some other women go on to commit crime in the first place. And it would be even less useful in explaining (1) why a few of all women lawbreakers go on to become recidivist criminals and prisoners and (2) why recidivist women criminals and female prisoners are disproportionately poor, black and with backgrounds involving childhood institutionalization (Carlen 1987).

It seemed, therefore, that what I should aim to achieve by analyzing the accounts of the women's criminal careers was an indication of at what stages (if any) race or class (and possibly age) had become more important than gender in the conditioning and occasioning of their lawbreaking, prosecution and imprisonment. I failed. In explaining the criminal careers of 39 women, more than a quarter of whom had at least one parent of Asian or Caribbean origin and who had also expressed awareness of being victimized by white racism, I erased the effects of racism on *black* women's criminal careers in the service of a more generalizable theory of *poor* women's criminal careers. I succumbed to the temptation of globalism. Yet if I had kept in mind a post-structuralist notion of the variability of meanings both within and between cultures I might have produced a theory that explained women's criminal careers in the fullness of *all* their contradictions and specificities. For as I myself had claimed: "By taking seriously women's own accounts of their criminal careers, there is first a refusal to reduce those lives to a sociology that erases the uniqueness of individual female experience; and, secondly, a commitment to deconstructing those careers into the elemental economic, ideological and political components which many of them share, albeit in the different combination that renders each unique" (Carlen 1988:72). The tensions between the generalizing and abstractionist tendencies of theoretical production and the political and policy concerns that need both to recognize and deny the specificities of individuals' shared experiences can, in my view, be best confronted by a poststructuralism that works on the contradiction that the already known has to be both recognized (in the service of politics) and denied (in the service of theory production).

Poststructuralist Perspectives

In view of my strictures against global theorizing, it may now seem perverse to attempt to argue for the possibilities of poststructural perspectives (on the relationships between economy, gender and race as constituents of crime discourses) that might be used cross-culturally and/or cross-nationally. Yet I think that from a poststructuralist perspective questions can be posed that could be used across a variety of cultural, economic and political contexts to call into question the official meanings of women in the criminal justice system as lawbreakers, convicts and prisoners. But first, some further discussion of poststructuralisms, global theories, and gender-centric theories is in order.

Poststructuralisms

Poststructuralisms are many, though they all share a "dissatisfaction with the subject as a 'programmed individual'" (Grbich 1991: 63). The poststructuralism that I am advocating both recognizes and denies structuralism. In relation to inequalities, the effectivity of the structures of social process and consciousness sociologically grouped (and often conflated) under the signs of "class," "gender" and "race" are recognized.

But they are then denied any necessary unitary being in theories, subjectivities or practices. Such a poststructuralism is structuralist insofar as it attributes a nominalist reality to the concepts of "class," "gender" and "race" and then poststructuralist in that it adopts the methodological protocol of Bachelard (1940) that systems of thought must say "no" to their own conventions and conditions of existence. It is structuralist insofar as it takes comfort from Saussurian linguistics, which demonstrate that individual words themselves have no essential meaning but acquire meaning only via syntagma, which through differentiation assign the value of a specific sign (Saussure 1974), and then becomes poststructuralist by raising the specter of otherness (Lacan 1977) or the desire for (and knowledge of) meanings that lie beyond the text (or context) but which also make possible (via "difference"—Derrida 1976) the construction and simultaneous deconstruction) of the text (context, theoretical object) itself. In other words, the poststructuralist perspective on inequality for which I am arguing is one that will allow recognition of the value (i.e., effectivity) of existing inequalities at the same time as denying that they always and already have perennial applicability to any specific society, social formation or individual subjectivity. Such a perspective will of course strive against both globalism and the advance privileging of any one structure of inequality in the deconstruction of specific, local or individual configurations of inequalities.

Globalism

By global theories I mean those that generalize from abstract theorizing that *may* be relevant to one group of women to account for the lawbreaking of all women. "Women's liberation leads to an increase in women's lawbreaking" is maybe the most notorious example of this kind of sociological globalism—though the biological type has also been well documented. Another brand of globalism can occur when a theorist develops a substantive theory to explain the situation of people of overlapping cultures within one nation purely in terms relevant to those of the dominant culture. Thus, as I have argued above, *Women, Crime and Poverty* is an example of globalism: although a quarter of the women in the study were black, the formalized substantive theory developed on the basis of the ethnography applied primarily to white women and, insofar as it applied to black women, only did so by putting their different histories as black women under an erasure.

Gender-centrism

Gender-centrism is often related to globalism, and in using the term I refer to academic work that either implies that concepts such as gender, class, race and racism must be set in hierarchies with gender *always* being the most important in terms of explanation or characterization of sets of relationships or that all theory should be "gendered." My reservation about the first version is rooted in campaigning and policy concerns. For if in explaining a set of relationships one starts from the assumption that, for instance, either patriarchal relations or a universal male violence must always-already provide the key to them, it may become very difficult indeed to use that theory to inform campaigning action aimed at decreasing the levels of oppression being suffered by women in a variety of very differently balanced material and ideological circumstances. This is not to assert that there is no need for studies and theories that privilege gender questions as the most important. It is to warn against conceptual conflation and/or conceptual imperialism, both of which might result in a theoretical closure.

The second version of gender-centrism involves a realism that assumes that all theories should have a one-to-one relationship or at least a verisimilitude with the empirical object. As I said, this is not a theoretical tenet that I hold. The task of theory is to produce new knowledge and not mirror the old. Moreover (and almost conversely), I believe that theoretical production still must *initially* essentialise certain relationships as objects of knowledge that are not reducible to each other (Fuss 1989). The empirically recognized relationships of class, gender and race are, in my opinion, pre-eminent amongst those that should initially be recognized separately, then have the basis of their power revealed through analytic deconstruction, and finally have the necessity for those relationships denied in theory production. This is not to argue that material relationships are not experienced as being simultaneously class dominated, gendered, racially or culturally specific or racist; it is to argue that it is quite permissible for a theorist initially to essentialise one dimension of multidimensional discourses and theorize it separately. Thereafter, the empirical/political meanings of the discourses have to be calculated according to the historical and prevailing material, ideological and political conditions in which they are constituted. Theories of class, racism and gender are non-assimilable and non-reducible both to each other (cf., Cain 1986) and empirical sets of relationships, and the ways in which they can be used either to produce new knowledge or reduce injustices will usually be matters of political calculation.

What then has a poststructuralism to offer? At this stage a quotation from Weedon (1987: 22) well summarizes what I see to be poststructuralisms' most important tenets:

> Neither social reality nor the "natural" world has fixed intrinsic meanings which language reflects or expresses. Different languages and different discourses within the same language divide up the world and give

it meaning in different ways which cannot be reduced to one another through translation or by an appeal to universally shared concepts of reflecting a fixed reality. For example, the meanings of femininity and masculinity vary from culture to culture and language to language. They even vary between discourses within a particular language, between different feminist discourses for instance, and are subject to historical change.

It is with such a poststructuralist perspective in mind that I have thought it possible to pose the following three interrelated questions, which might be just one way of productively interrogating the varying meanings of crime across a range of cultures and political contexts:

1. Why does a specific criminal justice discourse take the form that it does?
2. Which cultural, racial, class and other knowledges are constitutive of and/or silenced by a specific criminal justice discourse?
3. Which masculinities and femininities are constitutive of (recognized) and/or silenced (denied) by a specific criminal justice discourse?

Conclusion ... and Beginning Again

But what about the problems, the contradictions, the relativisms, the questions of agency, histories, essentialisms, translations, loss of meanings, and so on? The problems are endless. I'll now conclude by addressing just three of them.

Deconstruction and the Disappearing Women

Two related anxieties raised by feminists about post-structuralist analysis are (1) whether women's *histories* of oppression, resistance, etc., are made to disappear in the shifting semantics of deconstructionism and (2) whether the category "women" is erased out of all meaningful existence, making it impossible to talk of "women" at all. Yet there is nothing in poststructuralisms to necessitate the denial of history, and Riley (1988:1,2,5) has succinctly summarized its importance to one poststructuralist perspective: "'Women' is historically, discursively constructed, and always relatively to other categories which themselves change. . . . It's not that our identity is to be dissipated into airy indeterminacy, extinction . . . it is to be referred to the more substantial realms of discursive historical formation."

And why should a poststructuralism that both seeks to recognize discourses (for purposes of the analysis of their knowledge/power effects) and deny them (the necessity of the relationships preconditional to those knowledge/power effects) be at odds with any feminism that, as Riley describes it, assumes that "both a concentration on and a refusal of the identity of 'women' are essential to feminism" (Riley 1988:1)? The greater problem in my view lies with feminisms that in striving to retain the rich diversity of women's individual autobiographies argue against the possibility of making any theoretical statements at all about women (white or black) as a group.

Individualism and Systemicity

While some feminists fear that poststructuralisms erase the category of women via deconstruction, other feminists, conversely, are against theory per se. They claim that theory, in imposing limiting categories to universalism *some* meanings, also erases or silences others. Poststructuralists would agree. Yet, just as new knowledge can be created only out of the old already known knowledge (i.e., ideology), so too is deconstructionism dependent at least upon a *nominal* essentialism. As Diana Fuss (1989: 5) has written: "It is Locke's distinction between nominal and real essence which allows us to work with the category of 'women' as a linguistic rather than a natural kind, and for this reason Locke's category of nominal essence is especially useful for anti-essentialist feminists who want to hold on to the notion of women as a group without submitting to the idea that it is 'nature' that categorizes them as such." A poststructuralist perspective must engage in a nominalist essentialism in order to fully recognize that which it has to deny. In so doing it can also celebrate the range of women's individual experiences and subjectivities before deconstructing them into the constitutive ideological, economic and political discourses that many of them share in the different combinations that render them each unique.

The Question of Human Agency

A constant criticism of poststructuralisms is that they are deterministic and allow space neither for individual agency and responsibility nor for political struggle. If individuals are created in discourses, how can they be accountable for their actions or indeed ever get to change things? The charge of determinism is ill founded. Subject-positions are pre-given, but they also constantly change as different sets of subjects choose how to occupy them. The choices, however, are made under specific economic, political and ideological conditions that are not of the subjects' choosing. Arguments about degrees of culpability are tasks for political jurisprudence. The job of analytic deconstruction is to unravel the combinations of discourses and economic conditions within which crime and criminal justice discourses (including political jurisprudence) take a variety of forms. And this is precisely why I am *against* the tendency towards theoretical closure inherent in global gender-centric theories about the social control of women and the always-already unfinished interrogation of the "classes," "genders" and "racisms" so central to present understandings of inequalities and criminal justices.

Notes

1. For a comparative perspective on the search for a feminist jurisprudence, see Russell (1985) for Canada; Dahl (1987) for Norway; MacKinnon (1983) and Fineman and Thomadsen (1991) for the United States; Graycar (1990) and Grbich (1991) for Australia; and Smart (1984) for England.

PART FOUR

Linkages Among Forms of Social Control

9

Labor Markets and the Relationships Among Forms of the Criminal Sanction

James Inverarity

The form of the criminal sanction varies in diverse ways, reflecting variation in the underlying social structure. Consider, for example, two criminal prosecutions for attempted murder of a head of state. In 1757, Robert Damiens attacked King Louis XV with a penknife. Contemporary accounts suggest that Damiens was insane; nonetheless, he was convicted and subjected to a prolonged, torturous public execution in the center of Paris. In addition his immediate family was banished and their house razed (Kittrie 1971: 58; Foucault 1977: 3–6; McManners 1981:368). In 1981, John Hinckley shot President Ronald Reagan and several bystanders. He was found "not guilty by reason of insanity" and committed to a mental hospital until his mental illness is unlikely to result in harm to himself or others (Hans and Slater 1983; Low et al. 1986).

In the two hundred years between the criminal prosecutions of Damiens and Hinckley, the form of the criminal sanction has changed along several dimensions: the substitution of incarceration for execution, the elimination of punishment as a public spectacle, the abolition of vicarious liability for relatives of the offender, and the elaboration of medical and other systems of control as substitutes or adjuncts to the criminal sanction. Sociologists have sought not simply to chart such historical transformations but also to explain them in terms of corresponding changes in social organization (Garland 1990). While the changes represented by the Damiens and Hinckley prosecutions are complex and multifaceted, much of the transformation may be understood in terms of a labor theory of punishment proposed by Rusche and Kirchheimer (1939). This paper elaborates this theory, in part by integrating several cognate theoretical formulations of the relationship between social structure and criminal sanction. It then demonstrates that the labor theory of punishment explains better than alternative accounts several variations in the forms of the criminal sanction.

The Labor Theory of Punishment

Rusche and Kirchheimer envision transitions among forms of social control as directly related to transitions among modes of production: "Every system of production tends to discover punishments which correspond to its productive relationships" (1939:5).[1] They argue that criminal sanctions vary with the market value of human labor. Put simply, severe sanctions are associated with cheap labor; the cheaper the labor, the harsher the punishment. For example, in the late Middle Ages, "[a]s the price paid for labor decreased, the value set on human life became smaller and smaller. The hard struggle for existence molded the penal system in such a way as to make it one of the means of preventing too great an increase of population" (Rusche and Kirchheimer 1939: 20).

Punishment and Social Structure (Rusche and Kirchheimer 1939) collates historical cases illustrating how the form of the criminal sanction changed with fluctuations in the market value of human labor. This study portrays the criminal sanction as a form of human sacrifice that in economic terms diminishes the productive capacity of the individual. At any given historical period the dominant form of the criminal sanction—corporal punishment, execution, incarceration or fine—is best understood in terms of societal capacity to sustain such sacrifices. The earliest forms of incarceration, for example, sought to offset this cost by attempting to utilize productively the labor power of prisoners and by designing the prison to resocialize inmates into labor discipline. While these efforts have continued throughout the history of the prison, they have continually encountered obstinate structural limits on the capacity of the prison to produce value rather than consume societal resources.[2]

While several generations of sociologists have found Rusche and Kirchheimer's account compelling,[3] several deficiencies in the theory have inhibited the emergence of a systematic research program and stimulated vigorous critical assessments (Gardner 1987; Garland 1990; Zimring and Hawkins 1991). One of the most important impediments is that their study vaguely defines the central concept, the value of human labor. Our first task, therefore, is to consider two alternative formulations of the concept of labor value: human capital and moral individualism. We then consider how labor value may be connected to variation in the forms of criminal sanctions.

Value of Labor: Two Elaborations of the Concept of Human Capital

Becker (1975) introduced into the labor market literature the concept of human capital to refer to attributes of the individual worker that contribute to productivity: on-the-job training, schooling, skill level and health. Much of the research following this approach seeks to explain individual income differentials in terms of human capital investments, notably formal education. While formal education is the most accessible indicator, the concept of human capital entails several other dimensions. For example, Janoski (1990) argues that the U.S. and German labor markets are profoundly affected by differences in state emphases on vocational education and retraining. Years of schooling, thus, may disguise important variations in human capital investment.

In terms of Rusche and Kirchheimer's theory, Becker's concept of human capital can be viewed as a fairly straightforward extension of Marx's concept of the value of human labor power. It provides a way of transposing Rusche and Kirchheimer's theory into hypotheses about social indicators.

Moral Individualism

Durkheim (1947, 1973, 1978) connects the status of the individual and criminal sanctions in a more explicit fashion than does Becker's conception of human capital. The key concept in Durkheim's formulation is moral individualism (cf. Giddens 1971). Durkheim's theory portrays sacrifice of individuals as a routine consequence of the moral economy of mechanical solidarity, the life and welfare of a single individual being a small consideration before the collective need for rituals of reintegration. Organic solidarity sets different priorities; the individual, rather than the community, becomes the central focus of collective concern.

This moral individualism, Durkheim surmised, emerges because the only common values that can transcend the fragmented identities, privatized interests, and divided loyalties that result from a complex division of labor are those celebrating the integrity of the individual. Societies characterized by organic solidarity tend to avoid turning the individual offender into a communal scapegoat because

> the feelings of pity evoked in us by him who is struck by the punishment cannot be as easily nor as completely choked off by the sentiments which he violated and which react against him for both are of the same nature. The first are only a variety of the second. . . . [V]ery often the collective sentiments which the crime offends are also offended by the penalty. We have more pity for the guilty party. . . . It even happens that for a time the guilty one benefits more from this transformation than the victim. (Durkheim 1973: 175, 183)

Thus, as organic solidarity centers on moral individualism rather than a cult of the community, the criminal sanction is placed in recurrent double binds. Expulsion of the deviant continues to reinforce solidarity, but the value being so solidified emphasizes the rights and integrity of the individual. Many of the peculiar characteristics of the contemporary criminal sanction—its vacillation between rehabilitation and retribution, the emphasis on proportionality and concern with victim compensation, that social constituencies vary in demands for expulsion of the deviant—can perhaps be understood as symptoms of contradictions created by moral individualism (cf. Bottoms 1983: 198ff; Freiberg and O'Malley 1984; Friedman 1985; Burton et al. 1987).[4]

Dimensions of Labor Value

Rusche and Kirchheimer provide a cursory definition of the value of human labor, largely in terms of labor market supply and demand. Operationally, the indicators are simple: unemployment rates and wage levels. There are, however, several dimensions to labor value, which have been elaborated by other social theorists. Becker more precisely specifies additional economic components of labor productivity that may be more relevant than simply the unemployment or wage rates. Durkheim includes other aspects of value apart from the economic production. The sovereignty of the individual, expressed in terms of civil, political, and economic status,[5] may be as influential as economic productivity in affecting the form of the criminal sanction. Thus, the social status of the individual in the roles of consumer and voter as well as producer are collectively correlated but are potentially significant individual contributors to the changing forms of sanctions. In the absence of research delineating these dimensions, this paper will narrow the discussion to the relationship between human capital and penal sanctions, bearing in mind that this economic dimension may bear considerable excess baggage.

Current Research on Labor Value and Criminal Sanctions

The major current research program inspired by Rusche and Kirchheimer (1939) concentrates on limited dimensions criminal sanctions, imprisonment rates and time served. These studies share with more general "conflict theory" research (reviewed by Liska in this volume) a preoccupation with absolute and relative sizes of "threatening" populations. Intensity of punishment varies with the proportion of unemployed in the labor force or minorities in the general population (for overviews, see Melossi 1989; Chiricos and DeLone 1992). These labor market studies of variation in imprisonment only tangentially address variation among forms of the criminal sanction, largely because of the absence of long-term national statistics on probation, fines, and other alternatives to incarceration. Conversely, labor value appears only in the interstices of most current research on relationships among forms of criminal sanctions. This research focuses contemporaneously on the extent of trade-offs from one sanction to another or between criminal sanctions and other forms of social control (e.g., Austin and Krisberg 1981; but see McMahon 1990). The longitudinal version of this research question describes sanctions in terms of transitions; thus, lynchings are replaced by state executions; capital punishment is abolished and replaced by incarceration; probation and parole are developed as substitutes for incarceration.

A process of policy trade-offs assumes a common base among alternatives[6]; if the offender were not lynched, he would have been executed by the state. Systematic historical investigations of trends (Massey and Myers 1989; Myers 1991; Tolnay and Beck, in this volume) find little evidence of such trade-offs. While lynchings may have appeared to its participants as a substitution for ineffective law enforcement, the evidence increasingly suggests that the propensity to lynching was conditioned by a peculiar set of circumstances surrounding the crises of the Deep South's plantation agriculture in the late 1890s.

The central issue, however, perhaps should be framed more broadly than relationships among forms of criminal sanction. Criminal sanctions are but one mode of "social control" and relationships between labor value and criminal sanction may be conditioned by variation in welfare, mental hospitalization, military recruitment, and educational enrollments (cf. Piven and Cloward 1971; Mare and Winship 1984). Rusche and Kirchheimer's narrative touches upon the effects of labor markets on the military (1939: 29) but does not address the issue of simultaneous relationships among systems of social control (Inverarity and Grattet 1989; Lessan 1991).

The labor theory of punishment suggests a mechanism for these variations, contending that the criminal sanction attenuates in form and duration as human capital increases. This argument suggests an alternative perspective on the relationships among criminal justice and other interventions by the state. By raising levels of human capital investment, welfare and education reduce "labor-intensive" forms of criminal sanction.

Empirical Implications of Labor Theory of Punishment

Race and Region-Specific Rates

Although social scientists have for a long time written books about "the American criminal justice system" and routinely compared national aggregate indicators of crime and punishment to those of other nation-states, legal systems vary markedly among states and regions. These variations provide potentially fertile comparisons that bear on the labor theory of punishment since labor markets have varied substantially as well. Although a thorough test of the argument requires more fine-grained examination of trend data, some implications of theory may be illustrated by some simple, gross comparisons. Specifically, we will be looking here at how rates of execution and imprisonment vary by region.

Myers and Sabol (1987:50) have calculated race and region-specific rates of imprisonment (prison population/total population). Cahalan (1986:10, 14, 15) provides comparable data on rates of execution (including lynchings), whose trends may be interpreted in light of the labor theory of sanctions. Labor theory predicts that even controlling for differential involvement in crime, higher rates of execution and imprisonment for blacks would result from the historically lower levels of human capital investment in the black population. Furthermore, regional differentials in punishment should reflect regional differentials in human capital formation. And as levels of such investment increase, risk of execution should markedly decline.

These claims are broadly consistent with the gross rates of incarceration. Whether changes in racial disparity in punishment respond to changes in human capital cannot be assessed without more precise data. There are a few points of simple comparison, however, that are suggestive. For example, risk of execution is higher for Southern blacks, while Southern black incarceration rates are *lower*. The higher risk of executions for Southern blacks is well known and consistent with racial disparities generally. The lower incarceration rate for Southern blacks was first reported by Christianson (1981; see also Hawkins 1985; Bridges and Crutchfield 1988). Christianson attributed higher rates in the North to higher levels of racism, an explanation not only counter-intuitive but empirically counter to almost all other social indicators (such as income inequality and voter registration) on which African-Americans in the South are more disadvantaged (cf. Blalock 1967).

For the labor theory of punishment, the important variables are the racial and regional convergencies in human capital during the twentieth century. Schooling, to use one indicator, has become increasingly equalized between races and regions. Consistent with this trend, executions in the U.S. have undergone a secular decline beginning in the 1930s, most of which consists of a reduction in the execution of Southern blacks. The decline in executions parallels the regional convergence for blacks in incarceration rates over time.

The Incarceration of Women

The labor theory of punishment leads as well to some straightforward implications for the incarceration of women. Like blacks, women have been excluded from the labor market or relegated to marginal roles. Correspondingly, their rates of incarceration have been low. As labor force participation increased, the incarceration rate rose. Female incarceration, however, has more dimensions than fit this simple extrapolation. Female incarceration has always received the lowest priority in correctional resources (Rafter 1990). There are strong indications in the literature that variations in the social control of women is related to the extent and (perhaps more importantly) the nature of their involvement in the labor market (Bridges and Beretta, in this volume).

Gender division demarcates welfare and incarceration policies as well. The United States has provided more welfare payments for women, particularly mothers, because such subsidies support gender roles associated with industrial production (Abramowitz 1988). In contrast, Southern states concerned with maintaining cheap labor supplies have been much less concerned with financing this gender division (Piven and Cloward 1971). Such questions entail aspects of the labor market beyond the fluctuations of the business cycle. Assessment of variation and changes in human capital formation are likely to account for at least part of the variation in the criminal sanction.

Competing Theoretical Alternatives

The criminal sanction having long been a focus of social theorizing and systematic research, numerous explanations for changes in the forms of sanctions that compete with the labor theory alternatives are available. This section reviews three of the most prominent and attempts a tentative assessment of their comparative advantage over the labor theory.

Developmental Perspectives

Perhaps the most pervasive way of thinking about forms of criminal sanction is in terms of a developmental or evolutionary sequence. Usually this orientation is developed descriptively rather than theoretically. That is, seldom is the causal mechanism behind the sequencing of punishments specified. Much recent systematic research has been done on how forms of criminal sanction covary and how criminal sanctions vary with other state forms of social control like welfare payments, educational enrollments, military enlistments, and mental institutionalization.

Most developmental analysts have sought to advance one of two alternative empirical generalizations about trends. The first such generalization is an evolutionary/displacement theme, which views one form of the criminal sanction like probation sequentially overtaking another like incarceration. The most common version of this argument is the Whig history account of progressive humanitarianism: barbaric forms are replaced by more civilized forms. Black (1976: 107) provides a more value-neutral form of this generalization: "law varies inversely with other social control." Forms of social control, being functional equivalents, replace each other but in no particular historical order. The second recurrent theme in the general sociological theories is that of state expansion, which views new forms of the criminal sanction as incorporating ever larger domains of actors and activities. This was certainly the case with incarceration, which made it possible to punish a much wider range of offenders than the existing alternative sanctions. Current revisionist perspectives on "decarceration" (e.g., Austin and Krisberg 1981) draw similar conclusions about more recent innovations. Foucault (1977) provides the most important theoretic formulation of such developments, treating innovations in the criminal sanction as incremental expansions of state power.

Empirical assessments of evolutionary development and state expansion trends remain sharply divided (see, e.g., Bottoms 1983). Conceptually, these perspectives are fundamentally descriptive in character; as such they tend to be narrowly time and space bound, providing little information about generic factors underlying the observed developments. Relationships between forms of the criminal sanction, however, appear to be neither invariant nor independent of other institutions.

Priority of Politics

In rejecting as "deterministic" labor market explanations of variation in imprisonment rates, Rutherford (1984:47) argues that we ought instead to "regard prison populations as primarily the consequence of policy choices and practices." His is one manifestation of an independent causal role of elected officials and correctional bureaucracies that outweigh and outmaneuver such impersonal social forces as labor markets in determining the form and frequency of the criminal sanction.[7] Scull (1977) offers a variant of this position in his fiscal crisis theory of transitions in sanctioning. In particular, the use of institutionalization Scull traces not to societal forces but to budgetary constraints of the state administration.

Perhaps the most widely accepted version of this position assigns to the U.S. Supreme Court a central role in altering criminal sanctions. *Furman v. Georgia* (1972), for example, is often taken as the watershed Supreme Court decision in the administration of the death penalty. Both sides of the death penalty debate have looked to the Supreme Court as responsible for the abolition of the death penalty. Yet, when viewed from a longer historical perspective, the key court decisions came at the end of a long secular trend toward abolition (for a descriptive account of these developments, see especially Zimring and Hawkins 1986). The rate of decline is substantially greater for blacks, who since the 1930s moved from rural tenancy into urban labor markets. A case can be made here, as in other areas, that the Supreme Court has been less of an innovator in policy than a ratifier of policy that has emerged from other political—and perhaps social—forces (cf. Rosenberg 1991).

Generic Conflict Accounts

The third perspective principally derives from Blalock's (1967) social psychological theory of discrimination, which argues essentially that the percentage of minority population and relative size of minority resources create a threat to which the majority population responds with discrimination. This highly schematic theory, which is more akin to Simmel's formal theory than the substantive arguments of Marx or Weber, has found widespread reception among sociological researchers. It assigns centrality to universal demographic and social psychological variables: the greater the numbers, power and resources of a minority, the more discriminatory becomes the majority group. In contrast, the labor market perspective views correlations between the percentage of minority population and discrimination as being essentially coincidental associations with the role of minority populations in systems of production.[8]

Summary

Rusche and Kirchheimer (1939) propose a labor theory of criminal sanctions, which has only partially been explored by the research literature. Much of the evidence bearing on this thesis remains fragmentary and anecdotal. This is in large measure due to problems of conceptualization and measurement that remain to be resolved. This paper has suggested ways to approach these issues, drawing on the work of Becker, Durkheim and others who address cognate issues in other substantive areas. The work necessary to refine the theory is justified by the extent of circumstantial evidence of the role of labor value in punishment. Trends in execution and imprisonment compared across race and region give us some hints of the explanatory potential of the labor theory of punishment, as do some of the data on gender differentials in incarceration. Further support for the theory emerges by comparison with competing alternative explanations of changing forms of criminal sanction.

Making these claims for the labor theory of punishment does not preclude the role of political, ideological or other factors in shaping the form of sanctions. The relative role of labor value can be assessed only by an estimation equation that includes these alternatives along with measures of crime and controls for age composition. The narrowness of the discussion here reflects the preoccupation with the immediate task of theory construction, articulating a coherent, empirically testable connection. Such an examination may be of particular relevance for understanding the accelerating expansion of incarceration in the 1980s and the impediments to the search for policy alternatives. These developments are probably not coincidental with the declining role of human capital in manufacturing and the growth of employment in the secondary, service-industrial sector. While employment and earnings may exhibit some correlations with shifts in social control policies, understanding the market valuation of human labor power may prove to be critical.

Notes

1. This single sentence contains two ideas that bear significantly on current research designs. Note first that Rusche and Kirchheimer focus on *systems of production*, not nation-states or subsidiary levels of government (states, provinces, counties, municipalities). Second, the predicate is "tends to discover," which implies considerable variation in reality; any given system of production will tend to support any number of systems of punishment. The theoretical claim is about long-run, central tendencies of the sort that will become visible only in an analysis of aggregates. This latter emphasis largely lays to rest the objection of Garland (1990: 110) and others that Rusche and Kirchheimer are asserting a mechanistic economic determinism. The more valid objection is that the phrase "tends to" inherently contains the danger of granting their proposition immunity from empirical assessment. Claims about central tendency are best addressed through multivariate (and probably) quantitative assessments.

2. One such barrier, the principle of "less eligibility" (Rusche and Kirchheimer 1939: 151–155), limits the conditions of prison production. The continuing centrality of this concern appears in current discourse in the powerful and pervasive mythology of "country club" prisons. The questionable logic of having a job training program in computer technology for prison inmates but not for the general population is a recent example of a recurrent dilemma. The other barriers are the political constraints of labor unions and individual entrepreneurs threatened with competition by state-subsidized prison industry.

3. The role of labor value in shaping forms of dominant criminal sanctions can be supported by several mundane observations. Consider, for example, the virtual immunity from state criminal prosecution enjoyed by slaves. Only when the form of human capital changed from the laborer as the commodity to labor *power* did the state undertake an expansion of criminal sanctioning. The second mundane example is demographic. Currently and historically inmates of institutions have had the lowest levels of human capital formation in terms of educational attainment, job skills and work experience.

4. Consider, for example, the contradictory character of the repressive and restitutive elements of contemporary criminal sanctions in the development of procedural law on pretrial publicity. Where mechanical solidarity predominates, people "stop each other in the street, they visit each another, they seek to come together to talk of the event and to wax indignant in common. From all the similar impressions which are exchanged . . . there emerges a unique temper . . . which is everybody's without being anybody's in particular" (Durkheim 1947: 102). In

communities with mechanical solidarity, the public anger supports the communal value. Moral individualism, however, encompasses the perpetrator as well. This principle finds expression, for example, in *Irvin v. Dowd* (366 US 759, 1961), in which the Supreme Court ruled that "with his life at stake, it is not requiring too much that petitioner be tried in an atmosphere undisturbed by so huge a wave of public passion and by a jury other than one in which two-thirds of the members admit before hearing any testimony, to possessing a belief in his guilt."

5. Durkheim's discussion may be usefully supplemented with Marshall's (1965) formulation of the emergence of the welfare state as an extension of rights through three institutional spheres: civil right, political access and economic welfare. See also Schmid's (1986) application of Marshall's dimensions to recent development of rights for African-Americans.

6. A literature in political science elaborates the necessity of evaluating hypotheses about policy trade-offs in a multivariate (e.g., Garand and Hendrick 1981; Berry and Lowery 1990).

7. Skocpol and Amenta (1986: 136) state this position more generically: "Politics outweighs economic variables in determining state policies." For criminal justice policy, this argument has much surface validity. Crime control, along with taxation and conscription, was among the first arenas of nation-state expansion. Christie (1977) and Black (1983) discuss the problematic nature of state intervention in disputes. While the expansion of the state is linked to the emergence of the market economy, the precise connection has long been the subject of contentious study in the classical traditions of sociological theory. Among the more pervasive bodies of empirical evidence for this position is Therborn's (1977) cross-national survey of the expansion of legal rights.

8. Contrasts between labor market and generic conflict approaches have not yet been well defined in the literature. Among the interesting bases for comparing these positions may be the contrast between South Africa and the American South. For example, "in South Africa ... lynching has been virtually unknown, and other forms of private collective violence against blacks have been relatively rare" (Fredrickson 1981: 251).

10

Gender, Race, and Social Control: Toward an Understanding of Sex Disparities in Imprisonment

George S. Bridges and Gina Beretta

Few features of criminal justice in the United States are more striking than the pronounced disparities in imprisonment between men and women. Whereas men make up slightly less than one-half of the general population of the United States, they make up nearly 95 percent of the prison inmates in the country. Such disparity continues to stir controversy over gender differences in the administration of justice. Courts espouse a doctrine of "equal treatment under the law." Yet gender disparities in imprisonment suggest the possibility of discrimination in the administration of justice—discrimination in the form of less severe punishments for women than men. One writer recently described the differential treatment of men and women by the legal system as a matter of "unequal justice," a legal and social concern demanding rigorous empirical study (Rafter 1985).

Despite the importance of this issue, the relationships between gender, crime and criminal punishment are poorly understood. At least three aspects of previous writing and research are problematic. First, the contribution of sex differences in crime to sex differences in criminal punishment remains unclear. Some scholars attribute much of the variation in imprisonment disparity to the underrepresentation of women among persons committing the most serious and violent crimes. However, others suggest or imply that differences in criminal behavior are unimportant in explaining disparity (Steffensmeier 1978). Second, almost all of the empirical research published in recent years has ignored or omitted treatment of important characteristics of states and regions of the country that may cause sex differences in imprisonment. There is confusion over the process by which characteristics of states—for example, state laws, legal policies and structural differences in the social standing of women compared with men—foster differences in treatment by the administration of criminal justice. Third, there exists uncertainty over the role of race in explaining sex differences in imprisonment. Despite compelling historical evidence to the contrary, few studies offer convincing evidence that courts treat women of color much differently than white women (see, however, Spohn et al. 1981–82, 1985).

The present study is concerned with explaining gender disparities in imprisonment. The study focuses on whether characteristics of states such as state criminal laws, the administration of criminal justice and mental health services, the economic standing of women compared with men, and racial differences between men and women aid in explaining these disparities. Analyses presented in this chapter rest on the assumption that characteristics of states influence the likelihood of imprisonment for men and women above and beyond the characteristics of the individual defendants involved in criminal cases. The chapter examines the importance of these state characteristics to understanding disparity by comparing their differential influence on aggregate imprisonment rates for men and women. Further, the chapter examines the relationship between race and gender in contributing to disparities in imprisonment between men and women.

Gender, Crime, and Imprisonment

Much of the current writing on disparities in criminal punishment looks to differences in the legal system's treatment of men and women offenders (Rafter 1985; Simpson 1989). Written from Marxist/feminist or conflict perspectives, this literature reasons that imprisonment disparities are no more than a reenactment of the differential treatment afforded men and women by other social institutions (Cook 1987; Eaton 1987). Accordingly, courts may actually preserve and reinforce traditional images of women as passive, domestic, and needing protection by less frequently incarcerating women than men. Courts may impose less severe punishment on women because they see women as, among other things, inherently less dangerous and therefore less deserving of punishment than men.

Some critics of this perspective argue that Marxist/feminist and conflict theories ignore the fundamental relationship between punishment and crime. Many of the critics view gender disparities in imprisonment in terms of gender differences in criminal involvement, arguing that imprisonment disparities occur primarily because women commit crimes less frequently and in lesser seriousness than men (Steffensmeier, 1978, 1980). According to this perspective, criminal law is a set of codified norms applied equally for all law violators. Further, the severity of punishments imposed for crimes varies directly with the importance of the laws violated; as the importance of violated laws increases so does the severity of punishments imposed by the state (Durkheim 1947, 1973; Blumstein 1982; Langan 1985). Courts impose sanctions in relation to the seriousness of crimes committed, with the most serious penalties imposed only for the most serious and violent offenders. Thus, the administration of justice treats most defendants equally, without regard to their social standing or other personal characteristics.

According to this reasoning, gender differences in imprisonment and in other forms of criminal punishment occur primarily because women commit crimes less frequently and in lesser seriousness than men (Steffensmeier 1978, 1980; Steffensmeier and Kramer 1982). At the heart of this hypothesis of differential criminal involvement is the reasoning that the gender distribution of offenders imprisoned is therefore approximately equal to the distribution of persons arrested because no significant gender differences exist in the treatment of the accused following arrest—that is, at prosecution, conviction, sentencing, or in actual time served in prison (for reviews see Parisi 1982; Hagan et al. 1987; Simpson 1989). Thus, the differential involvement hypothesis predicts that courts imprison women at disproportionately lower rates than men in areas where women have disproportionately lower rates of arrest for serious and violent crimes. Further, disparities in imprisonment will be lowest in those areas where the arrest rates for men and women are approximately equal.

Although recent studies have sought more precise specification of the causes of imprisonment disparities (see, e.g., Bridges and Crutchfield 1988; Tittle and Curran 1988), there are few empirical tests that specifically apply to the linkages between gender, crime and criminal punishment. And among the studies, there are few consistent findings. Whereas some studies suggest that males are more likely to be sentenced to prison than women because men commit more serious and violent crimes (Simon 1975; Nettler 1978; Steffensmeier 1980), many other studies have shown that gender differences in crime fail to explain adequately gender differences in imprisonment (Parisi, 1982; Dobash et al. 1986; Daly 1987a, 1987b).

Scope of Previous Studies

Almost all of the empirical research published in recent years on sex differences in punishment has focused on the differential treatment of individual criminal defendants processed within a single jurisdiction or court. Analyses done at this level are unable to identify the full effects of such factors as (1) statewide sentencing laws or mental health policies regarding the institutionalization of the mentally ill and (2) areal or regional levels of social inequality on imprisonment practices. Nevertheless, areal characteristics have significant effects on rates of imprisonment, above and beyond the characteristics of individual defendants. For example, state parole policies and laws governing the sentencing of chronic or "habitual" criminal offenders yield pronounced black/white disparities in imprisonment across states and regions of the country (see, e.g., Bridges and Crutchfield 1988). Similarly, regional or state levels of social and economic inequality influence rates of imprisonment, independent of areal rates of serious and violent crime (Bridges et al. 1987; Bridges and Crutchfield 1988).

Although many of the more recent studies reveal pronounced differences in the treatment of men and women accused of crimes, there is confusion over the effects of major state characteristics on these differences. Factors such as state sentencing laws, practices of hospitalizing the mentally ill, and differences in the social standing of men and women may have differential effects on the imprisonment of men and women, causing excessively lenient dispositions for one group or excessively severe dispositions for another (Davis 1969). Further, no studies known to the authors specify the process by which legal or social characteristics of states are associated with differences in male and female rates of imprisonment.

Laws

At least three aspects of state laws and legal policies governing the punishment of criminal offenders may influence sex disparities in imprisonment. The first is whether states have enacted mandatory or determinate sentencing. Typically, these types of laws establish sentences—in the form of prescribed terms for major categories of crime—that must expire before a prisoner may be released. Mandatory and determinate sentencing laws may have many possible effects on sex disparities in imprisonment. The laws tend to increase the length of prison terms, on average, for persons convicted of the most serious and violent offenses. To the extent that sex disparities in imprisonment involve persons convicted of serious and violent offenses, and men are more heavily involved than women in these types of crime, mandatory sentencing laws may have the effect of increasing disparities by increasing the rate of imprisonment for men relative to women.

A different type of effect, however, is also possible. In practice, mandatory sentencing laws structure and limit the discretion afforded sentencing judges. With fixed sentence lengths for most classes of crime, judges have less freedom to be excessively lenient or excessively severe in meting out criminal punishments. Sentencing judges who may otherwise be predisposed to treat women offenders more leniently than men will be less able to do so in states with mandatory sentencing. Thus, it is anticipated that the existence of these laws may actually decrease disparities by "equalizing" the treatment of men and women offenders. In this instance, the expected effect would be to increase the rate of imprisonment for women compared with men. Second, laws that impose additional sentences on persons classified as "career criminals" or "habitual offenders" may also influence sex disparities in imprisonment. Typically, "habitual offender" laws result in longer prison terms for those offenders with extensive histories of criminal behavior. To the extent that women defendants are less likely than men to have criminal histories, they will on the average serve shorter prison terms in those states with habitual offender statutes. Habitual offender laws may exacerbate sex disparities in imprisonment by increasing the rate of imprisonment for men relative to women.

Third, many states use individualized parole processes that release inmates from prison before the expiration of their prison terms. Typically, early release is contingent upon three factors: (1) cooperation with institutional programs and rules; (2) diminished threat of criminal recidivism upon release; and (3) compliance with the conditions of release while on parole (Carroll and Mondrick 1976; Bynum 1981). Policies such as these place women at an advantage over men because women may be more capable than men of meeting release conditions. Men may be more likely than women to commit infractions of institutional rules, particularly rules prohibiting fighting with other inmates. Further, they are more likely to constitute a threat of recidivism following release (Parisi 1982). Finally, women are less likely, following release, to have their parole revoked for violation of parole conditions (Parisi 1982).

It is anticipated that sex disparities in imprisonment will be greater in states that use parole heavily. Women may be more likely than men to obtain early release and avoid parole revocation in those states. As a result, they are more likely to serve shorter terms of imprisonment than men for similar types of offenses.

Hospitalization of the Mentally Ill

Typically, societies use formal mechanisms of control such as the administration of criminal justice only when other control mechanisms fail. Most sociologists agree that societies use imprisonment in inverse proportion to other governmental and social institutions that enforce important social norms (Spitzer 1975; Black 1976; Scull 1977, 1982; Horwitz 1990). The greatest sex disparities in imprisonment would be expected in those areas where women who constitute problem populations are controlled or "taken care of" through other governmental agencies or institutions. One social institution that has been instrumental in the control of women, apart from prisons, is the psychiatric treatment of the mentally ill. Since the emergence of the mental asylum in the mideighteenth century, women have been much more vulnerable than men to being diagnosed or labelled as "mentally ill" (see, e.g., Rafter 1985; Morris 1987). And women continue to be more likely to define themselves and be defined by others as having serious mental problems (Schur 1983; Scheff 1984; Holstein 1987).

Sex differences in imprisonment, particularly the low rates of imprisonment of women, may in part stem from pronounced sex differences in institutionalization in mental hospitals. In effect, hospitalization may serve as a substitute for imprisonment as a mechanism of social control. If state officials are more likely to view women offenders as "mentally ill" or "disturbed" than men, they may more frequently hospitalize them as psychiatric patients and, thereby, channel them away from prison (Turk 1969a; Carlen 1983; Dobash et al. 1986; Holstein 1987; Morris 1987). In those regions of the country and historical periods where deviant women are processed primarily through mental health facilities, sex disparities in imprisonment may be particularly high. Women will be imprisoned at disproportionately lower rates than men in those regions where women are hospitalized at particularly high rates. Conversely, women will be imprisoned at disproportionately higher rates in those regions where the rate of hospitalization for women is low.

Social Standing

Much of the recent writing on criminal punishment reasons that rates of imprisonment have integral ties to the broader economic and social order in society. For example, Marxist and feminist writers interpret sex differences in punishment in terms of the social standing of women relative to men (Spitzer 1975; Carlen 1983; Dobash et al. 1986; Garland 1990). They reason that elites use mental health and legal institutions to subordinate women, particularly women who are not effectively regulated by informal or private mechanisms of control (Simpson 1989).

At least two aspects of the social standing of women are important to sex differences in crime and punishment. The first is the economic standing of women in society. Some writers argue that male elites are most likely to use the mental health system and the administration of criminal justice to enforce laws that preserve the existing economic order (Box and Hale 1984; Box 1987; Spitzer 1975, 1981). However, in communities and regions characterized by rigid economic stratification of women and men—that is, communities where women occupy primarily marginalized economic roles with low levels of participation in the labor force—

women may actually be regulated and controlled primarily through informal rather than formal mechanisms of control (Feeley and Little 1991).

This line of reasoning suggests that women will experience higher rates of imprisonment in those states and regions of the country where they play active participatory roles in the labor force compared with men. Thus, sex differences in imprisonment in those areas would be expected to be particularly small. In contrast, relatively large sex differences would be expected in those states and regions of the country where women have relatively low rates of labor force participation relative to men.

A second aspect of social standing involves the role of women in the domestic division of labor and specifically in the provision of child care. Courts may impose less severe punishment on women because adult women typically are responsible for children and child raising. Imprisoning them creates a serious and complicated labor problem in the caring for adolescents and young children (Parisi 1982; Dobash et al. 1986; Daly 1987a, 1987b). Women, more than men, occupy care-taking roles in families that cannot easily be replaced or supplanted by other forms of social or economic support. Being lenient on women, particularly women with dependent children, ensures that parental care of the children continues (Simon 1975; Steffensmeier 1980; Parisi 1982; Daly 1987a, 1987b). Such leniency is far less costly to the state. While "father surrogates exist in the form of welfare benefits and other state supports, ... mother surrogates in the form of foster or institutional care of children are more rare and expensive" (Daly 1987b: 287). Thus, sex disparities in imprisonment may be particularly large in those regions where the burden of dependent children is acute. Women will be imprisoned at disproportionately lower rates than men in those regions because of the heavy child-caring burden. Conversely, women will be imprisoned at disproportionately higher rates in those regions where the burden of dependent children is particularly low.

The Role of Race

In earlier historical periods, sex differences in punishment hinged in large part upon the race of the accused. Any leniency afforded women by courts was extended primarily to whites. Court officials in the nineteenth century viewed black women offenders much differently than white women, as "masculine and hence undeserving of protection" (Rafter 1985: 143). Thus, racial and ethnic differences directly influenced the gender/punishment relationship, conditioning how gender affected the actual outcomes of legal proceedings.

Most studies of contemporary courts examine the processing of individual defendants and offer conflicting accounts of race/sex interactions in punishment. Some studies show that courts are more likely to punish minority women severely for crimes than white women (Spohn et al. 1985, 1987). Others show that minority men receive more severe punishments for crimes than white men or minority or white women (Peterson and Hagan 1984; Kruttschnitt 1984; Schutt and Dannefer 1988). Many studies, however, find few or no interactions between race and gender in the severity of punishments (Curran 1983; Hagan and O'Donnel 1978).

At least two alternative lines of reasoning suggest that race and gender may interact in relation to areal rates of imprisonment but in very different ways. First, courts may be more likely to imprison racial minorities than whites because minorities may be more heavily involved in serious and violent crime (Blumstein 1982; Langan 1985). Minority men, particularly black men, commit serious and violent crimes at significantly higher rates than white men and women and minority women (Wolfgang 1958; Wolfgang et al. 1972; Hindelang et al. 1981; Tracey et al. 1990). Further, minority women are more likely to commit serious crimes than white women and some white men (Hindelang et al. 1981; Laub and McDermott 1984). It follows that minority men in particular will be imprisoned at higher rates than white men and all women in areas where they have disproportionate involvement in serious crime. To a lesser extent, courts will also imprison minority women at higher rates than white women for the same reasons. Courts will imprison minority men and women at lower rates than whites in those areas where they have disproportionately low levels of criminal involvement.

A second argument offers an altogether different line of reasoning. Courts may actually be less likely to imprison minority women than white or minority men because they may process minority women offenders more frequently through mental health agencies and hospitals. Historically, minority women have been more vulnerable than white women or men to being labeled mentally ill. In the nineteenth and early twentieth centuries, black women offenders were more likely than whites to be viewed as "undeveloped" or mentally defective (Rafter 1985). Further, contemporary mental health agencies and psychiatric professionals are more likely to define minority women's expressions of emotion and anger as "illness" (Gallagher 1980; Morris 1987). Perhaps as a result, minority women are processed and admitted as patients to mental hospitals with the most severe forms of chronic mental illness at rates significantly higher than white women, white men, or minority men (Gallagher 1990; Cockerham 1981). If minority women offenders are more likely to be viewed by justice and mental health officials as mentally ill than others, they may be much more likely to be hospitalized as psychiatric patients.

Further, they may be imprisoned at lower rates than white women or men in those regions of the country where they are hospitalized in mental health facilities at particularly high rates.

Methods of the Present Study

The study collected data on crime patterns, the administration of criminal justice and mental health, the social standing of men and women, and the demographic composition of all states in the United States for 1980, in addition to data on sex- and race-specific rates of imprisonment for each state for 1982. Measures constructed from these data—aggregated to the state level—provided indicators of (1) male and female rates of imprisonment; (2) aspects of the social and legal structure of states; and (3) levels of crime and arrests for crime, prison capacity and sex-specific rates of institutionalization for jails and mental hospitals.

The analysis of these data is based on the assumption that characteristics of states such as the laws and legal policies governing sentencing and parole have important effects on rates of imprisonment above and beyond the crime rate. We believe this to be a valid assumption for two reasons. First, laws and legal policies governing sentencing, for example, whether convicted defendants are sentenced under some form of determinate sentencing, typically have statewide jurisdiction. Thus, the effects of these laws on imprisonment, if any, will vary at the state level rather than across smaller jurisdictional areas (Bridges and Crutchfield 1988). Second, states are the appropriate unit of analysis for analyzing disparities in imprisonment as they are operationalized in this paper. The measure of disparity used in the analysis is as much a measure of length of stay as it is a measure of admission to prison. And because statewide sentencing laws and parole policies determine length of stay in prison, the appropriate unit of analysis is states, with a focus on differences across states in laws and legal policies.

Imprisonment Disparities

Imprisonment rates for men and women were computed by initially dividing the number of persons housed in state prisons as of December 31, 1982, by the total number of males or females in the state. These proportions were then multiplied by 10,000 to yield the measures of male and female imprisonment rates. The year 1982 was used to allow a lag in time between measures of our independent variables, all measured for 1980, and the dependent variables. The measure of disparity computed in the analysis is actually the ratio of the rates of imprisonment for men and women. Thus, a general measure of disparity was computed for each state by actually dividing the male imprisonment rate by the female imprisonment rate.

Serious and Violent Crime

Data on serious and violent crimes were drawn from the Uniform Crime Reports maintained by the FBI. Two types of information were collected. First, sex-specific arrest rates were collected on Part I Index Crimes (homicide, attempted homicide, rape, aggravated assault, assault, robbery, burglary, arson) for each state. The rates for men and women, aggregated across types of crime, are used as sex-specific measures of involvement in serious and violent crime. These offenses were selected primarily because they represent the types of crimes committed by offenders currently incarcerated in state prisons. Further, they are categories of crime that may translate into significant sex disparities in imprisonment because men are much more heavily involved in serious and violent offenses than women.

Second, general rates of violent crime (Part I Index Violent Crimes—homicide, attempted homicide, rape, aggravated assault, assault, robbery) were also included in the analyses. This factor has proven important in previous analyses of areal differences in rates of criminal punishment (Bridges and Crutchfield 1988). Justice officials may impose sanctions in relation to the perceived threat of violent crime (Spitzer 1975; Jacobs 1978). Severity and types of punishment may vary in relation to degree of threat. Because there exist no perceptual measures of crime threat across states, the violent crime rate was included in the analyses to adjust for differences across states in the actual threat of crime.

Laws and Treatment of the Mentally Ill

The study also collected data on state laws and legal practices and rates of institutionalization of the mentally ill. Information collected on state laws and legal policies included measures of (1) whether states had determinate sentencing and (2) the rate of parole use in releasing persons from prison. Determinate sentencing laws—that is, laws requiring the imposition of sentences or prison terms according to legislated guidelines or standards—restrict judicial discretion in sentencing decisions. Because determinate sentencing laws restrict discretion, it is anticipated that these laws may reduce sentencing disparities between men and women.

The rate of parole use reflects the extent to which state correctional systems use parole or early release as an alternative to long prison terms. Measured as the rate of persons released from prison on parole (early release) per 10,000 persons in the general population, the rate of parole use captures each state's reliance on individualized parole processes. In most states with parole policies, release on parole is discretionary—and contingent upon official assessments of a prisoner's likelihood of recidivism. To the extent that gender-based stereotypes of women as passive and less dangerous than men shape these assessments, parole release decisions may favor women prisoners over men.

To explore the relationship between sex differences in hospitalization in mental institutions and differences in imprisonment, data were also collected on male and female rates of institutionalization in state mental hospitals. These data were collected from the annual census of mental hospitals conducted for 1982 by the U.S. Department of Health and Human Services. As with the measurement of rates of imprisonment, hospitalization rates were computed by (1) dividing the number of men and women housed in state mental health facilities as of December 31, 1983, by the number of men and women in each state's total population and (2) multiplying each rate by 10,000.

Social Standing and Racial Composition

Four types of measures of state social structure were included in the analysis. The first type included sex-specific measures of labor force participation. Measured as the percent of men in the labor force and the percent of women in the labor force, labor force participation captures the degree to which persons are integrated into the labor force. For the sake of parsimony, these additional measures were omitted from subsequent parts of the analysis. The labor force participation rate for men and women captures the degree to which each group is economically marginalized. To the extent that levels of labor force participation differ between men and women and those differences have differential effects on imprisonment rates, they may help in explaining gender differences in imprisonment.

A second measure of social standing was the prevalence of dependent children in each state. Many recent studies suggest that any leniency afforded women by courts occurs because of burdens created by dependent children (Daly 1987a, 1987b). Measured as the percentage of the population under the age of six, this variable permits assessment of the child care burden in each state and whether rates of criminal punishment vary in relation to that burden.

Given the study's dual interest in gender and race, measures of the racial composition of states were also included in the analysis. These types of measures have proven extremely useful in previous analyses of racial disparities in criminal punishment (Myers and Talarico 1987; Bridges and Crutchfield 1988). The third measure of state social structure was percent black, the percent of each state's total population that is black. Perhaps most important for the present study, however, is the degree to which percent black reflects the degree of minority threat to the white population. In those areas where white elites are threatened by a minority population, they are most likely to use the legal process to discriminate against minorities. Many sociologists believe that this practice is most likely to occur in those states and regions of the country where minority populations are relatively large (Blalock 1957, 1967; Frisbie and Neibert 1976; Bridges and Crutchfield 1988).

Fourth, a measure of black/white urban concentration was included, that is, the degree of black representation among the urban population of each state compared with whites. This measure was computed by dividing the percent black living in the central cities of the state by the percent white living in central cities. Thus, this factor measures the extent to which blacks, compared with whites, are concentrated in urban, central city areas. The measure was included in the analysis because previous studies suggest that minority groups clustered in urban areas are more likely to be defined by law enforcement officials as a threat to community order and a legitimate target for social control (Bridges et al. 1987).

Results

To explore the relationships among these variables, multiple regression analyses were performed in which the logged rates of imprisonment for men and women were separately regressed on the full set of independent variables. The initial results are exhibited in Table 10.1. Four findings are particularly noteworthy. First, there is virtually no evidence supporting the assertion that differences in the levels of criminal involvement between men and women explain disparities in imprisonment. Sex differences in rates of arrest for violent crimes have almost no influence on differences in imprisonment, once other aspects of state law and social structure are taken into account. This finding is consistent with the results of other state- and county-level analyses of imprisonment showing a weak relationship between arrest rates for serious and violent crimes and imprisonment rates (Bridges et al. 1987; Bridges and Crutchfield 1988). Second, in sharp contrast is the relationship between the violent crime rate and imprisonment. States characterized by high rates of violent crime tend to have very high rates of imprisonment for both men and women. This finding is important, particularly when combined with the previous finding. It suggests that imprisonment is used in response to the threat of violent crime but not necessarily in direct relation to the rate of persons arrested for serious and violent crimes. Thus, rates of imprisonment may increase or decrease in relation to broad social conditions such as the rate of reported crimes—the "violent crime climate"—rather than the actual volume of offenders arrested for serious and violent crimes (Jacobs 1978).

TABLE 10.1 Determinants of Imprisonment Rates, by Gender

	Men			Women			
Factor	b^a	B^b	SE	b	B	SE	t(diff)
Arrest rate[c]	.034	.047	.090	−.028	−.038	.094	−.461
Violent crime rate	.299**	.342	.104	.287*	.256	.140	.327
Labor force participation	1.296	.115	.947	1.636*	.224	.628	−1.510
Dependent children	.170	.112	.148	.259	.133	.177	.348
Black/white urban concentration	−.208*	−.195	.090	−.232	−.169	.121	.000
Percent black	.216**	.598	.038	.317**	.684	.054	.092
Hospitalization rate	−.223*	−.180	.102	−.325**	−.264	.108	−.998
Determinate sentencing	−.052	−.104	.038	−.086	−.134	.052	.016
Parole use	−.351**	−.286	.101	−.400*	−.255	.133	−.045
Constant	−.072		1.932	−1.684		1.406	
R^2		.804			.774		
R^2 (adjusted)		.756			.720		

[a] Unstandardized coefficient.
[b] Standardized coefficient, with standard error (SE).
[c] Gender-specific arrest, hospitalization and unemployment rates are used. Thus, the male imprisonment rate is regressed on the arrest, hospitalization and unemployment rate for males; the female imprisonment rate is regressed on the female arrest, hospitalization, and unemployment rates. All measures are logged except determinate sentencing.
* $p = <.05$; ** $p = <.01$.

Third, state parole-use policies and practices of hospitalizing the mentally ill significantly influence the imprisonment rates of men and women, but the effects do not differ significantly by sex. For example, rates of hospitalization of the mentally ill have the anticipated negative effect on imprisonment rates, serving as an alternative to imprisonment as a form of social control. However, there is no evidence that hospitalization rates have a pronounced effect on the imprisonment of women relative to men. Although the effect is greater for women than men, the difference is not statistically significant. Finally, aspects of state social structure also influence rates of imprisonment. States characterized by relatively high rates of labor force participation by women have higher than average rates of imprisonment for women. Further, states with relatively high concentrations of blacks in the population have significantly higher than average rates of imprisonment for both men and women.

Perhaps most surprising, however, is the noticeable absence of statistically significant differential effects of state characteristics on imprisonment rates. Contrary to the expectations of some scholars that sex differences in criminal behavior are the primary cause of imprisonment differences, differences in crime between men and women, as measured by rates of arrest for violent crime, actually contribute little to variation in rates of imprisonment for either men or women. A similar pattern is observed regarding the effects of legal and mental health policies and practices of states. That determinate sentencing laws, parole-use policies and hospitalization rates have no significantly different effects on the imprisonment of men and women contradicts the prediction that these factors foster disparities in imprisonment.

Among women, high rates of labor force participation may disadvantage women more than men. Women are imprisoned at rates significantly higher than average in states where their rates of labor force participation are particularly high. Although the difference between the effects of labor force participation for men and women is not statistically significant, its amount is consistent with the prediction that women's increased involvement in the labor force is likely to subject them to increased formal control (Feeley and Little 1991). However, contrary to the arguments of some writers (Adler 1975; Simon 1975), increased participation in the labor force does not result in increased rates of imprisonment due to increased criminality by women. Criminal behavior plays no direct role in the labor force participation/imprisonment relationship.

Of particular concern to the present study is the role of race. Sex differences in punishment may hinge in large part upon the race of the accused (Rafter 1985), with any leniency afforded women by the administration of justice extended primarily to whites. Further, important racial differences in punishment persist even after controls are introduced for racial differences in involvement in crime. Blacks in urban areas may be more subject to attempts at formal social control and more vulnerable to those controls than whites (Bridges and Crutchfield 1988). To determine whether the effects of state characteristics on sex differences in imprisonment vary by racial group—that is, whether their effects interact with race—separate regression analyses were conducted for whites and blacks. The results of these analyses are reported in Table 10.2.

Among whites, state characteristics influence men and women's rates of imprisonment, but the effects do not differ significantly by sex. For example, rates of hospitalization of the mentally ill, as an alternative to imprisonment, advantages neither white men nor women. This finding contradicts the predictions of some scholars that hospitalization is more likely to serve as an alternative to imprisonment for women, particularly white women, as a form of social control. Similarly, rates of parole are associated with equally low rates of imprisonment for white men and women.

There are, however, two noteworthy differences between the equations for white men and women. The relationship between percent black and imprisonment is substantially stronger for white women than white

TABLE 10.2 Determinants of Imprisonment Rates, by Race and Gender

Factor	White Men			White Women			
	b^a	B^b	SE	b	B	SE	t(diff)
Arrest rate[c]	.038	.059	.110	.048	.069	.102	-.002
Violent crime rate	.386**	.488	.128	.259*	.252	.152	.753
Labor force participation	1.141	.112	1.168	1.478	.221	.679	-1.448
Dependent children	.207	.152	.184	.371	.210	.193	.716
Black/white urban concentration	-.256*	-.266	.108	-.504**	-.401	.130	-1.059
Percent black	.061	.188	.046	.176*	.414	.058	1.567
Hospitalization rate	-.294	-.263	.126	-.336*	-.298	.117	-.349
Determinate sentencing	-.061	-.134	.047	-.087	-.146	.056	-1.220
Parole use	-.321*	-.290	.125	-.330*	-.229	.144	.088
Constant	-.429		2.358	-2.268		1.510	
R^2		.633			.688		
R^2 (adjusted)		.544			.612		
	Black Men			Black Women			
Arrest rate	.091	.143	.136	-.187	-.279	.110	-1.219
Violent crime rate	.320**	.408	.154	.288*	.289	.164	-.170
Labor force participation	2.168	.215	1.408	1.605	.247	.732	.375
Dependent children	.332	.241	.228	-.046	-.026	.212	-1.069
Black/white urban concentration	.394*	.413	.130	.266	.218	.141	-.770
Percent black	-.051	-.159	.056	-.220*	-.532	.063	-2.490*
Hospitalization rate	-.029	-.026	.150	-.313*	-.286	.124	-1.201
Determinate sentencing	-.085	-.188	.056	-.137	-.238	.061	-.363
Parole use	-.274	-.249	.149	-.242	-.173	.156	-.301
Constant	-3.001		2.930	.582		1.586	
R^2		.446			.613		
R^2 (adjusted)		.311			.519		

[a] Unstandardized coefficient.
[b] Standardized coefficient, with standard error (SE).
[c] Gender-specific arrest, hospitalization and unemployment rates are used. Thus, the male imprisonment rate is regressed on the arrest, hospitalization and unemployment rate for males; the female imprisonment rate is regressed on the female arrest, hospitalization, and unemployment rates. All measures are logged except determinate sentencing.
* p = <.05; ** p = <.01.

men, suggesting that white women are more disadvantaged in states characterized by large black populations than white men and more advantaged in areas characterized by extremely small black populations. White women may also be more advantaged than white men in states characterized by black populations disproportionately concentrated in urban areas. The relationship between imprisonment and the degree of urban concentration of the state's black population is stronger for white women than white men. In effect, white women's imprisonment rates are lower than the rates of white men—other factors being equal—in areas where the black population is heavily urbanized.

The evidence for blacks is similar, although the sex differences are more pronounced. Perhaps most striking is the differential influence of percent black. Percent black and imprisonment is more strongly related for black women than black men. Black women are significantly more advantaged in states characterized by large black populations than black men and more disadvantaged in areas characterized by extremely small black populations. This finding is particularly important in light of the influence of percent black on white imprisonment rates. Among states where percent black is large, the imprisonment rates of white and black women are more likely to be equal. Black women's rates will be substantially lower and white women's rates will be substantially higher.

Among blacks, hospitalization for mental illness—as an alternative to imprisonment—may advantage women more than men. Black women are imprisoned at significantly lower rates in states where rates of hospitalization (for women) are particularly high. Although the difference between black men and women is not statistically significant, it sharply contrasts with the pattern observed among whites and is consistent with the prediction that hospitalization is more likely to serve as an alternative to imprisonment for women as a form of social control. It may also mean that hospitalization is rarely used as an alternative for imprisonment among black men.

Summary and Conclusions

This study has four noteworthy findings. First, sex differences in involvement in serious and violent crimes contribute substantially less to disparities in imprisonment than suggested or implied by many previous writers. Second, state laws, legal policies, and practices of hospitalizing the mentally ill have no differential influence on imprisonment disparity. And although there exist differences in the influence of rates of hospitalization between men and women, the differences are not pronounced. Third, minority men and women are no more likely than white men and women to be imprisoned at disproportionately high rates in states where they have disproportionate involvement in crime. Fourth, the concentration of blacks in the population has dramatically opposite effects on the imprisonment of white women and black women, significantly increasing the likelihood of imprisonment for white women while decreasing the likelihood of imprisonment for black women. The study results lend support to the perspective that state characteristics have *no* differential effects on the imprisonment of men and women. They imply that a common set of factors—more or less equally weighted for men and women—may be responsible for the patterns of imprisonment across states, including sex differences in imprisonment rates. Among these factors are sex-specific rates of labor force participation and hospitalization for mental illness. Sex differences in imprisonment rates will be greatest—other factors being equal—in those states where differences in sex-specific rates of labor force participation and hospitalization of the mentally ill are greatest.

These findings have clear implications for macro-sociological theories of gender, punishment and social control. Explanations of disparities in punishment must move away from perspectives that rely heavily on differences between men and women in criminal behavior or on the differential application of criminal laws or legal policies. More general theories of punishment are needed that clearly specify the linkages between the structural relations of men and women in the larger society and the application of formal social controls in preserving those relations. For example, the results of the present study suggest that a theory of punishment is needed that recognizes the importance of work and specifically the role of gender differences in the labor force in explaining sex differences in rates of imprisonment. Quite clearly, this theory must not ignore the role of crime, particularly violent crime, in explaining variation in the severity of punishments imposed. However, it must view crime as a general property of areas—an element of the social climate—rather than a behavioral characteristic of specific groups giving rise to societal reactions. The theory must also not ignore the role of laws and legal policies in explaining variation in the imposition of punishments. But it must view specific laws as not necessarily mediating between structural relations in the larger society and the severity and types of punishments imposed. Laws and legal policies must play a central role in explanations of punishment. However, this role is extraneous to the relationship between structural relations and the actual punishments society or groups within society impose.

Explanations of disparities in punishment must, simultaneously, move toward perspectives that view criminal punishments in the broader context of other social controls used within the society. Theories of punishment are needed that clearly specify the linkages between the application of punishments and the application of other types of formal controls. For example, any theory must specify the conditions under which the state or courts use institutionalization in mental hospitals as an alternative to incarceration for regulating individuals and groups threatening social relations. Further, the theory must also specify the linkages between the application of punishments and the extensiveness and effects of other less formal controls. Of concern is the relationship between criminal punishments and other institutions within the society—for example, work. A theory of gender, punishment and social control must explain the relationship between the informal controls placed upon men and women in a "gendered" division of labor and the pronounced sex differences associated with the application of criminal punishments.

Finally, sociological theories must view gender as one of many related markers of social standing that influence the imposition of punishments and other social controls. Further, any theory that ignores the linkages between these markers—for example, between gender and race—will be ineffective in explaining how society and its legal institutions impose punishments. Further, theories must specify how areal and temporal variation in the importance and meaning of these markers reflects the norms and values of communities, regions of the country, and specific historical periods. Because the significance of any one marker or set of markers may change across regions and historical periods—increasing or decreasing with changes in structural relations within each region and period—sociologists must explain how regional and temporal contexts frame the ways in which gender and other markers operate.

11

Lethal Social Control in the South: Lynchings and Executions Between 1880 and 1930

Stewart E. Tolnay and E. M. Beck

By the time Arthur Raper wrote his classic book, *The Tragedy of Lynching*, in 1933 the "tragedy" was already in its final act. At its peak, mob violence claimed nearly one hundred black victims annually. During some years of the late 1920s and early 1930s lynchings numbered only in the single digits. Even during the decades of extensive mob activity—for example, the bloody 1890s—the intensity of lynching varied substantially from year to year and from place to place. For instance, 46 southern blacks were lynched in 1890, compared with 99 victims in 1893. Moreover, many counties registered no lynchings during the decade of the 1890s, while 12 blacks were lynched in Shelby County, Tennessee, alone.

Contemporary observers of the lynching era, as well as more recent social scientists, have puzzled over the social forces that gave rise to southern lynchings and which might help to explain the considerable temporal and spatial variation in the distribution of lynchings. Recent studies of the lynching era have emphasized possible political and economic explanations for lynching. In brief, some have suggested that whites lynched blacks in order to neutralize their threat to the political hegemony enjoyed by southern whites—especially southern Democrats (e.g., Reed 1972; Corzine et al. 1983; Olzak 1990, 1992; Soule 1992). Others have claimed that lynchings were a reaction from an economically marginalized white population or the result of frustration stemming from stagnant or falling profits from cotton production (e.g., Corzine et al. 1988; Beck and Tolnay 1990). Few of the contemporary commentators would have pointed to such esoteric explanations, however. For them the answer was quite simple and obvious—southern whites lynched their black neighbors because (1) southern blacks were criminally inclined and

(2) the southern justice system, alone, was inadequate for dealing with black criminality.

Although dominant during the lynching era, little effort has been made to assess the empirical support for this "popular justice" interpretation of southern lynchings. In this paper we use time-series and cross-sectional methodologies to determine whether mob violence was, in fact, a reaction to a weak and inefficient legal system. Our objective is really exploratory—to sift the quantitative evidence that survives from the lynching era in order to determine whether the popular justice explanation for lynching, so popular in the southern mind and media during the period, was really more than a convenient rationalization.

Lynchings and Popular Justice

On July 14, 1898, a mob stormed the jail in Monticello, Arkansas, looking for Jim Redd and Alex Johnson. The two black men had been convicted of murdering W. F. Skipper, a rich white planter in Drew County. The vigilantes broke down the jail door, proceeded to the cell in which Redd and Johnson were held, and poured a volley of gunshots into the bodies of the two inmates. Both men eventually died from their wounds. Perhaps the mob was incensed over a recent ruling by the Arkansas Supreme Court that granted the two men a new trial. As the prospect of imminent execution for Redd and Johnson faded, the mob decided that it was appropriate and acceptable to intervene in the criminal justice process.

During the late nineteenth and early twentieth centuries similar incidents occurred in all southern states and with appalling regularity. Before the lynching era had run its course by the early 1930s, more than two thousand southern blacks had died at the hands of white mobs. Many of the victims were killed while in the custody of law enforcement officials, like Redd and Johnson. Still more were slain before the wheels of justice had begun to grind. For many white southerners, lynching was simply a form of "popular justice." It was widely perceived that the formal criminal justice system was too inefficient, or lenient, to guarantee the swift and severe punishment of criminals. And it was widely assumed that blacks were naturally prone to criminal behavior. Convinced of the existence of a bountiful supply of deviants to punish, and of the inherent weakness of formal mechanisms for carrying out the punishment, southern whites felt obligated and justified in "taking the law into their own hands."

There are ample cases of white mobs springing to action in the face of the possibility of an "unacceptable" formal response to black criminality. Only a few examples are necessary to illustrate the types of grievances that motivated whites to lynch blacks in order to inflict what they believed was "suitable" punishment. Claud Singleton was abducted from the sheriff of Poplarville, Mississippi, on April 18, 1918. He was hanged by a mob that was furious over Singleton's "lenient" life sentence for murder. Flannagan Thornton was taken from the jail in Morrillton, Arkansas, on April 19, 1893. Disappointed that Thornton had been indicted only for second degree murder in the killing of a policeman, the mob hanged him from a signboard. Will Echols of Quitman, Mississippi, was lynched in the early morning hours of September 12, 1920, after he received a stay of execution from the state Supreme Court. And, of course, the previously cited incident in Arkansas involving Jim Redd and Alex Johnson certainly fits within this general category. In many more cases, however, southern mobs intervened even before the arrest and trial of the accused—assuring the swift and severe punishment that white society demanded. In their own minds, at least, these white mobs were helping to preserve order in their communities, even if their intervention violated all notions of due process.

This conviction was shared by many in the broader white community, including the press. Southern newspapers were fascinated by lynchings. They often provided extended coverage of mob violence, including graphic detail of the suffering inflicted on the victim. Although the editorial positions on lynching naturally varied from paper to paper, the southern press often acted as an ardent apologist for mob justice. Their justification, or rationalization, for lynching generally emphasized the popular justice angle. In short, the press claimed that southern whites were pressed to extreme action by a criminal black population that needed to be controlled. While the drunken and unruly lynch mob typically was lamented, the orderly and efficient lynching of a suspected miscreant was often applauded (especially if the offense was interracial or particularly heinous).

An excellent example of the southern press's willingness to condone mob violence can be found in the New Orleans *Daily Picayune*'s treatment of the lynching of Reeves Smith in DeSoto Parish in 1886. Smith was accused of entering a house, and attempting to rape, "one of the most highly respected ladies of the parish." After a preliminary hearing, Smith was charged with attempted rape and deposited in the local jail. Late at night a mob of about eighty "of the best people in the parish" extracted Smith from his cell and hung him from a shade tree in front of the general store. In concluding its story about the lynching of Smith the *Daily Picayune* noted: "While we deplore the necessity for mob law, we must commend it in this instance, for if the accused had been convicted of an 'attempt at rape,' the penalty would only have been two years in the Penitentiary, which is worse than a farce. As we have said before, 'the will of the people is the law of the land,' and all such monsters should be disposed of in a summary manner."[1]

Early scholarship regarding lynching also acknowledged an important "popular justice" dimension to mob violence—sometimes approvingly, sometimes critically. James Cutler, one of the first social scientists to explore the complexities of the lynching phenomenon, strongly disapproved of the practice but claimed that the formal criminal justice system in the South was simply incapable of handling black criminality (Cutler 1905: 224–225). Winfield Collins, holder of advanced degrees (A.M. and Ph.D) but one of the most rabidly racist commentators on lynching, lent further "intellectual" credence to the popular justice mentality. Though far more sympathetic with the motives of white mobs, Collins (1918) agreed with Cutler that the southern justice system was incapable of dealing adequately with black criminality. He argued that separate systems of justice should be created for blacks and whites. Collins's special concern was with sexual attacks by black males on white women, and he considered lynching to be a form of self defense for the white population.

Relations Among Forms of Lethal Social Control

In fact, there may be a basis in social control theory for believing that the popular justice explanation for southern lynchings was more than post hoc rationalization. One school of thought has articulated what has become known as the substitution model of social control and southern lynchings. Essentially, this model describes *informal* vigilante efforts to maintain social control (e.g., lynching) as partially determined by the existence and strength of *formal* alternatives. Black's (1976: 107) observation that "law varies inversely with other social control" is often cited as a basis for the substitution model. Put simply, the substitution model predicts that lynchings should have been more common when, and where, formal alternatives were unsatisfactory to the white community.

Legal executions were the most likely "substitute" for lynchings and probably were equated in the southern mind. This is certainly consistent with the concerns expressed by numerous mobs that their lynch victims would have been treated too "leniently" by the criminal justice system had the law taken its course. In most cases they were disappointed that the accused had, or was expected to, escape the gallows. George Wright (1990) favors the substitution model as an explanation for the disappearance of lynchings in Kentucky during the early decades of the twentieth century. Although he offers no convincing empirical evidence, he suggests that lynchings declined because legal executions increased. In short, Wright argues that the state replaced the mob by conducting sham trials and carrying out public executions in order to placate the demands for vengeance from the white community.

To this point, however, empirical evidence regarding the substitution model of lynchings is mixed. Phillips (1987) provided supporting evidence for it when he concluded that trends in the frequencies of lynchings and executions in North Carolina before the turn of the twentieth century were *inversely* related. However, in a reanalysis of the data for North Carolina, and further investigation for Georgia, Beck et al. (1989) found no evidence that temporal swings in the intensity of lynching were negatively affected by concomitant trends in legal executions. Subsequent analysis by Massey and Myers (1989) also failed to reveal evidence of a negative association between the trends in lynchings and legal executions in Georgia between 1882 and 1935.

An alternative school of thought discounts both the importance of black deviance and the supposed ineffectiveness of the legal system as the cause of lynchings and views mob violence as part of a larger agenda by whites to maintain political, economic and social dominance in southern society. Since other forms of racial repression were motivated by the same concerns over white supremacy, they should have covaried *positively* with lynchings. According to the social conflict model, then, black lynchings and executions should be positively related over time and across space—both being reactions by the white community to perceived threats from the black community. The perceived "minority threat" became more salient when the dominance of the majority group was jeopardized by political, social or economic competition from the minority.

Empirical support for the social conflict model of lynching and executions is also relatively unimpressive. Beck et al. (1989) found a modest positive correlation of $r = +0.26$ between the annual numbers of lynchings and legal executions in Georgia from 1882 to 1930. On the other hand, in a more methodologically sophisticated analysis of roughly the same time period for Georgia, Massey and Myers (1989) found the two forms of lethal control to be virtually unrelated.

Finally, as Liska points out in this volume, it is possible for perceived racial threat to increase the white community's efforts to impose both types of lethal punishments (consistent with the social conflict model) *and* for lynchings and executions to be inversely related. Consequently, in order to estimate the relationship between these alternative forms of social control we must also consider how they are influenced by the level of racial threat perceived by southern white society. More will be said of this issue in the section on data and methods.

In sum, we are faced with two theoretical models that make opposite predictions about the relationship between black lynchings and executions in the South during the late nineteenth and early twentieth centuries. The substitution model is generally consistent with the popular justice explanation for lynching and places emphasis on the relative absence of formal social control alternatives. The social conflict model dismisses the implied association between black deviance and lethal violence and portrays both lynchings and executions as oppressive social control techniques exercised to blunt the competitive efforts of blacks. Moreover, we are still unable to draw confident conclusions about the accuracy of the two models. As mentioned, a few studies have examined the relationship between lynchings and legal executions in order to assess the competing models (Beck et al. 1989; Massey and Myers 1989; Phillips 1987). However, those analyses have been limited to descriptions of the temporal association between lynchings and executions and have examined a restricted geographic area—Georgia and North Carolina. In the following analyses we extend the search to include ten southern states, and we apply both time-series and cross-sectional methodologies.

Data and Methods

Data

Our geographic focus is the southern United States. We separate the entire South into the Deep South and Border South in order to explore for subregional differences in the effect of legal executions on lynching. The Deep South consists of Alabama, Georgia, Louisiana, Mississippi, and South Carolina. The Border South is Arkansas, Florida, Kentucky, North Carolina, and Tennessee.[2] Our temporal focus is the decades of the late nineteenth and early twentieth centuries.

The two key variables in our analyses are the numbers of blacks that were lynched or executed in the South between 1882 and 1930. A new inventory of black lynchings is used to measure the intensity of extralegal mob violence during this era. This inventory includes 2,314 black victims of white lynch mobs. All lynchings included in our study have been confirmed through independent verification by newspaper accounts in local or regional newspapers.[3] The execution data were obtained from Watt Espy's Capital Punishment Research Project. Espy's inventory of executions carried out under civil authority is widely regarded as the most extensive compilation of execution data in existence (e.g., Bowers 1984).[4] The record for each lynching and execution includes information about the exact date and specific location, allowing us to situate the event temporally and spatially.

A variety of other variables are also included in our analyses, primarily to avoid erroneous conclusions about the relationship between lynchings and executions based on spurious or suppressed effects. In both the time series and cross-sectional analyses, variables are included to control for variation in the racial composition of the population. The absolute size of the black population is included because the dependent variable is the raw number of black lynch victims—during a certain time period and within a specific locale. Percent black, including both linear and squared terms, is intended to represent the level of racial threat perceived by the white community. It is generally argued that the dominant majority group perceives a greater threat from a proportionately larger minority group and is therefore more willing to engage in discriminatory action. The potential for non-linearity is allowed, consistent with Blalock's hypotheses that economic and political competition between minority and majority groups will produce different types of non-linear relationships between minority concentration and discrimination (Blalock 1967). In both cases, the relationship is expected to be positive. However, where economic competition is dominant the association should become weaker at higher levels of minority concentration. Where political competition prevails, the relationship should intensify where the minority group is relatively larger.[5] The number of white lynch victims and the number of whites executed are also included in both types of analyses in order to reflect the general "punishment pattern", regardless of race, during the time period or in the county. In addition, our cross-sectional analyses include a measure of population density within the county to control for the fact that most lynchings (as opposed to executions) took place in more remote locations. Aside from lynchings and executions, all data have been drawn from decennial Agricultural and Population Census sources (ICPSR 1990: MRDF #0003).

Our general analytic strategy, in both the time series and cross-sectional approaches, is to first examine the bivariate association between black lynchings and executions. The social conflict model predicts a positive relationship since both types of punishment are functions of perceived racial threat. We next estimate the effect of executions on black lynchings while controlling for the level of racial threat. If the social conflict model is correct, the relationship between executions and lynchings should approach zero after controlling on racial threat.[6] The substitution model will be supported if the net effect of execution on lynching becomes negative.

Time Series Analyses

Our time series analyses cover the period from 1882 to 1930. We allow for a simultaneous effect of executions on lynchings, though the substantive findings are unchanged if the relationship is lagged by one year. After examining a variety of specifications we have chosen to report the results from a first-order moving-average model. According to this model, partial support for the conflict model can be inferred if the regression coefficient for the number of black executions (β_{exec}) is positive in sign. However, if the coefficient becomes negative when other factors are controlled, then the results also support the substitution model of social control and are consistent with the popular justice model of lynching. Conversely, a non-significant, or substantially attenuated, positive effect coefficient for black executions when other factors are controlled will contradict the substitution model and provide additional support for the social conflict model.

Cross-Sectional Analyses

When we shift to cross-sectional model estimation, our focus is on counties in the ten southern states and the question becomes, "Did areas that executed larger numbers of blacks experience fewer (or more) lynchings?" During the cross-sectional analyses, we still maintain a temporal dimension by examining the relationship between executions and lynchings during five separate time periods: 1882–1889, 1890–1899, 1900–1909, 1910–1919, and 1920–1929. This separation allows for the relationship between executions and lynchings to fluctuate over time and increases our chances of identifying periods during which the two may have been associated cross-sectionally. Because the dependent variable, the number of black lynch victims within each county during the decade, is a positively skewed count variable, we have estimated the parameters from the equation using Poisson regression rather than standard multiple regression techniques. Again, our focus will be on the coefficient, β_{exec}, which will indicate whether the frequencies of legal executions and black lynchings within counties were related. Support for the substitution or social conflict models will be inferred in the same fashion described above for the time series approach.

Results

Time-Series Findings

The Deep South accounted for the majority of lynchings and executions during this era—68 percent of all black lynchings and 66 percent of black executions between 1882 and 1930 occurred in these five states. Table 11.1 (columns 1 and 2) presents the results from the time series analysis for the Deep South. The bivariate equation (EQ. 1) suggests that lynchings and executions were positively associated, as hypothesized (β_{exec} = +.118). However, the coefficient is so small in relation to its standard error that we cannot reject the possibility that the two forms of punishment were actually unrelated in the Deep South throughout this period. This outcome supports neither the substitution model nor the social conflict model.

TABLE 11.1 Time-Series Regressions of Number of Black Lynch Victims, 1883–1930

Independent Variable	Deep South		Border South	
	EQ. 1	EQ. 2	EQ. 1	EQ. 2
Black executions	.118	.053	−.021	−.054
	(.826)[a]	(.341)	(−.136)	(−.326)
Black population (1,000s)	—	.017	—	.002
		(1.092)		(.038)
Percent black	—	4.075	—	1.710
		(1.696)		(.220)
White lynchings	—	.377	—	.467
		(.868)		(1.375)
White executions	—	.226	—	.019
		(.485)		(.061)
Moving-average coefficient	−.442	−.549	−.389	−.426
	(−3.251)	(−4.079)	(−2.822)	(−2.930)
Ljung-Box Q coefficient	21.855	26.148	30.399	33.472
Durbin-Watson statistic	1.897	1.776	1.876	1.851

[a] T-ratios in parentheses.

When additional predictors are added to the model (EQ. 2), the coefficient for black executions actually shrinks in size—as well as in relation to its standard error. It is clear from these findings that the pace with which blacks were legally executed had virtually no impact on the frequency of lynchings in the Deep South. Looking at other variables, we find that only percent black in the population was significantly related to the number of black lynchings. As anticipated, lynchings were more frequent when the relative size of the black population was greater. We were unable to include the quadratic term for percent black in the equation because of extreme collinearity between percent black squared and the other population composition variables.

Turning to the Border South, we find, again, an extremely anemic pattern of covariation between black lynchings and executions. The bivariate model (EQ. 1) for the Border South yields a negative coefficient (β_{exec} = −.021), which is very small relative to its standard error. Inclusion of the remaining predictor variables (EQ. 2) does not change appreciably this basic finding. Therefore, we must conclude once again that yearly fluctuations in the intensity of lynching in the Border South were impressively insensitive to the frequency with which blacks were marched to the gallows.

In sum, the time series analyses fail to lend support to either the substitution or the social conflict models of social control. We did not find the anticipated positive bivariate covariation between lynchings and executions—as predicted by the social conflict model. Nor, however, did we observe a negative effect of executions on lynchings after controlling for racial population concentration and other factors—as anticipated by the substitution model. It is possible that our inability to identify a meaningful relationship between trends in black executions and lynchings is due to the length of the time series being considered.

By lumping together all of the years between 1882 and 1930 into the same analysis, the traditional time series approach assumes that any relationship between executions and lynchings would have been invariant during this 49-year period. It is possible, however, that the absence of an overall relationship between 1882 and 1930 masks periods of significant association within shorter time periods. Isaac and Griffin (1989) refer to this as the "ahistorical" nature of traditional time series analysis and suggest a "moving regression" approach that derives parameter estimates for a series of shorter, overlapping intervals.[7] We use overlapping 15-year intervals, beginning with 1883–1897, followed by 1884–1898, and so on. The coefficients, representing the effect of legal executions on lynchings within each period, are plotted in relation to the effect of executions over the entire forty-nine years.[8]

In general, the evidence from the moving regression analyses, available on request, is consistent with that from the overall time series approach. That is, during most of the intervals the relationship between lynchings and executions is not statistically significant. However, there are a few exceptions to this overall pattern. Within the Deep South, lynchings and executions were significantly related only between 1903 and 1917. In the Border South, three periods exhibit significant association between black lynchings and executions: 1912–1926, 1913–1927, and 1915–1929.[9] Importantly, for all of these exceptions the association between lynchings and executions is positive, contrary to the predictions of the substitution model. These findings for the Border states suggest an intriguing emergence of coordinated formal and informal sanctioning of blacks during the latter part of our time period. While a definitive explanation for this development is beyond the scope of this paper, it is possible that state governments in the Border South used legal executions as a method for eradicating mob violence. That is, in response to intensive mob activity, perhaps courts in Border states began marching accused blacks off to the gallows more frequently in an effort to placate the mob-prone elements of the white community.[10]

If we concentrate less on sheer statistical significance and more on general patterns, a few additional observations can be made. First, until the early twentieth century, the coefficients in the Deep South were consistently positive in sign. As the century progressed, however, the relationship became more erratic—alternating between periods of positive and negative covariation. Second, the coefficients in the Border South are consistently positive throughout the era, turning negative only during a few of the 15-year intervals. While we are reluctant to overinterpret statistically non-significant effects, the evidence does hint at intriguing regional and temporal variation in the relationship between executions and lynchings.

In sum, our findings for the Deep and Border South regions partially confirm the conclusions reached by Massey and Myers (1989) for the state of Georgia. That is, when we focus on the longer-term patterns throughout the 49-year period, we find no evidence that southern whites reacted to the intensity of activity by the formal justice system when deciding whether to take an active role in the punishment of blacks. The findings in Table 11.1 suggest that they were not spurred to greater mob activity by the sight of relatively few blacks visiting the executioner—contrary to the expectations of the substitution model. Neither, however, did the two forms of lethal punishment share the same temporal swings. Thus, there is also no support for the predictions of the conflict model. At least in the broader temporal sense, lynchings and executions seem to have been invoked largely independently as mechanisms of social control over blacks.

When the effect of executions on lynchings is allowed to fluctuate during the longer 49-year period, we are still unable to infer a strong and consistent relationship. However, we do observe some abbreviated periods during which the two forms of punishment were positively related, especially in the Border states. Thus, the moving-regression time series analysis yields intriguing hints that the nature of the relationship between formal and informal lethal control was not invariant over time or across regions.

A possible limitation to the time series approach is that it lumps together vastly different social contexts—despite our separate treatment of the Deep and Border South regions. That is, each data point refers to the total number of black lynch victims for a single year aggregated over all areas within each subregion. That total, in turn, is regressed on the corresponding number of black executions during the same year, similarly aggregated. Perhaps such aggregation obscures real covariation (positive or negative) between the formal and informal punishment of blacks that prevailed within local areas or communities. An alternative approach is to consider smaller geographic units in an effort to capture processes that operated at the more local level.

Cross-Sectional Findings

We turn now to the cross-sectional analyses, which shift our attention to the distribution of black lynchings across southern counties rather than over time. Once again, the Deep South and Border South states are treated separately. A temporal dimension is maintained by examining the spatial variation in lynching within five distinct time periods between 1882 and 1930.

The findings for the Deep South, presented in Table 11.2, are only partially supportive of our hypotheses. Considering only the bivariate relationships between black lynchings and executions (EQ. 1), we observe the expected positive covariation for the middle three decades (1890–99, 1900–09 and 1910–19). Furthermore, in all three cases the significant positive bivariate relationship becomes negative, or is markedly attenuated, when controls, including racial threat, are introduced. These patterns are consistent with the predictions of the social conflict model. The bivariate association between lynchings and executions during the remaining two decades is negative, though statistically insignificant.

The multivariate results (EQ. 2) yield relatively little support for the substitution model. Only during the 1920s does it appear that black lynchings were significantly and negatively affected by the number of executions within the county. In all other decades, the net effect of executions on lynchings was either positive (1900–09), or statistically nonsignificant.

The evidence from the Border South in Table 11.3 provides relatively strong support for the social conflict model. In all decades but the 1880s, the bivariate association between lynchings and executions is positive and statistically significant, as anticipated. Furthermore, in those same decades the strength of the relationship is substantially attenuated when the control variables, including racial threat, are introduced. Only during the earliest decade does the bivariate relationship between lynchings and executions fail to attain statistical significance—though it, too, is positive in sign.

The lone bit of support for the substitution model in the Border South is observed for the 1880s when the net relationship between black lynchings and executions is negative and statistically significant. During all other decades, the results of the multivariate equations (EQ. 2) reveal a positive association between lynchings and executions. And, during the two latest decades, lynchings were significantly greater in counties in which more blacks were legally executed.

Considering the cross-sectional evidence for the Deep and Border South, we believe that the findings yield moderate, though not unblemished, support for the social conflict model. In seven out of the ten equations, the bivariate association between black lynchings and executions was positive and statistically significant. Furthermore, in those seven cases the relationship became substantially weaker with the introduction of controls for racial threat—as anticipated by the social conflict model. On the other hand, in only two equations (the Border South in the 1880s

TABLE 11.2 Poisson Regressions of Number of Black Lynch Victims, Deep South States, by Decade

Independent Variable	1882–89 EQ.1	1882–89 EQ.2	1890–99 EQ.1	1890–99 EQ.2	1900–09 EQ.1	1900–09 EQ.2	1910–19 EQ.1	1910–19 EQ.2	1920–29 EQ.1	1920–29 EQ.2
Black executions	-.006 (-.077)[a]	-.118 (-1.275)	.080 (2.143)	-.001 (-.030)	.097 (4.327)	.079 (2.408)	.135 (2.758)	-.031 (-.441)	-.064 (-.656)	-.250 (-2.032)
Black population (1,000s)	—	.033 (3.297)	—	.040 (3.579)	—	.019 (1.693)	—	.010 (1.037)	—	.037 (2.597)
Percent black	—	.059 (3.112)	—	.044 (3.054)	—	.048 (3.021)	—	.083 (4.223)	—	.094 (3.759)
(Percent black)²	—	-.0006 (-2.911)	—	-.0005 (-3.210)	—	-.0003 (-2.357)	—	-.0006 (-3.315)	—	-.0009 (-3.540)
White lynchings	—	.658 (3.724)	—	.212 (3.424)	—	.493 (2.244)	—	1.350 (4.198)	—	.550 (1.708)
White executions	—	-.246 (-.729)	—	.021 (.105)	—	.349 (1.816)	—	.582 (3.887)	—	.084 (.578)
Density	—	-.008 (-1.337)	—	-.005 (-2.403)	—	-.013 (-2.712)	—	-.005 (-1.482)	—	-.005 (-1.389)
Constant	-.445 (-4.739)	-1.890 (-4.119)	.186 (2.305)	-.889 (-2.606)	-.095 (-1.192)	-1.290 (-3.173)	-.387 (-4.487)	-2.789 (-5.421)	-1.225 (-12.679)	-3.560 (-5.846)
Scale parameter	1.684	1.541	2.279	2.101	2.004	1.775	1.731	1.422	1.011	.930
Number of cases	368	368	367	367	377	377	395	395	414	414

[a] Asymptotic t-ratios are in parentheses.

TABLE 11.3 Poisson Regressions of Number of Black Lynch Victims, Border South States, by Decade

Independent Variable	1882–89 EQ.1	1882–89 EQ.2	1890–99 EQ.1	1890–99 EQ.2	1900–09 EQ.1	1900–09 EQ.2	1910–19 EQ.1	1910–19 EQ.2	1920–29 EQ.1	1920–29 EQ.2
Black executions	.007 (.049)[a]	-.466 (-2.925)	.455 (7.327)	.122 (1.211)	.168 (2.809)	.101 (1.071)	.476 (7.007)	.212 (2.344)	.409 (8.152)	.205 (3.732)
Black population (1,000s)	—	.053 (1.849)	—	.066 (3.659)	—	.009 (.392)	—	.061 (4.102)	—	.098 (5.871)
Percent black	—	.128 (5.924)	—	.052 (3.853)	—	.100 (5.956)	—	.063 (4.301)	—	.092 (5.560)
(Percent black)²	—	-.002 (-5.220)	—	-.0006 (-3.404)	—	-.001 (-4.831)	—	-.0006 (-3.537)	—	-.001 (-5.230)
White lynchings	—	.290 (2.343)	—	.244 (1.877)	—	.678 (2.666)	—	.261 (.681)	—	.351 (.813)
White executions	—	.462 (2.182)	—	-.474 (-1.525)	—	-.018 (-.076)	—	-.225 (-.843)	—	-.045 (-.249)
Density	—	-.002 (-.579)	—	-.009 (-2.396)	—	-.009 (-1.836)	—	-.016 (-3.121)	—	-.034 (-6.073)
Constant	-1.355 (-12.892)	-3.238 (9.173)	-.817 (8.700)	-1.429 (-5.802)	-.976 (-9.975)	-2.203 (-6.910)	-1.501 (-14.028)	-2.211 (-6.786)	-1.887 (-17.785)	-2.453 (-7.177)
Scale parameter	1.060	.909	1.531	1.373	1.473	1.262	1.053	.874	.744	.546
Number of cases	418		417		432		435		444	

[a] Asymptotic t-ratios are in parentheses.

and the Deep South in the 1920s) does the relationship between lynchings and executions become negative (and statistically significant) after the introduction of controls, as expected by the substitution model.

Still, the findings seem to suggest that the association between lynchings and executions was somewhat "time dependent." This observation is generally consistent with the patterns discerned in the moving regression time series analyses. For example, the significant and positive cross-sectional effect of executions in the Deep South during the 1900s is compatible with the significant effect inferred from the moving regression analysis for the 1903–1917 period. In addition, the positive effect of executions during the 1910s and 1920s inferred from the cross-sectional analyses for the Border South agrees with the series of positive and statistically significant moving regression coefficients for 1912–1926, 1913–1927, and 1915–1929.

Some of the other results contained in Tables 11.2 and 11.3 are worthy of brief comment. First, we find impressive consistency in the relationship between lynchings and the racial composition of southern counties. In every decade, for the Deep and Border South alike, percent black has a significant and non-linear relationship with black lynchings. Furthermore, the negative sign for the squared term indicates a weakening association in counties with particularly high concentrations of black population. The form of this non-linearity is supportive of Blalock's economic competition hypothesis (see, e.g., Blalock 1967; Corzine et al. 1983; Tolnay et al. 1989) and has appeared consistently in our other empirical analyses of spatial patterns in black lynchings during this time period (Tolnay and Beck 1994). Second, with a few exceptions, the number of whites lynched within a county varies directly with the number of black lynch victims. This suggests that an underlying atmosphere of extra-legal violence permeated some communities and affected both black and white residents. Finally, lynchings were more common in less densely settled areas, though this pattern was somewhat more consistent within Border states.

Interpretation and Conclusions

Contemporaries of the lynching era often explained it as the white community's response to a criminal black population and an inefficient and lenient southern criminal justice system. The substitution model provides deeper insight into the popular justice explanation for lynchings by positing an inverse relationship between formal and informal types of punishment. According to both, we should expect to find that the frequency of mob violence and legal executions in the South were negatively related over time and across space. That is, as southerners gained confidence in the efficiency and certainty of punishment meted out by the state, they had less reason to resort to alternative forms of social control such as lynching. However, the findings reported here offer paltry support for the popular justice model of lynching. There is little evidence that white southerners abandoned the rope and faggot where or when state authorities more vigorously executed convicted blacks. Our time-series investigation provided no evidence supporting the substitution model. The cross-sectional approach hinted at a substitution process only for the Border South during the 1880s and the Deep South during the 1920s. In sum, even though the individual members of white lynch mobs may have thought they were engaged in acts of popular justice, the aggregate historical record of their activity largely, though not completely, contradicts that image.

On the other hand, the empirical evidence is somewhat more consistent with exactly the opposite hypothesis—that the frequency of mob activity and the intensity of legal executions were positively related. The first hint of positive covariation between black lynchings and executions emerged in the moving regression component of the time-series analysis. Especially noteworthy was the statistically significant positive relationship observed for the Border states after about 1910. Further evidence of this positive association was gleaned from the cross-sectional analyses, especially in the Border South. While not unanimous, this evidence is consistent with the social conflict model's description of lynchings and executions as two elements of the southern white community's broader armamentarium for subjugating and controlling its black population.

Additional evidence from the cross-sectional analyses also favors a social conflict model of southern lynchings. For every decade, in the Deep and Border South alike, the relative size of the black population had a significant and non-linear effect on mob violence. Consistent with Blalock's "economic competition" model, this relationship between percent black and lynchings grew weaker at higher concentrations of black population. As we have described elsewhere, race relations in the southern states were exacerbated seriously by economic conditions during this era (Beck and Tolnay 1990; Tolnay and Beck 1992b, 1994). Black and white poor dirt farmers competed with each other for the shrinking number of prime parcels of land—either for tenancy or ownership. White planters were dependent on cheap black labor but also benefitted from an antagonistic racial climate that reduced the chances of a coalition between black and white workers. Combine these volatile conditions with wildly fluctuating cotton prices, and the basis for conflict becomes all too apparent. As the most vulnerable group in southern society, blacks were a natural target for the conflict, competition and hostility that brewed in this southern cauldron. Our findings show that black lynching, and in some cases executions, were the end result.

However, as Tittle suggested earlier in this volume, the social conflict model is not necessarily the only theoretical perspective to predict the disproportionate exposure of southern blacks to social control (either lynchings or executions) during this era. For instance, he notes that consensus theory predicts that "those behaviors, individuals, subgroups, and categories of people that are thought to actually threaten the survival or continuity of society or that are believed by most to undermine its basic values will be regarded as dangerous and bad and will be prohibited, punished, and blocked." There can be little doubt that southern whites shared a strong consensus that blacks were just such a threat to the integrity of their cherished society.

Finally, we must emphasize the lack of perfect consistency in our findings. Both the results of our moving regression time-series analyses and the cross-sectional findings suggest that forces unique to different time periods, as well as to specific locales, may have played an important role in determining the nature of the relationship between lynchings and executions. This raises interesting questions about the underlying causes of the changes in society's dependence on alternative forms of social control. Why, for example, should the two forms of punishment covary positively in the Border South after 1900 but not in the Deep South? How should we interpret their negative relationship during the 1880s in the Border South? What should we conclude from the hints of temporal variation in the effect of executions on lynchings that emerge from the moving regression time-series analyses?

Liska has argued in this volume that the relationship between alternative forms of social control may be complex. Further, he states that successful empirical estimation of the covariation between forms of social control requires correctly specified models that are consistent with relevant theory. Within the constraints of available data we have attempted to identify and estimate appropriate models. It may be, however, that the social processes were more complex than can adequately be represented by the historical data at our disposal. Perhaps this partially accounts for the inconsistency in our results across time periods and geographic areas. Furthermore, it must be kept in mind that lethal punishment was not the only option available to the southern white community. They also had access to less drastic mechanisms for controlling competitive blacks, including Jim Crow restrictions, disenfranchisement, debt peonage, economic discrimination, and non-lethal intimidation.

In sum, although southern lynch mobs may have argued that they were attempting to compensate for weaknesses in the criminal justice system, the surviving statistical evidence of their grisly deeds fails to support such a pious claim. More likely, they were responding to perceived threats to their traditional social advantage and in the process victimizing their vulnerable black neighbors. This chapter has presented tantalizing support for the latter interpretation, but the definitive story must await additional corroboration.

Notes

1. Details about the lynching of Reeves Smith were taken from the *Daily Picayune* of New Orleans (October 25, 1886: 8).

2. The remaining southern states (e.g., Oklahoma, Texas, Virginia and West Virginia) are omitted because we have been unable to confirm a large enough percentage of their reported lynchings.

3. For more information about this lynching inventory, see Beck and Tolnay (1990) or Tolnay and Beck (1994). Construction of the inventory was partially supported by grants from the University of Georgia Research Foundation and the Sociology Program of the National Science Foundation (SES-8618123) to Stewart E. Tolnay, E.M. Beck, and James L. Massey.

4. A publicly available version of Espy's execution data has been prepared by ICPSR. We have obtained our execution data directly from Watt Espy. According to Espy (personal communication), there are substantial differences between our data and the version released by ICPSR. Since preparation of the ICPSR version, Espy has made several additions to his inventory as well as corrections based on further research. These are included in our data base. Thus, the execution data used in our analyses are more complete and accurate than those publicly available through ICPSR. We wish to thank M. Watt Espy, Jr. for his cooperation and assistance in the early phases of this research.

5. Elsewhere we have argued that direct measures of perceived minority threat are preferable to the more indirect measure on relative size of the minority population (Tolnay and Beck 1992a). In this chapter, however, we are less interested in articulating the specific threats (economic, political or status) that resulted in lynching than in simply controlling for the level of threat as we estimate the relationship between lynchings and executions. Supplementary analyses that included direct measures of racial competition or threat yield findings basically similar to those reported here.

6. This assumes that we are able to partial all our influences of racial threat. To the extent that this assumption is invalid, however, we may expect to find a residual positive effect of executions on lynchings, after controlling for racial threat.

7. See Beck and Tolnay (1990) for an application of the moving regression approach to supplement a traditional time series analysis.

8. It is necessary to begin with year 1883 since the data are differenced once. Because of collinearity problems, we once again dropped the variable, percent black squared, from the equations used to produce the parameter estimates.

9. While these intervals may not appear to be the most extreme points, they are the largest in relation to their standard errors.

10. This interpretation is somewhat consistent with Wright's (1990) argument that executions replaced lynchings in Kentucky during the first few decades of the century. Wright's framework describes an inverse relationship between lynchings and executions, consistent with the substitution model. However, it is possible that during the initial phase of a "replacement" process executions were more frequent when mob activity was vigorous.

12

Double Jeopardy: The Abuse and Punishment of Homeless Youth

John Hagan and Bill McCarthy

The state usually is assigned primacy in sociological discussions of sanctioning.[1] However, it is crucial to understand that the family also plays a major role in social sanctioning and that the state and the family are interrelated sanctioning systems. In many ways legal sanctions act as a subset of social sanctions enforced by the authority of government within the larger social system that includes the family. Thus legal and social sanctions are connected in a variety of ways, sometimes opposing and sometimes reinforcing one another.

Examples of opposing and reinforcing relationships are common. An example of the former relationship occurs when folkways or customs take on the force of law. Alternatively, an oppositional relationship occurs when violence is defined and sanctioned as criminal. As Donald Black (1983) has shown, in some cases the violent act can itself be understood as a form of social control (i.e., a social sanction) but one that is sometimes opposed by the legal system and controlled through legal sanctions. The provision that this is only sometimes true is particularly apparent in the context of family violence.

Black's conception of violence as a form of social control is aptly applied to family violence against children, since violence against children within the family can itself be understood as a process of social sanctioning. Thus, coercive as well as consensual sanctions are imposed within the family. Coercive sanctioning of children by parents often is called discipline, even when it is abusive. This coercion occurs whenever one family member uses physical force or its threat as a sanction to control the behavior of other family members. Often this coercive sanctioning compels compliance with intra-family norms and is used to control behavior that varies from these norms. These norms include definitions of power and authority in the family. Recent writing about child abuse includes efforts to understand how the state reinforces this system of private sanctions.

The state reinforces the family as a sanctioning system through norms of legitimation and privacy. A norm of legitimacy establishes and maintains the exercise of adult power over children. This norm is reflected in the widespread belief that parents have a right to control their children. Although this norm may not be linked directly to the use of violence against children within the family, it can indirectly encourage such violence by establishing and maintaining the legitimacy of the unequal power of parents over children and the right of parents to control children within the home.

The problem is that norms that legitimate the use of less severe forms of physical force against children in the family create conditions that allow use of more severe force. For example, like many U.S. state criminal codes, the Criminal Code of Canada (Watt and Fuerst 1989: 79–80) provides that "every schoolteacher, parent or person standing in the place of a parent is justified in using force by way of correction toward a pupil or child, as the case may be, who is under his care, if the force does not exceed what is reasonable under the circumstances." Moreover, even those who recognize the seriousness of child maltreatment continue to disagree about the definition of abuse. Some argue that current legal definitions are over-inclusive (e.g., Besharov 1988), whereas others maintain that they are adequate (e.g., Finkelhor 1990). Thus, neither legal codes nor child-protection advocates have established a clear boundary on the extent to which parents can use physical force to legally coerce compliance by children.

A norm of privacy augments the norm of legitimacy. Conceptually, the norm of privacy implies a right to control without external intervention. Although there is no natural law basis to a claim that the family has inherent rights to non-interference, legal codes frequently incorporate this definition into statutes that involve the family. Thus, for the most part the family is seen as a private world where activities are the concern of family members and into which law should intrude very selectively. This is not to suggest that the norm of family privacy is sacrosanct. Rather, there are many historical instances (e.g., compulsory education) in which the state acts in the presumed public interest and disregards any conceivable inherent right to non-interference in the family. Nonetheless, when it comes to the use of physical force by parents against children, the norm of privacy establishes the family as an entity of its own, analogous to the state, with powers to create and enforce its own norms. The effect of this norm of privacy is to restrain the use of state sanctions and legitimate the non-interference by legal authorities (police and courts) and other social actors such as doctors, social workers, teachers, and neighbors.

In everyday practice, the norms of legitimation and privacy take effect through restrictive definitions of what constitutes child abuse and subsequently high thresholds for intervention by social and legal actors, including the police and courts (see Olsen 1985; Rose 1987). Again, the effects of these norms are not to directly encourage violence against children but rather to indirectly create the conditions in which child abuse can flourish (Gil 1978:124).

As we have argued elsewhere (Hagan et al. 1990), child welfare schemes have proven a poor remedy for these problems. Normative disputes about reasonable limits of physical discipline and tolerable levels of public intrusion into the family characteristically have resulted in definitions of "children in need of protection" that set high thresholds for findings of abuse. Thus, it is not surprising that child protection workers often see themselves as caught between the dual demands of protecting children and not interfering with families (Kamerman and Kahn 1990). A result is that discovery of abuse remains highly problematic, even with the introduction of mandatory child abuse reporting legislation in most jurisdictions over the past decade. For example, Burgdorf (1980) estimates that in the United States only about one-third of all instances of child abuse are reported to officials, of which fewer are investigated and of which only a small proportion ever go to court (also see American Humane Association 1984; Health and Welfare Canada 1989). As well, there is evidence that educators and health practitioners are often reluctant to report cases of abuse (see Swoboda et al. 1978; Muehlman and Kimmons 1981; Nightingale and Walker 1986; McIntyre 1987).

Furthermore, even when abuse is reported, most child protection agencies operate with insufficient resources and therefore must restrict their activities to only the most severe cases. Zellman and Antler (1990) surveyed 1,196 child care professionals (including pediatricians, social workers, psychiatrists, school principals) and found that "virtually all" agencies screen reported cases of child maltreatment on the basis of a priority scale, and "[t]he press of more serious calls often results in failure to ever respond to the lowest-ranked cases." (32). Thus most parents remain unsanctioned for the use of violence against their children.

However, our concerns go beyond those that result from the socially constructed circumstances that lead to the legal neglect of violence against children within a family, for the interrelationship between state and family sanctioning is more problematic than we have yet suggested.

The further, and in some ways more serious, problem is that although most cases of parental abuse against children are not subject to state sanctioning, behaviors that may be causally linked to this abuse, including leaving home and consequent involvement in juvenile delinquency, are subject to state sanctioning.

Research on Abused Youth

Four kinds of literature are germane to the issues raised in this paper: studies of child maltreatment, links between maltreatment and adolescent homelessness, maltreatment and delinquency, and homelessness and delinquency. The literature on child maltreatment suggests that the parental use of force against children is seen as an acceptable child-rearing practice by many parents and that it is a common occurrence (e.g., see Straus et al. 1980; Caplan et al. 1984; Gelles and Straus 1987). Moreover, these studies report that parents who use force employ it periodically, not episodically, and that for most victims, physical maltreatment begins in early childhood and often continues through adolescence (for a review, see Health and Welfare Canada 1989; Justice and Justice 1990).

There is also much evidence that parental maltreatment (both physical and sexual) is common among those adolescents who leave home. Although early studies of adolescents who have left home rarely considered the prevalence of abuse (see Brennan et al. 1978 for review), more recent research confirms that adolescents who leave home are disproportionately the victims of abuse. Reported rates of physical abuse among adolescents who flee from their homes range from between 40 percent to over 80 percent (Farber et al. 1984; Janus et al. 1987; Stiffman 1989; Powers et al. 1990; Whitbeck and Simons 1990).

The results of previous research on the relationship between physical maltreatment and delinquency are less consistent than those on physical abuse and leaving home. Although many studies report that abused youth are at a higher risk of crime, others fail to find evidence of this relationship (Garbarino and Plautz, 1986). For example, Doerner (1988) found positive associations between physical abuse and self-reported serious and minor crime in a sample of 221 college students. Using a "specialized cohorts" design, Widom (1989a, 1989b) compared the juvenile probation and adult criminality records of 908 victims of court-substantiated child abuse and neglect (aged eleven or less at the time of abuse) with 667 individuals from a control group. She reports that compared to their controls, victims of childhood physical abuse or neglect (the two are joined) are significantly more likely to have juvenile and adult criminal records, 17 percent versus 26 percent and 21 percent versus 29 percent respectively (also see Hunner and Walker 1981; McCord 1983; Dembo et al. 1989; Wauchope and Straus, 1990).

Nonetheless, a number of other studies failed to find a relationship between physical punishment and self-reported delinquency (e.g., Nye 1958; McCord et al. 1959; Brown 1984). A possible source of the divergent findings involves offsetting interactions and sampling differences. For example, Agnew (1983) analyzed data from the Youth in Transition survey (N = 2213, tenth-grade males) and found a negative relationship between delinquency and parental slapping in cases in which the parental demands are highly consistent but a positive relationship in families when parental demands are inconsistent (also see Kruttschnitt et al. 1987). As well, Whitbeck and Simons (1990) point to the possibility of a gender interaction: in a study of runaways, they found a direct positive relationship between abuse and delinquency on the street for adolescent males but not for females.

The relationship between delinquency and adolescent homelessness is also uncertain. For example, Brennan et al. (1984) found that youth who left home reported substantial involvement in crime while on the street: 33 percent pilfered objects worth less than $5, 15 percent stole things of greater value, and 20 percent sold marijuana. Brennan et al. also found that compared with adolescents who never left home, these youth were significantly more delinquent during the time they lived at home. Although a number of other studies allude to a relationship between adolescent homelessness and crime, they fail to provide data that adequately support this hypothesis (e.g., see Palenski 1984; Janus et al. 1987).

In contrast, Goldmeier and Dean (1972) failed to find a relationship between leaving home and delinquency in their study of 57 adolescent "runaways." Shellow et al. (1972) also found that the great majority of 776 "runaways" did not get into trouble with the law either before or after leaving home and that the former were not significantly different in their criminality from 1,327 non-runners. However, Shellow et al. did find a relationship between leaving home and delinquency for adolescents who left home on more than one occasion. Gold and Reimer (1974) also failed to find a strong relationship between leaving home and crime. In their analysis of the 1972 National Survey of Youth, they found that fewer than 10 percent of adolescents who leave home reported committing a delinquent act while not at home. However, those who did leave home reported greater involvement in crime while living at home.

Although the incongruent findings from studies on crime and abuse and homeless are troubling, they are somewhat expected given the variation in when the research was done, sampling techniques, indicators, and specification of effects. For example, a number of the studies that failed to find a relationship between delinquency and either abuse or crime were conducted more than a generation ago (e.g. Nye 1958; McCord et al. 1959; Goldmeier and Dean 1972; Shellow et al. 1972). Adolescents from latter years may belong to a cohort with dramatically different experiences. As well, the divergent results may be influenced by sampling procedures. Whereas some studies have used national, regional, or municipal probability samples and thus have obtained only a small number of abused or homeless persons (e.g., Gold and Reimer 1974; Agnew 1983; Brennan et al. 1984), others have overrepresented these groups by using samples collected from institutions or social service agencies (e.g., Shellow et al. 1972; Gil 1978; Doerner 1988; Dembo et al. 1989; Widom, 1989a). Unfortunately, these approaches have rarely been combined. There is also considerable variation in the measurement of physical abuse, ranging from parental slapping (e.g., Agnew 1983) to severe beatings or weapon-based assaults (e.g., Dembo et al. 1989) and a range in between (e.g., Kruttschnitt et al. 1987). Lastly, the failure of a number of studies to consider the possibility of indirect and interactive effects may also explain the inconsistent results.

Notwithstanding the preceding, studies on abuse, homelessness, and delinquency gain additional meaning when placed in the context of our previous discussion of private and public sanctions. These studies imply that when state sanctions do make their way into the lives of those who experience child abuse, they tend to fall on the victims rather than the perpetrators of this violence; moreover, from the perspective of social control, these sanctions can be viewed as responding to the symptoms rather than the causes of the underlying social problems involved. The research that follows is an attempt to make explicit and explore links between parental abuse of children (which, we have observed, is in general legally unsanctioned) and other types of behavior, such as leaving home and delinquency (which are more likely subjects of legal sanctions).

The Present Study

As noted above, past research on child abuse and homelessness has used data gathered from a variety of sources, ranging from agency registers of special populations of abused or runaway children to national surveys. The analytical problems, of course, are the infrequency of child abuse in the general population and the need to experimentally or statistically control for factors associated with abuse in order to assess its presumed effects. Thus, unstratified samples of the general population yield fewer cases than are needed for multivariate analysis of the causes and consequences of abuse, whereas samples of special populations known to be abused allow no comparative assessment of populations unaffected by abuse. Our response to this problem is a compromise that incorporates a sample that is highly stratified by the location and circumstances in which adolescent respondents live.

The respondents for this sample were selected from street and school settings in the city of Toronto (Canada). Toronto is a city with a growing street population. The street setting was chosen because youth in it are known as a high-risk population for child abuse (e.g., Lamphear 1985). The street sample was developed between spring 1987 and spring 1988, through purposive sampling from nine social service agencies (e.g., shelters and drop-in centers) and from a number of non-agency locations suggested by agency workers and homeless youth (e.g., streets and city parks of downtown Toronto). One of the authors developed the sample over a twelve-month period using an anonymous self-report survey instrument that also was used in schools, as described below (for a detailed description see Hagan and McCarthy 1992). Ten-dollar food certificates were used as inducements, and efforts were made to systematize the selection of subjects over a range of sites and times. Coverage of times and places was extensive, and refusals were infrequent (57 of 475 potential respondents). The street portion of the sample includes 390 youth (an 82 percent response rate) who were thirteen to nineteen years of age. While it is impossible to know if our sample is "representative" of the Toronto homeless youth population, the age and gender distribution of our sample is quite similar to that reported in social service agency figures and other studies of Canadian street youth (Janus et al. 1987; Kufeldt and Nimmo 1987).

School youth for the sample were selected during the spring of 1988 through a probability sampling of classes in three metropolitan schools serving socially heterogeneous parts of the city. Invitations to participate during lunch period were distributed in randomly selected ninth- through twelfth-grade classes, with a choice of popular album tapes as an inducement. Signed parental permission forms indicated that participating students were thirteen to nineteen years of age and living with parents. The school survey was administered by the authors and research assistants to groups of up to forty students. The school portion of the sample includes 562 students, with a response rate of 68 percent. This level falls in the range of between 60 percent and 75 percent reported for most self-report studies of delinquency (e.g., Elliott and Ageton 1980; Hindelang et al. 1981; Thornberry and Christenson 1984).

Like other voluntary survey measures, the self-report questions used in our study are open to measurement error. However, we incorporated a number of techniques recommended (Sudman and Bradburn 1983) for reducing reactivity error (e.g., time clues, anonymity, deliberate loading, and familiar wording). The strong correlations between diverse measures of criminal activity at home and on the street (including items on non-serious and serious theft, drug use, drug-selling, and violence), family dynamics, and school experiences inspire further confidence in the data (Hagan and McCarthy 1992). As well, the relatively low reporting of abuse within the homeless sample suggests that the findings are not adversely affected by a retrospective inflating of abuse. For example, although 60 percent of homeless youth reported that a parent had hit them with enough force to cause a bruise or bleeding, only 17 percent said that this happened more than twice. Moreover, only 6 percent of this sample reported that they were sexually abused. Nonetheless, the results of this study should be viewed with the same degree of caution usually accorded self-reported retrospective data collected from volunteer samples: they should be viewed as provisional rather than as definitive.

The combined school and street sample includes 952 youth. For the analysis that follows, we have weighted this sample back to an estimated population of Toronto school and street youth. In 1988 there were approximately 150,000 youth attending public and private schools in Toronto. "Expert estimates" by representatives from nine street agencies included in this study indicate that the population of comparable street youth in Toronto is between 10,000 and 20,000. This is consistent with a recently published account that reports that there are "12,000 hard-core street kids who make downtown Toronto their home" (Kelly 1988: A4; see also Toronto Star, July 13, 1985:A1; April 30, 1987:B1). Our conservative estimate is that over the approximate year of the study, for every twenty youth in school in Toronto, there was one on the street; in other words, we use a population estimate of 7,500 for homeless youth. We use the ratio of twenty to one to weight our stratified sample back to the population of adolescents in Toronto.[2]

The Analysis

The analysis we present seeks to make explicit the relationship between the use of coercive sanctions by the family and the state. The core of the model we examine asserts a causal sequence in which parental child abuse leads youth to the streets, which in turn causes delinquent behavior on the street and leads to police sanctioning.[3] The implication of this model is that state sanctions are imposed on the victims rather than the perpetrators of family violence. However, before this implication is drawn, it is necessary to establish that the core relationships asserted by this model hold and that they are not altered by taking into account the effects of other correlated variables that may render the core paths in our causal framework spurious.

Descriptive information on the observed variables included in our analysis is presented in Table 12.1. Symbols used to represent these variables are presented in the first column of this table, followed by brief item descriptions and means and standard deviations for the unweighted combined sample and the separate street and school samples.

The first set of observed variables consists of exogenous factors that might predetermine relationships between the core variables in our causal model. These exogenous variables include age, gender, unemployment of family head, and intactness of family of origin. As expected, on average and compared to school youth, the street youth are disproportionately older, male, and from families that have an unemployed head and are not intact (i.e., one or more biological parent has left). It is possible, if not likely, that street youth are more prone to police sanctioning because they have these background characteristics rather than because they are abused or on the street. We assess this possibility in the multivariate analysis presented below.

The first of the observed endogenous variables in the core of our causal model are our measures of physical child abuse. These variables consist of responses to (1) an open-ended question asking the respondent to describe problems s/he experienced at home and (2) a more direct question asking whether s/he had ever been struck so hard by a parent or guardian as to cause a bruise or bleeding. We recognize that the restriction of these items to physical forms of child abuse ignores sexual and other forms of psychological abuse that are also in need of study; however, our goal is to reduce definitional uncertainty about the kind of abuse being studied. As in past research, the street youth in this study are more strongly represented on both of the physical abuse measures. Further issues associated with the measurement of abuse are addressed below.

The next set of observed variables consists of two measures of homelessness: whether the respondent was currently living away from home and how often the respondent reported having left home in the past. These measures are intended to reflect the fact that homelessness can be a transitory state, perhaps often very brief and less often of long duration. Note that in Toronto leaving home is *not* an offense for adolescents age 16 and over. Consequently, we define youth who leave home as "homeless" (since they are) and not "runaways" (since this is often a misnomer). The stratification of our sample guaranteed that a large portion of our sample (about 40 percent) would be currently homeless, but some school youth also reported having left home in the past.

A third set of endogenous observed variables consists of two summed measures of "common" and "serious" delinquency. Past research on delinquency suggests that most "common" delinquency involves little threat to persons and property, while some less frequent forms of

TABLE 12.1 Coding and Descriptive Statistics for Variables, by Type of Youth

Variable	Coding	Full Sample (n = 952) Mean (SD)	School Youth (n = 562) Mean (SD)	Street Youth (n = 390) Mean (SD)
ε_1 Age				
x_1 Reported age	Years	17.027 (1.460)	16.632 (1.326)	17.597 (1.457)
ε_2 Gender				
x_2 Reported sex	Dummy coded Male = 1	.544 (.498)	.458 (.499)	.667 (.472)
ε_3 Unemployed head				
x_3 Reported unemployment	Dummy coded Unemployed = 1	.043 (.203)	.021 (.145)	.074 (.263)
ε_4 Family intact				
x_4 Reported family	Dummy coded Intact = 1	.442 (.498)	.718 (.451)	.313 (.464)
n_1 Child abuse				
y_1 "Have you ever been intentionally struck so hard by a parent or guardian that it caused bruise or bleeding?"	0–4[a]	.737 (1.079)	.409 (.824)	1.210 (1.220)
y_2 Voluntarily described familial physical abuse	Dummy coded Abuse = 1	.098 (.297)	.027 (.161)	.200 (.401)
n_2 Homelessness				
y_3 Currently Homeless	Dummy coded Homeless = 1	.410 (.936)		
y_4 "Have you ever run away from home and stayed overnight?"	0–5[b]	.996 (1.335)	.263 (.676)	2.054 (1.341)
n_3 Delinquent behavior				
y_5 Common delinquency	0–5[c]	1.164 (2.205)	1.467 (1.926)	3.169 (2.197)
y_6 Serious delinquency	0–5[d]	1.037 (1.882)	.387 (1.193)	1.974 (2.263)
n_4 Police sanctions				
y_7 "How often, if ever, have you been picked up by the police?"	0–5[e]	1.044 (1.782)	.206 (.757)	2.254 (2.112)
y_8 "How often, if every, have you been charged by the police?"	0–5[e]	.684 (.496)	.066 (.374)	1.577 (1.981)

[a] For street youth, coded as never (0); once or twice (1); sometimes (2); often (3); always (4). For youth at home, coded as never (0); once or twice (1); three to nine (2); ten to nineteen (3); twenty or more (4).

[b] Coded as never (0); one to two (1); three to four (2); five to nine (3); ten to nineteen (4); twenty or more (5).

Double Jeopardy 205

delinquency are more "serious" in the sense of presenting greater threats to persons and property. The former kinds of delinquent behavior are represented in six items included in a scale developed by Hirschi (1969) and the second in a scale of four items developed by Hindelang, Hirschi and Weis (1981: 220). Our measures of street youth delinquency are limited to events that took place since leaving home, and our measures of delinquency among school youth are restricted to those events that occurred in the year prior to the survey. We restricted our measure of delinquency to the last year for school youth to make their reports correspond as closely as possible to the street youth, close to half of whom have been on the street less than a year. Street youth score higher on both scales than school youth. To assure that our street sample results were not biased by including homeless youth who were on the street longer than the reporting period for school youth, we estimated two additional models like that reported below. In the first model the homeless sample was restricted to those youth who were on the street one year or less (this reduced the street sample from 390 to 187); in the second model, we used a measure of crime for school youth based on responses to questions that asked if they had *ever* participated in the activity. The results from estimating these models are strikingly similar to those reported below and are available on request.

The final set of observed variables consists of measures of police sanctioning, which ask about being picked up and charged by the police. Again, school youth measures are restricted to the year preceding the survey, and street youth measures are limited to the period since leaving

---

[c] The scale was constructed from items asking how often youths had done these things: (1) Not counting fights with brothers or sisters, beaten up someone on purpose? (2) Taken things worth less than $5 that didn't belong to you? (3) Taken things worth over $50 that didn't belong to you? (4) Taken family member's car for a ride without permission? (5) Banged up something that didn't belong to you? The responses were coded as: never (0); once (1); twice (2); three times (3); four times (4); five or more times (5). For school youth, these refer to events that occurred in the past year. For street youth, they refer to events that have occurred since leaving home.

[d] The scale was constructed from items asking how often youths had done these things: (1) Taken a car belonging to someone you didn't know for a ride without the owner's permission? (2) Taken things from a store worth more than $50? (3) Taken things from a car (tape deck, etc.)? and (4) Broken into a house or building and taken something? The responses were coded as never (0); once (1); twice (2); three times (3); four times (4); five or more times (5). For school youth, these refer to events that ocurred in the past year. For street youth, they refer to events that have occurred since leaving home.

[e] The responses were coded as never (0); once (1); twice (2); three times (3); four times (4); five or more times (5). For school youth, these refer to events that occurred in the past year. For street youth, they refer to events that have occurred since leaving home.

home. As is the case with delinquency, street youth score higher on this scale than school youth. Police sanctioning is the ultimate endogenous outcome variable in our analysis.

The statistical method we use to explore the causal model introduced above is known as LISREL, a program developed to estimate relationships among sets of manifest or observed variables in terms of a typically smaller number of latent or unobserved variables (Joreskog and Sorbom 1985).

Results

The causal model we initially test involves the twelve observed variables and eight unobserved concepts described in Table 12.1 and is identical to the model presented in Figure 12.1, if causal arrows are added between child abuse and delinquent behavior and police sanctions respectively. We will refer to this as Model A. This model posits a causal sequence among its endogenous variables in which physical child abuse leads to homelessness and directly and indirectly to delinquent behavior and police sanctions. Note that the sanctions posited here are applied not to parents who have imposed the physical abuse but to the adolescents who are the victims of this abuse and who are involved in subsequent delinquent behavior. Meanwhile the exogenous variables (age, gender, unemployed family head, and family intactness) in Model A all directly influence abuse and homelessness, and age and gender directly influence delinquent behavior. These exogenous variables are added to the model to control for plausible spurious sources of influence that otherwise would be attributed to the endogenous variables, most notably abuse and homelessness.

Overall, the proposed model (Model A) satisfies many of the fit and specification requirements demanded of structural equation models. The model's Chi-square (140.46) is statistically significant beyond the .001 level, which is not surprising given the sensitivity of chi-square to large samples. With a sizeable sample, a significant Chi square does not necessarily mean that the theoretical model poorly fits the observed data. Rather, in such samples small differences are detectable as being more than mere sampling fluctuations (Joreskog and Sorbom 1985). To adjust for this problem, Joreskog (1973) suggests dividing Chi square by the degrees of freedom. Wheaton et al. (1977) propose that a Chi square five times the degrees of freedom is adequate, while Carmines and McIver (1981) suggest that two or three times is more acceptable. The ratio for Model A is between four and five.

The LISREL program encourages model modification. The first modification we make to our model involves four pairs of correlated error

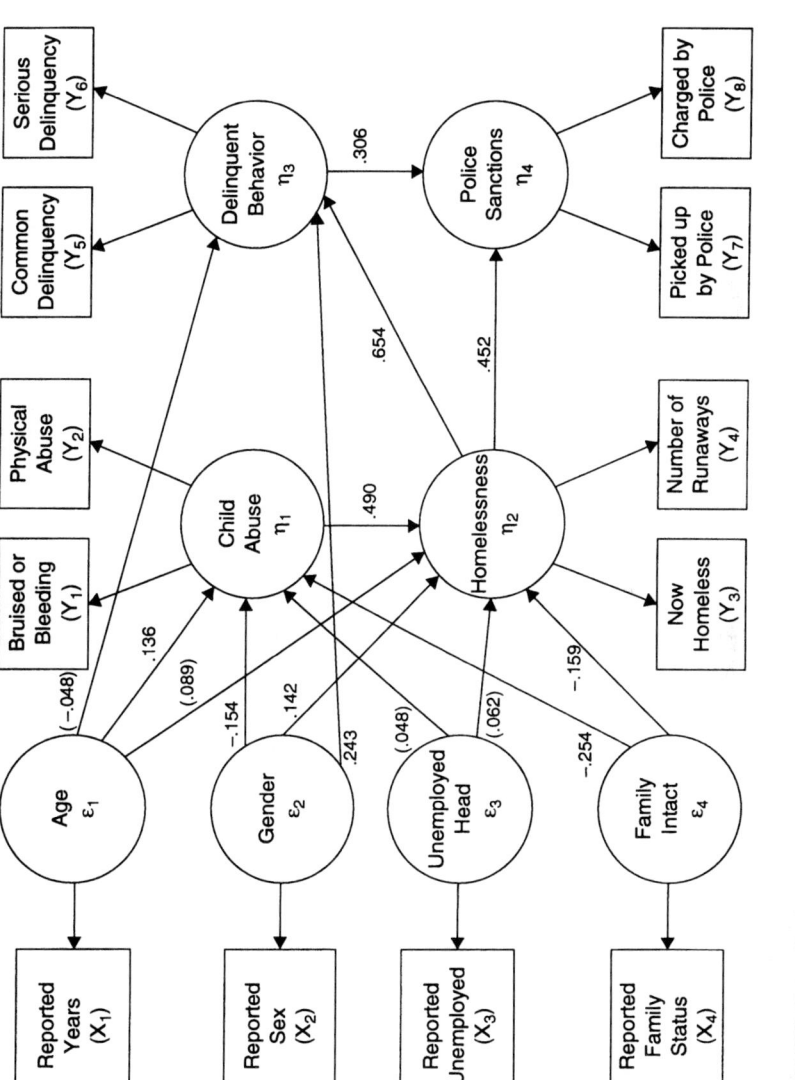

FIGURE 12.1 Revised model with standardized effects (paths with coefficients in parentheses are included in estimated model but are statistically non-significant; other reported effects are significant at .05 level)

terms between homelessness and common delinquency, serious delinquency and arrest, and between serious delinquency and arrest. This does not seem unreasonable. While we postulate that homelessness is a direct cause of common and serious delinquency and arrest, and that involvement in serious delinquency leads to arrest, it also seems likely that these variables share other causes in common beyond those introduced in our model. Including these correlated error terms significantly reduces the chi-square value of Model B (56.08) and reduces the chi-square/degrees of freedom ratio to less than two.

The next modification that we introduce in Model C concerns the relationship between child abuse and delinquency. Much of the literature on child abuse implies that there is a strong positive and direct causal effect of child abuse on various types of deviant behavior, including delinquency (Hunner and Walker 1981; Cohen and Densen-Gerber 1982; Lynch and Roberts 1982; Silbert and Pines 1982). However, it may also be that this effect is entirely indirect, operating through the desperation that results from leaving abusive homes and taking to the streets. To date, the research literature largely has been reduced to assessing the effects of abuse within homeless populations, which is a faulty foundation for causal inferences. To more adequately test the significance of a direct effect of child abuse on delinquency, we specify the effect of child abuse on delinquency in Model C as operating entirely indirectly through homelessness. Model C increases the degrees of freedom by one, but it does not significantly increase the Chi-square value (56.31). Apparently physical child abuse does not have a significant direct effect on delinquency. To put it differently, we can reject the hypothesis that Model B with this direct effect is a statistically significant improvement over Model C without it. We further consider the indirect effect of child abuse on delinquency below.

Another modification assesses an effect postulated in much work on the relationship between legal sanctioning and criminal and other kinds of behavior defined as disreputable. Specifically, a number of writers (Foote 1956; Chambliss 1964; Hay et al. 1975; Thompson 1975) observe that the criminal law often is used to sanction individuals for being in disreputable conditions apart from actual involvement in crime. Vagrancy laws have often been used in this way. If this is the case in the current setting, homelessness should directly effect police sanctioning, apart from any indirect effect that operates through delinquent behavior. To test the significance of such a direct effect, we delete this direct path in the estimation of Model D. The result is an increase of one degree of freedom and a jump in the Chi square of 44.05. This indicates that being homeless directly leads to police sanctioning, aside from involvement in delinquency and other variables operating in the model.

A final attempt to improve the fit of our model to the observed data involves restoring the direct effect of homelessness on police sanctions while removing the effect of child abuse on police sanctions. Recall that the latter sanctions are imposed on adolescents, not their abusive parents. There is no particular reason to assume that such abuse, in itself, should lead directly to police sanctions. Certainly our thesis is not that the police intentionally seek to punish the victims of this problem. Rather, the police indirectly do so in response to the homelessness and delinquency that results in sequence from the abuse of these youth. So in model E we delete the direct effect of physical child abuse on police sanctions.

The appropriate comparison to assess this modification is between Models C and E. The change results in an increase of one degree of freedom and only a minor change in the value of Chi square (from 56.31 to 59.90). Overall, this model fits the observed data well. The Chi-square value is less than two, the goodness of fit index is .99, and only one standardized residual is greater than one. Perhaps most important, the model makes substantive sense.

Having established a model that fits our observed data well, we can turn finally to estimates of causal effects, as summarized in Figure 12.1. All effects discussed are significant at the .05 level or beyond.

We first consider effects of the exogenous control variables in this model. As expected, abuse mildly increases with age and more strongly reduces with family intactness. We did not know what if any relationship to expect between gender and abuse, but this relationship is mild and negative, indicating that girls report slightly more abuse than boys. Meanwhile, family intactness also reduces homelessness, while boys are more likely to be homeless than girls. Finally, gender has a strong positive effect on delinquent behavior, indicating that boys are much more heavily involved in this behavior than girls. The remaining exogenous effects are nonsignificant, and those significant exogenous effects we have reported are taken into account in the estimation of the endogenous influences we report next.

As expected, physical abuse has a strong positive effect on homelessness; homelessness has a strong positive effect on delinquent behavior; and both homelessness and delinquent behavior have strong positive effects on police sanctions. This set of effects offers substantial support for the argument that physical child abuse is associated with delinquency through an indirect causal sequence that involves the adolescents in question being pushed out of the home and that ultimately results in these adolescent victims themselves often becoming offenders and subject to police sanctions. If there is a further surprise in these findings, it is that these adolescents are subject to police sanctioning not just because they may become involved in delinquency but also as a result of being homeless in and of itself. In either case the law responds to the symptoms rather than to the causes of child abuse and homelessness among young people. In neither case are the causes of physical child abuse addressed or their perpetrators santioned.

Discussion and Conclusion

We have conceptualized the context of parental violence against children as involving a linkage between family and state sanctioning. In doing so we have argued that parental use of force can be viewed as a form of social sanctioning that is imposed to control parentally defined deviant behavior within the family. State-based legal sanctions are presumed to control the use of forceful sanctions within the family. However, norms of legitimacy and privacy historically and presently restrict the use of state sanctions for this purpose, making the state control of parental maltreatment infrequent and ineffectual. Meanwhile, state-based legal sanctions frequently are used to control the delinquent behaviors of children who are pushed out of abusive homes and onto the street.

More specifically, our research demonstrates an indirect causal link between the family sanctions involved in the abuse of children and the state sanctions involved in the policing of adolescents. This link is misguided in that its consequence is to punish the victims rather than the perpetrators of parental child abuse. Our study suggests that parental maltreatment leads youth to leave home and take to the streets, where they encounter police sanctions for being homeless as well as for the delinquent behavior that sometimes follows from homelessness. This link between family and state sanctions is illegitimate in that it places abused youth in double jeopardy. This response to the conditions and consequences of homelessness among adolescents is inefficient in responding to the symptoms rather than the causes of adolescent homelessness and is unjust in punishing the victims rather than the perpetrators of the parental child abuse that often underlies this social problem.

Notes

1. The order of authorship is alphabetized and does not reflect seniority or priority. This research was made possible by a grant from the Social Sciences and Humanities Research Council of Canada.

2. Obviously, our approach involves sampling on an endogenous variable, a reasonable approach when standard sampling practices fail to provide a sufficient representation of a rare but important category of an endogenous variable, here, adolescent homelessness (see Xie and Manski 1989). In other analyses (Hagan and McCarthy 1992), we use weighted maximum likelihood estimates of

logit response functions, with the response and residual samples weighted in proportion to their representation in the general population. The results of these analyses indicate that weighting the sample produces little substantive difference in results. Although the estimation technique used in this paper does not lend itself to logit response functions for sampling corrections, widely varying the specific weights also failed to noticeably alter the findings.

3. This sequence seems reasonable, given the findings of previous research. The child abuse literature indicates that parental use of force most often begins in early childhood (Strauss et al. 1980; Wilson et al. 1980; Wilson and Daly 1987). Delinquency research (e.g., Hirschi and Gottfredson 1983), in contrast, affirms that participation in delinquency is most often delayed until adolescence.

PART FIVE
Human Agency

13

Eugenics, Class, and the Professionalization of Social Control

Nicole Hahn Rafter

This paper analyzes the social origins of the U.S. eugenics movement, which advocated prevention of reproduction as a means of bringing the "unfit" under control. I will be conceptualizing social control as a process that generates knowledge about social problems as well as sets of regulations, and I will be focusing on situational factors that prompted eugenicists to undertake their campaigns against the unfit. Drawing on the professionalization thesis advanced by recent histories of deviance and social control, I will suggest that the professionalization of social control work helps account for both the class content of eugenics doctrine and the movement's extraordinary success.

In what follows, after briefly summarizing the U.S. eugenics movement, I review what we already know about its social origins, arguing that currently available accounts fail to explain why a specific group ("social control workers") was primarily responsible for the production, dissemination, and application of eugenics theory. I reason that professionalization of the type of work in which members of this group were engaged (social control itself) does much to explain their involvement in eugenics. The professionalization of social control and the production of eugenics theory were interdependent and mutually supportive phenomena: social control workers used eugenics as a vehicle for professionalization, and the movement triumphed partly because it was backed by social control workers who could implement its recommendations.

The U.S. Eugenics Movement

In the United States, the eugenics movement started in the 1870s, peaked in popularity about 1910, and began losing credibility about

1920.[1] Past historians sometimes dismissed eugenics as a fad that attracted only a few ultra-conservative crackpots and had little impact on actual social policies. *Conscience and Convenience* (Rothman 1980), the standard history of early twentieth-century criminal justice policies, mentions eugenics only in passing. But, as other historians have shown, liberals and socialists as well as right-wing racists endorsed eugenics (Haller 1963; Pickens 1968; Jenkins 1982; Kevles 1985), and eugenicists profoundly affected the lives of those they deemed unfit (Gould 1985; Noll 1990, forthcoming; Reilly 1991; Rafter 1992a). Eugenicists not only biologized class relationships; they also imposed a form of social control rarely achieved, the prevention of reproduction.

Eugenicists somaticized inequality in a period when workers were mobilizing a strong socialist movement, women and emancipated blacks were entering the paid work force in significant numbers, and immigrants were flooding American shores. Rates of unemployment and crime shot up in the wake of the Civil War; economic depressions spread severe poverty even among the employed. Alarmed by these threats to stability and traditional values, eugenicists drew on nineteenth-century interpretations of evolution and heredity, concluding that socially problematic groups must be biologically unfit. They did not question the heredity of the industrial magnates on whom they relied for funds (Haller 1963; Hahn 1980; Kevles 1985; Allen 1986), but their ideal was the middle-class professional whose good works demonstrated inherent worthiness.

For eugenicists, one of the surest signs of healthy heredity was "intelligence": the fit were bright, energetic achievers like themselves. After decades of estimating intelligence by informal methods, they found a seemingly more scientific method in Binet-testing, introduced by eugenicist Henry H. Goddard (1910). Goddard's mental tests, with their poorly standardized scales, overly difficult questions, and generous definitions of intellectual subnormality (Terman 1912; Sarason and Doris 1969; Gould 1981), provided eugenicists with a high-powered tool for identifying the unfit.

Eugenicists equated the "unfit" with those whom they and other social scientists also called "the dependent, defective, and delinquent classes" (e.g., U.S. Department of the Interior 1883; Henderson 1893). Turn-of-the-century Americans did not clearly distinguish these three groups. Indeed, they believed that *dependents* (paupers), *defectives* (the mentally retarded, the insane, and others whose diseases seemed constitutional), and *delinquents* (criminals, wayward children, and loose women) were interrelated through the common denominator of bad heredity or "degeneration."

Degeneration theory offered the most plausible nineteenth-century account of the nature and transmission of social problems (Nye 1984; Chamberlin and Gilman 1985; Pick 1989). Degenerationists conceived of bad heredity as a kind of inner rot that could manifest itself in any number of forms: one family member might be an imbecile, others paupers, insane, or criminal. The outward expression mattered little; much more important was the apparent fact that the unfit passed their degenerative tendency on to subsequent generations through their "blood," or germinal matter. In the degenerationist view, dependents, defectives, and delinquents formed an unholy trinity, seamlessly allied (e.g., Dugdale 1877). The first eugenicists shared this belief (Lowell 1879; Reynolds 1879). Like other degenerationists, they considered the poor to be next-of-kin to—indeed, interchangeable with—other problem groups. Degenerationism gave eugenicists the hereditarian theory on which they based their doctrine of class inequality.

Eugenicists developed a number of policies to prevent the unfit from multiplying. Some lobbied for the immigration restriction legislation that eventually limited the influx of swarthy skinned foreigners from southern and eastern Europe. Others endorsed coercive sterilization, a method that was used into the 1960s and resulted in the "desexualization" of at least 60,000 men and women (especially women, during some decades) (Reilly 1991). A third and much more popular measure was prophylactic institutionalization—incarcerating the unfit through their reproductive years. Eugenicists utilized this third tactic most extensively with the "feeble minded" (mentally retarded), whom they regarded as both a prolific source of degenerate germ plasm and inherently criminalistic. Institutions for the feeble minded, most of them superintended by eugenicists, expanded in number and size during the late nineteenth and early twentieth centuries (Fernald 1917; Tyor and Bell 1984). The vast majority of their inmates came from poor families, and many were the feeble-minded women whom eugenicists considered a particularly fertile source of defective progeny (Neff 1910; Kuhlmann 1916; Tyor 1977; Rafter 1992a).

In addition to developing policies to reduce the ranks of the unfit, eugenicists worked at reforming the criminal justice system. Their concept of degeneration meshed well with the nascent medical interpretation of criminality as a biological sickness or abnormality. Eugenicists promoted their constitutional version of the so-called medical model of deviance (Conrad and Schneider 1980) by endorsing first criminal anthropology and, after 1910, the enormously popular theory of defective delinquency, according to which criminals break the law because they are too feeble minded to restrain their primitive instincts (e.g., Hart 1912). Eugenicists introduced court "clinics" and prison "laboratories" where offenders were classified by biological condition (Anderson 1914–1915; Fernald

1917). In several states, they established institutions for defective delinquents, prisons where inmates' fixed sentences automatically became prophylactic, up-to-life terms (Branham 1926; Gordon and Harris 1950; Hahn 1978).

Eugenicists' greatest achievements lie in areas that cannot be quantified. Applying the *parens patriae* concept to adults—full-grown "morons," criminals who flunked intelligence tests, prostitutes—they championed justifications for state intervention that subsequent generations took for granted. They defined a new type of "dangerous individual" (Foucault 1988), the lawbreaker who repeatedly commits minor crimes or is only a potential offender, a criminal without crime (e.g., Fernald 1909–1910). As Garland (1985: 142) points out with regard to British eugenics, although "the eugenics programme soon disappeared from respectable political discourse, it did not disappear without a trace. Many of its strategies, techniques and proposals were in fact to become inscribed in the new complex of social and penal regulation," our modern system of regulation by experts. And eugenicists legitimated assumptions about what makes people good and bad, valuable or worthless, that still have currency. Present-day attitudes toward welfare mothers, for example, echo the eugenic belief that feeble-minded women automatically bear numerous unfit children, and our new genetic and reproductive technologies are often applied to cases that turn-of-the-century eugenicists, too, would have deemed unfit (Miringoff 1991).

The eugenics movement, then, constituted an important chapter in the history of social control, giving us a highly articulated theory of the origins of social problems, techniques for improving the nation's health, and potent images of good and evil. Why did it flourish in the late nineteenth and early twentieth centuries?

Explanatory Frameworks for Eugenics

We have some fairly good general answers to the question of why eugenics thrived in the United States between 1870 and 1930. This was a period of profound shifts in the social class structure. The nation developed a large underclass at one end of the spectrum and an elite of wealthy industrialists at the other. Urbanization, industrialization, and immigration also upset the old order, in which members of the middle class had enjoyed status by virtue of who they were. At times, in fact, class warfare threatened to eliminate traditional middle-class privileges entirely. Hofstadter (1955) describes the middle-class predicament in terms of a "status upheaval" that left its members overshadowed by the new corporate millionaires, deprived of their old prerogatives and anxious to preserve their respectability. They began searching for a new basis on which to rebuild their authority and prestige.

Members of the traditional middle class reestablished their position partly by participating in the multipronged reform efforts that began after the Civil War and became known as "progressive."[2] Grappling with the forces of disruption, they instituted changes that made government more "scientific" and "efficient"—and left them in charge. As they became progressives, they also became professionals—those who, by virtue of their specialized knowledge, are entitled to supervise others. Whereas Hofstadter (1955) views progressivism in part as a middle-class attempt to regain lost status, Wiebe (1967: 111–113) emphasizes the "strong professional aspirations" that characterized the "new middle class," the ways that "identification by . . . their skills gave them the deference of their neighbors." In his interpretation, the old middle class did not merely react but actively "transcended" the past by becoming progressive. Whichever perspective we prefer, it is clear that middle-class membership now had to be earned; that it could be earned through professionalization; and that middle-class professionals led both the eugenics movement and related progressive reforms, introducing innovative methods of social and cultural control (Bledstein 1976).

Much as postbellum shifts in the class structure help explain why inequality and social control became major middle-class concerns, so too do Darwinism and degeneration theory help explain why those middle-class progressives who became eugenicists pitched their reforms on hereditarian foundations. To many, Darwin's theory suggested that humans had evolved from lower to higher, from a savage to a civilized state. It followed that criminals, imbeciles, and other uncivilized types must constitute primitive forms of life, unfit for advanced society. Degeneration theory, in turn, accounted for the apparently protean and hereditary nature of social problems. From Darwinism and degeneration theory, some nineteenth-century reformers took the short step to formulating a program to eliminate the unfit.[3] What they knew about evolution and heredity indicated that society would be well served by curbs on the reproduction of dependents, defectives, and delinquents.

These social-context factors—shifts in the social class structure and popular concepts of evolution and heredity—go far toward explaining the emergence and content of eugenics doctrine. Yet there remains a gap that they cannot fill. The problem is this: since 1963, when Haller published the first contemporary study of eugenics, we have known that the movement was led by a highly specific group. It did, of course, attract a variety of adherents, including geneticists (Ludmerer 1972), university presidents and professors, women involved in social purity campaigns (Gordon 1977), and politicians such as Theodore Roosevelt. But the movement was spearheaded by an alliance of criminologists, institutional superintendents, penologists, psychiatrists, psychologists, and social workers (Haller 1963: 5, 25–26).

Whereas many members of the middle class endorsed eugenics, these particular men and women *generated* it. They did not merely join forces with the eugenics movement; to a large degree, they *were* that movement. Why did they, and not some other group such as politicians or academics, form the movement's backbone? To my knowledge, none of the secondary literature on U.S. eugenics even poses this question (but see, with regard to English eugenics, Garland 1985).

We cannot answer the question without finding a way to conceptualize and designate this group. We might call its members "charity" or "social welfare" workers (Trattner 1986). However, "social control" workers better reflects their own conception of their work. Moreover, because "social control" is a somewhat broader term than "charity" or "welfare," it can encompass the intelligence testers and criminal anthropologists whose work related only tangentially to philanthropy and social welfare but who were nonetheless influential eugenicists. Finally, the label "social control" links these key eugenicists with the philosophy of *Social Control*, a book that Edward A. Ross, the nation's most respected sociologist, published in 1901. Ross's recommendations for steps that an industrial mass society should take to maintain order were widely read by his contemporaries and expressed convictions that many of them shared.[4]

We might hypothesize that social control workers formed the generative core of the eugenics movement because many of them worked closely with dependents, defectives, and delinquents. But that answer begs the question by assuming that they would have discovered unfitness in their charges. Conceivably, close association might have made them *more* tolerant of the feeble minded, the poor, and even the criminal. Earlier, it did: before the eugenics movement began, those responsible for problem populations demonstrated considerable sympathy for their charges (e.g., Backus 1846, 1847). But social control specialists, unlike their untrained and minimally skilled predecessors, were engaged not only in managing deviants but also in professionalizing their work.

The Professionalization of Social Control Work

Some historians argue that when professional groups generated hereditarian theory, the result (if not the conscious aim) was to strengthen their claims to expertise in social problems. With varying degrees of emphasis, this professionalization thesis appears in much of the recent literature on eugenics. But it has not yet been articulated so as to specify the role played by professional interests in the sponsorship of eugenics by American social control specialists.

Foucault and Dowbiggin make the professionalization argument in histories of psychiatry, with Foucault (1988: 133–134) arguing that nineteenth-century psychiatrists pathologized the criminal body to secure and justify a new "modality of power," authority over public hygiene. Psychiatry desired "not . . . to take over criminality, but . . . to justify its [own] functions: the control of the dangers hidden in human behavior" (Foucault 1988: 135). Dowbiggin (1991: 6) claims that "the nineteenth-century French psychiatric fondness for the theory of hereditary degeneracy largely derived from the attempt to solve professional difficulties" such as lack of a set body of knowledge and accepted therapeutic practices.[5]

Varying the professionalization thesis, MacKenzie (1981: 12) explains the intersection of the development of statistics with the British eugenics movement by contending that the "shape" of English statisticians' "science . . . was partially determined by eugenic objectives." Perhaps due to the nature of the profession he analyzes, MacKenzie's view of the link between professionalization and hereditarianism is less instrumentalist than that of Foucault and Dowbiggin. He interprets statisticians' attraction to eugenics in terms of cultural authority and social values: "The rationale of professionalisation is to give an occupation special status by implying that its work is based on its accredited possession of a body of systematic knowledge" (MacKenzie 1981: 27). According to MacKenzie, eugenics appealed to professionals because it taught that "social position was (or at least should be) the consequence of individual mental ability. There was a natural hierarchy of talent which could be translated into a social hierarchy of occupations. At the top were the professions. . . . For the old criteria of wealth and honor it [eugenics] substituted mental ability" (MacKenzie 1981: 29).

In *Punishment and Welfare* (1985), David Garland took the important step of extending the professionalization thesis to social control work itself. Before publication of this book, it was difficult to conceptualize the relationship of professionalization to eugenics because most professionalization studies had focused on a single type of work (psychiatry, social work, statistics). Eugenics never became a distinct discipline (Proctor 1981), nor did eugenicists fit into a single occupational category. Garland observed the rise of a new type of expert who, *irrespective* of training or title, produced knowledge about the unfit. Combining instrumentalist with cultural explanations, moreover, he pointed out that eugenics "ensured the advancement and promotion of a cadre of administrators, experts and intellectuals and the professional middle class from which they were drawn" (Garland 1985: 152). In short, Garland tied the emergence of those whom I call social control workers to the emergence of the professional middle class. Garland focuses on Britain, but as I showed earlier, in the United States, too, the appearance of the social control occupations was linked to the rise of the professional middle class.

These histories establish theoretical groundwork for positing the professionalization of social control work as one source of eugenic ideas. However, they do little to specify the nature of that relationship. In the next section, I try to map out the relationship as it developed in the United States.

Eugenics and the Professionalization of Social Control

Eugenics offered practical solutions to problems with which social control workers struggled daily in their encounters with dependents, defectives, and delinquents. It also helped them deal with dilemmas they faced as members of newly forming occupations. Eugenics provided a coherent explanation of social problems (the "unfit") and a program for solving those problems (prevention of reproduction). It gave institutional superintendents, criminologists, mental testers, and psychiatrists a rationale for expanding their domains of authority. In eugenics theory, those who attempted to rehabilitate deviants found an explanation for why some individuals could not be reformed. Eugenics supplied a research methodology favored by social control specialists, genealogical investigations of degenerate families such as the Kallikaks (Goddard 1912) and the Hill Folk (Danielson and Davenport 1912). It created a need for experts who could identify the unfit and decipher the world in terms of heredity. By affiliating with eugenics, social control workers could establish themselves as members of the eugenic aristocracy and ultimate authorities on social matters. Intelligence testing, for instance, not only identified the unfit; it also confirmed the testers' intelligence.

The relationship was reciprocal—the professionalization of social control work in turn promoted eugenics. By demonstrating the ability of experts to govern, social control specialists reinforced the eugenic equation of the middle class with the fit. The more professional they were, the greater the eugenics movement's prestige and cultural authority. More practically, the meetings and journals of the control specialists' new professional associations disseminated eugenics doctrine. As professionals, social control workers could identify the unfit; they could also establish and operate institutions that would prevent degenerates from breeding.

Although I have been separating the professionalization of social control and the production of eugenics discourse for analytical purposes, in practice they were indistinguishable. Their symbiosis occurred spontaneously, a result of control workers' involvement with deviants and their occupations' immaturity (for a related argument, see Brown 1992). Eugenics did not "cause" the professionalization of social control work (after all, at the time numerous occupations were professionalizing), but it did promote it. The professionalization of social control did not, in and of itself, "cause" eugenics, but it contributed forcefully to the movement's growth and success. This conjunction of interests and reciprocity of influence helps explain why a specific group led the movement, why the movement succeeded, and why it equated the fit with the middle class. Eugenics naturally enshrined middle-class professionals: it was produced by them. The plutocrats who became the movement's patrons signed on to identify themselves with the professionals who constituted the eugenic elite.

Social control specialists seldom became full professionals in the sense of monopolizing the markets for their skills or tightly regulating access to their occupations.[6] Indeed, there is no reason to think that these aims, although pursued by contemporary lawyers and physicians, held much interest for the majority of them. Yet social control workers adopted many facets of the professional model. Negotiating new roles in the division of labor, they developed careers that (in contrast to the mere jobs of, for example, mid-nineteenth century prison custodians and poorhouse keepers) conferred social status, confirmed middle-class standing, and involved a sense of calling and personal commitment. They established workplace organizations that gave their occupations identity, goals, and means to disseminate information. They legitimated the claim "to know better than their clients what ails them" that, in the words of Everett Hughes (1965: 2), "is the essence of the professional idea." And—yet another index of professionalism—they produced knowledge: records, reports, research, policy recommendations.

That practitioners, as many of these social control specialists were, produce authoritative information about social problems may seem peculiar, for we are accustomed to distinguishing those who apply knowledge from those who generate it. During the period under consideration, however, there was as yet no clear distinction between practitioners and the academics who became the "true" social scientists. The issue of the nature of social science was debated well into the twentieth century (Furner 1975; Haskell 1977; Cravens 1985; Brown and van Keuren 1991; Ross 1991; Brown 1992; Rafter 1992b). Social control work drew from both "the field" and the university; those who advanced knowledge in the area of social control often combined the roles of reformer and researcher. Katharine B. Davis, for instance, was an innovative prison administrator *and* a pioneer in the mental testing of criminals (Fitzpatrick 1990; Rafter 1990). The groups later distinguished as "applied" and "pure" social scientists were both professionalizing; neither was as yet clear about their relationship, relative status, or task differences. Practitioners could help lead the eugenics movement precisely because they had not yet been relegated to a secondary position in terms of "capacity" to produce creditable data. Thus they could, with authority, generate eugenic information.

For social control specialists as for other occupational groups that began to scientize, standardize, and streamline their work in the late nineteenth century, professionalization was less a goal than a process. Those who professionalized social control did so in search of solutions to daily dilemmas—problems "on the job" (managing deviants) and problems "of the job" (establishing their types of work). Professionalization was a lengthy, broadly based endeavor, the ends and means of which were often unclear to participants. It was a "project" in the sense defined by Magali Larson (1977: 6): because it "emphasizes the coherence and consistence that can be discerned ex post facto in a variety of apparently disconnected acts." The social control workers who produced eugenics sometimes aimed self-consciously at what we perceive as professionalization; often they did not, even while contributing strongly to that result. Their involvement in eugenics was part of this largely undeliberate professionalization process.

While the production of eugenics and the professionalization of social control reinforced one another in the practical ways outlined earlier, the two processes were also joined at the cultural level, by the concept of altruism. In her sensitive study of Sir Francis Galton, the Englishman who coined the term eugenics, Cowan traces his eugenicism back to his desire to be helpful: through eugenics Galton hoped to be "'advantageous to future inhabitants of the earth'" (Cowan 1985: 53, quoting from *Hereditary Genius*). Other eugenicists, especially those who made careers as "professional altruists" (Lubove 1965), shared Galton's service ideal. They wanted to ensure the future health of their society and at the same time to demonstrate, through their benevolent behavior, the worthiness that other eugenicists recognized as a reliable sign of hereditary fitness. Altruism was also intrinsic to professionalism: to distinguish their work from other occupations, professionals need to demonstrate that they labor for a worthwhile cause, not money alone. Altruistic behavior, moreover, confirms "distinction" and middle-class standing (Bledstein 1976; Bourdieu 1984).

But altruism requires an object for its attention; there can be no altruism without an Other. "Altruism" in fact derives from *alter*, "other," in Latin. Social control specialists defined degenerates in ways that indicated all that they themselves were not. Constructing the unfit, they simultaneously constructed themselves as altruistic, fit and worthy. They elaborated these definitions until about 1920, when, with their occupations firmly established and the threat of lower-class insurrection fading, demonstrations of altruism began to seem less necessary. Gradually social control workers lost interest in eugenics.[7]

By recognizing the altruistic content of eugenics, we can avoid interpreting the doctrine in purely instrumentalist terms. It is certainly true that by facilely equating social classes with degrees of worthiness and by carelessly demanding the life incarceration and even death (McKim 1900) of threatening inferiors, eugenics practically begs for an instrumentalist interpretation. It is also true that eugenicists were deeply concerned with class control and, to a degree, realized it. But they achieved powers far more extensive and subtle than those of heavy-handed oppression. If we take the connections among altruism, professionalization, and social class into account, we can move beyond the self-interest explanation (itself facile and tinged with a Darwinian view of human struggles [for a related argument, see Ignatieff 1981]) to see that eugenicists achieved social control by establishing themselves as authorities, with powers to diagnose and treat individuals and society itself—by gaining the cultural legitimation that being expert confers. We can avoid casting eugenicists as mere villains and perhaps understand them and even learn from the ways they stumbled on the path of doing good (see also Rothman 1978).

Conclusion

I have proposed a way to account for the U.S. eugenics movement's leadership and phenomenal success. Had it not been promoted by social control specialists, the movement could scarcely have achieved so many of its goals. To completely understand why it flourished, we must of course place it in the context of middle-class defensiveness and hereditarian interpretations of social problems. We also need to acknowledge more peripheral factors, not mentioned above, such as eugenicists' ability to attract funding from the wealthy elite, the willingness of impoverished families to institutionalize retarded children, and prisoners' difficulties in resisting diagnoses of degeneracy. Nonetheless, a crucial (though previously little-noticed) element in the movement's success lay in its symbiotic relationship with the professionalization of the social control specialities.

Like other labels, the terms "eugenicists," "social control workers," and "professionalization" obscure individual differences, local variations, and contested processes. My purpose, however, has been not to present a picture of the eugenics movement in all its complexity but to theorize its social origins and success. Moreover, I suspect that historians will be unable to assemble full pictures of specific eugenics campaigns if they do not take the more general professionalization of social control work into account.

Notes

For helpful comments on earlier versions, I thank Kathleen Daly, Steven Noll, Alexandra Todd, and Diane Vaughan.

 1. Eugenics theory still has its advocates (see, e.g., Wattenberg 1987; Wilson 1989). Kevles (1985) and Proctor (1991) provide useful analyses of the resurgent

interest in eugenic issues. For critiques and warnings, see Miringoff (1991) and Neuhaus (1988).

2. Although historians usually treat progressivism as a phenomenon that started around the turn of the century, its characteristic managerial and scientific approach actually emerged decades earlier in the area of social control. On defining progressivism, see Rodgers (1982).

3. After 1900, when a version of inheritance based on the ideas of Weismann and Mendel came into vogue, eugenicists translated degeneration theory into Mendelian terms (e.g., Danielson and Davenport 1912). Mendelism gave eugenics theory an additional source of plausibility. However, aside from forcing eugenicists to abandon their earlier belief in the inheritance of acquired characteristics, Mendelism had little effect on their basic concepts.

4. On the respect accorded to Ross and *Social Control* (1901), see Weinberg (1972) and Bannister (1979). *Social Control* was reprinted ten times over the next quarter of a century.

5. For a critique of both positions, see Pick (1989).

6. The view of professions as autonomous and monopolistic, emphasized by Freidson (1988) and Larson (1977), has recently been challenged; see, in particular, Abbott (1988: 71), who distinguishes between dominant and subordinate professions, the latter having less-than-full jurisdiction. With the exception of psychiatry, no social control occupation in the United States has become a profession by the criterion of monopoly over markets, and it is unlikely that any will: the skills involved are not sufficiently arcane, and government plays too strong a regulatory role. Criteria such as monopolistic control and self-regulation are too constricting to be useful here for another reason: I am concerned with the evolution of professionalization rather than its end products.

7. The eugenics movement began later and lasted farther into the twentieth century in the South than the North and Midwest (Noll 1990, forthcoming), probably because the social control occupations professionalized later in that region. This explanation, if correct, would tend to confirm my hypothesis about the relationship between eugenics and the professionalization of social control work.

14

Children in the Therapeutic State: Lessons for the Sociology of Deviance and Social Control

John R. Sutton

This essay is not about children and their doings. Rather it is about the institutional process by which the troublesome child has been construed as a qualitatively distinct type of deviant in modern Western societies and about the implications of that process for theories about the role of inequality in the shaping of crime and social control. In adopting this focus, I intend to ignore the vast mass of conventional positivist, individual-level research on the causes and etiology of delinquent behavior. Work of this sort is uninteresting for our purposes because it takes for granted the very concepts that should be at issue—specifically, the socially constructed nature of childhood, delinquency, and deviance more generally. In the positivist tradition, childhood is treated as a natural phase of intense socialization, and delinquency is conceptualized as the violation of formal-legal precepts applicable to children. Inequality is operationalized as a set of individual attributes (SES, gender, race, IQ) that can be combined with other attributes (e.g., social bonds, association with delinquent peers, learning) to yield linear-additive models of the forces that compel young people to norm-violating behavior. These models are often elegant and, to a point, convincing precisely because they are circular and self-referential. If we want seriously to address the issues of inequality, deviance, and social control in terms of children, we must choose an approach that radically problematizes not only specific taxonomies and theories of delinquency but also the very notions of childhood as a natural phenomenon and of delinquency as a distinct and scientifically accountable form of behavior.

Thus in this essay the emphasis shifts from inner compulsion to what one might call the "opportunity structure" of delinquency. The term opportunity structure here refers to something much broader than the economic and cultural stratification systems discussed by Merton (1957) or Cloward and Ohlin (1960). It incorporates the range of institutions that encode human differences, sort individuals in terms of their social and legal statuses, and ascribe identities to them based on those statuses. In particular, I am concerned with the origins of those institutions and their impact on the life courses of individuals; my perspective, thus, is primarily historical and processual.

The issues of childhood and delinquency offer a privileged point of access to the broader issue of inequality and social control. Age grading is obviously one of the most highly codified, pervasive, and fateful forms of stratification in modern Western societies. Virtually every institution, from education and the labor market to courts and prisons, is fundamentally structured around age differences. The family has adapted to incorporate modern conceptions of childhood and the life cycle. Indeed Ariès (1962), the most influential early historian of family life, argues that the modern family exists *primarily* to embody a historically constructed conception of childhood as an extended period of vulnerability and dependence.

Recognition of the historical nature of childhood is fundamental to this discussion; but in another sense, to say that age influences everything is to say nothing. To place the issue of child control within the broader terrain of deviance and social control, I begin by describing two intellectual problems that are brought to the fore by a historical approach to delinquency. The first problem is a paradox: American policies toward children are notable for the degree to which they use formal, legal mechanisms to address forms of misbehavior that are mainly noncriminal and typically intrafamilial. In the mid- to late 1970s, much more so than today, the popular and policy literature was very much concerned with the "status offender," by which is meant a child who has committed no criminal act but who has violated some law—against running away or being out after curfew or being "incorrigible"—that applies only to minors. At about the same time, attention began to focus on the plight of neglected and abused children; this concern has not abated but has gradually grown to address the taboo subject of sexual abuse. Juvenile justice system data showed that Americans deployed a great deal of resources to punish a large number of children for defying, leaving, or being victimized by their parents. Historical research on the problem, including my own, showed that this problem was not new: policies of this sort could be traced back, through at least a nominal line of succession, to legislation in seventeenth-century Massachusetts Bay. From that time to the present—through the asylum reforms of the Jacksonian period and the Progressive-era juvenile court reforms to the decarceration reforms of the 1960s and 1970s—Americans have expressed their abiding concern for childhood by drawing increasingly invidious distinctions between the legal status of children and adults and by broadening the discretionary authority of officials to intervene in the family (Hawes 1973; Rothman 1971: ch. 9, 1980: ch. 6–8; Mennel 1973; Scull 1977; Sutton 1988). The paradox is not that these often well-intentioned reforms had inhumane results; that is an old story. The more important *theoretical* paradox is that this trend runs counter to hallowed expectations, running from Weber to Parsons and beyond about the increasing formal rationality of Western law. It also contradicts conventional ideas about American attitudes toward the family and obscures the cherished distinction between public and private spheres in American political discourse. This paradox calls for nothing less than a re-theorization of the developmental dynamic of Western law.

The second intellectual problem posed by the study of delinquency is the gradual, but seemingly inexorable, dominance of a medical model of juvenile deviance and the development of an array of putatively therapeutic institutions and policies. By "medical" and "therapeutic" I mean, in this context, three things: that the enterprise of juvenile justice is informed by the discourse of the helping professions; that the agencies that make up the juvenile justice "system" are invested with significant discretionary authority; and that this authority is legitimized by the goal of prevention as well as rehabilitation. While the medical model has for the time being been eclipsed by a more punitive, law-and-order approach to crime, it persists in the basic ideology of delinquency as a pathology of family and community life in urban society. Simply to frame the issue of medicalization in these terms partially solves the initial paradox concerning legal development: professionals' claims to scientific expertise and demands for professional autonomy have provided the justification for increased intervention into families. Official child regulators have expanded their domain by enlisting the helping professions, and the professionals themselves have enhanced their prestige and authority by becoming subcontractors to the state (cf. Polsky 1991). My own work on American juvenile justice suggests that professional ideologies informed the making of legal policy and influenced the flow of children among institutional settings in the United States (Sutton 1988, 1990). As Donzelot (1979) has shown, similar patterns are apparent in French family policy. But in another sense, the paradox only deepens. The therapeutic paradigm consolidated in the late nineteenth and early twentieth centuries persists, despite its demonstrated inability to produce conformity. By what means have helping professionals become integral to child-control policy? How are the diagnostic discourse of medicine and the judgmental discourse of law accommodated within the same institutional framework?

The issue of the medicalization of delinquency is crucial because it implicitly broadens the scope of the inquiry and considerably raises the theoretical payoff to research. When delinquency-control policies are viewed in their historical context, it is apparent that they have repeatedly served as prototypes for a much broader transformation in the ways Americans responded to criminals, the insane, and even the poor. Thus, for example, the first specialized public institutions for children—the houses of refuge created in the 1820s and 1830s—were prototypes for adult reformatories created in the 1870s and 1880s; the juvenile court paved the way for adult probation and parole; and the diversion and deinstitutionalization policies of the 1960s and 1970s were prototypes for a much larger array of community treatment programs for criminals, drug addicts, and mental patients. More generally, the overt paternalism of the juvenile justice system has been echoed in the more discreet administrative condescension of the welfare state. In all of these areas, the basic dynamic is the same: therapeutic discourse provides a veneer of legitimacy for a system that is fundamentally punitive. Children have repeatedly been used as guinea pigs in social control experiments; it seems only fair, as well as analytically strategic, to treat juvenile justice reformers as subjects in our own research on social control.

The mainstream literature on crime and delinquency has offered little in the way of theoretical leverage on these problems. In their survey of the social control literature, Humphries and Greenberg (1981) identified two competing sets of accounts, which they refer to as "systems" and "agency" models. Systems models include accounts offered by some historians, functionalist sociologists, and policy analysts, all of which express a naive faith in the efficacy of control institutions. From this perspective, the rehabilitative paradigm is a progressive improvement—both more humane and more effective—over punitive strategies of control; the chronic decay of therapeutic regimes into regimes of custody and repression is seen as a regrettable accident resulting from inadequate knowledge, planning, or resources. The neo-Marxist studies that began to appear in the 1960s were overtly critical of such whiggish accounts but shared their basic functional logic. Here, the argument went, social control institutions serve the imperatives of capitalism. The therapeutic model appears in some Marxist accounts as an ideological veneer over an intentionally punitive system and in others as an effective strategy to chastise and resocialize potentially troublesome members of the surplus labor army. These revisionist models, like the whig accounts that preceded them, have attracted criticism from many quarters for their dogmatic determinism and lack of attention to historical agency (see, e.g., Greenberg 1976; Hagan and Leon 1977; Hagan 1980; Ignatieff 1981; Mennel 1983; Rothman 1983).

Agency models, in contrast, focus more closely on the active roles of reformers and social movements in the creation of rules and the construction of social control institutions. Sociologists in the 1960s built on Hofstadter's (1955) "status politics" argument to argue that specific reforms are often promoted by entrepreneurial groups for their symbolic significance, independent of their instrumental value or function in the social system. Gusfield (1963), for example, described the American temperance movement, which culminated in the odd experiment of Prohibition, as a drive by native white Protestants to reassert their cultural dominance over growing populations of immigrants. Becker (1963) coined the term "moral entrepreneurs" in his deft analysis of American anti-drug policies. The virtue of this line of research is that it portrays social control reform as a somewhat arbitrary, often haphazard, and always deeply ironic process. Yet these case studies did not add up to a convincing theoretical paradigm because they typically failed to specify how reform groups gained the political leverage to translate their parochial morality into policy—in other words, they threw the "baby" of structure out with the "bathwater" of functionalism. Perhaps most relevant to this discussion, Anthony Platt's (1969) justly famous study of juvenile court reform in Chicago fell short in ways typical of both systems and agency models. The "child savers" succeeded, he argues, because they served the interests of a backstage industrial elite. Issues left unexamined were precisely why "capitalism" should be interested in the moral socialization of children; whether, in fact, the juvenile court had any demonstrable and general effect on immigrant children; and how the (presumably convergent) interests of capitalists and child savers were articulated.

My research took this theoretical impasse as a starting point and sought to develop a historical account of American juvenile justice policy as a *political* response to the vicissitudes of state building in a dynamic and often troubled society. This task required that I move beyond the mainstream crime and delinquency literature to incorporate theoretical insights from other subfields of sociology and historical analyses of a broad range of social movements. I will not review the results of that research here.[1] Instead I propose, in the next section, to describe some scholarly currents that flowed strongly into my work and the work of others on these issues. Following that, I attempt to rework this material and present in more formal terms the elements of a synthetic model of deviance and control.

Influences and Lessons

My main goal in this section is to identify important sources of theoretical insight that appear to be useful for any attempt to broaden our discussions of deviance and social control. Some of these sources lie outside the conventional deviance–social control domain, indeed outside sociology proper. I find three such sources; there are probably more.

Deviance and Societal Reaction

First, while I argue mainly for a macro-historical perspective on the social construction of delinquency, it is imperative that such a perspective be firmly grounded in a realistic micro-level account of the process of deviant attribution. I would argue that the most likely source of such an account is the classic literature on societal reaction theory and more specifically the version of that approach developed by Edwin Lemert. In contrast to conventional models, which assumed that social sanctions are more or less mechanical responses to deviant behavior, Lemert argued that the application of sanctions is largely "adventitious" in nature and that the interventions of social control agents can in some cases stabilize individuals in a deviant identity by cutting off access to more reputable definitions of self (Lemert 1967a). The societal reaction tradition has been caricatured, both by Lemert's imitators and by his positivist critics, as arguing that deviant attributions are arbitrary and random and that rates of deviation can be explained primarily by sanctions.[2] Lemert himself eschewed such a position (1974); indeed, he insisted that exclusionary practices are generic to social groups and that the process of deviant attribution begins with some quite real act or condition that sets the individual apart from the group. The causes of this vast mass of "primary" deviation are neither analyzable nor interesting; the focus of interest, he argued, should be on the operation of forces that influence the adoption and stabilization of deviant identities. Thus, the paranoid insane he studied (1967c) all began with some kind of "status loss," such as a stigmatic scar or a recent job demotion. The interesting issue here is not whether deviance actually occurred but rather how generally troublesome or unpleasant behavior becomes interpreted as a specific form of deviance, resulting in a diagnosis of schizophrenia. Similarly, check forgers really do forge checks, and Lemert argued that an important determinant of their career trajectories is the fact that they know their actions to be illegal and they expect to be aggressively prosecuted (1967d).

The societal reaction perspective opens two doors that we should keep open. First, it has encouraged a vibrant line of research on the ways in which bureaucratic and institutional priorities influence the process of attribution. One relevant landmark in this regard is Cicourel's *Social Organization of Juvenile Justice* (1968), which shows in abundant and subtle detail how juvenile justice personnel use their discretionary authority to negotiate invidious outcomes with their clients. Another is Emerson's ethnography of an urban juvenile court, *Judging Delinquents* (1969). Emerson's analysis shows that the actions of juvenile court officials are often influenced by the need to maintain harmonious working relationships with other agencies, such as schools and the police. Both Cicourel and Emerson illuminate the subtle ways in which gender and social class enter into the attribution process. These and other related studies show that the process of deviant attribution is neither mechanical nor natural but rather an interpretive, sense-making activity. Official taxonomies of deviance—whether in legal codes or psychiatric nosologies—are discursive resources that social control agents use strategically to transform ambiguous trouble situations into successfully closed cases; the application of deviant labels is heavily influenced both by organizational priorities and by the ascriptive status of clients (see, e.g., Sudnow 1965; Emerson and Messinger 1977; Emerson 1983, 1991).

This insight opened a second door, but only a crack. Work in the societal reaction tradition suggested that the rules defining various kinds of deviance and the organizations set up to do social control work play an important role in the shaping of deviant careers. It seems apposite, then, to move to a higher level of analysis and begin to analyze the origins of those rules and organizational systems. However, it seems, the stubborn ethnographic bias of this tradition discouraged the kind of macro-level inquiry that was needed. The "moral entrepreneur" tradition I have already discussed obviously attempts to move in this direction. The labeling and social movement perspectives were brought together most creatively by Becker (1963); Lemert has also offered provocative studies of juvenile justice reform in California (1970) and Italy (1986). But again, these studies tend to focus on the making of specific rules defining specific types of deviance; they rarely aspire to a more general theoretical analysis of the rule-making process.

Neoinstitutional Theory

To address broader questions about the formation of social control regimes we must move outside the deviance literature toward theories of organizational and political structure. The approach that proved most useful to me was provided by neoinstitutional theory. In contrast to functionalism, neoinstitutional theorists argue in Weberian terms that formal policies and administrative structures—including juvenile justice institutions—are embedded in a wider scheme of canonical norms; that the primary focus of any such structure is not on the achievement of stated goals, but rather on its own survival; and that survival is likely to be dependent less on efficiency than on legitimacy. Substantive theories in this vein range widely, from Meyer's emphasis on rationalized "myths" (Meyer and Rowan 1977) to Skocpol's (1985) concern with the mechanisms of state building and policy making.

Research inspired by neoinstitutional theory has thoroughly revolutionized the sociological understanding of childhood and education, pushing aside functionalist accounts in favor of models that emphasize the role of the state in structuring the life course of individuals. Boli-Bennett and Meyer (1978), for example, draw attention to transnational ideological currents that influence the social construction of childhood. Ramirez and Boli (1987) argue that modern European educational systems are a by-product of political development rather than economic modernization. Similarly, findings by Meyer et al. (1979) suggest that the expansion of schooling in the U.S. was an ideological project that was closely related to a rural Protestant image of social order.[3] This approach has successfully problematized the notions of education and schooling in the way that I would like to problematize notions of delinquency, deviance, and social control. The old view that has implicitly informed scholarly and policy debates—that "schooling" is a more or less effective way of doing "education"—is no longer tenable; it has been replaced by the view that institutionalized forms of schooling *constitute* education in a given society, with analyzable effects on, for example, the nature of the life course, the distribution of cultural capital, structural opportunities for mobility, and the definition of citizenship.

In the same way, neoinstitutional theorists have attempted to de-naturalize social control institutions by treating them as politically contingent and constitutive of the domain of deviance. The earliest applications of this approach to crime and deviance are John Hagan's studies of the adoption and impact of probation policies (Hagan 1979; Hagan et al. 1979). In these studies, Hagan argued that probation was a "ceremonial" reform in the sense that it lent the criminal court an aura of therapeutic justice—thus co-opting its politically troublesome critics—but did not alter its underlying punitive agenda. Hagan's work inspired me to pursue these insights in a more sustained and systematic way.

Drawing largely on my own research (especially Sutton 1988, 1990), I would identify three conspicuous lessons of neoinstitutional theory for the study of reform in juvenile justice. First, the watershed reforms that created the contemporary juvenile justice system—from colonial "stubborn child" laws to the houses of refuge in the Jacksonian period, to the Progressive-era juvenile courts and the decarceration movement of the 1960s and 1970s—were deeply embedded in a broader pattern of institutional re-evaluation that involved the fate of criminals, the insane, and the poor. For three hundred years discussions of child welfare have provided an arena within which Americans debated, in coded language, the moral contours of their society. Thus at every stage in the history of juvenile justice reform, wider political crises—especially those involving the political status of immigrants and minorities—contributed to the partial delegitimation of existing policies of child control. System incumbents responded in defense of their cultural ideals and institutional authority by attempting to co-opt their critics and developing more elaborate professional ideologies of treatment. Reforms, thus, tended increasingly to be symbolic rather than substantive in nature, designed more to demonstrate legitimacy than to influence routine decision-making practices.

Second, contrary to the imagery of "moral entrepreneur" models, reforms did not erupt spontaneously from private, voluntary social movements. Rather, the state was an active player in the reform process at every stage. In all modern societies, including the United States no less than the more centralized European democracies, the state bears primary responsibility for the maintenance of social order. The United States is peculiar, however, in the sense that it lacks both a tradition of aristocratic hierarchy and a strong bureaucratic center (Skowronek 1982; Hamilton and Sutton 1989). The ideological attachment to popular sovereignty and the structural diffusion of authority throughout the polity contributes to chronic uncertainty about the stability of the social order and discourages the formation of universalistic policies and strong administrative agencies to deal with problems of crime and dependency. Private-sector activists, organized originally along religious and charitable lines and later in the form of professional associations, rushed to fill this void, but they were heavily dependent on the state for fiscal support and legal authority. Reformers adapted their appeals to local political circumstances; perhaps the strongest finding of my research is that the outcomes of reform, at least through the early twentieth century, were heavily dependent on the political contours of the American states.

The third lesson is that juvenile justice reform is a symbolic process, accountable less in terms of the goals it claims to achieve than the cultural norms it embodies. Struggles over juvenile justice reform brought into focus a much wider set of cleavages in American society: between natives and immigrants, Protestants and Catholics, bureaucratic state builders and party politicians. Americans have typically responded to divisive crises by attempting to resocialize threatening groups into a common moral community rather than by making fundamental changes in the economy and polity. The perceived source of these threats has shifted, from religious heretics to immigrants and people of color, and strategies of resocialization have shifted as well, away from religious conversion toward professional therapeutic treatment. These strategies persist not because they are effective at the individual level but because they achieve a satisfactory level of political unity. The juvenile justice system that has developed from these struggles, I have argued, derives its greatest strength from its weaknesses: it is diffuse enough to incorporate a broad range of public and private vested interests within a dense web of patronage exchanges, and it is decentralized enough to adapt at the periphery to shifting public attitudes toward delinquency and dependency.

The New Social History

The last feeder stream is what has come to be called the "new social history." Like neoinstitutional theory, the new social history can best be characterized in terms of what it has superseded. Traditionally historical research has been preoccupied with the doings of elites, in large part because elites left the most extensive written records. Recent historiography attempts to redress this bias by writing history "from the bottom up," focusing in particular on the private lives of members of the middle and lower classes. The exemplar in the history of childhood is, of course, Ariès (1962).

This literature offers two lessons for the study of social control. First, it reminds us that the activities of reformers and their clients are historically situated and local and deserve to be located within the intimate contexts of family, neighborhood, precinct, and parish. But this is no justification for narrowness; on the contrary, the texture of social life cannot be understood within the rigid institutional frameworks we now often take for granted. While Foucault is not exactly a social historian, his work is widely influential in this regard: the history of the prison (1977) and the asylum (1965) cannot be understood apart from each other or the trend toward wholesale confinement in the eighteenth century; this trend, in turn, must be related to the normalizing tendencies of medical discourse and to the increasing influence of that discourse in the more general ordering of the social mind in the Enlightenment.

Invocation of Foucault threatens to send us in the other direction, toward unfocused generality and impotent calls for interdisciplinarity. There is a substantive point here, however: social marginality is a generic phenomenon. Societies establishment of boundaries between acceptable and unacceptable behavior and how they cut up the terrain of deviance are variable. This variability is the thing to be explained, not taken for granted—thus social history meets labeling theory. This is especially relevant for the study of children: in all modern Western societies, discussion of the fate of children implies also the fate of women and families. My research argues strongly that debates over juvenile justice were in part symbolic debates over the construction of an American welfare state. These symbolic debates had real policy consequences: by precariously combining institutional attributes of law and social welfare, and public authority with private enterprise, the American juvenile justice system embodies American ambivalence toward poverty and social misfortune in general. Thus, contrary to those who argue that social welfare is an extension of social control (most notably, Piven and Cloward 1971), I would argue that juvenile justice agencies, mental hospitals, and even prisons in the United States are forms of social policy—all such institutions are built on the idea that individual moral reform is the only viable means of achieving social order.

The second lesson of social history is the power of the powerless. Because social control policies have broad cultural referents does not mean that they are uncontested. Indeed, specific policies are likely to emerge from struggles for control over institutional resources. As Thompson (1975) and the allied Warwick group (Hay et al. 1975) have shown, popular pressure forced concessions in eighteenth-century British penal policy; Katz (1983, 1986) demonstrates the active role played by the immigrant poor in the administration of welfare services in Progressive-era America; and Brenzel (1983) describes the negotiation of order between inmates and staff in the first American women's reformatory. My research has focused mainly on the activities of elite reformers, but even from their rather smug discourse one gets a strong sense of the struggle waged by the immigrant poor to control the fate of their families (National Conference on Charities and Correction 1904: 573–574).

Poor families often required assistance because they were vulnerable to extremely high rates of disease and industrial injury. In the absence of outdoor relief, which was extremely rare and never adequate, parents pieced together support from a number of unattractive sources: from extended kin if they had any, or from political machines, fraternal and religious associations, and especially the Catholic church. Placing children in institutions was usually a last resort. Lacking any other alternatives, Catholic parents preferred Catholic institutions, not only to protect their children from Protestant heresy but also because these institutions encouraged parents to reclaim their children when they felt able to care for them. Mainstream reformers argued that leaving such decisions to parents encouraged irresponsibility and freeloading; on this basis they promoted laws that clearly limited parental authority. We cannot know how, in any individual instance, a particular family's poverty or other circumstances may have contributed to their willingness actually to pursue institutional care for their children. Perhaps some immigrant parents were cynical manipulators of the court and church, obtaining desired social services for their children at no personal expense. But we *do* know that, from the reformer's point of view, such parents personified a dangerous and much more general inclination among some immigrants to seek security for their children without fully yielding to the paternalistic embrace of the official child-control system. Such instances typified, in a negative way, a much broader class of claims to which reformers were vulnerable.

The various conflicts that were symbolized in juvenile justice reform reached their peak in the early years of the twentieth century and were resolved, albeit precariously, by the institutionalization of a medical model of delinquency and child welfare. In adopting this model as their official program, reformers reworked longstanding Protestant doctrine about the redeemability of the human soul into an ideology of social pathology. In terms of practical action, this diffuse ideology justified policies of institutional discretion that met the needs of diverse constituencies. Perhaps more important, it preserved the central cultural myth of the individual origins of social problems and helped forestall reforms of structural inequities.

Toward a Generic Model of Deviance and Social Control

This expanded view of childhood and delinquency offers some starting points for a new, and hopefully generic, model of deviance and social control. It is reasonable to ask why we need such a model. If you are on the same publishers' mailing lists as I am on and read some of the same journals that I read, you are probably aware that putatively revolutionary theories of crime and deviance appear every month. But there is nothing really new; our texts and readers continue to round up the usual theoretical suspects with numbing regularity. The content of these texts has not changed much in 20 years; what is worse, most of the theories they present are aimed exclusively at crime or more narrowly still at juvenile delinquency.[4] Criminology may usefully be viewed as a subset of deviance, but it hardly exhausts the field. Criminological theories cannot hope to account for such obvious forms of deviance as mental illness or unconventional sexuality or less obvious forms such as poverty and bad table manners.

An additional reason for a fresh approach is that empirical research on deviance, while continuing at a high level of quantity, has become progressively more detached from the mainstream research traditions in sociology. Areas such as comparative-historical sociology, political sociology, organizations, stratification, and the sociology of culture have undergone significant revival and revision in the last several years and have become less specialized and more open to cross-fertilization; the study of deviance has been unable to partake in this spirit of post-Parsonsian adventure and has instead become more isolated and internally incoherent. This is more than a subjective impression. Recent network studies of sociology by Burt et al. (1990), Ennis (1992), and Cappell and Guterbock (1992) show that the crime and deviance community is moderately large but internally fragmented and peripheral to the rest of the discipline.[5] This may be of no concern to many, but it raises serious barriers to our attempts to discuss the relationships of crime and social control to inequality.

This section draws on the foregoing lessons to suggest some elements of a model that (1) takes issues of power and inequality seriously and (2) is potentially applicable to a wide range of social control settings. Any analytical model must, of course, have a target, some empirical variation that it seeks to explain. In the area of deviance and social control, two sets of empirical issues stand out. The first is the organization of the deviant terrain in a given social and historical context: How is the symbolic boundary drawn between acceptable and unacceptable behavior? How many kinds of deviance are there? How, and to what degree, are specialized institutions created to manage the various types of deviance? The second issue is the volume of control in various settings: How much deviance does a given society produce overall? What is the rate at which bodies flow through various institutional pathways? What is the relationship between these flows and other ascribed characteristics of individuals—in particular, characteristics of class, race, gender, and age?

My most radical proposal, and one I mean about half seriously, is to discard the terms "deviance" and "social control" in favor of terms that more successfully convey the generic nature of our enterprise. The very term "deviance" tends to reify a phenomenon that deserves critical scrutiny: it implies a substantive focus that includes, certainly, crime, mental illness, drug abuse, and sexual misconduct. It may include as well, for example, poor table manners, talking out loud during movies, police misconduct, and corporate dumping of toxic substances; it never seems to include such topics as poverty, racial and sexual discrimination,[6] or political oppression. Likewise the term "social control" is freighted with functionalist baggage. Mostly it is an American concept; its coinage signifies a highly ideological attempt to account for behavioral regularity without invoking European notions of hierarchy and political sovereignty (e.g., Ross 1901; Mead 1924–1925; Hamilton and Sutton 1989; Melossi 1990). As such it has two meanings: first, it projects an assumption that individuals act on the basis of deeply internalized norms; second, it implies that these norms represent some broader and typically impalpable set of interests (of society as a whole or of a conspiratorial ruling class). Thus individuals are "cultural dopes" (Garfinkel 1967), helpless in the grip of a "social control" machinery that is merely the servant of some more sublime hegemony. I have sought, so far in vain, for a substitute euphemism that effectively captures the constitutive relationship between "social control" activities and the domain of "deviance" ("the production of marginality" is the closest I've come). I will probably continue to use the terms deviance and social control but beg that they be heard in quotation marks.

My second point is probably not controversial at all. Research in deviance and social control typically focuses on one institutional sector (e.g., crime, delinquency, mental illness) within one country. Our research must become more comparative, along two dimensions. First and most obviously, we can account for the rise of specific social control regimes only by comparing societies in which they vary. Moreover, any such research—on, for example, policies for dealing with juvenile delinquency and dependency—must take into account the cross-societal diffusion of the very concepts we are studying. I have argued elsewhere (Sutton 1988) that Americans pretty much invented the concept of delinquency, along with the therapeutic armamentarium it was designed to justify. What has been the fate of this new social problem as it was exported to other societies? This requires us to treat the world system as a legitimate level of analysis. Second, we must compare patterns of development across institutional sectors. Courts, prisons, welfare agencies, mental hospitals, and reformatories are in varying degrees administratively and politically interdependent; so, then, are the relative official rates of crime, poverty, mental illness, and delinquency.

My suggestions so far have been mainly strategic; my third point is more substantive. To develop a generic model of deviance and social control, or even to have interesting conversations across subdisciplinary boundaries, we must draw upon and begin to synthesize research at three levels of analysis—what I call the cultural or social structural level, the institutional or political level, and the interactional or life-course level. Here I will only sketch the outlines of such a model; it should be read very much as a work in progress.

At the broadest level of culture and social structure, Durkheim provides a starting point. This may seem an odd place to begin, since Durkheim's best-known work laid the foundation for two of the most conspicuous variants of positivist deviance theory (especially Merton [1957] and Hirschi [1969]). Durkheim was explicitly concerned only with crime and not with other forms of deviance. His famous hypotheses about the stability of sanctioning rates (Durkheim 1938: 65–70) and the evolution of punishment (1978) reflect a faith in the invisible hand of social structure that is both logically and empirically untenable (see, e.g., Berk et al. 1981; Lukes and Scull 1983; Garland 1990: ch. 2). But there is another, until recently neglected, aspect of Durkheim's thought that can be freed from his more problematic functional assumptions and used as the foundation for a more flexible model. The key idea here is Durkheim's argument that societies define their collective experience primarily in terms of the symbolic boundaries they draw between acceptable and unacceptable behavior—an idea first laid out in his discussion of the "normality of deviance" in *Division of Labor* (1947) and developed in more abstract discussions of ritual and taboo in his later sociology of religion (1915). To Durkheim, deviance is as generic to societies as the fundamental distinction between "us" and "them." Societies produce deviance through ritual acts of punishment; punishment is not, moreover, an instrumental attempt to eradicate deviance or correct deviants but rather a celebration of a common moral order. Punishment *constitutes* deviance.

The anthropologist Mary Douglas (1966, 1982) has done the most to elaborate the cultural and symbolic aspects of Durkheim's thought. Douglas explicitly rejects Durkheim's evolutionary functionalism, along with any instrumental account of social organization, in favor of a structuralist approach (following Lévi-Strauss) that emphasizes its communicative significance. Most important for our purposes, Douglas strongly emphasizes the cultural importance of boundaries in producing social order. Human beings, she argues, strongly crave a sense of order, of homology between the humble experiences of the body and the shape of the cosmos. Social organization is the text that encodes cosmological meaning into the routine activities of everyday life. Pollution, taboo, or—in our terms—deviance consist of "things out of place" (Douglas 1966: 2), actions or objects whose location violates the natural order of things. Thus, to use one of her favorite illustrations, shoes on the kitchen table may evoke outrage far out of proportion to the hygienic threat they present; likewise a homeless man in Beverly Hills presents a more dangerous threat to propriety than property.

Douglas moved beyond Durkheim in another way, by suggesting in a more nuanced way how codes of pollution and taboo vary with social organization. Her famous "grid-group" scheme (1982) is an attempt to capture salient aspects of societal structure and relate those to characteristic forms of deviance. Group-oriented societies are concerned with boundaries that divide them from others and tend to be preoccupied with the dangers of heresy and subversion. Grid-oriented societies are focused internally, on the maintenance of proper hierarchical and lateral role relationships; deviance in this setting is viewed more as the result of individual weakness, excessive hubris, or bad luck. One may, with some imagination, treat Douglas's concepts of grid and group as rough analogs to therapeutic and punitive styles of social control—though the fit is far from exact—and begin to generate hypotheses about when one or the other is likely to predominate.[7] The fit is far from exact, however, and in any event Douglas vehemently denies that her model is applicable to cross-societal analyses. This is a major limitation of her work for our purposes. Another is that she does not address the issue of why a given society emphasizes external threats or internal order at any given time. She seems to take it for granted that a society's taboos reflect its real social-organizational needs; I would argue on the contrary that these matters are political constructions. But whether Douglas's specific model proves to be useful or not, her general approach suggests a fruitful way to update Durkheim's emphasis on the cultural nature of deviance.

Space forbids a nuanced discussion of a cultural approach to deviance,[8] for now three implications may be mentioned. First, the task at this level of analysis is primarily interpretive rather than explanatory, and the goal is to decode social practices of stigmatization and marginalization for their symbolic meanings and their implications for the construction of the moral order. Thus the putative instrumental impact of deviance and control—retribution, say, or rehabilitation, even "control" itself—is treated not as an explanation of a given practice but as one more aspect of a historically contingent cultural account. Second, the meanings of social practices are neither static nor uncontested, and individuals are not cultural dopes. Rather, as Douglas (1966) points out, symbols are ambivalent: the most cherished symbols of purity contain elements of pollution, and the most dangerous taboos hold fascination and allure. The moral order is made up of an array of such symbols, which competent social members use as a "tool kit" (Swidler 1986) in an active and strategic attempt to navigate the hazards of social life with a more-or-less intact sense of self. Third, while symbolic meaning is ambivalent, it is not arbitrary: the valence of specific symbols and their organization into larger genres is a collective process in which matters of power figure prominently.

The issue of power propels us to the second level of analysis, where the focus is on the role of political institutions in the construction of deviance. This is the level at which cultural reproduction takes place: political actors appropriate cultural symbols of deviance and normality to legitimize policies of social control. As policies become institutionalized, they feed back into, and in varying degrees transform, the larger cultural framework. The practical dynamics of this process are suggested by neoinstitutional theory: the political and bureaucratic survival of a given policy generates a widening circle of patrons and constituents and thus enhances its aura of legitimacy. Political legitimacy provides prima facie evidence that the program is effective—that the problem it is designed to address is real and that its approach is rational—independent of its instrumental value. This scenario may seem to suggest that policy is constrained to move in one direction only, and indeed cultural discourse limits the range of speakable policies. But within that range, conflict and change are possible because, as Douglas reminds us, symbols are ambivalent. In the American context, therapeutic and punitive modes of managing deviance represent contending interpretations of the meaning of individualism in liberal society; behind these interpretations are arrayed the broader contending constituencies of professional expertise and the rule of law.[9]

At this level of analysis, empirical attention focuses on the organizational sites where symbols are infused with power: the state and its constituent agencies, including public and private social control bureaucracies; professional groups; and voluntary associations. As I have already suggested, the literature on "moral entrepreneurs" has provided abundant examples of the ways in which reform groups manipulate cultural levers in pursuit of their parochial ideals; the task now is to frame such activities in a more systematic context. This requires a political economy of deviance that treats the state as an active participant in the definition of social problems.

Such an approach would have two broad foci. The first focus is the state itself, and the relative vulnerability of various political regimes to transient moral panics. Erikson's (1966) study of three "crime waves" in colonial Massachusetts Bay is an early exemplar of such an inquiry. Erikson frames his analysis as a synthesis of Durkheimian functionalism and societal reaction theory and argues that the apparently cyclical nature of repression in Massachusetts Bay supports Durkheim's hypothesis about the stability of punishment rates. Read more closely, however, the analysis suggests that repression occurred not in defense of social order as such, but rather in defense of the political authority of the colony's ruling elite. The Congregationalist oligarchy sought to stifle chronic demands by internal dissenters and English authorities for a more open system of governance; successive campaigns of repression against the Antinomians, the Quakers, and local witches occurred at times when these demands erupted into full-blown political crises and usefully symbolized those crises as threats to the sacred mission of the commonwealth. In short, the symbolic boundaries of colonial society were drawn by visible political interest, not by invisible societal imperatives. One might, in passing, draw a direct line from these events through the Palmer Raids and the McCarthy era and finally to the recent pathetic celebrity of Willie Horton. In the post–Cold War period, deprived as we are of convincing external enemies, moral threat is personified by a black rapist and a gullible liberal governor.

In seeking to discover the political correlates of moral panics, one likely factor is the strength of the state, and in particular the relative centralization and bureaucratization of agencies chartered to administer marginal populations. Strong agency structures signify institutionalized definitions as well as solutions to social problems; in decentralized and weakly bureaucratized polities such as the United States, fuzzy agency boundaries signify that social problems have not been rationalized and tamed. Such conditions likely provide fertile grounds for moral crusades. The second focus is on private-sector activists, both amateur and professional. Here the point is not to pile up more case studies but to follow the social movements literature in developing a more systematic understanding of the appearance of such groups, the formation of network linkages among reform organizations and between reformers and the state, and the rationalization of reform ideologies. Two recent studies of reform organizations stand out as exemplars of this approach. Reinarman's (1988) study of Mothers Against Drunk Drivers (MADD) effectively places that group in the context of American attitudes toward alcohol and recent Republican Party politics. On this foundation, Reinarman accounts for the MADD ideology—which seeks to punish individual drivers and leaves the beverage industry unscathed—and assesses its impact on federal and state policies. Beisel (1990) presents a comparative analysis of anti-pornography campaigns in New York, Boston, and Philadelphia, using network analysis of relations among cultural elites to explain their varied success.

Finally, at the interactional or life-course level we can begin to place individuals in the context of cultural, political, and organizational forces. Here the issue is how symbolic attributions are negotiated among social control agents and their clients and the consequences of those negotiated outcomes for individual moral careers. As I suggested earlier, we are blessed with a wealth of empirical case studies on this topic but little in the way of theoretical synthesis.

The first step toward such a synthesis is to conceptualize the notion of the deviant career in a way that permits more systematic comparisons across various settings and types of deviance. Too often in the deviance literature the notion of the deviant career has been interpreted as applying only to "career criminals," and there is a somewhat tedious debate about whether such a species exists. But recently some writers have suggested reconceptualizing the deviant career in terms of the broader life-course literature, treating "deviant or criminal acts as movements of individuals through positions in a system, with these movements often given form and coherence by the reactions and designations of control agents" (Hagan and Palloni 1988; Sampson and Laub 1990; Arnold and Hagan 1992). This approach encourages us to theorize links between macro- and micro-levels of analysis and between neoinstitutional and societal reaction perspectives. Hagan and Palloni (1990), for example, have sought to do exactly this in their analysis of the intergenerational transmission of criminal careers in working-class London. A more general, comparative research program might go on to ask, for example, whether deviant careers are typically stable or unstable, whether they are inclusive or exclusive of other roles, and whether they are transient or enduring. All of these questions can be respecified to take into account ascriptive inequalities, as for example in Arnold and Hagan's (1992) study of professional deviance among lawyers.

In conceptual terms, we can identify two general routes by which organizational forces bring cultural categories to bear on the structuration of deviant careers. One route, which we have already attended to in our discussion of societal reaction theory, is through the behavior of social control agents. Here the central focus should be on the use of lay stereotypes, or conceptions of "normal" deviance (Sudnow 1965; Cicourel 1968), in the sorting of cases. Studies in this tradition have repeatedly uncovered the existence of informal rules that guide the sorting process, often in defiance of formal agency prescriptions (i.e., legal rules or professional diagnostic criteria). Rigorous comparative analyses across different agency settings can move us toward *generalizable* conclusions about the stereotyping process. Neoinstitutional theory offers a wealth of hypotheses in this regard—for example, we would expect that agencies with "loosely coupled" authority structures (Weick 1976) and those that are highly professionalized are likely to have more elaborated structures of "normal" stereotypes.

The second route is through the representations deviants make about themselves. This leads us, willy-nilly, to a reconsideration of two hallowed concepts in the deviance literature: neutralization and deviant subcultures. For the most part, studies of neutralization consist of descriptive lists of the accounts deviants give for their behavior, with arguments about the role of neutralization strategies in the stabilization of deviant identities (most notably, Sykes and Matza 1957; see also Goode 1984: 63–70). Little attention has been paid to the origins of these accounts, how they vary across settings, or how effective they are (do some neutralization strategies "work" better than others?). The issue of subcultures arises here, since a large body of literature argues that gangs, neighborhood cultures, and other stable deviant associations provide collective accounts that can be deployed by individual members to ward off disreputable attributions. But by treating neutralization work as something only deviants do, and by treating deviant subcultures as inherently pathological, the conventional literature has missed a valuable opportunity for theoretical synthesis. The multilevel approach suggested here would place neutralization within the larger context of cultural accounting. Such an effort would begin with the assumption that all competent members of society engage in a constant process of self-rationalization in order to ascribe meaning to their past actions and to choose among future courses of actions. They do not do so in a vacuum, however, but by drawing on a collectively validated repertoire of symbols—a "tool kit" of representations (Swidler 1986)—from which to construct a reputable self-image. These symbols are a form of cultural capital, and like any resource, they are not evenly distributed across society (Bourdieu 1977, 1984). Some people's tool kits are more complete than others, and one's choice of neutralization strategies is likely to depend systematically on access to symbolic resources. Some kinds of cultural accounts lie ready to hand—for example, Scully (1990) found that convicted rapists account for their behavior in terms of common gender stereotypes, and Levi (1981) suggests that the ethos of a professional murderer is not unlike that of your average aggressive businessman. But more important, differential access to self-justifying accounts is likely to depend on membership in social groups of various types; thus deviance in the processual sense is theoretically linked to more general stratification processes. For example, crack smoking has an entirely different meaning and has entirely different consequences for the definition of the self, depending on whether the smoker is a white member of the ABA or a black member of the Fifty-fourth Street Crips.[10] Research from this perspective should begin with the proposition that the ability of individuals to sustain a reputable identity, or construct a stable deviant identity, is a function of the size, prestige, economic power, and internal organization of the groups to which they are linked.[11]

Finally, note that from this perspective official social control agencies are treated as one more set of groups contending to define the boundaries of reputability. Their role is relatively powerful in cases involving low-status persons who have little access to alternative definitions of self, such as children and minorities. Within the system, specific agencies are salient for different ascriptive groups. For example, the mental health system provides accounts that are particularly suited to the social roles of whites and women, the criminal justice system specializes in black men, and the social welfare system in black women.

Conclusion

This paper has drawn on research on the social control of children to suggest some new directions for the sociology of deviance. The issue of inequality was not the starting point of the discussion, but my argument suggests that stratification plays into the attribution process in three important ways. First, inequality may operate as an independent variable that encourages bias in the attribution of deviance. Many studies have explored whether blacks and whites, the rich and the poor, and males and females incur differential risks of being officially sanctioned for similar behaviors; what is remarkable about this literature is the frequent absence of clear associations between inequality and sanctions. Thus, second, this paper has encouraged reflection and research on the ways status attributes of class, race, gender, and age may be constitutive of certain types of deviance and thus may produce differential sanctioning outcomes even in the absence of subjective, individual bias. This is true by definition in the case of delinquency; in addition, certain forms of mental illness are historically associated more with women than men, and stereotypes of "normal crimes" suggest that embezzlers will be middle-class whites and drug dealers will be lower-class blacks. Thus, third, it is important to understand the historical origins and workings of institutions that encode these typifications—either explicitly in their formal structure (e.g., juvenile courts) or implicitly through the informal "working knowledge" of experienced participants (e.g., public defenders).

I have argued, first, that we need to clear the ground of accumulated brush and return to Durkheim's formulation of deviance as a normal and symbolically central aspect of social organization. To understand what I have called the "production of deviance" in these terms, it seems important to incorporate elements of neoinstitutional theory, which contains important lessons about the ways in which values are encoded into policy, and comparative social history, which exposes us to the variability and genetic origins of deviant typifications. The resulting theoretical framework suggests that the production of deviance is a process of cultural accounting that operates both through institutional mechanisms and face-to-face interactions. In the institutional sphere, state officials, professional associations, and voluntary groups negotiate formal policies that define a given set of deviant typifications as natural and rational. Naturalizing analogies also play a role in face-to-face interactions, as family members and peers seek to assign meaning to the deviant's actions and social control agents attempt to fit ambiguous trouble into categories defined by official taxonomies. Institutional and societal-reaction accounts meet where social control work is done.

Notes

1. I report results from my analysis of the development of American juvenile Justice reforms elsewhere (Sutton 1988). At that point, it seemed useful to inquire into the effects of these reforms (and other factors) on the volume of control in institutional settings, and I stumbled across data that allowed me to carry out some analyses in the context of the Progressive era (1880 through the early 1920s). This inquiry expanded to include not only studies of public and private juvenile institutions (Sutton 1990) but also prisons, jails and mental hospitals (Sutton 1987, 1991). In collaboration with Gary Hamilton, the theoretical aspects of this work were development further in a broad-scale account of social control in the United States (Hamilton and Sutton 1989).

2. The collection of articles edited by Gove (1980a) gives a thorough sense of the positivist rejection of societal reaction theory. For an elegant defense of that perspective, which in essence says that positivists miss the point, see Kitsuse's rejoinder in that volume.

3. See also Meyer (1977) for a general theoretical statement of the neoinstitutionalist view of education.

4. The most influential of these, Hirschi's (1969) control theory, addresses delinquency exclusively, if only because the self-report methods on which it relies cannot be used with adults. Social disorganization and differential association theories are applicable only to crime, and conflict theory is about property crime. Merton's version of anomie theory claims to account for a number of different kinds of deviance but is notoriously difficult to operationalize and therefore enjoys almost no empirical support.

5. Indeed, these studies probably underestimate the size, fragmentation, and peripheralization of crime-deviance research, since they focus either on mainstream sociology journals (Burt et al. 1990) or members of the American Sociological Association (Cappell and Guterbock 1992; Ennis 1992). Thus, they exclude the many scholars who publish primarily in specialty journals and who participate in professional criminological associations rather than the ASA.

6. For a notable exception, see Schur (1983). A remarkable feature of this book is that it not only addresses institutionalized forms of deviance committed by women (e.g., women and crime), it also treats gender itself as a form of stigma. It is, in that sense, exemplary of the direction I am suggesting.

7. Bergesen (1977), for example, has explicitly applied Douglas's ideas in a comparative analysis of political witch hunts.

8. For a good introduction to Douglas and her relationship to Durkheim, see Wuthnow et al. (1984: ch. 3). On a cultural approach to the making of moral order, see Wuthnow (1987). A recent volume, edited by Lamont and Fournier (1992), includes a number of relevant articles on the relationship between culture and inequality. For a particularly fine attempt to reformulate the sociology of punishment in cultural terms, including an exemplary reworking of Durkheim, see Garland (1990).

9. See, for example, Garland's (1985) erudite discussion of the meaning of individualism and individualization in the discourse of British penal reform.

10. Again, Lemert's (1967d) analysis of check forgers is relevant here: the peculiarly self-destructive trajectory of the forger's career is due in large part to the fact that he or she has no group, other than the social control system itself, from which to draw exculpatory images of self.

11. This point was originally made by Goffman thirty years ago in his discussion of group alignment and ego identity (1963: ch. 3).

15

Crime and the Social Control of Blacks: Offender/Victim Race and the Sentencing of Violent Offenders

Cassia Spohn

Research investigating the relationship between the defendant's race and sentence severity has not consistently supported the conflict perspective's contention that blacks will be sentenced more harshly than whites. Although a number of studies have uncovered such a link (Spohn et al. 1981–1982; Petersilia 1983; Zatz 1984), others have found either that there are no significant racial differences (Klein et al. 1990) or that blacks are sentenced more leniently than whites (Levin 1972; Bernstein et al. 1977; Gibson 1978). The failure of research to produce uniform findings of racial discrimination in sentencing has led to conflicting conclusions. Some researchers (Hagan 1974; Kleck 1981; Pruitt and Wilson 1983) assert that racial discrimination in sentencing has declined over time and contend that the predictive power of race, once relevant legal factors are taken into account, is quite low. Others (Klepper et al. 1983; Zatz 1987) claim that discrimination has not declined or disappeared but simply has become more subtle and difficult to detect. These researchers argue that race affects sentence severity *indirectly* through its effect on variables such as bail status (Lizotte 1978; LaFree 1985) or type of attorney (Spohn et al. 1981–1982) or that race *interacts* with other variables and affects sentence severity only in particular types of cases (Barnett 1985; Spohn and Cederblom 1991) or for particular types of defendants (Peterson and Hagan 1984; Walsh 1987; LaFree 1989).

Hawkins (1987) and LaFree (1989) present an analogous but somewhat different argument. Hawkins (1987: 721) argues that many of the so-called anomalies or inconsistencies in sentencing research reflect "oversimplification" of conflict theory. He contends that the work of early conflict theorists such as Quinney (1970) and Chambliss and Seidman (1971) does not support the proposition that "blacks or other nonwhites will receive more severe punishment than whites for all crimes, under all conditions, and at similar levels of disproportion over time" (Hawkins 1987: 724). Similarly, LaFree (1989) criticizes sentencing research for its failure to consider the relationship between the victim and the offender. He maintains that conflict theory is not disproved "if research demonstrates that sanctions are not particularly harsh when relatively powerless persons in society murder and rape each other" (LaFree 1989: 48).

Hawkins proposes a revision of the conflict perspective to account for the possibility of interaction between defendant race and other predictors of sentence severity and especially between defendant race, victim race, and the type of crime committed by the offender. He argues that differences in the level of social control used against blacks and against whites may vary depending upon the race of the victim and the type of offense; those who victimize whites or who commit crimes deemed "racially inappropriate" would be punished more harshly than those who victimize blacks or who commit race-appropriate crimes. Hawkins thus argues for the development of a more comprehensive conflict theory that embodies these race-of-victim and type-of-crime effects.

In this paper we incorporate Hawkins's suggestions concerning conflict theory. We begin with the presumption that there is a "hierarchy of seriousness based on the race of the victim and offender" (Hawkins 1987: 724). We examine the impact of the racial composition of the offender-victim dyad on sentences imposed on black and on white defendants convicted of serious felonies in Detroit Recorder's Court. We also analyze the impact of offender and victim race on sentence severity for a variety of crimes; we perform separate analyses on defendants convicted of homicide, sex offenses, robbery, and assault. We hypothesize that an interactive relationship exists between the victim's race, the defendant's race, the type of crime, and the severity of the sentence.

Previous Research

Research exploring the impact of offender and victim race on criminal justice decision making has generally focused on either homicide or rape cases. There is a substantial body of research demonstrating that blacks who murder whites are much more likely to be sentenced to death than blacks who murder blacks or than whites who murder blacks or whites (Arkin 1980; Bowers and Pierce 1980; Radelet 1981; Baldus et al. 1983, 1985; Paternoster 1984; Gross and Mauro 1989; Keil and Vito 1989). The most widely cited of these studies (Baldus et al. 1985) found that defendants convicted of killing whites were over four times as likely to receive a death sentence as defendants convicted of killing blacks. Baldus and his colleagues also found that blacks who killed whites had the greatest likelihood of receiving the death penalty.

Some commentators have questioned the national significance of findings of victim-based racial discrimination in the capital sentencing process, noting that almost all of the studies address capital sentencing in southern states. Recent research by Gross and Mauro (1989), however, demonstrates that discrimination based on the race of the victim is not confined to southern states. Gross and Mauro found capital sentencing disparities by the race of the victim in each of the eight states included in their study—Florida, Georgia, Illinois, Oklahoma, North Carolina, Mississippi, Virginia, and Arkansas. They concluded that their data showed "a clear pattern" of victim-based discrimination "unexplainable on grounds other than race" (Gross and Mauro 1989: 110).

There have been a number of studies comparing the processing of interracial and intraracial sexual assaults. LaFree (1989) examined the impact of offender and victim race on the disposition of sexual assault cases in Indianapolis, Indiana. He found that black men who assaulted white women were charged with more serious crimes and were sentenced more severely than were other defendants. LaFree concluded that his results highlighted the importance of examining the race composition of the offender-victim dyad. Because the law was applied *most* harshly to blacks charged with raping white women but *least* harshly to blacks charged with raping black women, simply examining the overall disposition of cases with black defendants would have produced misleading results.

Walsh (1987) reached a similar conclusion. When he used an additive model to examine the sentences imposed on black defendants and white defendants convicted of sexual assault in a metropolitan Ohio county, he found that neither the defendant's race nor the victim's race influenced sentencing in the predicted manner. Use of a race-specific model, however, revealed that black-on-white sexual assaults received more severe sentences than black-on-black assaults. As Walsh explained, the high sentence severity mean for blacks who sexually assaulted whites and the low sentence severity mean for blacks who sexually assaulted other blacks "had the effect of moving the black grand mean to a value not significantly different from the white offender mean" (Walsh 1987: 170). Discrimination against black defendants, in other words, was masked by the additive model.

Explanations for Disparate Treatment

Researchers have advanced two interrelated explanations for the harsher treatment of crimes involving black offenders and white victims and for the more lenient treatment of crimes involving black offenders and black victims. One explanation focuses on the racial composition of the victim-offender dyad; the other focuses on the victim's race alone.

The first explanation builds on conflict theory's premise that the law is applied to maintain the power of the dominant group and to control the behavior of individuals who threaten that power (Turk 1969a; Quinney 1970). It suggests that crimes involving black offenders and white victims are punished most harshly because they pose the greatest threat to "the system of racially stratified state authority" (Hawkins 1987: 726). Researchers have advanced a similar explanation for the harsher treatment of blacks who sexually assault whites. Using the concept of sexual stratification, LaFree (1989) argues that one measure of the dominant group's power is its ability to control sexual access to women in the dominant group, who are regarded as the scarce and valuable sexual property of men of their own race. The sexual assault of a white woman by a black man, then, threatens the power of the dominant group by violating the group's sexual property rights. This, according to Walsh (1987: 155) "accounts for the strength of the taboo attached to inter-racial sexual assault." It also explains why sexual assaults of black women, who are seen as less valuable sexual "commodities," are perceived as less serious crimes.

The second explanation for the harsher penalties imposed on those who victimize whites emphasizes the race of the victim rather than the racial composition of the victim-offender dyad. This explanation suggests that crimes involving black victims are not taken seriously and/or that crimes involving white victims are taken very seriously; it suggests that the lives of black victims are devalued relative to the lives of white victims. Thus, crimes against whites will be punished more severely than crimes against blacks regardless of the race of the offender.

Most researchers have failed to explain adequately *why* those who victimize whites are treated more harshly than those who victimize blacks. Gross and Mauro (1989) suggest that the explanation, at least in capital cases, may hinge on the degree to which jurors are able to identify with the victim. The authors argue that jurors take the life-or-death decision in a capital case very seriously. To condemn a murderer to death thus requires something more than sympathy for the victim. Jurors will not sentence the defendant to death unless they are particularly horrified by the crime, and they will not be particularly horrified by the crime unless they can identify or empathize with the victim. According to the authors, "In a society that remains segregated socially if not legally, and in which the great majority of jurors are white, jurors are not likely to identify with black victims or to see them as family or friends. Thus jurors are more likely to be horrified by the killing of a white than of a black, and more likely to act against the killer of a white than the killer of a black" (Gross and Mauro 1989: 113). The same line of reasoning obviously could be applied to judicial sentencing decisions. One might argue that judges, the majority of whom are white, will identify more readily with white victims and thus will be more horrified by crimes against whites. As a consequence, they will be more willing to impose harsh penalties on those who victimize whites.

Explanations for the harsher treatment of blacks who victimize whites have not generally considered the effect of type of crime. In fact, some researchers have implied that the effect of race is constant across crime types and that nonwhites will be sentenced more harshly than whites for all crimes. This is not necessarily true. Conflict theorists argue that "the probability that criminal sanctions will be applied varies according to the extent to which the behaviors of the powerless conflict with the interests of the power segments" (Quinney 1970: 18). As Hawkins (1987) notes, some crimes may be seen as relatively unthreatening to the system of white authority and thus may not produce harsher penalties for blacks who commit those crimes.

Differences in the degree of social control imposed on blacks and on whites may also reflect the fact that some crimes are perceived as more "normal" or "appropriate" for one racial group than another. Hawkins (1987) argues that offenders will be punished most harshly for committing "racially inappropriate" crimes. He contends that white-collar crimes are deemed more appropriate for white offenders while street crimes, particularly violent street crimes, are viewed as more appropriate for black offenders. Similarly, black-on-black crimes are perceived as more appropriate than black-on-white crimes. Given this, one would expect greater differentials in the sentences imposed on black offenders convicted of white-collar crimes than on black offenders convicted of street crimes. One also would expect an interaction between the type of crime and the racial combination of the offender-victim dyad; the effect of offender/victim race would be greatest for racially inappropriate crimes.

Objectives of the Study

This study responds to Hawkins's (1987: 740) call for a "systematic rethinking of the conflict perspective." Our first objective is to determine if the race of the offender-victim dyad affects the severity of the sentences imposed on felony defendants. We hypothesize that the race of the victim will not have an independent effect on sentence severity but will interact with the race of the defendant to produce harsher penalties for blacks who victimize whites and more lenient penalties for blacks who victimize other blacks. Like the early conflict theorists (Johnson 1941), we expect the sentences imposed on whites who victimize other whites to be more severe than those imposed for black-on-black crime and less severe than those imposed for black-on-white crime.

Our second objective is to analyze the effect of offender/victim race on sentence severity for a variety of crimes. We noted above that most studies have included only homicide or rape cases. In this study we examine the relationship between offender/victim race and the harshness of the sentence imposed on defendants convicted of homicide, sex crimes, robbery, and assault. In line with previous research, we expect to find that blacks who murder or sexually assault whites face harsher penalties than blacks who murder or sexually assault other blacks. In line with Hawkins's (1987) assertion that black-on-white crimes will be perceived as less appropriate than black-on-black crimes, we expect offender/victim race to affect the sentences for robbery and assault in a similar manner.

The third objective of our study is to test for interaction between offender/victim race and the relationship between the offender and victim. Black (1976) and other social control theorists have asserted that the victim-offender relationship is an important predictor of the outcome of legal proceedings. They argue that crimes among intimates are perceived as less serious than crimes among strangers. Studies of decision making by criminal justice officials have confirmed this. Crimes involving strangers are more likely than crimes involving acquaintances to result in an arrest (Black 1971; Oppenlander 1982; Baumgartner 1988). In addition, offenders who victimize strangers are more likely to be prosecuted (Bernstein et al. 1977; LaFree 1980; Radelet and Pierce 1985) and to be found guilty (Williams 1978; Feeley 1979; Myers 1980); they also tend to receive harsher sentences than those who victimize acquaintances (Walsh 1987). This research suggests that crimes involving strangers will be taken seriously regardless of the race of the offender or the race of the victim. We therefore hypothesize that offender/victim race will affect judges' sentencing decisions only for crimes involving non-strangers.

Research Design and Methods

The data for this study were collected by Colin Loftin and Milton Heumann (see Heumann and Loftin 1979; Loftin et al. 1983) for their analysis of the impact of the Michigan Felony Firearm Law on the processing of defendants in Detroit Recorder's Court.[1] The sample includes all defendants who were originally charged with at least one of eleven violent felonies[2] during 1976, 1977, and 1978. The data file includes detailed information on the characteristics of defendants and the processing of their cases. Although the original file included information on 8,414 defendants, information on the victim's race and gender was available for only a subset of the sample. Because we were interested in the effect of victim race on sentencing decisions, we eliminated cases (mainly 1976 cases) where the race of the victim was missing (N = 2,856) or where there was no victim (N = 112); we also eliminated cases in which all charges were dismissed or in which the defendant was acquitted of all charges. We intended to compare the sentences imposed on black defendants and white defendants, so we eliminated cases where the defendant's race was unknown. Because of the small number of cases with female defendants (particularly white female defendants), we also eliminated these cases. These procedures left 2,858 cases; of these cases, 1,830 involved black offenders and black victims, 596 involved black offenders and white victims, 379 involved white offenders and white victims, and 53 involved white offenders and black victims.

Dependent Variables

In sentencing convicted offenders, judges must make two distinct and somewhat independent decisions. They must first decide whether to incarcerate the offender. Once this decision has been made, they then must determine the length of the prison sentence. Research has demonstrated that these decisions are empirically distinct; that is, different variables, or different sets of variables, are associated with each decision (Sutton 1978; Spohn et al. 1981–1982). Consequently, we analyzed the two decisions separately.

We used a dichotomous dependent variable to measure whether the offender was sentenced to prison. Our second dependent variable, the expected minimum sentence (EMS) measures the amount of time (in days) a defendant could expect to spend in confinement. For this part of the analysis, we included only defendants who were sentenced to prison; defendants who were given non-incarceration sentences were excluded. The EMS, developed by Loftin and Heumann to "avoid problems posed by indeterminate sentencing, suspended sentences, good-time discounts, life sentences, and the like" (Loftin et al. 1983: 290), requires some explanation. The measure reflects the minimum prison sentence imposed by the judge minus the maximum amount of good-time credit available to the defendant.[3] All life sentences, and minimum sentences of more than ten years after applying the good-time discount, were recorded as ten-year sentences; this is consistent with Michigan Department of Corrections' Policy, which grants the parole board jurisdiction over cases after ten calendar years of imprisonment. As the authors note, the EMS "roughly corresponds to the expected length of sentence, but more precisely it is the length of time to first possible release" (Loftin et al. 1983: 291).

Independent Variables

In all of our analyses, we control for the racial combination of the offender-victim dyad.[4] Because there were only 53 white offender/black victim cases (and only 30 of these were sentenced to prison), we eliminated these cases from the analysis. The race of the offender and the race of the victim were then combined to form three dummy variables—black offender/black victim, black offender/white victim, and white offender/ white victim. Black offender/white victim is the omitted category; our hypothesis is that defendants in this category will receive harsher sentences than defendants in either of the other two categories.

We also controlled for the gender of the victim and for other variables that have been shown to affect judges' sentencing decisions. We controlled for the defendant's age and number of prior felony convictions and we included a number of measures of the seriousness of the crime committed by the defendant: the most serious conviction charge,[5] the number of conviction charges, whether the defendant used a gun to commit the crime, whether the defendant injured the victim, or whether the defendant victimized a stranger rather than an acquaintance. Finally, we controlled for characteristics of the defendant's case that might influence the severity of the sentence imposed by the judge. We took into account whether the defendant was represented by a private attorney or was released pending trial, the type of disposition in the case,[6] and the race of the sentencing judge. These variables, their codes, and their frequencies are displayed in Table 15.1.

Analytic Procedures

We initially analyzed the data using both ordinary least squares regression analysis and probit analysis. We used regression to analyze the EMS, an interval-level measure. Since many consider OLS regression inappropriate for the analysis of dichotomous dependent variables, we analyzed the incarceration rate using both OLS regression and probit analysis. Because the results of the analyses were identical[7] and because the regression results are more interpretable, we present the regression results.

We used a two-stage analytic procedure to explore the relationship between offender/victim race and sentencing. We first estimated the additive effects of offender/victim race on the two sentencing outcomes, controlling for defendant and case characteristics. We then explored the possibility of an interactive relationship between offender/victim race, the conviction charge, the relationship between the victim and the offender, and sentence severity. We performed separate analyses on each type of conviction charge[8], and on cases involving strangers and nonstrangers.

TABLE 15.1 Coding and Descriptive Statistics for Variables

Variable	Coding	N	Mean	%
Prison sentence	0 = no	666		23.7
	1 = yes	2,139		76.3
Minimum expected sentence	Days		1,478	
Race of offender/victim	Dummy-coding			
Black/black		1,830		65.2
White/white		379		13.5
Black/white (omitted category)		596		21.2
Gender of victim	0 = male	1,609		57.4
	1 = female	1,195		42.6
Age of offender	Years		26.4	
Prior felony convictions	0–18		.9	
Most serious conviction charge	Dummy-coding			
First-degree murder		78		2.8
Second-degree murder		243		8.7
Manslaughter		131		4.7
Rape		238		8.5
Robbery		1,041		37.1
Other sex offenses		188		6.7
Assault		644		23.0
Other felony (omitted category)		242		8.6
Number of conviction charges	1–9		1.5	
Pretrial release	0 = no	2,082		75.1
	1 = yes	692		24.9
Type of disposition	Dummy-coding			
Guilty plea		2,114		75.4
Jury trial		276		9.8
Bench trial (omitted category)		415		14.8
Private attorney	0 = no	2,050		74.3
	1 = yes	709		25.7
Gun present	0 = no	1,230		43.9
	1 = yes	1,573		56.1
Victim injury	0 = no	1,707		60.9
	1 = yes	1,096		39.1
Victim a stranger	0 = no	1,213		43.8
	1 = yes	1,558		56.2
Race of judge	0 = white	1,574		60.1
	1 = black	1,045		39.9

Results

Additive Analyses

The results of the additive analyses are displayed in Table 15.2. Black offender/white victim is the omitted category in the analysis; therefore, the coefficient for each of the two included categories reflects the difference in the incarceration rates for cases in that category and for cases in

TABLE 15.2 The Effects of Offender/Victim Race on Sentence

Variable	Prison Sentence			Expected Minimum Sentence		
	b	Beta	T	b	Beta	T
Race of offender/victim						
Black/black	-.02	-.02	.12	-64.53	-.03	1.17
White/white	-.10	-.08	4.05***	-22.61	-.01	0.28
Gender of victim	-.02	-.03	1.58	69.33	.03	1.78
Age of offender	-.002	-.05	2.59**	-5.71	-.04	2.10*
Prior felony convictions	.02	.09	5.03***	154.66	.22	11.09***
Most serious conviction charge						
First-degree murder	.33	.12	6.27***	1,713.40	.26	10.38***
Second-degree murder	.41	.27	11.01***	1,667.24	.43	12.87***
Manslaughter	.30	.15	7.16***	647.75	.11	4.20***
Rape	.34	.22	9.00***	842.88	.20	6.34***
Robbery	.37	.42	12.96***	667.84	.28	6.06***
Other sex offenses	.10	.06	2.44*	367.36	.06	2.36*
Assault	.16	.16	5.49***	-17.50	-.01	0.15
Number of conviction charges	.04	.08	4.54***	105.59	.08	4.14***
Pretrial release	-.25	-.26	13.99***	-253.86	-.07	3.82***
Type of disposition						
Guilty plea	.02	.02	0.81	-33.98	-.01	0.41
Jury trial	.14	.12	4.72***	716.11	.23	7.57***
Private attorney	-.04	-.04	2.15*	-68.38	-.02	1.27
Gun present	.05	.06	2.88**	174.58	.07	3.37***
Victim injury	.02	.02	0.93	168.96	.07	2.80**
Victim a stranger	.04	.05	2.73**	181.63	.07	3.50***
Race of judge	-.03	-.03	1.96*	-14.88	-.01	0.33
R^2		.36			.40	

NOTE: b = unstandardized coefficient; B = standardized coefficient. * $p < .05$; ** $p < .01$; *** $p < .001$.

which the offender is black and the victim is white. A statistically significant coefficient for the black/black variable, then, reflects disparity based on the race of the victim; it indicates that blacks who victimized blacks were treated differently than blacks who victimized whites. A statistically significant coefficient for the white/white category, on the other hand, reflects disparity based on the race of the *offender*; it indicates that blacks who victimized whites were sentenced differently than whites who victimized whites.

The data presented in Table 15.2 reveal that offender/victim race did not affect the expected minimum sentence at all and did not affect the incarceration rate in the predicted way. We hypothesized that the race of the victim would interact with the race of the offender to produce significantly more severe sentences for blacks who victimized whites than for blacks who victimized other blacks; we expected the sentences for whites who victimized other whites to fall in the middle. This hypothesis was not confirmed. The difference in the incarceration rates for black-on-black and black-on-white crimes was only two percentage points and was not statistically significant. There was, on the other hand, a significant difference in the rates for white-on-white and black-on-white crimes. As explained above, this difference reflects disparity based on the race of the offender; the incarceration rate for whites who victimized whites was ten percentage points lower than the rate for blacks who victimized whites.

The results presented in Table 15.2 also reveal that the effect of the offender/victim race variables, even where significant, is clearly overshadowed by the effect of the other independent variables. Judges' sentencing decisions are determined, first and foremost, by the seriousness of the crime committed by the offender and by the offender's prior criminal record—factors of explicit legal relevance. Not surprisingly, offenders convicted of a more serious charge or of a number of charges are punished more severely, as are offenders who used a gun, injured the victim, or victimized a stranger. The gender of the victim, on the other hand, did not influence either sentencing decision.

The results of the additive analyses, then, reveal that the race composition of the victim-offender dyad does not affect sentence severity in the expected way. As will become apparent, it has an impact, but only under certain circumstances.

Interactive Analyses of Incarceration

We analyzed the effect of offender/victim race separately for each type of crime and for strangers and non-strangers. The results displayed in Table 15.3 reveal that the impact of offender/victim race on incarceration is confined to sex crimes. Consistent with the sexual stratification hypothesis, blacks who sexually assaulted whites were incarcerated at a much higher rate than blacks who sexually assaulted other blacks. The disparity between blacks who assaulted whites and whites who assaulted whites is even larger. In fact, the two offender/victim race variables were the best predictors of incarceration after the seriousness of the offense (forcible rape or some other offense); they were better predictors than the defendant's prior criminal record.

We used the results of the regression analysis to calculate adjusted incarceration rates for each of the three offender/victim racial combinations.[9] We did this for offenders convicted of all felonies and for offenders convicted of sex crimes only. These adjusted rates take all of the other independent variables listed in Table 15.1 into account. The rates for offenders convicted of all felonies are remarkably similar: 79 percent for blacks who victimized whites, 77 percent for blacks who victimized

TABLE 15.3 The Effects of Offender/Victim Race on Prison Sentence, by Type of Crime and Offender-Victim Relationship

Variable[a]	b	Beta	T
Type of Crime			
Murder[b]			
Black offender/black victim	-.004	-.01	0.09
White offender/white victim	.02	.02	0.36
Sex crimes[c]			
Black offender/black victim	-.20	-.20	2.89**
White offender/white victim	-.31	-.27	3.92***
Robbery			
Black offender/black victim	-.008	-.02	0.48
White offender/white victim	-.02	-.03	0.76
Assault			
Black offender/black victim	.05	.05	0.95
White offender/white victim	-.05	-.04	0.72
Other felony			
Black offender/black victim	-.06	-.06	0.66
White offender/white victim[d]			
Offender/victim relationship			
Strangers			
Black offender/black victim	-.004	-.005	0.21
White offender/white victim	-.04	-.04	1.52
Non-strangers			
Black offender/black victim	-.10	-.09	2.14*
White offender/white victim	-.22	-.17	4.07***
Sex crimes only: Race and relationship[e]			
Black/black/strangers	-.13	-.12	1.50
Black/black/non-strangers	-.25	-.26	3.17**
White/white/strangers	-.32	-.24	3.49***
Black/white/non-strangers	.08	.03	0.61
White/white/non-strangers	-.33	-.17	2.98**

[a] Regression analyses included all of the variables listed in Table 15.1. Black offender/white victim is the omitted category.

[b] Regression analysis of defendants convicted of murder (first-degree murder, second-degree murder and manslaughter) included controls for first- and second-degree murder.

[c] Regression analysis of defendants convicted of sex crimes (rape and other sex offenses) included a control for rape.

[d] There were too few cases in this category for analysis.

[e] Black offender/white victim/strangers is the omitted category. Thus, the coefficients reflect differences between that category and the included categories.

* $p < .05$; ** $p < .01$; *** $p < .001$.

blacks, and 69 percent for whites who victimized whites. These similarities stand in stark contrast to the differences in the rates for sex crimes. Eighty-six percent of the blacks convicted of sexually assaulting whites were sentenced to prison, compared to only 66 percent of the blacks convicted of sexually assaulting blacks and 54 percent of the whites convicted of assaulting whites.

Table 15.3 reveals that the effect of the race-combination variables on sentence severity also is conditioned by the relationship between the offender and the victim. As expected, offender/victim race affected the incarceration rate only for crimes on non-strangers. The adjusted rates for the three categories are nearly identical when the offender and victim are strangers. Among offenders and victims who are acquainted, on the other hand, blacks who victimized whites faced a greater likelihood of incarceration (77.7 percent) than either blacks who victimized other blacks (68.0 percent) or whites who victimized whites (55.9 percent).

The findings discussed thus far suggest the possibility of an interaction between offender/victim race and offender/victim relationship for sex crimes; they suggest that the effect of offender/victim race on the incarceration rate for sex crimes may be confined to cases in which the victim and the offender are acquainted. To explore this possibility, we created six offender race/victim race/relationship interaction terms: black offender/black victim/stranger; black offender/black victim/non-stranger; black offender/white victim/stranger; black offender/white victim/non-stranger; white offender/white victim/stranger; and white offender/white victim/non-stranger. The omitted category was black offender/white victim/stranger; our assumption was that the incarceration rate would be highest for blacks who sexually assaulted white strangers.

The results in Table 15.3 indicate that the incarceration rate for the black/white/non-stranger category was actually slightly higher than the rate for the black/white/stranger category; the difference, however, was not statistically significant. The difference between the black/white/stranger category and the black/black/stranger category also was not significant. As predicted, the rates for the other three categories were substantially lower than the rate for the omitted category.

The adjusted means, available on request, illustrate more clearly the differences among the six categories. The most striking differences are found for sexual assaults involving black offenders and white victims and those involving white offenders and white victims. For these two combinations, the offender/victim relationship is irrelevant. The incarceration rates for *black* offenders convicted of sexually assaulting white acquaintances (94.2 percent) or strangers (85.6 percent) are substantially higher than the rates for *whites* convicted of assaulting white acquaintances (53.4 percent) or strangers (52.7 percent). These differences may reflect discrimination based on the race of the offender. Table 15.3 may reveal discrimination based on the race of the victim, but here the relationship between the offender and the victim does come into play. There are no significant differences in the incarceration rates for blacks convicted of sexually assaulting white strangers, blacks convicted of sexually assaulting white non-strangers, and blacks convicted of sexually assaulting black strangers. The differences between these three categories and the black/black/non-stranger category, on the other hand, *are* statistically significant. Discrimination based on the race of the victim, in other words, may be confined to cases involving black offenders convicted of sexually assaulting black acquaintances.

Interactive Analysis of Expected Minimum Sentence

We also examined the effect of offender/victim race on the expected minimum sentence for the various types of crimes and for cases involving strangers and non-strangers. As Table 15.4 indicates, the race-combination variables affected the EMS only for murder cases. The EMS for blacks convicted of murdering whites was significantly longer than the EMS for blacks convicted of murdering blacks (a difference of 548 days); it also was significantly longer than the EMS for whites convicted of murdering other whites (a difference of 675 days). These results signal discrimination in sentence length based on the race of the victim *and* the race of the offender.

In contrast to our findings on the incarceration rate, we did not find an interaction between offender/victim race and the relationship between the offender and victim. In fact, when we analyzed the EMS for murder using the offender race/victim race/relationship dummy variables, we found that the sentences imposed on blacks convicted of murdering either white acquaintances or white strangers were significantly longer than the sentences imposed on the other four categories. And the sentences for intraracial murders did not vary depending upon the victim-offender relationship. These results are also displayed in Table 15.4.

Summary and Discussion

In this study we hypothesized that victim race would interact with defendant race to produce more severe sentences for blacks who victimized whites and less severe sentences for blacks who victimized blacks. We expected the sentences for whites who victimized whites to fall in between the other two categories. This hypothesis was not confirmed. Offender/victim race did not affect the expected minimum sentence (for all felony defendants) at all and did not affect the incarceration rate in the predicted way. The incarceration rate for the black offender/white victim category was nearly identical to the rate for the black offender/black victim category. And the rate for the white offender/white victim category was significantly *lower* than the rate for the other two categories. These results signal discrimination in sentencing based on the race of the *offender* rather than the race of the victim.

The results discussed above were obtained when we examined the

TABLE 15.4 The Effects of Offender/Victim Race on Expected Minimum Sentence, by Type of Crime and Offender-Victim Relationship

Variable[a]	b	Beta	T
Type of Crime			
Murder[b]			
Black offender/black victim	−547.68	−.19	3.23**
White offender/white victim	−675.06	−.17	2.84**
Sex crimes[c]			
Black offender/black victim	−226.25	−.09	1.28
White offender/white victim	−71.18	−.02	0.31
Robbery			
Black offender/black victim	43.44	.02	0.61
White offender/white victim	111.39	.03	0.90
Assault			
Black offender/black victim	−56.52	−.03	0.41
White offender/white victim	−44.92	−.02	0.27
Other Felony			
Black offender/black victim	−208.05	−.14	0.98
White offender/white victim	−216.17	−.10	0.75
Offender/victim relationship			
Strangers			
Black offender/black victim	−51.91	−.02	0.82
White offender/white victim	20.51	.005	0.20
Non-strangers			
Black offender/black victim	−198.58	−.06	1.63
White offender/white victim	−198.84	−.05	1.32
Murder only: Race and relationship[d]			
Black/black/strangers	−470.76	−.17	2.49*
Black/black/non-strangers	−639.50	−.27	3.61***
White/white/strangers	−747.14	−.15	2.72**
Black/white/non-strangers	6.87	.00	0.02
White/white/non-strangers	−586.49	−.09	−1.96*

[a] Regression analyses included all of the variables listed in Table 15.1. Black offender/white victim is the omitted category.

[b] Regression analysis of defendants convicted of murder (first-degree murder, second-degree murder and manslaughter) included controls for first- and second-degree murder.

[c] Regression analysis of defendants convicted of sex crimes (rape and other sex offenses) included a control for rape.

[d] Black offender/white victim/strangers is the omitted category. Thus, the coefficients reflect differences between that category and the included categories.

* p < .05; ** p < .01; *** p < .001.

sentences imposed on all felony defendants, controlling for the seriousness of the crime and for case and defendant characteristics. When we analyzed the effect of offender/victim race on sentence severity *separately* for the various types of crimes and for strangers and non-strangers, we found a number of significant effects. Most important, we found that offender/victim race influenced judges' sentencing decisions in sexual assault and murder cases. Blacks who sexually assaulted whites faced a greater risk of incarceration than either blacks who sexually assaulted blacks or whites who sexually assaulted whites; similarly, blacks who murdered whites received longer sentences than did offenders in the other two categories. For these two crimes, then, we found discrimination based on the race of the offender and the race of the victim.

We also found an interaction between offender/victim race, the relationship between the offender and the victim, and the type of conviction charge. When we examined the sentences imposed on all felony defendants, we found some support for our hypothesis that offender/victim race would affect judges' sentencing decisions only for crimes involving non-strangers. Offenders who victimized strangers, regardless of their race or the race of their victims, were sentenced to prison at about the same rate; among non-strangers, the incarceration rate was significantly higher for black-on-white crimes than for either black-on-black or white-on-white crimes. The offender/victim race variables, on the other hand, had no effect on the expected minimum sentence for either strangers or non-strangers.

The results of our comparison of the incarceration rates for defendants convicted of sex crimes and of the EMS for defendants convicted of murder, on the other hand, did not support our hypothesis. We found that offender/victim race affected judges' sentencing decisions for crimes involving strangers as well as non-strangers. Among defendants convicted of sex crimes, for example, the incarceration rate for whites who sexually assaulted white strangers was much lower than the rates for blacks who assaulted either white or black strangers. And the incarceration rate for blacks who sexually assaulted white acquaintances was much higher than the rate for blacks who assaulted black acquaintances or for whites for assaulted white acquaintances. Similarly, when we examined the EMS for offenders convicted of murdering strangers, we found significantly longer sentences for black-on-white crimes than for either black-on-black or white-on-white crimes.

These findings call into question Black's (1976: 44) assertion that the relationship between the victim and the offender "predicts and explains the outcomes of legal proceedings." At least in this jurisdiction, offenders who murder and sexually assault strangers are not necessarily sentenced more harshly than those who murder and sexually assault relatives and acquaintances. Instead, blacks who murder white strangers *or* acquaintances receive significantly longer sentences than other defendants. And blacks who sexually assault white strangers, white acquaintances, *or* black strangers are sentenced to prison at a higher rate than are other offenders. This suggests that research investigating the link between race and sentencing should consider the relationship between the offender and the victim, the racial combination of the offender-victim dyad, and the interaction between the two.

Our findings also indicate that researchers should heed Hawkins's (1987: 721) call for a revision of the conflict perspective on race and sentencing "to address more specifically the question of the role played by various contingencies or mediating factors." The results discussed above add to a growing body of literature demonstrating that the relationship between race and sentencing is nonlinear and nonadditive. The effect of race may be mediated by the race composition of the offender-victim dyad and by the type of conviction charge; for some types of crimes, it also may be mediated by the relationship between the offender and the victim. Researchers who simply test for the direct effect of defendant race may incorrectly conclude that race does not affect sentence severity. They may miss the subtle and potentially more interesting interactive effects uncovered here.

The results of our study also demonstrate the importance of explicitly testing for type-of-crime effects. Researchers should not assume that blacks who victimize whites will be punished more harshly regardless of the type of crime. Our results suggest otherwise. We found that although offender/victim race did not have the predicted effects on the severity of the sentences imposed on defendants convicted of all felonies, it did influence the incarceration rate for sexual assault and the expected minimum sentence for murder.

Our finding that offender/victim race was one of the *strongest* predictors of sentence severity for murder and for sexual assault supports the conflict perspective's contention that judges apply the law to control the behavior of those who threaten the power of the dominant group. More to the point, the more serious penalties imposed on black-on-white homicides and sexual assaults suggest that "the more powerful the group to which the victim belongs vis-à-vis the group to which the offender belongs, the greater the seriousness of the violation and hence the more severely the crime is treated by the legal system" (LaFree 1989: 115). Because homicides and sexual assaults against blacks do not involve victims from the dominant social group, and because white-on-white homicides and sexual assaults do not involve the crossing of racial or class lines, these crimes are perceived as less threatening and therefore as less serious.

Interpretation of the results for sexual assault is complicated by our finding that black-on-black sexual assaults involving strangers were more likely to result in incarceration than black-on-black sexual assaults involving acquaintances. The incarceration rates for black-on-white and for white-on-white sexual assaults, on the other hand, were not affected by the relationship between the victim and the defendant. Estrich (1987) has suggested that the most serious disposition is reserved for the aggravated rape case involving a stranger, multiple assailants, or extrinsic violence; the simple rape case involving an acquaintance who acts alone and who does not beat his victim or threaten her with a dangerous weapon is punished less harshly. Our results indicate that this applies only to black men who sexually assault black women. Crimes involving black men and white women are punished harshly regardless of whether the offender and the victim are strangers or acquaintances.

Taking all of our findings concerning sexual assault into account, it appears that judges impose the harshest sentences on black men who assault white women *and* on black men who assault black women who are strangers. Judges believe these are serious crimes that generally merit incarceration. Sexual assaults involving white offenders and white victims are punished more leniently, not because crimes with white victims are deemed less serious than crimes with black victims, but because crimes involving *white offenders* are regarded as less serious than crimes involving *black offenders*. The more lenient punishment of sexual assaults involving black offenders and black victims who are acquainted, on the other hand, suggests that judges downplay the seriousness of this type of simple rape. It suggests that some judges may regard black-on-black rapes involving acquaintances as "'normal' behavior within the black subculture" (Walsh 1987: 154).

Our finding that the impact of offender/victim race is limited to homicide and sexual assault cases indicates that there is a "race/crime-specific perception of the appropriateness of criminal behavior that affects racial differentials in criminal sentencing" (Hawkins 1987: 730). More to the point, it suggests that there is something about murder and sexual assault that prompts judges to impose more severe sentences on blacks who cross racial lines to commit these crimes. Although we can only speculate, judges may regard black-on-white murder and rape as a more serious threat to the power and status of the dominant group than black-on-white robbery or assault. This, of course, assumes that judges apply the law to preserve the power of the dominant group. It is also possible that it is the intimate and interpersonal nature of murder and sexual assault—the violent violation of a person's body—that evokes racially biased sentencing discrimination. Future research should address this issue.

Notes

1. The data used in this manuscript were made available by the Inter-university Consortium for Political and Social Research. Neither the original collectors of the data nor the Consortium bear any responsibility for the analyses or interpretations presented here.

2. The eleven felonies are first-degree murder, second-degree murder, manslaughter, criminal sexual conduct (first degree), criminal sexual conduct (second degree), criminal sexual conduct (third degree), armed robbery, assault with intent to commit murder, assault with intent to commit great bodily harm, assault with intent to rob and steal (armed), and felonious assault.

3. Loftin and his colleagues (1983: 291) report that in calculating good-time credit they used the same procedures used by the Michigan Department of Corrections. These procedures are outlined in Section 33, Act No. 118 as amended, Section 800.33, Compiled Laws of 1948.

4. We did run the regression analyses with a dummy variable for victim race (black = 1; white = 0). We found that victim race did not have a significant effect on either dependent variable.

5. All defendants were originally charged with one of eleven violent felonies. Defendants were, however, convicted of a variety of crimes in addition to these felonies. We used eight dummy variables measuring type of crime in the multivariate analyses. FIRST-DEGREE MURDER, SECOND-DEGREE MURDER, and MANSLAUGHTER are self-explanatory. RAPE includes first- and third-degree criminal sexual conduct. OTHER SEX OFFENSES includes second- and fourth-degree criminal sexual conduct, assault with intent to rape, and attempted CSC1, CSC2, CSC3 and CSC4. ROBBERY includes armed robbery, unarmed robbery (there were too few cases to analyze separately), assault with intent to rob, and attempted robbery. ASSAULT includes assault and battery, aggravated assault, felonious assault, and attempted assaults. OTHER FELONY includes burglary, larceny and other theft offenses, drug offenses, and weapons offenses.

6. We created three dummy variables to measure the type of disposition in the case. PLEA indicates if the defendant pled guilty; BENCH indicates if the defendant was tried by a judge; and JURY indicates if the defendant was tried by a jury. In the multivariate analyses, BENCH is the omitted category. We used all three dispositions, rather than simply trials and guilty pleas, because of the case assignment system used in Detroit. Cases first go by blind draw to one of the floor executive judges, who are not known for imposing the harshest sentences. Their role is to try to work out a plea agreement or to encourage waiver trials, and they do not take any jury trials. If a plea or waiver trial is not agreed to with the floor executive judge, then the case goes by blind draw to one of the other judges. (The incarceration rates for the dispositions are 70 percent for guilty pleas, 64 percent for bench trials, and 95 percent for jury trials.)

7. The results of the probit analysis of the incarceration rate (for all felonies) were as follows: black offender/black victim (MLE = $-.132$; SE = $.09$; MLE/SE = 1.46); white offender/white victim (MLE = $-.399$; SE = $.11$; MLE/SE = 3.41^{***}). The results of the analysis of sex crimes were black offender/black victim (MLE = $-.62$; SE = $.23$; MLE/SE = 2.69^{**}); white offender/white victim (MLE = $-.81$; SE = $.25$; MLE/SE = 3.31^{***}). Complete results of the analysis are available from the author.

8. Because we intended to analyze each crime separately, and because of the small number of cases involving white offenders for some of the crimes, we combined first-degree murder, second-degree murder, and manslaughter into

MURDER. We also combined rape and other sex offenses into SEX CRIME. The regression analyses for MURDER included two dummy variables (first-degree murder; second-degree murder; manslaughter was the omitted category). Similarly, the analyses of SEX CRIME included a dummy variable that indicated whether the defendant was convicted of rape or a lesser offense.

9. Technical details are available from the author on request.

16

The Symbolic Punishment of White-Collar Offenders

Celesta A. Albonetti

This chapter explores the sanctioning of white-collar offenders by focusing on the decision to suspend a sentence. It draws from earlier findings of the relationship between socioeconomic status and sentence outcomes in the federal district courts (Hagan et al. 1980, 1982; Wheeler et al. 1982, 1988; Weisburd et al. 1991). I examine this relationship from an organizational perspective that considers the criminal justice system as an interdependent network of decision-makers who relate to each other primarily within an input/output arrangement of case processing. From this perspective, I suggest that the offender's socioeconomic status is relevant to sentencing outcomes only to the extent that the offender's status is related to priorities of efficient case processing. This is not to say that offenders with financial means to afford an adversarial private attorney do not enjoy an advantage over offenders without such means. What I do suggest is that, relative to prosecutorial and judicial concerns for efficient case processing, the offender's socioeconomic status is not an important determinant of whether a white-collar offender receives a suspended sentence. Of importance are case characteristics that make it worthwhile for the prosecuting attorney and the judge to offer a suspended sentence in exchange for a guilty plea.

Drawing from Hagan et al. (1982) and others (Reiss 1971, 1974; Meyer and Rowan 1977; Hagan and Bernstein 1979; Katz 1979), this chapter empirically explores the effect of offender characteristics (i.e., socioeconomic status, gender, race, record of felony convictions), outcomes at earlier stages of case processing (i.e., pretrial detention, guilty plea), and offense characteristics (i.e., case complexity, maximum sentence statutorily available) on the likelihood of a suspended sentence. This research goes beyond a focus on offender characteristics as central to understanding discretionary decision-making in the sentencing of white-collar offenders by considering how subsystem priorities and interests in case management affect the imposition of punishment. Implications for future research on the relationship between offender social status and sentence severity are noted.

Social Class and Punishment

To date, most of the research on the relationship between the defendant's social class and sentencing has sought to test the relevance of conflict theory to the operations of the criminal justice system. According to conflict theory (Chambliss and Seidman 1971) and other propositions (Black 1976), increases in social status produce increasingly less serious levels of punishment. Most of the empirical research relied on data of case processing for common crime offenders. Some studies report a weak, positive relationship (Chiricos and Waldo 1975), while other research indicates a strong inverse relationship (Farrell and Swigert 1978; Lizotte 1978). The limited variation on the defendant's social class, reflected in common crime data, makes it difficult to statistically test the proposed association.

Within the past decade attention has shifted to exploring the relationship between social class and punishment using data on white-collar crimes.[1] This body of research has produced inconsistent findings of the relationship between the offender's social class and punishment severity. Research on the ten largest federal district courts (Hagan et al. 1980; Hagan et al. 1982; Nagel and Hagan 1982) found that social class, measured by education level and income, was unrelated to length of imprisonment and whether the offender received a prison term compared to a less severe form of punishment such as a fine or probation. However, Wheeler et al. (1982) and Weisburd et al. (1990), using Duncan's Socioeconomic Index to measure social class, found that white-collar offenders of higher socioeconomic status were more likely to be incarcerated. They argued that judges viewed these offenders as more blameworthy than offenders of lower social status and therefore deserving of more severe punishment. However, for incarcerated offenders, they found that social class was unrelated to length of imprisonment. Using Wheeler et al.'s (1982) data and a relational class indicator derived from Wright (1985), Weisburd et al. (1990) found that (1) the Duncan SEI effect is positive but trivial in magnitude and (2) only the contrast of officer with worker produced a significant effect of the likelihood of imprisonment. The findings indicated that officers were less likely to receive a prison term.

In contrast, other researchers (e.g., Benson and Walker 1988) found that the offender's socioeconomic status was not significantly related to the probability of incarceration or the length of sentence.[2] Their findings supported Hagan and Palloni's (1986) conclusion that after Watergate white-collar offenders were incarcerated at a higher rate, but there was no relationship between the offender's social class and probability of imprisonment or length of incarceration.

Theoretical Perspective

To broaden recent discussion of the determinants of sentence severity in white-collar cases, this chapter draws from an organizational perspective of the criminal justice system developed by Hagan and others (Reiss 1974, 1971; Hagan et al. 1979, 1982; Albonetti 1987). This perspective begins by focusing on the social organization of the criminal justice system. Reiss (1971, 1974) suggested that the criminal justice system operates as a system of interdependent subsystems that are held together by the task of processing defendants from the initial decision to prosecute through sentencing. Albonetti (1986, 1987, 1991) suggested that a key feature of this system is a shared interest in avoiding uncertainty at each stage of decision-making. Sources of uncertainty affect outcomes at various stages of the criminal justice system (Albonetti 1987, 1989) and can be a basis for the development of subsystem linkages.

Applying Meyer and Rowan's (1977) concept of a "loosely coupled system" to the criminal justice system, Hagan et al. (1982) examined the operational relationship between prosecuting attorneys and judges in the processing of white-collar offenders. They hypothesized that the coupling between the prosecuting attorney and judge will be tightened when decision makers in the criminal justice system place a high priority on proactive prosecution of white-collar offenses. They argued that proactive prosecution is essential for obtaining a conviction in white-collar crime cases because these cases "usually involve a diffuseness and subtlety of victimization that removes victims themselves as sources of information about the criminal events of concern" (Hagan et al. 1982: 261–262). They argued that effective prosecution of white-collar offenders required a tightening of the otherwise loose coupling between the prosecuting attorney and the sentencing judge. This tightening facilitated the collection and management of evidence, information, and witnesses, which were made particularly difficult because of the structural complexity of white-collar crime compared to common crime. As Hagan et al. (1982: 264) note, "In other words, prosecutors must overcome the tendency toward loose coupling between most parts of the criminal justice system, establishing instead a direct connection between plea bargaining and sanctioning decisions in white-collar cases." Hagan et al.'s hypothesis was tested and verified in their analysis of the determinants of sentence severity in a U.S. attorney's office in a federal district that placed a high priority on prosecuting white-collar crime compared to other districts without such a proactive policy.

Several hypotheses emerge from the theoretical perspective above. First, I hypothesize that for guilty pleas, evidence of a tight coupling between prosecutorial and sentencing subsystems increases the likelihood that the offender receives a suspended sentence. This is consistent with the assertion and findings of Hagan et al. (1982). Second, from an uncertainty avoidance perspective (March and Simon 1958; Thompson 1967; Albonetti 1987), I expect that, among white-collar cases, the effect of pleading guilty on the likelihood of a suspended sentence is conditioned by case complexity. Because guilty pleas facilitate bureaucratic interests in efficient case processing, the rewards for cooperating will be greater for white-collar cases posing higher uncertainty of a trial conviction. In the situation of prosecuting a structurally complex white-collar case, the hypothesized increase in reward associated with a guilty plea disposition is evidence of a tightening between prosecuting attorney and sentencing judge. As a result of this coupling, concessions at sentencing take the form of symbolic punishment for white-collar offenders who are convicted of complex white-collar crime.

What case characteristics are associated with high levels of complexity? For the purpose of this analysis, complex white-collar cases involve both an overarching plan of illegal acts and placement at a high level in an organization. Compared to less complex white-collar crime and common crime, complex white-collar crime requires greater proactive prosecution and is characterized by higher levels of uncertainty of a conviction, if taken to trial. In these complex cases, it is necessary to devote substantial investigative and prosecutorial resources to constructing the illegal events, with no assurance of obtaining a conviction should the case go to trial. These complex white-collar offenses are categorically different than other white-collar crime and common crimes because of the absence of presumptive evidence of a crime. Finally, I hypothesize that the offender's socioeconomic status is related to the imposition of the most lenient of sentences—a symbolic punishment—to the extent that it is related to concerns for avoiding uncertainty in a trial conviction.

Data and Methods

The data were originally gathered from presentence investigation reports for a sample of offenders convicted of one of eight statutory categories, considered as white-collar offenses (Wheeler et al. 1982; Weisburd et al. 1990). Wheeler and his colleagues provided the data for the present analysis. The statutory categories in the federal system are antitrust, securities and exchange violations, postal and wire fraud, false claims and statements, credit and lending institution fraud, bank embezzlement, tax evasion and bribery. The sample was obtained for fiscal years 1976, 1977, and 1978 for the following districts: Central California (Los Angeles), Northern Georgia (Atlanta), Northern Illinois (Chicago), Maryland (Baltimore), Southern New York (Manhattan and the Bronx), Northern Texas (Dallas), and Western Washington (Seattle).

The analysis involves three stages. First, a logistic regression equation of the variables affecting the likelihood of a suspended sentence is estimated for the pooled offenders. Interest centers on the effects of the defendant's social class measures (i.e., education and net worth) and pleading guilty. The effects of the defendant's race, impeccability, bail outcome, and case information (i.e., type of offense, duration) are also estimated. In the second stage of the analysis, white-collar offenses are collapsed into four levels of case complexity. Two indicators of complexity[3] are used as the basis for determining placement. The first indicator is that the illegal activity happened on a number of separate occasions with an overarching plan or that the illegal activity involved a number of activities (discrete or continuous) that had a cumulative effect. The second indicator is the level of organization at which the illegal activity occurred. Both indicators are consistent with Katz's (1979) and Wilson and Matz's (1977) specification of offense characteristics that make investigation and prosecution particularly difficult and uncertain. For each white-collar offense, the percent of cases characterized by both of these two indicators was calculated. The obtained percentages produced four levels of case complexity. Offense type was then collapsed into one of these four levels. These categories are used in the third stage of the analysis.

In order to test the hypothesis that case complexity conditions the effect of pleading guilty on the likelihood of a suspended sentence, the suspended sentence equation is estimated separately for each category of case complexity. Differences in logistic coefficients for pleading guilty and the defendant's social class are examined across the four equations.

Results

Table 16.1 provides descriptive information and coding for the variables included in the logistic regression equation. Table 16.2 provides the logistic regression estimates, their respective standard errors and odds for the variables included in the suspended sentence equation. It indicates that the two defendant social class measures, education and net worth, fail to produce a significant effect on the likelihood of receiving a suspended sentence. Of interest, however, is the finding that defendants who plead guilty are significantly more likely to receive a suspended sentence. This translates into a 2.05 to 1 odds of a suspended sentence. The

TABLE 16.1 Coding and Descriptive Statistics for Variables

Variables	Coding	Frequency	Mean (SD)	Percent
Sentence	1 = Suspended	678		49
	0 = Not suspended	719		51
Processing variables				
Plea	1 = Guilty plea	1,171		84
	0 = Trial	226		16
Pretrial release	1 = Detained	101		7
decision	0 = Not detained	1,296		93
Counsel	1 = Private	561		40
	0 = Public/court appointed	836		60
Offender characteristics				
Race	1 = Minority	342		25
	0 = Non-minority/white	1,055		75
Gender	1 = Male	1,175		84
	0 = Female	222		16
Evidence of remorse	1 = Yes	252		18
	0 = No	1,145		82
Education	1 = High school or more	588		42
	0 = Less than high school	809		58
Net worth	Assets-Liabilities ($1,000)		28.3 (328)	
Impeccability[a]	−2 to +3		1.2 (1.4)	
Prior record	1 = Prior arrests	114		8
	0 = No prior arrests	1,283		92
Offense characteristics				
Dollar victimization	0 = None	13		1
	1 = $100 or less	13		1
	2 = $101–$500	63		4
	3 = $501–$1,000	43		3
	4 = $1,001–$2,500	98		7
	5 = $2,501–$5,000	92		6
	6 = $5,001–$10,000	95		7
	7 = $10,001–$25,000	119		8
	8 = $25,001–$100,000	558		40
	9 = $100,001–$500,000	134		10
	10 = $500,001–$1,000,000	35		3
	11 = $1–$2.5 million	53		4
	12 = $2.5 million or more	81		6
Duration	1 = Less than 1 month	197		12
	2 = 1 month to 1 year	592		36
	3 = 1 year to 3 years	504		31
	4 = 3 years or more	358		21
Defendant's role	1 = Secondary	316		23
	0 = Primary	1,081		77
Sentence severity	Years		6.2 (8.9)	

TABLE 16.1 (continued)

Variables	Coding	Frequency	Mean (SD)	Percent
District	Dummy-coding			
Central California		234		17
Northern Illinois		166		12
Maryland		119		9
Southern New York		292		21
Northern Texas		212		15
Western Washington		159		11
Northern Georgia (omitted category)		215		15

[a] The impeccability scale, developed by Wheeler et al. (1982), uses the following information: defendant raised in an intact family, parents'/guardians' ability to provide necessities of life, living arrangements, type of residence, length at residence, neighborhood of residence, number of residences in past five years, overall academic performance, social adjustments to school, religious preference, frequency of church attendance, involvement with drugs/alcohol, military record, number of jobs held in past five years, employment history, general reputation in the community, favorable letters of recommendation at presentence hearing. Wheeler et al. (1990) report a Cronbach's alpha = .80.

question examined later in the analysis is whether this positive effect is invariant across levels of case complexity. Before that question, it is informative to point out the effects of other variables included in the analysis.

Table 16.2 indicates that offender characteristics that significantly influence the probability of a suspended sentence are gender, showing remorse for the illegal activity, and the offender's impeccability score. These findings indicate that male defendants are less likely than female defendants to receive a suspended sentence. Defendants who expressed remorse for their illegal activity and those who score high on Wheeler et al.'s (1982) impeccability scale are more likely to receive a suspended sentence.

The alternative perspective examined in this paper suggests that case complexity, measured in terms of an overarching plan of illegal activities and level of organizational involvement, conditions the effect of pleading guilty on the likelihood an offender receives a suspended sentence. Put differently, the effect of pleading guilty on sentences varies across levels of case complexity. For defendants convicted of complex white-collar offenses, pleading guilty will have a substantial positive. For defendants convicted of less complex white-collar cases, however, the effect of pleading guilty will be small or nonexistent. In less complex white-collar cases the offender may reap some rewards from a guilty plea, but I suggest that the reward will not be great enough to include a suspended

TABLE 16.2 Logistic Estimates and Odds Predicting a Suspended Sentence

Variables	Estimate	Standard Error	Odds[a]
Processing variables			
Plea	.72**	.18	2.04
Pretrial release decision	−2.04**	.34	.13
Counsel	.21	.14	
Offender characteristics			
Race	−.03	.16	
Gender	−1.13**	.19	.07
Evidence of remorse	.37*	.16	1.45
Education	.18	.13	
Net worth	.0001	.0001	
Impeccability	.17**	.06	1.19
Prior record	−.09	.22	
Offense characteristics			
Dollar victimization	−.21**	.03	.81
Duration	−.23**	.07	.79
Defendant's role	.77**	.15	2.16
Sentence severity	−.06**	.01	.94
District			
Central California	−.07	.21	
Northern Illinois	−.67**	.23	.51
Maryland	−.50*	.25	.61
Southern New York	.14	.19	
Northern Texas	−1.33**	.24	.26
Western Washington	−.58*	.25	.56
Intercept	2.66**	.42	
−2 Log Likelihood	1593.08		
Chi square (20 df)	324.37**		

[a] Odds provided for statistically significant estimates.
* $p < .05$; ** $p < .01$.

sentence. Guilty plea offenders may receive a more lenient sentence than offenders who pursued a trial disposition, but the leniency will be in the form of a reduced prison term or a smaller fine. Clearly, these forms of reward are not to be minimized, but the biggest return on a guilty plea is evidenced in receiving a suspended sentence.

To pursue the question of the invariance of the effect of pleading guilty on the likelihood of a suspended sentence, the original suspended sentence equation is estimated separately for each level of case complexity. As noted earlier, each offense type was located in one of the level of case complexity based on the percentage of cases that were characterized as involving both a high level of planning and a high level of organization placement. Consistent with Katz (1979), antitrust and securities and exchange violations have the highest percentage of such cases (95 percent and 86 percent, respectively). Both bribery and postal and interstate wire frauds have the same percentage of cases so characterized in terms of complexity (40 percent). These offenses are assigned a medium level of case complexity. The third level of case complexity is made up of offenses of false claims/statements fraud (27 percent), lending and credit institution fraud (22 percent), income tax evasion (23 percent), and income tax felony (18 percent). These offenses are assigned a medium-low level of complexity. The offenses characterized as lowest in case complexity are embezzlement (8 percent), forgery (2 percent), and larceny and theft (0 percent). The variation in the percentage of cases within offense type meeting both criterion of complexity is clear and striking. Using these four levels of case complexity, the following analysis explores whether case complexity conditions the effect of pleading guilty on the likelihood of a suspended sentence.

To pursue the suggested alternative theoretical perspective, the original logistic equation is estimated separately for each of the four levels of case complexity. Again, primary interest lies with determining whether there is a significant difference in the coefficient estimates for the effect of pleading guilty on the likelihood of a suspended sentence. Invariance of other estimates is also discussed. Table 16.3 provides the logistic estimates, significance level, and odds for the variables included in each of the suspended sentence equations. Consistent with expectations under the proposed alternative perspective, the effect of pleading guilty on the likelihood of receiving a suspended sentence is substantial and positive for offenders convicted of a white-collar crime characterized as complex. However, for offenders convicted of white-collar crimes characterized as medium or low in level of case complexity, the effect of pleading guilty on the probability of a suspended sentence is nonsignificant. Offenders in these types of cases simply do not reap the same benefit from their guilty plea as those offenders convicted of crimes involving a higher level of complexity.

At first glance, the significant effect of pleading guilty on the suspended sentence for offenders convicted of white-collar crimes characterized by a medium low level of case complexity is not expected under the proposed alternative perspective. However, Katz's (1979) research provides insight into what may account for this finding. Katz (1979) notes that tax evasion cases, similar to security and exchange violations, are cases that must be investigated and prosecuted in a proactive manner due to the lack of presumptive evidence. Tax evasion cases, included in the medium low category, are also characterized by the absence of a ready victim as a source of information about the illegal activity. In this way these cases share in common an important feature that characterized the offenses included in the high complexity category. With this in mind,

TABLE 16.3 Logistic Estimates and Odds Predicting a Suspended Sentence, by Offense Complexity

Variables	High Est.	High Odds[a]	Medium Est.	Medium Odds	Medium Low Est.	Medium Low Odds	Low Est.	Low Odds
Processing variables								
Plea	1.46**	4.31	.58		1.19**	3.29	.18	
Pretrial detention	—	—	-1.78**	.17	-1.97**	.14	-2.40**	.09
Counsel	-.31		.13		-.15		-.17	
Offender characteristics								
Race	—	—	-.52		.46		-.23	
Gender	—	—	-.78		-1.48**	.23	-1.10**	.33
Remorse	.49		.22		.05		1.07**	2.92
Education	-.20		-.20		.49*	1.63	.18	
Net worth	.001**	1.00	-.001		.00		-.00	
Impeccability	-.09		.21		.28**	1.32	.11	
Prior record	-.71		.20		-.44		.38	
Offense characteristics								
$ Victimization	-.14		-.14		-.22**	1.25	-.17**	.84
Duration	.07		-.57**	.57	.08		-.54**	.58
Defendant role	1.04**	2.83	1.25**	3.49	.46		.69*	1.99
Sentence severity	-.02		-.08*	.92	-.21**	.81	-.003	
Type of offense								
Bribery			1.11*	3.03				
Securities	-1.75**	.17						
District								
Northern Illinois					-1.24**	.29		
Maryland					-1.07**	.34		
Northern Texas			-1.90**	.15	-1.08**	.34	-.68	.21
Intercept	1.66		2.54**		2.33**		2.83**	
-2 Log Likelihood	243.06		316.44		459.44		475.56	
Chi square (df)	71.59** (12)		109.20** (16)		118.53** (17)		141.34** (15)	

[a] Odds provided for significant coefficients.
* p < .05; ** p < .01.

the findings become understandable and actually support the underlying argument linking uncertainty in going to trial with the added value placed on guilty pleas. This finding points to a need for future research on sentence outcome to explore dimensions of uncertainty that are unrelated to level of planning and organizational placement.

Additional findings reported in Table 16.3 warrant attention. Level of case complexity clearly conditions the effect of both offender and offense characteristics. The effect of the defendant's net worth, a social status indicator, is significant only in white-collar cases involving a high level of complexity. But it must be noted that the effect is trivial in magnitude.

Conclusion

This chapter explored the question of whether the offender's socioeconomic status is related to the probability of receiving a suspended sentence. Using a measure of social control that distinguishes between white-collar offenders who avoid punishment by a suspended sentence and those who actually serve time in prison, this paper explored (1) the relationship between the offender's educational level, net worth and punishment and (2) the merits of an organizational perspective that emphasizes relationships between interdependent subsystems in the criminal justice system. The proposed alternative perspective suggests that social control in the sentencing of white-collar offenders is influenced not by the offender's social class but by a tightening of the coupling between the prosecuting attorney and the sentencing judge, evidenced by the effect of guilty pleas on the likelihood of receiving a suspended sentence.

For the debate over the relevance of social class to punishment in white-collar cases, three findings are particularly noteworthy. First, findings from the present research indicate that social class, measured by the offender's educational level and net worth, does not substantially and significantly influence the likelihood of receiving a suspended sentence. This is evidenced in the analysis of the pooled offenders and in the across-group analysis. I will return to this point below.

Second, findings suggest general support for the proposed perspective. Compared to offenders convicted of less complex white-collar crimes, offenders convicted of complex white-collar crimes receive a greater return from a guilty plea. Because of the greater uncertainty of winning a trial conviction and the need for greater proactive prosecution of these cases, negotiated pleas for the latter group of offenders reap greater rewards in terms of concessions of leniency at sentencing. This is evidenced by the significant, and stronger, effect of pleading guilty on the likelihood of a suspended sentence for offenders who are convicted of the most complex of the white-collar crimes included in this analysis.

These offenders are in a better bargaining position over the sentence that will be imposed. The need to proactively prosecute complex white-collar cases actually advantages offenders convicted of these crimes.

The findings herein can be viewed in a larger cultural-penal context articulated by Garland (1990). He argues that "if we wish to understand the cultural messages conveyed by punishment we need to study not just the grandiloquent public statements which are occasionally made but also the programmatic repetitive routines of daily practice, for these routines contain within them distinctive patterns of meaning and symbolic forms which are enacted and expressed every time a particular procedure is adopted, a technical language used, or a specific sanction imposed" (Garland 1990: 255). Garland invites us to explore the practical routines to uncover "the values, meanings, and conceptions which are embodied and expressed in penality (1990: 255). For Garland, the declaration of a sentence expresses a symbolic statement that implies a particular understanding of the relations between actors in society. These actors are typically the offender and the victim. Garland's assertion is evidenced in Wheeler et al.'s (1988) research based on interviews with judges sentencing white-collar offenders. As one judge noted, "I tend to sentence more heavily in cases where the crime is continued over a long period of time, and appears not to be impulsive but rather willful and planned (Wheeler et al. 1988: 69). From this rationalization of judicial discretion to sentence more severely, the message, according to Garland, would be clear. Namely, that white-collar victimization that is planned and that continues over an extended period of time results in greater social harm and therefore warrants a more severe punishment.

Clearly, judges do send messages when they sentence. However, the findings of my research suggest that the message associated with a sentence may be as much, if not more, a product of informal practical practices of case processing that are tied to professional and subsystem interests in efficient and proactive disposition of case, influenced by the very structure of the offense.

Third, the findings that case complexity conditions the effect of pleading guilty on the likelihood of a suspended sentence offers a context for further specifying a relationship between social class and social control. The findings herein suggest that to the extent that higher-status offenders are more likely to be charged with *complex* white-collar crimes, they benefit from the complex nature of their crimes. Offenders of higher net worth and higher educational levels are represented with greater frequency in the complex crime category. This finding, taken together with the findings for education and net worth reported in Table 16.3, suggests an indirect effect of social class on the likelihood of receiving a suspended sentence. Because officials are willing to negotiate levels of punishment in the pursuit of convictions in complex and difficult cases, offenders of high social class are more likely to avoid punishment. This conclusion speaks to Shapiro's (1985) findings for sentence outcomes for offenders in SEC violations. She concluded that "despite the greater seriousness of their misdeeds, the cohort of convicted upper status offenders is no more vulnerable to incarceration, a finding that should surprise no one" (Shapiro 1985: 214). My research indicates that actually they are better able to avoid incarceration by their increased likelihood of a suspended sentence.

From the findings herein, several points of departure for future research are suggested. First, future research should identify other shared subsystem-defined priorities that influence the exercise of discretion at other stages of the criminalization process. Do these operating priorities structurally favor one social class while disadvantaging another? Second, research should address the consequences of failing to maintain linkages across subsystems. Under what conditions, organizationally and offense related, are linkages between subsystems in the criminal justice system (i.e., various federal investigative agencies and the prosecuting attorney's office) maintained?

Finally, research should further explore how organizational interests in efficiency and finality in case processing influence the relationship between social class and punishment. Offenders of high social class may be well positioned to avoid severe punishment simply because they are more likely to commit offenses that are complex in nature. Future research should address how the form of punishment varies across social class and how occupants of the upper class are better able to protect their liberty by the way they translate their occupational position and distance from victims into advantage within the structures of the criminal justice system. Findings from this research suggest that advantage in the criminal justice system is not merely a matter of location in a social class, as suggested by traditional theories of crime and punishment.

Notes

1. Representative examples of this work include Hagan et al. (1980), Nagel and Hagan (1982), Wheeler and Rotham (1982), Wheeler et al. (1982, 1988), Hagan and Parker (1985), Hagan and Palloni (1986), Benson and Walker (1988), and Weisburd et al. (1990, 1991).

2. It is important to note that unlike other researchers (e.g., Hagan et al. 1980; Nagel and Hagan 1982; Wheeler et al. 1982; Weisburd et al. 1990), Benson and Walker's (1988) analysis did not include SEC violations, antitrust and bribery offenses. Both SEC and antitrust violations are more likely than other white-collar offenses to be committed by higher-status persons. Excluding these offenses may

substantially decrease variation in the offender's social class, resulting in a less rigorous test of the relationship between class and sentencing.

3. Wheeler et al. (1982) and Weisburg et al. (1990) used four indicators of case complexity: (1) the number of persons other than the defendant who participated in the actual offense; (2) duration of the offense; (3) whether the offense involved a single event or a number of actions with an overall plan; and (4) location of the defendant in the organization. Given my interest in a measure that is sensitive to the difficulties encountered when obtaining a conviction, I use only the latter two dimensions.

References

Abbott, Andrew. 1988. The System of Professions: An Essay on the Division of Expert Labor. Chicago: University of Chicago Press.

Abramovitz, Mimi. 1988. Regulating the Lives of Women: Social Welfare Policy from Colonial Times to the Present. Boston: South End Press.

Adamson, Christopher R. 1984. "Toward a Marxian Penology: Captive Criminal Populations as Economic Threats and Resources." Social Problems 31:435–58.

Adler, Freda. 1975. Sisters in Crime: The Rise of the New Female Criminal. New York: McGraw-Hill.

Adler, Zsuzsanna. 1987. Rape on Trial. London: Routledge & Kegan Paul.

Agnew, Robert. 1983. "Physical Punishment and Delinquency: A Research Note." Youth and Society 15: 225–36.

Albonetti, Celesta A. 1985. "An Integration of Theories to Explain Judicial Discretion." Social Problems 38: 247–66.

———. 1986. "Criminality, Prosecutorial Screening, and Uncertainty: Toward a Theory of Discretionary Decision Making in Felony Case Processing." Criminology 24:623–44.

———. 1987. "Prosecutorial Discretion: The Effects of Uncertainty." Law & Society Review 21:291–313.

———. 1991. "An Analysis of Judicial Discretion: Toward a Reconceptualization of the Variables Affecting Sentence Severity." Social Problems 38: 247–60.

———, Robert M. Hauser, John Hagan and Ilene Nagel. 1989. "Criminal Justice Decision Making as a Stratification Process: The Role of Race and Stratification Resources in Pre-Trial Release." Journal of Quantitative Criminology 5: 57–82.

Alexander, Jeffrey C. (ed.) 1985. Neofunctionalism. Newbury Park, Calif: Sage Publications.

Alexander, John K. 1973. "Poverty, Fear and Continuity: An Analysis of the Poor in Late Eighteenth-Century Philadelphia," in Allen F. Davis and Mark H. Haller, eds., The Peoples of Philadelphia: A History of Ethnic Groups and Lower-Class Life, 1790–1940. Pp. 13–31. Philadelphia: Temple University Press.

Allen, Garland E. 1986. "The Eugenics Record Office at Cold Spring Harbor, 1910–1940: An Essay on Institutional History." Osiris, 2d series, 2: 225–64.

Allen, Hilary. 1987. Justice Unbalanced: Gender, Psychiatry and Judicial Decisions. Philadelphia: Open University Press.

American Friends Service Committee. 1971. Struggle for Justice. New York: Hill and Wang.

American Humane Association. 1984. Trends in Child Abuse and Neglect: A National Perspective. Denver: The American Humane Association.
Andersen, Margaret L., and Patricia Hill Collins (eds.) 1992. Race, Class and Gender: An Anthology. Belmont, Calif.: Wadsworth.
Anderson, Benedict. 1991. Imagined Communities: Reflections on the Origin and Spread of Nationalism. London: Verso.
Anderson, Victor V. 1914–1915. "The Laboratory in the Study and Treatment of Crime." Journal of Criminal Law and Criminology 5:840–850.
Antunes, George, and Erik J. Scott. 1981. "Calling the Cops: Police Telephone Operators and Citizen Calls for Service." Journal of Criminal Justice 9:165–179.
Aries, Philippe. 1962. Centuries of Childhood. New York: Vintage.
Arkin, Steven D. 1980. "Discrimination and Arbitrariness in Capital Punishment: An Analysis of Post-Furman Murder Cases in Dade County, Florida, 1973–1976." Stanford Law Review 33: 75–101.
Arnold, Bruce L., and John Hagan. 1992. "Careers of Misconduct: The Structure of Prosecuted Professional Deviance Among Lawyers." American Sociological Review.
Arvanites, Thomas M. 1992. "The Mental Health and Criminal Justice Systems: Complementary Forms of Coercive Control," in Allen E. Liska, ed., Social Threat and Social Control. Pp. 131–150. Albany: State University of New York Press.
Austin, James, and Barry Krisberg. 1981. "Wider, Stronger and Different Nets: The Dialectics of Criminal Justice Reform" Journal of Research in Crime and Delinquency 18: 165–96.
Austin, Thomas L. 1981. "The Influence of Court Location on Type of Criminal Sentence: The Rural-Urban Factor." Journal of Criminal Justice 9: 305–16.
Bachelard, Gaston. 1940. The Philosophy of No: A Philosophy of the New Scientific Mind. New York: Orion Press.
Backus, Frederick F. 1846. Report of the Committee on Medical Societies and Medical Colleges, on that Portion of the Census Relating to Idiots. New York Sen. Doc. No. 23.
———. 1847. Report of the Committee on Medical Societies and Medical Colleges, Relative to the Bill Proposing the Establishment of an Asylum or School for Idiots, &c. New York Sen. Doc. No. 44.
Baker, Paula. 1984. "The Domestification of Politics: Women and American Political Society, 1780–1920." American Historical Review 89: 620–47.
Baldus, David C., Charles A. Pulaski, Jr., and George Woodworth. 1983. "Comparative Review of Death Sentences: An Empirical Study of the Georgia Experience." Journal of Criminal Law and Criminology. 74: 661–753.
———. 1986. "Arbitrariness and Discrimination in the Administration of the Death Penalty: A Challenge to State Supreme Courts." Stetson Law Review 15: 133–261.
Baldus, David C., George Woodworth and Charles Pulaski. 1985. "Monitoring and Evaluating Contemporary Death Sentencing Systems: Lessons From Georgia." U.C. Davis Law Review 18: 1375–1407.

Bannister, Robert C. 1979. Social Darwinism: Science and Myth in Anglo-American Social Thought. Philadelphia: Temple University Press.
Banton, Michael. 1964. The Policeman in the Community. New York: Basic.
Barak, Gregg (ed.) 1991. Crimes by the Capitalist State: An Introduction to State Criminality. Albany: State University of New York Press.
Barnett, Arnold. 1985. "Some Distribution Patterns for the Georgia Death Sentence." U.C. Davis Law Review 18: 1327–74.
Barrett, Michele and Mary McIntosh. 1991. The Anti-Social Family. London: Verso.
Bartlett, Katharine T., and Rosanne Kennedy. (eds.) 1991. Feminist Legal Theory. Boulder, Colo.: Westview.
Baumgartner, Margaret P. 1988. The Moral Order of a Suburb. New York: Oxford University Press.
Bayley, David H. 1985. Patterns of Policing: A Comparative International Analysis. New Brunswick, N.J.: Rutgers University Press.
Beck, E. M., and Stewart E. Tolnay. 1990. "The Killing Fields of the Deep South: The Market for Cotton and the Lynching of Blacks, 1882–1930." American Sociological Review 55: 526–39.
Beck, E. M., James L. Massey and Stewart E. Tolnay. 1989. "The Gallows, The Mob, The Vote: Lethal Sanctioning of Blacks in North Carolina and Georgia, 1882 to 1930." Law & Society Review 23: 317–31.
Becker, Gary S. 1968. "Crime and Punishment: An Economic Approach." Journal of Political Economy 76:169–217.
———. 1975. Human Capital. 2nd edition. New York: National Bureau of Economic Research.
Becker, Howard S. 1963. Outsiders: Studies in the Sociology of Deviance. New York: Free Press.
Beisel, Nicola. 1990. "Class, Culture, and Campaigns Against Vice in Three American Cities, 1872–1892." American Sociological Review 55: 44–62.
Bell, Derrick A., Jr. 1980. Race, Racism, and American Law. Boston: Little Brown.
Benson, Michael L., and Esteban Walker. 1988. "Sentencing the White-Collar Offender." American Sociological Review 53: 294–302.
Ben-Yehuda, Nachman. 1980. "The European Witch Craze of the 14th and 17th Centuries: A Sociologist's Perspective." American Journal of Sociology 86:1–31.
Bergesen, Albert. 1977. "Political Witch Hunts: The Sacred and Subversive in Cross-National Perspective." American Sociological Review 42: 220–33.
———. 1984. "The Cultural Anthropology of Mary Douglas," in Robert Wuthnow, James Davison Hutton, Albert Bergesen, and Edith Kurtzweil, eds., Cultural Analysis: The Work of Peter L. Berger, Mary Douglas, Michel Foucault, and Jurgen Habermas. Pp. 77–132. Boston: Routledge & Kegan Paul.
Berk, Richard A., Sheldon L. Messinger, David Rauma, and J.E. Bercochea. 1983. "Prisons as Self-Regulating Systems: A Comparison of Historical Patterns in California for Male and Female Offenders." Law & Society Review 17: 547–86.
Berk, Richard A., David Rauma, Sheldon L. Messinger, and Thomas F.

Cooley. 1981. "A Test of the Stability of Punishment Hypothesis: The Case of California 1851–1970." American Sociological Review 46: 805–29.
Bernard, Thomas J. 1983. The Consensus-Conflict Debate: Form and Content in Social Theories. New York: Columbia University Press.
Bernstein, Basil B. 1971. Class Codes and Control Vol. I. London: Routledge & Kegan Paul.
———. 1973. Class Codes and Control Vol. II. London: Routledge & Kegan Paul.
———. 1979. Class Codes and Control Vol. III. London: Routledge & Kegan Paul.
Bernstein, Ilene Nagel, William R. Kelly, and Patricia A. Doyle. 1977. "Societal Reaction to Deviants: The Case of Criminal Defendants." American Sociological Review 42: 743–95.
Berry, William D., and David Lowery. 1990. "An Alternative Approach to Understanding Budgetary Trade-offs." American Journal of Political Science 34: 671–705.
Besharov, Douglas. (ed.) 1988. Protecting Children from Abuse and Neglect: Policy and Practice. Springfield, Ill.: C.C. Thomas.
Bhabha, Homi K. (ed.) 1990. Nation and Narration. London: Routledge.
Bickle, Gayle S., and Ruth D. Peterson. 1991. "The Impact of Gender-based Family Roles in Criminal Sentencing." Social Problems 38: 372–94.
Bittner, Egon. 1970. The Functions of Police in Urban Society. Bethesda, Md.: National Institute of Mental Health.
Black, Donald. 1971. "The Social Organization of Arrest." Stanford Law Review 23: 1087–1111.
———. 1976. The Behavior of Law. New York: Academic Press.
———. 1980. Manners and Customs of the Police. New York: Academic Press.
———. 1983. "Crime as Social Control." American Sociological Review 48: 34–45.
———. 1989. Sociological Justice. New York: Oxford University Press.
Blalock, Hubert M. 1956. "Economic Discrimination and Negro Increase." American Sociological Review 21: 584–88.
———. 1957. "Percent Nonwhite and Racial Discrimination in the South." American Sociological Review 22: 677–82.
———. 1967. Toward a Theory of Minority Group Relations. New York: John Wiley and Sons.
Blauner, Robert. 1972. Racial Oppression in America. New York: Harper and Row.
Bledstein, Burton J. 1976. The Culture of Professionalism. New York: W. W. Norton.
Blumstein, Alfred. 1982. "On the Racial Disproportionality of United States' Prison Populations." Journal of Criminal Law and Criminology 73: 1259–81.
———, and Jacqueline Cohen. 1973. "A Theory of the Stability of Punishment." Journal of Criminal Law and Criminology 64: 198–207.
———, and Souymo D. Moitra. 1979. "Growing or Stable Incarceration Rates:

A Comment on Cahalan's Trends in Incarceration in the United States since 1880." Crime and Delinquency 25: 91–4.
Blumstein, Alfred, Jacqueline Cohen, and David Nagin. 1976. "The Dynamics of a Homeostatic Punishment Process." Journal of Criminal Law and Criminology 67: 317–34.
———. 1978. Deterrence and Incapacitation: Estimating the Effects of Criminal Sanctions on Crime Rates. Washington, D.C.: National Academy of Science.
Blumstein, Alfred, Jacqueline Cohen, Susan E. Martin, and Michael H. Tonry. (eds.) 1983. Research on Sentencing: The Search for Reform, Vol 1. Washington, D.C.: National Academy Press.
Bogardus, Emory S. 1928. Immigration and Race Attitudes. Boston: D.C. Heath.
———. 1933. "A Social Distance Scale." Sociology and Social Research 17: 265–71.
———. 1959. Social Distance. Yellow Springs, Oh.: Antioch Press.
Boli-Bennett, John, and John W. Meyer. 1978. "The Ideology of Childhood and the State: Rules Distinguishing Children in National Constitutions." American Sociological Review 43: 797–812.
Bonger, Willem A. 1943. Race and Crime. New York: Columbia University Press.
———. 1969 [1916]. Criminality and Economic Conditions. Abr. by Austin T. Turk. Bloomington: Indiana University Press.
Boris, Eileen. 1991. "Reconstructing the 'Family': Women, Progressive Reform, and the Problem of Social Control," in Noralee Frankel and Nancy S. Dye, eds., Gender, Class, Race and Reform in the Progressive Era. Pp 73–86. Lexington: University Press of Kentucky.
Boswell, John. 1990. "Revolutions, Universals, and Sexual Categories," in Martin B. Duberman, Martha Vicinus, and George Chauncey, Jr., eds., Hidden from History: Reclaiming the Gay and Lesbian Past. Pp. 17–53. New York: Meridian.
Bottoms, Anthony E. 1983. "Neglected Features of Contemporary Penal Systems," in David Garland and Peter Young, eds., The Power to Punish: Contemporary Penality and Social Analysis. Pp. 166–202. London: Heineman Educational Books.
Bourdieu, Philippe. 1962. The Algerians. Boston: Beacon.
———. 1977. Outline of a Theory of Practice. New York: Cambridge University Press.
———. 1981. "The Specificity of the Scientific Field," in Charles C. Lemert, ed., French Sociology: Rupture and Renewal since 1968. Pp. 257–92. New York: Columbia University Press.
———. 1984. Distinction: A Social Critique of the Judgement of Taste. Cambridge, Mass.: Harvard University Press.
———. 1988. Prestige. Cambridge, Mass.: Harvard University Press.
———. 1990a. The Logic of Practice. Stanford, Calif.: Stanford University Press.
———. 1990b. Photography: A Middle-Brow Art. Stanford, Calif.: Stanford University Press.

———. 1991. Language and Symbolic Power. Edited and with an introduction by John P. Thompson. Cambridge, Mass.: Harvard University Press.
———, and Jean-Claude Passeron. 1977. Reproduction in Education, Society and Culture. Beverly Hills, Calif.: Sage Publications.
———, and Loic J.D. Wacquant. 1992. An Invitation to Reflexive Sociology. Chicago: University of Chicago Press.
Bowers, William J. 1984. Legal Homicide: Death as Punishment in America, 1864–1982. Boston: Northeastern University Press.
———, and Glenn L. Pierce. 1980. "Arbitrariness and Discrimination Under Post-Furman Capital Statutes." Crime and Delinquency 26: 563–635.
Box, Steven, and Chris Hale. 1982. "Economic Crisis and the Rising Prison Population in England and Wales." Crime and Social Justice 17:20–35.
———. 1984. "Liberation/Emancipation, Economic Marginalization, and Less Chivalry." Criminology 22:473–97.
———. 1985. "Unemployment, Imprisonment and Prison Overcrowding." Contemporary Crisis 9:209–28.
Braithwaite, John. 1989. Crime, Shame and Reintegration. New York: Cambridge University Press.
Branham, Vernon C. 1926. "The Classification and Treatment of the Defective Delinquent." Journal of Criminal Law and Criminology 17:183–217.
Brennan, Tim, David Huizinga, and Delbert S. Elliott. 1978. The Social Psychology of Runaways. Lexington, Mass.: Lexington Books.
Brenzel, Barbara M. 1983. Daughters of the State. Cambridge, Mass.: MIT Press.
Bridges, George S., and Robert D. Crutchfield. 1988. "Law, Social Standing and Racial Disparities in Imprisonment." Social Forces 66: 601–18.
———, Robert D. Crutchfield and Edith E. Simpson. 1987. "Law, Social Standing and Racial Disparities in Imprisonment." Social Problems 34: 345–65.
Brown, JoAnne. 1992. The Definition of a Profession. Princeton, N.J.: Princeton University Press.
———, and David K. van Keuren. (eds.) 1991. The Estate of Social Knowledge. Baltimore, Md.: The Johns Hopkins University Press.
Brown, M. Craig, and Barbara D. Warner. 1992. " Immigrants, Urban Politics, and Policing in 1900." American Sociological Review 57: 293–305.
Brown, Stephen E. 1984. "Social Class, Child Maltreatment, and Delinquent Behavior." Criminology 22: 259–78.
Browne, Angela. 1987. When Battered Women Kill. New York: Free Press.
Bruner, Edward M. 1986. "Ethnography as Narrative," in Victor W. Turner and Edward M. Bruner, eds., The Anthropology of Experience. Pp. 137–155. Urbana: University of Illinois Press.
Bull, David, and Wilding, Paul. (eds.) 1983. Thatcherism and the Poor. London: Child Poverty Action Group.
Burgdorf, Ken. 1980. Recognition and Reporting of Child Maltreatment. Rockville, Md.: Westat.
Burke, Kenneth. 1969. A Grammar of Motives. Berkeley: University of California Press.
Burt, Ronald S., Hajdeja Iglic, and Charlene Vannuci. 1990. "Sociology

Markets." Department of Sociology, Columbia University. Unpublished manuscript.
Burton, Velmer S., Jr., Francis T. Cullen and Lawrence F. Travis III. 1987. "The Collateral Consequences of a Felony Conviction: A National Study of State Statutes." Federal Probation 51: 52–60.
Buzawa, Eva Schlesinger, and Carl G. Buzawa. 1990. Domestic Violence: The Criminal Justice Response. Newbury Park, Calif.: Sage Publications.
———. (eds.) 1992. Domestic Violence: The Changing Criminal Justice Response. Westport, Conn.: Auburn House.
Bynum, Tim. 1981. "Parole Decision-Making and Native Americans," in Robert McNeely and Carl Pope, eds., Race, Crime, and Criminal Justice. Pp. 75–87. Beverly Hills, Calif.: Sage Publications.
Cahalan, Margaret S. 1979. "Trends in Incarceration in the United States since 1880: A Summary of Reported Rates and the Distribution of Offenses." Crime and Delinquency 25: 9–41.
———. 1986. Historical Corrections Statistics in the United States, 1850–1984. Washington, D.C.: Bureau of Justice Statistics.
Cain, Maureen. (ed.) 1986. "Realism, Feminism, Methodology and Law." International Journal of the Sociology of Law 14: 255–67.
———. 1989. Growing Up Good: Policing the Behavior of Girls in Europe. Newbury Park, Calif: Sage Publications.
———. 1990. "Toward Transgression: New Directions in Feminist Criminology." International Journal of the Sociology of Law 18: 1–18.
———, and Alan Hunt. 1982. Marx and Engels on Law. New York: Academic Press.
Caplan, Paula, Jessie Watters, Georgina White, Ruth Parry, and Robert Bates. 1984. "Toronto Multi-Agency Child Abuse Research Project: The Abused and the Abuser." Child Abuse and Neglect 8: 343–51.
Cappell, Charles L., and Thomas M. Guterbock. 1992. "Visible Colleges: The Social and Conceptual Structure of Sociology Specialties." American Sociological Review 57: 266–73.
Carlen, Pat. 1983. Women's Imprisonment. London: Routledge & Kegan Paul.
———. 1987. "Out of Care, into Custody," in Pat Carlen and Anne Worrall, eds., Gender, Crime and Justice. Pp. 126–69. Philadelphia: Open University Press.
———. 1988. Women, Crime and Poverty. Philadelphia: Open University Press.
Carmichael, Stokely, and Charles Hamilton. 1967. Black Power: The Politics of Liberation in America. New York: Vintage Books.
Carmines, Edward, and John McIver. 1981. "Analyzing Models with Unobserved Variables: Analysis of Covariance Structures," in George W. Bohrnstedt and Edgar F. Borgatta, eds., Social Measurement: Current Issues. Pp. 65–115. Beverly Hills, Calif.: Sage Publications.
Carr-Hill, Roy A., and Nicholas Herbert Stern. 1979. Crime, the Police, and Criminal Statistics. New York: Academic Press.
Carroll, Leo, and Margaret E. Mondrick. 1976. "Racial Bias in the Decision to Grant Parole." Law & Society Review 11: 93–107.

Center for Research on Criminal Justice. 1977. The Iron Fist and the Velvet Glove: An Analysis of the U.S. Police. 2nd edition. Berkeley, Calif.: Center for Research on Criminal Justice.
Central Statistical Office. 1987. Key Data. London: HMSO.
Chamberlin, J. Edward, and Sander L. Gilman. (eds.) 1985. Degeneration: The Dark Side of Progress. New York: Columbia University Press.
Chambliss, William J. 1964. "A Sociological Analysis of the Law of Vagrancy." Social Problems 12: 67–77.
———. 1973. "Elites and the Creation of Criminal Law," in William J. Chambliss, ed., Sociological Readings in the Conflict Perspective. Pp. 430–44. Reading, Mass.: Addison-Wesley.
———, and Robert B. Seidman. 1971. Law, Order and Power. Reading, Mass.: Addison-Wesley.
Chaudhuri, Molly, and Kathleen Daly. 1992. "Do Restraining Orders Help? Battered Women's Experience with Male Violence and Legal Process," in Eve Buzawa and Carl Buzawa, eds., Domestic Violence: The Changing Criminal Justice Response. Pp. 227–252. Westport, Conn.: Auburn House.
Chesler, Phyllis. 1972. Women and Madness. Garden City, N.Y.: Doubleday.
Chiricos, Theodore G., and Miriam A. DeLone. 1992. "Labor Surplus and Punishment: A Review and Assessment of Theory and Evidence." Social Problems 39: 421–46.
———, and Gordon P. Waldo. 1975. "Socioeconomic Status and Criminal Sentencing: An Empirical Assessment of a Conflict Perspective." American Sociological Review 40: 753–72.
Christianson, Scott. 1981. "Our Black Prisons." Crime and Delinquency 27: 364–75.
Christie, Nils. 1977. "Conflicts as Property." British Journal of Criminology 17: 1–15.
Cicourel, Aaron. 1968. The Social Organization of Juvenile Justice. New York: John Wiley.
Clark, Alexander L., and Jack P. Gibbs. 1965. "Social Control: A Reformulation." Social Problems 12: 398–415.
Clarke, John. 1991. New York and Old Enemies: Essays on Cultural Studies and America. London: Harper Collins Academic.
Clark, Terry Nichols. 1975. "Community Power," in Alex Inkeles, James Coleman and Neil Smelser, eds., Annual Review of Sociology, Vol 1. Pp. 271–95. Palo Alto, Calif.: Annual Reviews, Inc.
Cloward, Richard A., and Lloyd E. Ohlin. 1960. Delinquency and Opportunity: A Theory of Delinquent Gangs. Glencoe, Ill.: The Free Press.
Cloyd, Jerald W. 1977. "The Processing of Misdemeanor Drinking Drivers: The Bureaucratization of the Arrest, Prosecution, and Plea Bargaining Situations." Social Forces 56: 385–407.
Cockerham, William C. 1981. The Sociology of Mental Disorder. Englewood Cliffs, N.J.: Prentice-Hall.
Cohen, Frederick S., and Judianne Densen-Gerber. 1982. "A Study of the Relationship Between Child Abuse and Drug Addiction in 178 Patients: Preliminary Results." Child Abuse and Neglect 6: 383–87.

Collins, Randall. 1975. Conflict Sociology: Toward an Explanatory Science. New York: Academic Press.
Collins, Winfield H. 1918. The Truth About Lynching and the Negro in the South. New York: The Neale Publishing Company.
Connor, Walter. 1972. "The Manufacture of Deviance: The Case of the Soviet Purge, 1936–1938." American Sociological Review 37: 403–13.
Conrad, Peter, and Joseph W. Schneider. 1980. Deviance and Medicalization: From Badness to Sickness. St. Louis, Mo.: C.V. Mosby Company.
Cook, Dee. 1987. "Women on Welfare: In Crime or Injustice," in Pat Carlen and Anne Worrall, eds., Gender, Crime and Justice. Pp. 28–42. Philadelphia: Open University Press.
Cook, Philip J. 1977. "Punishment and Crime: A Critique of Current Findings Concerning the Preventive Effect of Criminal Sanctions." Law and Contemporary Problems 41: 164–204.
Cooper, Lynn, and Anthony Platt. 1968. Policing America. Englewood Cliffs, N.J.: Prentice-Hall.
Corzine, Jay, James Creech and Lin Corzine. 1983. "Black Concentration and Lynchings in the South: Testing Blalock's Power-Threat Hypothesis." Social Forces 61: 774–796.
———, Lin Huff-Corzine and James C. Creech. 1988. "The Tenant Labor Market and Lynching in the South: A Test of Split Labor Market Theory." Sociological Inquiry 58: 261–78.
Cousins, Mark. 1978. "Material Arguments and Feminism." M/F 2: 63–70.
———. 1980. "Men's Rea: A Note on Sexual Difference, Criminology and the Law," in Pat Carlen and Mike Collison, eds., Radical Issues in Criminology. Pp. 109–22. Totowa, N.J.: Barnes & Noble.
Cowan, Ruth Schwartz. 1985. Sir Francis Galton and the Study of Heredity in the Nineteenth Century. New York: Garland.
Cravens, Hamilton. 1985. "History of the Social Sciences." Osiris, 2d series, 1:183–207.
Crenshaw, Kimberle. 1989. "Demarginalizing the Intersection of Race and Sex: A Black Feminist Critique of Antidiscrimination Doctrine, Feminist Theory, and Antiracist Politics." The University of Chicago Legal Forum: 139–167.
Cumming, Elaine, Ian Cumming, and Laura Edell. 1962. "Policeman as Philosopher, Guide and Friend." Social Problems 12:276–286.
Curran, Debra. 1983. "Judicial Discretion and Defendant's Sex." Criminology 21: 41–58.
Currie, Elliot P. 1968. "Crimes without Criminals: Witchcraft and Its Control in Renaissance Europe." Law & Society Review 3: 7–32.
Cunningham, Hugh. 1991. The Children of the Poor: Representations of Childhood since the Seventeenth Century. Oxford: Basil Blackwell.
Cutler, J. E. 1905. Lynch-Law: An Investigation into the History of Lynchings in the United States. New York: Longsman Green.
Dahl, Tove Stang. 1987. Women's Law: An Introduction to Feminist Jurisprudence. Oslo: Norwegian University Press.
Dahrendorf, Ralf. 1959. Class and Class Conflict in Industrial Society. Stanford, Calif.: Stanford University Press.

———. 1968. Essays in the Theory of Society. Stanford, Calif.: Stanford University Press.

Daly, Kathleen. 1987a. "Discrimination in the Criminal Courts: Family, Gender and the Problem of Equal Treatment." Social Forces 66: 152–75.

———. 1987b. "Structure and Practice of Familial-Based Justice in a Criminal Court." Law & Society Review 21:267–290.

———. 1989a. "Neither Conflict nor Labeling nor Paternalism will Suffice: Intersections of Race, Ethnicity, Gender, and Family in Criminal Court Decisions." Crime & Delinquency 35: 136–168.

———. 1989b. "Criminal Justice Ideologies and Practices in Different Voices: Some Feminist Questions about Justice." International Journal of the Sociology of Law 17: 1–18.

———. 1990. "Reflections on Feminist Legal Thought." Social Justice 17: 7–24.

———. Forthcoming. Gender, Crime, and Punishment: Problems of Equality and Justice. New Haven, Conn.: Yale University Press.

———, and Rebecca L. Bordt. 1991. "Gender, Race, and Discrimination Research: Disparate Meanings of Statistical 'Sex' and 'Race Effects' in Sentencing." University of Michigan, Ann Arbor, Mich. Unpublished manuscript.

Danielson, Florence H., and Charles B. Davenport. 1912. "The Hill Folk: Report on a Rural Community of Hereditary Defectives," in Nicole H. Rafter, ed., White Trash: The Eugenic Family Studies, 1877–1919. Pp. 81–163. Boston: Northeastern University Press.

Davis, Kenneth Culp. 1969. Discretionary Justice. Chicago: University of Chicago Press.

Davis, Kingsley. 1976 [1961]. "Sexual Conduct," in Robert K. Merton and Robert Nisbet, eds., Contemporary Social Problems. 4th edition. Pp. 221–61. New York: Harcourt, Brace, Jovanovich, Inc.

———, and Wilbert E. Moore. 1945. "Some Principles of Stratification." American Sociological Review 10: 242–49.

Davis, Mike. 1990. City of Quartz: Excavating the Future in Los Angeles. London: Verso.

Davis, Phillip. 1983. "Restoring the Semblance of Order: Police Strategies in the Domestic Dispute." Symbolic Interaction 6:261–78.

Delgado, Richard. 1989. "Storytelling for Oppositionists and Others: A Plea for Narrative." Michigan Law Review 87: 2411–41.

Dembo, Richard, Linda Williams, Lawrence LaVoie, Estrellita Berry, Alan Getreu, Eric D. Wish, James Schmeidler, and Mark Washburn. 1989. "Physical Abuse, Sexual Victimization, and Illicit Drug Use: Replication of a Structural Analysis Among a New Sample of High Risk Youth." Violence and Victims 4: 121–38.

Dentler, Robert A., and Kai T. Erikson. 1959. "The Functions of Deviance in Groups." Social Problems 7: 98–107.

Denzin, Norman. 1984. "The Phenomenology of Domestic, Family Violence." American Journal of Sociology 90: 483–513.

Derrida, Jacques. 1976. Of Grammatology. Baltimore, Md.: The Johns Hopkins University Press.

Deutsch, Sarah. 1987. No Separate Refuge: Culture, Class, and Gender on the Anglo-Hispanic Frontier in the American Southwest, 1880–1940. New York: Oxford University Press.
DiMaggio, Paul. 1979. "Review essay on Pierre Bourdieu." American Journal of Sociology 84:1460–74.
Dobash, Russell P., R. Emerson Dobash and Sue Gutteridge. 1986. The Imprisonment of Women, New York: Basil Blackwell.
Doerner, William G. 1988. "Child Maltreatment Seriousness and Juvenile Delinquency." Youth and Society 19: 197–224.
Donzelot, Jacques. 1979. The Policing of Families. New York: Pantheon.
Douglas, Mary. 1966. Purity and Danger. London: Routledge & Kegan Paul.
———. 1982. Natural Symbols. New York: Pantheon.
Dowbiggin, Ian. 1991. Inheriting Madness: Professionalization and Psychiatric Knowledge in Nineteenth-Century France. Berkeley: University of California Press.
DuBois, W.E.B. 1899. The Philadelphia Negro. New York: Benjamin Blom.
———. (ed.) 1904. Proceedings of the Ninth Atlanta Conference for the Study of the Negro Problems, Volume 2. Atlanta: Atlanta University.
Duff, John B. 1971. The Irish in the United States. Belmont, Calif.: Wadsworth.
Dugdale, Richard L. 1877. "The Jukes": A Study in Crime, Pauperism, Disease and Heredity; also Further Studies of Criminals. New York: G. P. Putnam's Sons.
Dunford, Franklyn, David Huizinga, and Delbert S. Elliott. 1990. "The Role of Arrest in Domestic Assault: The Omaha Police Experiment." Criminology 28:183–206.
Durkheim, Emile. 1915. Elementary Forms of the Religious Life. New York: Free Press.
———. 1938. The Rules of Sociological Method. Glencoe, Ill.: Free Press.
———. 1947. The Division of Labor in Society. Glencoe, Ill.: Free Press.
———. 1973. "Individualism and the Intellectuals," in Robert N. Bellah, ed., Emile Durkheim on Morality and Society. Pp. 43–57. Chicago: University of Chicago Press.
———. 1978. "Two Laws of Penal Evolution," in Mark Traugott, ed. and trans., Emile Durkheim on Institutional Analysis. Pp. 153–80. Chicago: University of Chicago Press.
Eagleton, Terry. 1991. Ideology: An Introduction. London: Verso.
Eaton, Mary. 1987. "The Question of Bail: Magistrates' Responses to Applications for Bail on Behalf of Men and Women Defendants," in Pat Carlen and Anne Worrall, eds., Gender, Crime and Justice. Pp. 95–107. Philadelphia: Open University Press.
Edwards, Susan S. M. 1984. Women on Trial: A Study of the Female Suspect, Defendant and Offender in the Criminal Law and the Criminal Justice System. Manchester, U. K.: Manchester University Press.
Ehrenreich, Barbara, and Deirdre English. 1978. For Her Own Good. Garden City, N.Y.: Anchor.
Ehrlich, Isaac. 1973. "Participation in Illegitimate Activities: A Theoretical and Empirical Investigation." Journal of Political Economy 81: 521–64.

Elliott, Delbert S., and Suzanne S. Ageton. 1980. "Reconciling Race and Class Differences in Self-Reported and Official Estimates of Delinquency." American Sociological Review 45: 95–119.

Emerson, Robert M. 1969. Judging Delinquents: Context and Process in Juvenile Court. Chicago: Aldine.

———. 1983. "Holistic Effects in Social Control Decision-Making." Law & Society Review 17: 425–55.

———. 1991. "Case Processing and Interorganizational Knowledge: Detecting the 'Real Reason' for Referrals." Social Problems 38: 198–212.

———. 1992. "Typification and Social Control Decision-Making." Unpublished paper presented at the State-of-the-Art Conference on Inequality, Crime, and Social Control, University of Georgia, April.

———, and Sheldon L. Messinger. 1977. "The Micro-Politics of Trouble." Social Problems 25: 121–34.

Ennis, James G. 1992. "The Social Organization of Sociological Knowledge: Modeling the Intersection of Specialties." American Sociological Review 57: 259–65.

Ericson, Richard V. 1981. Making Crime: A Study of Detective Work. Toronto: Butterworths.

———. 1982. Reproducing Order: A Study of Police Patrol Work. Toronto: University of Toronto Press.

———. 1989. "Patrolling the Facts: Secrecy and Publicity in Policework." British Journal of Sociology 40: 205–26.

———. 1991. "Mass Media, Crime, Law, and Justice." British Journal of Criminology 31: 219–49.

Erikson, Kai T. 1966. Wayward Puritans: A Study in the Sociology of Deviance. New York: Wiley.

Estrich, Susan. 1987. Real Rape. Cambridge, Mass.: Harvard University Press.

Fanon, Franz. 1965. The Wretched of the Earth. New York: Grove.

Farber, Edward D., Cecilia Kinast, W. Douglas McCoard, and Deborah Falkner. 1984. "Violence in Families of Adolescent Runaways." Child Abuse and Neglect 8:295–99.

Farley, Reynolds. 1990. "Blacks, Hispanics and White Ethnic Groups: Are Blacks Uniquely Disadvantaged?" The American Economic Review 80: 237–41.

Farnworth, Margaret. 1989. "Theory Integration Versus Model Building," in Steven F. Messner, Marvin D. Krohn and Allen E. Liska. eds. Theoretical Integration in the Study of Deviance and Crime: Problems and Prospects. Pp. 93–103. Albany: State University of New York Press.

Farrell, Ronald A., and Victoria Swigert. 1978. "Legal Disposition of Intergroup and Intra-group Homicides." Sociological Quarterly 19:565–76.

Feeley, Malcolm. 1970. "Coercion and Compliance: A New Look at an Old Problem." Law & Society Review 4: 505–19.

———. 1979. The Process is the Punishment: Handling Cases in a Lower Criminal Court. New York: Russell Sage Foundation.

———, and Deborah Little. 1991. "The Vanishing Female: The Decline of Women in the Criminal Process, 1687–1912. " Law & Society Review 25: 19–57.

References

Fernald, Guy G. 1917. "The Psychopathic Clinic at Massachusetts Reformatory." Journal of Psycho-Asthenics 21:73–81.
Fernald, Walter E. 1909–1910. "The Imbecile with Criminal Instincts." Journal of Psycho-Asthenics 14:16–36.
——. 1917. "The Growth of Provision for the Feeble-minded in the United States." Mental Hygiene I:34–59.
Ferraro, Kathleen J. 1989. "Policing Woman Battering." Social Problems 36: 61–74.
Ferdinand, Theodore N. 1967. "The Criminal Patterns of Boston since 1849." American Journal of Sociology 73:84–99.
Fineman, Martha Albertson, and Nancy Sweet Thomadsen. (eds.) 1991. At the Boundaries of Law: Feminism and Legal Theory. New York: Routledge, Chapman and Hall, Inc.
Finkelhor, David. 1990. "Is Child Abuse Overreported?" Public Welfare 48: 22–9.
——, Richard J. Gelles, Gerald T. Hotaling, and Murray Straus. 1983. The Dark Side of Families: Current Family Violence Research. Beverly Hills, Calif.: Sage Publications.
Finstad, Liv. 1990. "Sexual Offenders Out of Prison: Principles for a Realistic Utopia." International Journal of the Sociology of Law 18: 157–77.
Fitzpatrick, Ellen. 1990. Endless Crusade: Women Social Scientists and Progressive Reform. New York: Oxford University Press.
Flowers, Ronald Barri. 1988. Minorities and Criminality. Westport, Conn.: Greenwood Press.
Foucault, Michel. 1965. Madness and Civilization. New York: Vintage.
——. 1977. Discipline and Punish. New York: Pantheon.
——. 1978. The History of Sexuality. Volume 1: An Introduction. New York: Random House.
——. 1988. "The Dangerous Individual," in Lawrence D. Kritzman, ed., Michel Foucault: Politics, Philosophy, Culture—Interviews and Other Writings, 1977–1984. Pp. 126–51. New York: Routledge.
Foote, Caleb. 1956. "Vagrancy Type Laws and Their Administration." University of Pennsylvania Law Review 104: 603–50.
Frankel, Marvin. 1972. Criminal Sentences. New York: Hill and Wang.
Frankel, Noralee, and Nancy S. Dye. (eds.) 1991. Gender, Class, Race and Reform in the Progressive Era. Lexington: University Press of Kentucky.
Frazier, Charles E., E. Wilbur Bock, and John C. Henretta. 1983. "The Role of Probation Officers in Determining Gender Differences in Sentencing Severity." The Sociological Quarterly 24: 305–18.
Fredrickson, George M. 1981. White Supremacy: A Comparative Study in American and South African History. Oxford: Oxford University Press.
Freiberg, Arie, and Pat O'Malley. 1984. "State Intervention and the Civil Offense." Law & Society Review 18: 373–94.
Freidson, Eliot. 1988. Profession of Medicine: A Study of the Sociology of Applied Knowledge. Chicago: University of Chicago Press.
Friedman, Lawrence. 1981. The Roots of Justice: Crime and Punishment in Alameda County, California, 1870–1910. Chapel Hill: University of North Carolina Press.

———. 1985. Total Justice. Boston: Beacon Press.
Frisbie, W. Parker, and Lisa Neibert. 1976. "Inequality and the Relative Size of Minority Populations: A Comparative Analysis." American Journal of Sociology 82: 1007–30.
Furner, Mary O. 1975. Advocacy and Objectivity: A Crisis in the Professionalization of American Social Science. Lexington: University Press of Kentucky.
Fuss, Diana. 1989. Essentially Speaking: Feminism, Nature, Difference. London: Routledge & Kegan Paul.
Gallagher, Bernard. 1980. The Sociology of Mental Illness. Englewood Cliffs, N.J.: Prentice-Hall.
Garand, James C., and Rebecca H. Hendrick. 1981. "Expenditure Tradeoffs in the American States: A Longitudinal Test, 1948–1984." Western Political Quarterly 44: 915–40.
Garbarino, James, and Margaret C. Plantz. 1986. "Child Abuse and Juvenile Delinquency: What are the Links?," in James Garbarino, Cynthia J. Shellenbach, and Janet M. Sebes and Associates, eds., Troubled Youth, Troubled Families. Pp. 27–39. New York: Aldine de Gruyter.
Garber, Steven, Steven Klepper, and Daniel Nagin. 1983. "The Role of Extralegal Factors in Determining Criminal Case Disposition," in Alfred Blumstein, Jacqueline Cohen, Susan E. Martin, and Michael H. Tonry, eds., Research on Sentencing: The Search For Reform. Pp. 129–83. Washington, D.C.: National Academy Press.
Gardner, Gil. 1987. "The Emergence of the New York State Prison System: A Critique of the Rusche-Kirchheimer Model." Crime and Social Justice 29: 88–109.
Garfinkel, Harold. 1967. "Studies in the Routine Grounds of Everyday Activities," in Harold Garfinkel, Studies in Ethnomethodology. Pp. 35–75. Englewood Cliffs, N.J.: Prentice-Hall.
Garland, David. 1990. Punishment in Modern Society: A Study in Social Theory. Chicago: University of Chicago Press.
———. 1985. Punishment and Welfare: A History of Penal Strategies. Brookfield, Vt.: Gower.
———, and Peter Young. (eds.) 1983. The Power to Punish: Contemporary Penality and Social Analysis. London: Heineman Educational Books.
Gelles, Richard J. 1979. Family Violence. Beverly Hills, Calif.: Sage Publications.
Gelles, Richard J., and Murray Straus. 1987. "Is Violence Toward Children Increasing? A Comparison of 1975 and 1985 National Survey Rates," in Richard J. Gelles, ed., Family Violence. Pp. 78–88. Beverly Hills, Calif.: Sage Publications.
Gibson, James L. 1978. "Race as a Determinant of Criminal Sentences: A Methodological Critique and a Case Study." Law & Society Review 12: 455–78.
Giddens, Anthony. 1971. "The 'Individual' in the Writings of Emile Durkheim." European Journal of Sociology 12: 210–28.
———. 1981. Power, Property and the State. London: Macmillan.

———. 1984. The Constitution of Society. Berkeley: University of California Press.
Gil, David. 1978. "Unravelling Child Abuse," in Joanne Valiant Cook and Roy Tyler Bowles, eds., Child Abuse: Commission and Omission. Pp. 119–28. Toronto: Butterworth.
Gilligan, Carol. 1982. In a Different Voice. Cambridge, Mass.: Harvard University Press.
Gilroy, Paul. 1987. There Ain't No Black in the Union Jack: The Cultural Politics of Race and Nation. London: Unwin Hyman.
Goddard, Henry H. 1910. "Four Hundred Feeble-Minded Children Classified by the Binet Method." Journal of Psycho-Asthenics 15: 17–30.
———. 1912. The Kallikak Family: A Study in the Heredity of Feeble-mindedness. New York: Macmillan.
Goffman, Erving. 1961. Asylums. New York: Anchor.
———. 1963. Stigma: Notes on the Management of Spoiled Identity. Englewood Cliffs, N.J.: Prentice-Hall.
Golab, Caroline. 1973. " The Immigrant and the City: Poles, Italians, and Jews in Philadelphia, 1870–1920," in Allen F. Davis and Mark H. Haller, eds., The Peoples of Philadelphia: A History of Ethnic Groups and Lower Class Life, 1790–1940. Pp. 203–30. Philadelphia: Temple University Press.
Gold, Martin, and David Reimer. 1972. Testimony presented on the "Runaway Youth Act" to the Subcommittee on Equal Opportunity of the United States House Committee on Education and Labour, 93 Congress, 2nd Session. Pp. 274–80. Washington, D.C.: Government Printing Office.
Goldmier, John, and Robert Dean. 1972. "The Runaway: Person, Problem or Situation." Paper in the United States Senate Hearings on Runaway Youth Before the Subcommittee to Investigate Juvenile Delinquency, Committee on the Judiciary, 92 Congress, First Session. Pp. 233–38. Washington, D.C.: Government Printing Office.
Goldstein, Herman. 1990. Problem-Oriented Policing. New York: McGraw-Hill.
Goode, Erich. 1984. Deviant Behavior. 2nd edition. Englewood Cliffs, N.J.: Prentice-Hall.
Gordon, Efrem A., and Lewis Harris. 1950. "An Investigation and Critique of the Defective Delinquent Statute in Massachusetts." Boston University Law Review 30: 459–501.
Gordon, Linda. 1977. Women's Body, Women's Right: Birth Control in America. New York: Penguin.
Gould, Stephen Jay. 1981. The Mismeasure of Man. New York: W. W. Norton.
———. 1985. The Flamingo's Smile: Reflections in Natural History. New York: W. W. Norton.
Gouldner, Alvin W. 1959. "Organizational Analysis," in Robert K. Merton, Leonard Broom, and Leonard S. Cottrell, Jr., eds., Sociology Today. Pp. 400–10. New York: Basic Books.
———. 1968. "The Sociologist as Partisan: Sociology and the Welfare State." American Sociologist 3: 103–16.
———. 1973. "Metaphysical Pathos and the Theory of Bureaucracy," in Wil-

liam J. Chambliss, ed., Sociological Readings in the Conflict Perspective. Pp. 337-52. Reading, Mass.: Addison-Wesley.

Gove, Walter. (ed.) 1980a. The Labelling of Deviance: Evaluating a Perspective. Beverly Hills, Calif.: Sage Publications.

———. 1980b. "The Labelling Perspective: An Overview," in Walter R. Gove, ed., The Labelling of Deviance: Evaluating a Perspective. 2nd edition. Pp. 9–33. Beverly Hills, Calif.: Sage Publications.

Graycar, Regina. (ed.) 1990. Dissenting Opinions: Feminist Explorations in Law and Society. North Sydney, NSW : Allen and Unwin Australia.

Grbich, Judith E. 1991. "The Body in Legal Theory," in Martha Albertson Fineman and Nancy Sweet Thomadsen, eds., At the Boundaries of Law: Feminism and Legal Theory. Pp. 61–76. New York: Routledge, Chapman and Hall, Inc.

Greeley, Andrew M. 1972. That Most Distressed Nation: The Taming of the American Irish. Chicago: Quadrangle Books.

Greenberg, David F. 1976. "On One-Dimensional Marxist Criminology." Theory and Society 3: 611–21.

Greenberg, David, and Drew Humphries. 1980. "The Cooptation of Fixed Sentencing Reform." Crime and Delinquency 26: 206–223.

Gross, Samuel R., and Robert Mauro. 1989. Death and Discrimination: Racial Disparities in Capital Sentencing. Boston: Northeastern University Press.

Gruhl, John, Susan Welch, and Cassia Spohn. 1984. "Women as Criminal Defendants: A Test for Paternalism." Western Political Quarterly 37: 456–67.

Gusfield, Joseph R. 1963. Symbolic Crusade: Status Politics and the American Temperance Movement. Urbana: University of Illinois Press.

Gutierrez, Ramon. 1991. When Jesus Came, The Corn Mothers Went Away: Marriage, Sexuality, and Power in New Mexico, 1500–1846. Stanford, Calif.: Stanford University Press.

Guttentag, Marcia, and Paul F. Secord. 1983. Too Many Women? The Sex Ratio Question. Beverly Hills, Calif.: Sage Publications.

Hagan, John. 1974. "Extra-Legal Attributes and Criminal Sentencing: An Assessment of a Sociological Viewpoint." Law & Society Review 8: 357–83.

———. 1977a. "Criminal Justice in Rural and Urban Communities: A Study of the Bureaucratization of Justice." Social Forces 55:597–612.

———. 1977b. "Finding 'Discrimination': A Question of Meaning." Ethnicity 4: 167–76.

———. 1979. "Symbolic Justice: The Status Politics of the American Probation Movement." Sociological Focus 12: 295–309.

———. 1980. "The Legislation of Crime and Delinquency: A Review of Theory, Method, and Research." Law & Society Review 14: 603–28.

———, and Ilene Bernstein. 1979. "The Sentence Bargaining of Upperworld and Underworld Crime in Ten Federal District Courts." Law & Society Review 13: 467–78.

———, and Kristin Bumiller. 1983. "Making Sense of Sentencing: A Review and Critique of Sentencing Research," in Alfred Blumstein, Jacqueline Cohen, Susan E. Martin, and Michael H. Tonry, eds., Research on Sentencing: The Search for Reform, Vol. 2. Pp. 1–54. Washington, D.C.: National Academy Press.

———, and Jeffrey Leon. 1977. "Rediscovering Delinquency: Social History, Political Ideology and the Sociology of Law." American Sociological Review 42: 587–98.

———, and Bill McCarthy. 1992. "Streetlife and Delinquency." British Journal of Sociology 43: 533–62.

———, and Nancy O'Donnel. 1978. "Sexual Stereotyping and Judicial Sentencing: A Legal Test of Sociological Wisdom." Canadian Journal of Sociology 3: 309–23.

———, and Alberto Palloni. 1986. " 'Club Fed' and the Sentencing of White-Collar Offenders Before and After Watergate." Criminology 24: 603–22.

———, and Alberto Palloni. 1988. "Crimes as Social Events in the Life Course: Reconceiving a Criminological Controversy." Criminology 26: 87–100.

———, and Alberto Palloni. 1990. "The Social Reproduction of a Criminal Class in Working Class London, Circa 1950–1980." American Journal of Sociology 96: 265–99.

———, and Patricia Parker. 1985. "White-Collar Crime and Punishment: The Class Structure and Legal Sanctioning of Securities Violations." American Sociological Review 50:302–16.

Hagan, John, John D. Hewitt, and Duane F. Alwin. 1979. "Ceremonial Justice: Crime and Punishment in a Loosely Coupled System." Social Forces 58: 506–27.

Hagan, John, and Ilene H. Nagel (Bernstein) and Celesta A. Albonetti. 1980. "The Differential Sentencing of White-Collar Offenders in Ten Federal District Courts." American Sociological Review 45: 802–20.

———. 1982. "The Social Organization of White-Collar Sanctions: A Study of Prosecution and Punishment in the Federal Courts," in Peter Wickerman and Timothy Dailey, eds., White-Collar and Economic Crime. Pp. 259–74. Lexington, Mass.: Lexington Books.

Hagan, John, Carol Rogerson and Bill McCarthy. 1990. "Family Violence: A Study in Social and Legal Sanctions," in Martin Lawrence Friedland, ed., Securing Compliance: Seven Case Studies. Pp. 392–440. Toronto: University of Toronto Press.

Hagan, John, Edward T. Silva, and John H. Simpson. 1977. "Conflict and Consensus in the Designation of Deviance." Social Forces 56: 320–61.

Hagan, John, John Simpson, and A.R. Gillis. 1987. "Class in the Household: A Power-Control Theory of Gender and Delinquency." American Journal of Sociology 92: 788–816.

Hahn, Nicolas F. 1978. "The Defective Delinquency Movement." Ph.D. thesis, State University of New York at Albany.

———. 1980. "Too Dumb to Know Better: Cacogenic Family Studies and the Criminology of Women." Criminology 18:3–25.

Hale, Chris. 1989. "Economy, Punishment and Imprisonment." Contemporary Crisis 13: 327–50.

Hall, Stuart. 1988a. The Hard Road to Renewal: Thatcherism and the Crisis of the Left. London: Verso.

———. 1988b. "New Ethnicities." ICA Documents 7:27–31.
———. 1990. "Cultural Identity and Diaspora," in Jonathan Rutherford, ed., Identity: Community, Culture, Difference. Pp. 222–37. London: Lawrence and Wishart.
Hall, Stuart, Charles Critcher, Tony Jefferson, John Clarke and Brian Roberts. 1978. Policing the Crisis: Mugging, the State and Law and Order. London: Macmillan.
Haller, Mark H. 1963. Eugenics: Hereditarian Attitudes in American Thought. New Brunswick, N.J.: Rutgers University Press.
———. 1973. "Recurring Themes," in Allen F. Davis and Mark H. Haller, eds., The Peoples of Philadelphia: A History of Ethnic Groups and Lower-Class Life, 1790–1940. Pp. 277–90. Philadelphia: Temple University Press.
Hamilton, Gary G., and John R. Sutton. 1989. "The Problem of Control in the Weak State: Domination in the U.S., 1880–1920." Theory and Society 18: 1–46.
Handlin, Oscar. 1941. Boston's Immigrants, 1790–1865: A Study in Acculturation. Cambridge, Mass.: Harvard University Press.
Hans, Valerie P., and Dan Slater. 1983. "John Hinckley, Jr. and the Insanity Defense: The Public's Verdict." Public Opinion Quarterly 47: 202–12.
Harring, Sidney L. 1983. Policing a Class Society: The Experience of American Cities, 1865 to 1915. New Brunswick, N.J.: Rutgers University Press.
Hart, Hastings H. 1912. "Extinction of the Defective Delinquent: A Working Program." American Prison Association Proceedings 1912: 205–25.
Hartmann, Heidi. 1981. "The Unhappy Marriage of Marxism and Feminism: Toward a More Progressive Union," in Lydia Sargent, ed., Women and Revolution: A Discussion of the Unhappy Marriage of Marxism and Feminism. Pp.1–42. Boston: South End Press.
Haskell, Thomas. 1977. The Emergence of Professional Social Science. Urbana: University of Illinois Press.
Hawes, Joseph M. 1971. Children in Urban Society: Juvenile Delinquency in Nineteenth-Century America. New York: Oxford University Press.
Hawkins, Darnell F. 1985. "Trends in Black-White Imprisonment: Changing Conceptions of Race or Changing Patterns of Social Control?" Crime and Social Justice 24: 187–209.
———. 1987. "Beyond Anomalies: Rethinking the Conflict Perspective on Race and Criminal Punishment." Social Forces 65: 719–45.
———. 1990. "Explaining the Black Homicide Rate." Journal of Interpersonal Violence 5: 151–63.
———. 1993. "Crime and Ethnicity," in Brian Forst, ed., The Socioeconomics of Crime and Justice. New York: M.E. Sharpe.
Hawkins, Keith. 1986. "On Legal Decision-Making." Washington and Lee Law Review 43: 1161–1242.
Hay, Douglas, Peter Linebaugh, John G. Rule, E. P. Thompson, and Cal Winslow. 1975. Albion's Fatal Tree. New York: Pantheon.
Health and Welfare Canada. 1989. Family Violence: A Review of Theoretical and Clinical Literature. Ottawa: Minister of Supply and Services.

Heidensohn, France. 1985. Women and Crime. New York: New York University Press.
Henderson, Charles R. 1893. An Introduction to the Study of the Dependent, Defective and Delinquent Classes. Boston: D. C. Heath and Company.
Henry, Stuart, and Dragan Milovanovic. 1991. "Constitutive Criminology: The Maturation of Critical Theory." Criminology 29: 293–315.
Hess, Henner von, Martin Moerings, Dieter Paas, Sebastian Scheerer, and Heinz Steinert. 1988. Angriff auf das Herz des Staates: Soziale Entwicklung und Terrorismus. Frankfurt: Suhrkamp.
Heumann, Milton. 1977. Plea Bargaining. Chicago: University of Chicago Press.
———, and Colin Loftin. 1979. "Mandatory Sentencing and the Abolition of Plea Bargaining." Law & Society Review 13: 393–430.
Hindelang, Michael J., Travis Hirschi and Joseph G. Weis. 1981. Measuring Delinquency. Beverly Hills, Calif.: Sage Publications.
Hindus, Michael. 1980. Prison and Plantation: Crime, Justice and Authority in Massachusetts and South Carolina, 1767–1878. Chapel Hill, N.C.: University of North Carolina Press.
Hirschi, Travis. 1969. Causes of Delinquency. Berkeley: University of California Press.
———. 1989. "Exploring Alternatives to Integrated Theory," in Steven F. Messner, Marvin D. Krohn and Allen E. Liska, eds., Theoretical Integration in the Study of Deviance and Crime: Problems and Prospects. Pp. 37–50. Albany: State University of New York Press.
———, and Michael Gottfredson. 1983. "Age and the Explanation of Crime." American Journal of Sociology 89:552–84.
Hobbs, E. A. 1943. "Criminality in Philadelphia: 1790–1810 compared with 1937." American Sociological Review 8: 198–202.
Hofstadter, Richard. 1955. The Age of Reform. New York: Vintage.
Holmstrom, Lynda Lytle and Ann Wolbert Burgess. 1978. The Victim of Rape: Institutional Reactions. New York: Wiley.
Home Office. 1985. Prison Statistics England and Wales 1984. Cmnd.9622 London: HMSO.
Hooks, Bell, and Cornel West. 1991. Breaking Bread: Insurgent Black Intellectual Life. Boston: South End Press.
Horton, John, and Anthony Platt. 1986. "Crime and Criminal Justice Under Capitalism and Socialism." Crime and Social Justice 25:115–135.
Horwitz, Allen V. 1990. The Logic of Social Control. New York: Plenum.
Holstein, James A. 1987. "Producing Gender Effects on Involuntary Mental Hospitalization." Social Problems 34: 141–55.
Hudson, Barbara. 1984. "Femininity and Adolescence," in Angela McRobbie and Mica Nava, eds., Gender and Generation. Pp. 31–53. London: Macmillan.
Hughes, Everett C. 1965. "Professions," in Kenneth S. Lynn, ed., The Professions in America. Pp. 1–14. Boston: Houghton Mifflin.
Humphries, Drew, and David F. Greenberg. 1981. "The Dialectics of Crime

Control," in David F. Greenberg, ed., Crime and Capitalism. Pp. 209–54. Palo Alto, Calif: Mayfield.
Hunner, Robert J., and Yvonne Elder Walker. (eds.) 1981. Exploring the Relationship Between Child Abuse and Delinquency. Montclair, N.J.: Allanheld, Osmun.
Hunt, Jennifer. 1984. "The Development of Rapport through the Negotiation of Gender in Fieldwork among the Police." Human Organization 43: 283–96.
Hutter, Bridget, and Gillian Williams. 1981. Controlling Women: The Normal and the Deviant. London: Croom Helm.
Ignatieff, Michael. 1978. A Just Measure of Pain: The Penitentiary in the Industrial Revolution, 1750–1850. New York: Columbia University Press.
———. 1981. "State, Civil Society and Total Institution: A Critique of Recent Social Histories of Punishment," in Michael Tonry and Norval Morris, eds., Crime and Justice: An Annual Review of Research, vol. 3. Pp. 153–92. Chicago: University of Chicago Press.
Inciardi, James A., Alan A. Block, and Lyle A. Hallowell. (eds.) 1977. Historical Approaches to Crime: Research Strategies and Issues. Beverly Hills, Calif.: Sage Publications.
Inter-University Consortium for Political and Social Research. 1990. Guide to Resources and Services, 1989–1990. Ann Arbor: Inter-University Consortium for Political and Social Research.
Inverarity, James, and Rykken Grattet. 1989. "Institutional Responses to Unemployment: A Comparison of U.S. Trends, 1947–1985." Contemporary Crises 13: 351–70.
Inverarity, James, and Daniel McCarthy. 1988. "Punishment and Social Structure Revisited: Unemployment and Imprisonment in the U.S.: 1948–1984." The Sociological Quarterly 29:263–79.
Isaac, Larry, and Larry Griffin. 1989. "Ahistoricism in Time-Series Analyses of Historical Process: Critique, Redirection, and Illustrations from U.S. Labor History." American Sociological Review 54: 873–90.
Isaac, Larry, and William R. Kelly. 1981. "Racial Insurgency, the State, and Welfare Expansion: Local and National Level Evidence from the Postwar United States." American Journal of Sociology 86: 1348–86.
Jacobs, David. 1978. "Inequality and the Legal Order: An Ecological Test of the Conflict Model." Social Problems 25: 515–25.
Janoski, Thomas. 1990. The Political Economy of Unemployment: Active Labor Market Policy in West Germany and the United States. Berkeley: University of California Press.
Janus, Mark-David, Arlene McCormack, Ann Wolbert Burgess, and Carol Hartman. 1987. Adolescent Runaways: Causes and Consequences. Lexington, Mass.: D.C. Heath.
Jaynes, Gerald D., and Robin M. Williams (eds.) 1989. A Common Destiny: Blacks and American Society. Washington, D.C.: National Academy Press.
Jenkins, Philip. 1982. "The Radicals and the Rehabilitative Ideal, 1890–1930." Criminology 20:347–72.
Johnson, David R. 1973. "Crime Patterns in Philadelphia, 1840–70," in Allen

F. Davis and Mark H. Haller, eds., The Peoples of Philadelphia: A History of Ethnic Groups and Lower-Class Life, 1790–1940. Pp. 89–100. Philadelphia: Temple University Press.
———. 1979. Policing the Urban Underworld. Philadelphia: Temple University Press.
Johnson, Guy B. 1941. "The Negro and Crime." Annals of the American Academy of Political and Social Science 217: 93–104.
Joreskog, Karl G. 1973. "A General Method for Estimating a Linear Structural Equation System," in Arthur S. Goldberger and Otis Dudley Duncan, eds., Structural Equation Models in the Social Sciences. Pp. 85–112. New York: Seminar Press.
———, and Dag Sorbom. 1985. Lisrel VI: User's Guide. Uppsala, Sweden: University of Uppsala.
Justice, Blair, and Rita Justice. 1990. The Abusing Family. Rev. edition. New York: Plenum.
Kamerman, Sheila B., and Alfred J. Kahn. 1990. "If CPS is Driving Child Welfare-Where Do We Go from Here?" Public Welfare 48: 9–14.
Karabel, Jerome, and A. H. Halsey. (eds.) 1977. Power and Ideology in Education. New York: Oxford University Press.
Katz, Jack. 1979. "Legality and Equality: Plea Bargaining in the Prosecution of White-Collar and Common Crimes." Law & Society Review 13:431–59.
———. 1988. Seductions of Crime: Moral and Sensual Attractions in Doing Evil. New York: Basic.
Katz, Michael. 1983. Poverty and Policy in American History. New York: Academic Press.
———. 1986. In the Shadow of the Poorhouse. New York: Basic Books.
Keil, Thomas J., and Gennaro F. Vito. 1989. "Race, Homicide Severity, and Application of the Death Penalty: A Consideration of the Barnett Scale." Criminology 27: 511–31.
Kelly, Francis. 1989. "Drugs Darken Yonge St. Strip." Toronto Star, June 30, 1989: A4.
Kempf, Kimberly, and Roy Austin. 1986. "Older and More Recent Evidence on Racial Discrimination on Sentencing." Journal of Quantitative Criminology 2:29–47.
Kephardt, William, and William W. Zellner. 1991. Extraordinary Groups: An Examination of Unconventional Life-Styles. 4th edition. New York: St. Martin's Press.
Kevles, Daniel J. 1985. In the Name of Eugenics: Genetics and the Uses of Human Heredity. New York: Knopf.
King, Deborah K. 1988. "Multiple Jeopardy, Multiple Consciousness: The Context of Black Feminist Ideology." Signs: Journal of Women in Culture and Society 14: 42–72.
Kittrie, Nicholas N. 1971. The Right to be Different: Deviance and Enforced Therapy. Baltimore, Md.: The Johns Hopkins University Press.
Kleck, Gary C. 1981. "Racial Discrimination in Sentencing: A Critical Evaluation of the Evidence with Additional Evidence on the Death Penalty." American Sociological Review 43: 783–805.

Kleiman, Mark. 1992. Against Excess: Drug Policy for Results. New York: Basic Books.
Klein, Stephen, Joan Petersilia and Susan Turner. 1990. "Race and Imprisonment Decisions in California." Science 247: 812–16.
Klepper, Steven, Daniel Nagin and Luke-Jon Tierney. 1983. "Discrimination in the Criminal Justice System: A Critical Appraisal of the Literature," in Alfred Blumstein, Jacqueline Cohen, Susan E. Martin and Michael H. Tonry, eds., Research on Sentencing: A Search for Reform, Vol. 2. Pp. 55–128. Washington, D.C.: National Academy Press.
Kluegel, James R., and Eliot R. Smith. 1986. Beliefs about Inequality: Americans' Views of What is and What Ought to Be. New York: Aldine De Gruyter.
Kornhauser, R. 1978. Social Sources of Delinquency. Chicago: University of Chicago Press.
Kruttschnitt, Candace. 1980–81. "Social Status and Sentences of Female Offenders." Law & Society Review 15: 247–65.
———. 1982a. "Women, Crime, and Dependency." Criminology 19: 495–513.
———. 1982b. "Respectable Women and the Law." Sociological Quarterly 23: 221–34.
———. 1984. "Sex and Criminal Court Dispositions: The Unresolved Controversy." Journal of Research in Crime and Delinquency 21:213–32.
———, and Donald E. Green. 1984. "The Sex-Sanctioning Issue: Is It History?" American Sociological Review 49: 541–51.
———, David Ward and Mary Ann Sheble. 1987. "Abuse-Resistant Youth: Some Factors That May Inhibit Violent Criminal Behavior." Social Forces 66: 501–19.
Kufeldt, Kathleen, and Margaret Nimmo. 1987. "Youth on the Street: Abuse and Neglect in the Eighties." Child Abuse and Neglect 11:531–43.
Kuhlmann, Fred. 1916. "Part Played by the State Institutions in the Care of the Feeble-minded." Journal of Psycho-Asthenics 21: 3–24.
Lacan, Jacques. 1977. Ecrits: A Selection. New York: Norton.
LaFree, Gary D. 1980. "The Effect of Sexual Stratification by Race on Official Reactions to Rape." American Sociological Review 45: 842–854.
———. 1985. "Official Reactions to Hispanic Defendants in the Southwest." Journal of Research in Crime and Delinquency 22: 213–237.
———. 1989. Rape and Criminal Justice: The Social Construction of Sexual Assault. Belmont, Calif.: Wadsworth.
Lamont, Michéle, and Marcel Fournier. (eds.) 1992. Cultivating Differences: Symbolic Boundaries and the Making of Inequality. Chicago: University of Chicago Press.
Lamphear, Vivian Shaw. 1985. "The Impact of Maltreatment on Children's Psychosocial Adjustment: A Review of the Research." Child Abuse and Neglect 9: 251–63.
Lane, Roger. 1967. Policing the City: Boston, 1822–1885. Cambridge, Mass.: Harvard University Press.
———. 1979. Violent Death in the City. Cambridge, Mass.: Harvard University Press.

———. 1986. Roots of Violence in Black Philadelphia, 1860–1900. Cambridge, Mass.: Harvard University Press.
Langan, Patrick. 1985. "Racism on Trial: New Evidence to Explain the Racial Composition of Prisons in the United States." The Journal of Criminal Law and Criminology 76: 666–83.
Langworthy, Robert H. 1986. The Structure of Police Organizations. New York: Praeger.
Larson, Magali Sarfatti. 1977. The Rise of Professionalism: A Sociological Analysis. Berkeley: University of California Press.
Laub, John, and M. Joan McDermott. 1985. "An Analysis of Serious Crime by Young Black Women." Criminology 23:81–98.
Lauderdale, Pat. 1976. "Deviance and Moral Boundaries." American Sociological Review 41: 660–76.
———, Phil Smith-Cunnien, Jerry Parker, and James Inverarity. 1984. "External Threat and the Definition of Deviance." Journal of Personality and Social Psychology 46: 1058–68.
Lemert, Edwin M. 1967a. "The Concept of Secondary Deviation," in Edwin M. Lemert, Human Deviance, Social Problems, and Social Control. Pp. 40–66. Englewood Cliffs, N.J.: Prentice-Hall.
———. 1967b. Human Deviance, Social Problems, and Social Control. Englewood Cliffs, N.J.: Prentice-Hall.
———. 1967c. "Paranoia and the Dynamics of Exclusion," in Edwin M. Lemert, Human Deviance, Social Problems, and Social Control. Pp. 197–211. Englewood Cliffs, N.J.: Prentice-Hall.
———. 1967d. "Role Enactment, Self, and Identity in the Systematic Check Forger," in Edwin M. Lemert, Human Deviance, Social Problems, and Social Control. Pp. 119–34. Englewood Cliffs, N.J.: Prentice-Hall.
———. 1970. Social Action and Legal Change: Revolution Within the Juvenile Court. Chicago: Aldine.
———. 1974. "Beyond Mead: The Societal Reaction to Deviance." Social Problems 21: 457–67.
———. 1986. "Juvenile Justice Italian Style." Law & Society Review 20: 509–44.
Lempert, Richard. 1989. "Humility is a Virtue: On the Publicization of Policy-Relevant Research." Law & Society Review 23:145–61.
Lessan, Gloria T. 1991. "Macro-economic Determinants of Penal Policy: Estimating the Unemployment and Inflation Influences on Imprisonment Rate Changes in the United States, 1948–1985." Crime, Law and Social Change 16: 177–98.
Levi, Ken. 1981. "Becoming a Hit Man: Neutralization in a Very Deviant Career." Urban Life 10: 47–63.
Levin, Martin A. 1972. "Urban Politics and Policy Outcomes: The Criminal Courts," in George F. Cole, ed., Criminal Justice: Law and Politics. Pp. 348–67. Belmont, Calif.: Wadsworth.
Lipton, Lawrence. 1966. The Erotic Revolution. New York: Pocket Books.
Liska, Allen E. (ed.) 1992. Social Threat and Social Control. Albany: State University of New York Press.

———, Joseph J. Lawrence, and Michael Benson. 1981. "Perspectives on the Legal Order: The Capacity for Social Control." American Journal of Sociology 87: 412–26.
Liska, Allen E., Marvin D. Krohn and Steven F. Messner. 1989. "Strategies and Requisites in the Study of Crime and Deviance," in Steven F. Messner, Marvin D. Krohn and Allen E. Liska, eds., Theoretical Integration in the Study of Deviance and Crime: Problems and Prospects. Pp. 1–20. Albany: State University of New York Press.
Lizotte, Alan J. 1978. "Extra-legal Factors in Chicago's Criminal Courts: Testing the Conflict Model of Criminal Justice." Social Problems 25: 564–80.
Loftin, Colin, and David McDowall. 1982. "The Police, Crime and Economic Theory." American Sociological Review 47: 393–401.
Loftin, Colin, Milton Heumann and David McDowall. 1983. "Mandatory Sentencing and Firearms Violence: Evaluating an Alternative to Gun Control." Law & Society Review 17: 287–318.
Loseke, Donileen R. 1992. The Battered Woman and Shelters: The Social Construction of Wife Abuse. Albany: State University of New York Press.
Low, Peter W., John C. Jeffries, Jr., and Richard J. Bonnie. 1986. The Trial of John Hinckley, Jr.: A Case Study in the Insanity Defense. Mineola, N.Y.: Foundation Press.
Lowell, Josephine Shaw. 1879. "One Means of Preventing Pauperism." Conference of Charities, 6th Proceedings 1879: 189–200.
Lubove, Roy. 1965. The Professional Altruist: The Emergence of Social Work as a Career, 1880–1930. Cambridge, Mass.: Harvard University Press.
Ludmerer, Kenneth M. 1972. Genetics and American Society. Baltimore, Md.: The Johns Hopkins University Press.
Lukes, Steven, and Andrew Scull. 1983. "Introduction," in Steven Lukes and Andrew Scull, eds, Durkheim and the Law. Pp. 1–32. New York: St. Martin's Press.
Lynch, Margaret A., and Jacqueline Roberts. 1982. Consequences of Child Abuse. New York: Academic Press.
MacKenzie, Donald A. 1981. Statistics in Britain, 1865–1930: The Social Construction of Scientific Knowledge. Edinburgh: Edinburgh University Press.
MacKinnon, Catharine A. 1983. "Feminism, Marxism, Method and the State: Toward Feminist Jurisprudence," Signs: Journal of Women in Culture and Society 8: 635–58.
———. 1987. Feminism Unmodified. Cambridge, Mass.: Harvard University Press.
Mann, Coramae R. 1984. "Race and Sentencing of Female Felons: A Field Study." International Journal of Women's Studies 7: 160–72.
Manning, Peter K. 1977. Police Work. Cambridge, Mass.: MIT Press.
———. 1982. "Organisational Work: Enstructuration of the Environment." British Journal of Sociology 33: 118–39.
———. 1988. Symbolic Communication: Signifying Calls and the Police Response. Cambridge, Mass.: MIT Press.
———. 1992. "Screening Calls," in Eva S. Buzawa and Carl G. Buzawa, eds.,

Domestic Violence: The Changing Criminal Justice Response. Pp. 42–58. Boston: Auburn House.

March, James G., and Herbert A. Simon. 1958. Organizations. New York: Wiley Publishers.

Marcus, Isabel, Paul Spiegelman, Ellen DuBois, Mary Dunlap, Carol Gilligan, Catherine MacKinnon, and Carrie Menkel-Meadow. 1985. "Feminist Discourse, Moral Values, and the Law—A Conversation." Buffalo Law Review 34: 11–87.

Mare, Robert D., and Christopher Winship. 1984. "The Paradox of Lessening Racial Inequality and Joblessness among Black Youth: Enrollment, Enlistment, and Employment, 1964–1981." American Sociological Review 49: 39–55.

Marshall, Thomas H. 1965 [1949]. "Citizenship and Social Class," in Marshall, Thomas H., Class, Citizenship and Social Development. Pp. 71–134. New York: Anchor.

Marx, Gary T. 1989. Undercover: Police Surveillance in America. Berkeley: University of California Press.

Massey, James L., and Martha A. Myers. 1989. "Patterns of Repressive Social Control in Post-Reconstruction Georgia, 1882–1935." Social Forces 68:458–88.

Martin, Roscoe. 1934. The Defendant and Criminal Justice. Austin, Tex.: University of Texas Bulletin No. 3437, Bureau of Research in the Social Sciences, Study No. 9.

Mather, Lynn. 1979. Plea Bargaining or Trial? Lexington, Mass.: Lexington Books.

Mathiesen, Thomas. 1974. The Politics of Abolition. London: Martin Robertson.

Matthews, Roger and Jock Young. (eds.) 1986. Confronting Crime. Beverly Hills, Calif.: Sage Publications.

———. 1992. Issues in Realist Criminology. Newbury Park, Calif.: Sage Publications.

Matza, David. 1964. Delinquency and Drift. New York: Wiley.

Maynard, Douglas. 1982. "Defendant Attributes in Plea Bargaining: Notes on the Modeling of Sentencing Decisions." Social Problems 49: 347–60.

———. 1984. Inside Plea Bargaining. New York: Plenum.

McCaughan, Ed. 1991. "Class, Race, Nation, and Ethnicity Within Theories of Social Structure and Human Agency." Department of Sociology, University of California, Santa Cruz, Calif. Unpublished manuscript.

McCord, Joan. 1983. "A Forty Year Perspective on Effects of Child Abuse and Neglect." Child Abuse and Neglect 7: 265–70.

McCord, William Maxwell, Joan McCord and Irving Kenneth Zola. 1959. Origins of Crime. New York: Columbia University Press.

McIntyre, Thomas C. 1987. "Teacher Awareness of Child Abuse and Neglect." Child Abuse and Neglect 11: 133–35.

McKim, W. Duncan. 1900. Heredity and Human Progress. New York: G. P. Putnam's, The Knickerbocker Press.

McMahon, Maeve. 1990. "'Net-Widening': Vagaries in the Use of a Concept." British Journal of Criminology 30: 121–49.

McManners, John. 1981. Death and the Enlightenment. New York: Oxford University Press.
McPheters, Lee R., and William B. Stronge. 1974. "Law Enforcement Expenditures and Urban Crimes." National Tax Journal 27: 633–44.
Mead, George Herbert. 1924–25. "The Genesis of the Self and Social Control." International Journal of Ethics 35: 251–77.
Meier, Robert F. 1982. "Perspectives on the Concept of Social Control," in Ralph H. Turner and James F. Short, Jr., eds., Annual Review of Sociology. Pp. 35–65. Palo Alto, Calif.: Annual Reviews.
Meierhoefer, Barbara S. 1992. The General Effect of Mandatory Minimum Terms. Washington, D.C.: Federal Judicial Center.
Melossi, Dario. 1989. "An Introduction: Fifty Years Later, Punishment and Social Structure in Comparative Analysis." Contemporary Crises 13:311–26.
———. 1990. The State of Social Control. New York: St. Martin's Press.
Mennel, Robert M. 1973. Thorns and Thistles: Juvenile Delinquents in the American States, 1825–1940. Hanover, N.H.: University Press of New England.
———. 1983. "Attitudes and Policies Toward Juvenile Delinquency in the United States: A Historiographical Review." Crime and Justice 4: 191–224.
Merton, Robert K. 1957. Social Theory and Social Structure. Glencoe, Ill.: The Free Press.
Messerschmidt, James W. 1986. Capitalism, Patriarchy and Crime: Towards a Socialist Feminist Criminology. Totowa, N.J.: Rowman and Littlefield.
Meyer, John W. 1977. "The Effects of Education as an Institution." American Journal of Sociology 83: 55–77.
———, and Brian Rowan. 1977. "Institutionalized Organizations: Formal Structure as Myth and Ceremony." American Journal of Sociology 83: 340–63.
Meyer, John W., David Tyack, Joane Nagel, and Audri Gordon. 1979. "Public Education and Nation-Building in America: Enrollments and Bureaucratization in the American States, 1870–1930." American Journal of Sociology 85: 591–613.
Miller, Wilbur R. 1977. Cops and Bobbies: Police Authority in New York and London, 1830–1870. Chicago: University of Chicago Press.
Mink, Gwendolyn. 1990. "The Lady and the Tramp: Gender, Race, and the Origins of the American Welfare State," in Linda Gordon, ed., Women, The State, and Welfare. Pp. 92–122. Madison: University of Wisconsin Press.
Miringoff, Marque-Luisa. 1991. The Social Costs of Genetic Welfare. New Brunswick, N.J.: Rutgers University Press.
Monkkonen, Eric H. 1975. The Dangerous Class: Crime and Poverty in Columbus, Ohio, 1860–1885. Cambridge, Mass.: Harvard University Press.
———. 1981. Police in Urban America, 1860–1920. New York: Cambridge University Press.
———. 1992. "History of the Urban Police, " in Michael H. Tonry and Norval Morris, eds., Modern Policing. Pp. 547–80. Chicago: University of Chicago Press.
Morris, Allison. 1987. Women, Crime and Criminal Justice. Oxford: Basil Blackwell.

Morris, Norval. 1981. "Punishment, Desert, and Rehabilitation," in Hyman Gross and Andrew von Hirsch, eds., Sentencing. Pp. 257–71. New York: Oxford.
Muehleman, Thomas, and Cheryl Kimmons. 1981. "Psychiatrists' Views on Child Abuse Reporting, Confidentiality, Life and the Law: An Exploratory Study." Professional Psychiatry 12: 631–38.
Muir, William K., Jr. 1977. The Police: Streetcorner Politicians. Chicago: University of Chicago Press.
Muncy, Robyn. 1991. Creating a Female Dominion in American Reform, 1890–1935. New York: Oxford University Press.
Myers, Martha A. 1980. "Predicting the Behavior of Law: A Test of Two Models." Law & Society Review 14: 835–57.
———. 1990. "Economic Threat and Racial Disparities in Incarceration: The Case of Postbellum Georgia." Criminology 28:627–56.
———. 1991. "Economic Conditions and Punishment in Postbellum Georgia." Journal of Quantitative Criminology 7:99–121.
Myers, Martha A., and Susette M. Talarico. 1986. "Urban Justice, Rural Injustice?: Urbanization and its Effect on Sentencing." Criminology 24: 367–91.
———. 1987. The Social Contexts of Criminal Sentencing. New York: Springer-Verlag.
Myers, Samuel L., Jr., and William J. Sabol. 1987. "Business Cycles and Racial Disparities in Punishment." Contemporary Policy Issues 5:46–58.
Nagel, Ilene H. 1989. "Presentation" for Panel V, Equality versus Discretion in Sentencing [from the Second Annual Lawyers Convention of the Federalist Society: The Constitution and Federal Criminal Law]. American Criminal Law Review 26: 1815–19.
———, and John Hagan. 1982. "The Sentencing of White-Collar Criminals in Federal Courts: A Socio-legal Explanation of Disparity." Michigan Law Review 80:1427–65.
Nardulli, Peter F., James Eisenstein, and Roy B. Flemming. 1988. The Tenor of Justice. Urbana: University of Illinois Press.
National Advisory Commission on Civil Disorders. 1968. Report of the National Advisory Commission on Civil Disorders. New York: Bantam Books.
National Commission on Law Observance and Enforcement. 1931. Report on Crime and the Foreign-Born. Washington, D.C.: U. S. Government Printing Office.
Neff, Joseph S. 1910. The Degenerate Children of Feeble-Minded Women. Philadelphia: Department of Public Health and Charities.
Nelli, Humbert S. 1970. Italians in Chicago, 1880–1920. New York: Oxford University Press.
Nettler, Gwynn. 1978. Explaining Crime. 2nd edition. New York: McGraw-Hill.
Neuhaus, Richard John. 1988. "The Return of Eugenics." Commentary 85: 15–26.
———. 1979. "Criminal Justice." American Review of Sociology 5: 27–52.
Nightingale, Narina N., and Elaine F. Walker. 1986. "Identification and Re-

porting of Child Maltreatment by Head Start Personnel: Attitudes and Experiences." Child Abuse and Neglect 10: 191–99.
Noll, Steven. 1990. "Care and Control of the Feeble-minded: Florida Farm Colony, 1920–1945." Florida Historical Quarterly 69: 57–80.
——. Forthcoming. Feeble-minded in Our Midst: Institutions for the Mentally Retarded in the South, 1910–1940. Chapel Hill: University of North Carolina Press.
Nye, F. Ivan. 1958. Family Relationships and Delinquent Behavior. New York: Wiley.
Nye, Robert A. 1984. Crime, Madness, and Politics in Modern France: The Medical Concept and National Decline. Princeton, N.J.: Princeton University Press.
O'Connor, James. 1973. The Fiscal Crisis of the State. New York: St. Martin's Press.
Odem, Mary. 1991. "Single Mothers, Delinquent Daughters, and the Juvenile Court in Early 20th Century Los Angeles." Journal of Social History 25: 27–43.
Olsen, Frances. 1985. "The Myth of State Intervention in the Family." University of Michigan Journal of Law Reform 18: 835–64.
Olzak, Susan. 1990. "The Political Context of Competition: Lynching and Urban Racial Violence, 1882–1914." Social Forces 69: 395–421.
——. 1992. The Dynamics of Ethnic Competition and Conflict. Stanford: Stanford University Press.
Oppenlander, N. 1982. "Coping or Copping Out: Police Service Delivery in Domestic Disputes." Criminology 20: 449–65.
Palenski, Joseph E. 1984. Kids Who Run Away. Saratoga, Fla.: R&E Publishers.
Parisi, Nicolette. 1982. "Are Women Treated Differently? A Review of the Theories and Evidence on Sentencing and Parole Decisions," in Nicole Hahn Rafter and Elizabeth Anne Stanko, eds., Judge, Lawyer, Victim, Thief: Women, Gender Roles and Criminal Justice. Pp. 205–20. Boston: Northeastern University Press.
Park, Robert, Edward W. Burgess, and R.D. McKenzie. 1928. The City. Chicago: University of Chicago Press.
Parker, Andrew, Mary Russo, Doris Sommer and Patricia Yaeger. (eds.) 1992. Nationalisms and Sexualities. London: Routledge.
Parsons, Talcott. 1951. The Social System. New York: Free Press.
Paternoster, Raymond. 1984. "Prosecutorial Discretion in Requesting the Death Penalty: A Case of Victim-Based Racial Discrimination." Law & Society Review 18: 437–478.
Pepinsky, Harold E., and Richard Quinney. (eds.) 1991. Criminology as Peacemaking. Bloomington: Indiana University Press.
Petersilia, Joan. 1983. Racial Disparities in the Criminal Justice System. Santa Monica, Calif.: Rand.
Peterson, Ruth D., and John Hagan. 1984. "Changing Conceptions of Race: Towards an Account of Anomalous Findings of Sentencing Research," American Sociological Review 49: 56–70.

Pettigrew, Thomas F. (ed.) 1980. The Sociology of Race Relations: Reflection and Reform. New York: The Free Press.
Phillips, Charles D. 1987. "Exploring the Relations Among Forms of Social Control: The Lynching and Execution of Blacks in Georgia and North Carolina, 1889–1918." Law & Society Review 21: 361–74.
Phillips, Llad, and Harold L. Votey Jr. 1981. The Economics of Crime Control. Beverly Hills, Calif.: Sage Publications.
Pick, Daniel. 1989. Faces of Degeneration: A European Disorder, c. 1848–c. 1918. New York: Cambridge University Press.
Pickens, Donald K. 1968. Eugenics and the Progressives. Nashville, Tenn.: Vanderbilt University Press.
Pisciotta, Alexander W. 1981. "Corrections, Society, and Social Control in America: A Metahistorical Review of the Literature." Criminal Justice History: An International Annual 2: 109–30.
Piven, Frances Fox and Richard Cloward. 1971. Regulating the Poor: The Functions of Public Welfare. New York: Vintage Books.
Platt, Anthony M. 1969. The Child Savers: The Invention of Delinquency. Chicago: University of Chicago Press.
———. 1977. The Child Savers: The Invention of Delinquency. 2nd edition. Chicago: University of Chicago Press.
———. 1991. "If We Know, Then We Must Fight: The Origins of Radical Criminology in the United States," in Martin Oppenheimer, Martin J. Murray and Rhonda F. Levine, eds., Radical Sociologists and the Movement: Experiences, Lessons, and Legacies. Philadelphia: Temple University Press.
Pogrebin, Mark R., and Eric D. Poole. 1988–89. "South Korean Immigrants and Crime: A Case Study." The Journal of Ethnic Studies 17: 47–80.
Polsky, Andrew J. 1991. The Rise of the Therapeutic State. Princeton, N.J.: Princeton University Press.
Polsky, Ned. 1967. Hustlers, Beats, and Others. Chicago: Aldine.
Powell, Elwin H. 1966. "Crime as a Function of Anomie." Journal of Criminal Law, Criminology, and Police Science 57: 151–71.
Powers, Jane Levin, John Eckenrode and Barbara Jaklitsch. 1990. "Maltreatment among Runaway and Homeless Youth." Child Abuse and Neglect 14:87–98.
Proctor, Robert N. 1991 "Eugenics among the Social Sciences." in JoAnne Brown and David K. van Keuren, eds. The Estate of Social Knowledge. Pp. 175–208. Baltimore, Md.: The Johns Hopkins University Press.
Pruitt, Charles R., and James Q. Wilson. 1983. "A Longitudinal Study of the Effect of Race on Sentencing." Law & Society Review 7: 613–35.
Quinney, Richard. 1970. The Social Reality of Crime. Boston: Little Brown.
———. 1974. Critique of the Legal Order. Boston: Little Brown.
———. 1977. Class State and Crime. New York: David McKay Co.
Rachman, Stanley. 1974. The Meaning of Fear. Baltimore: Penguin Books.
Radelet, Michael L. 1981. "Racial Characteristics and the Imposition of the Death Penalty." American Sociological Review 46: 918–27.
———, and Glenn L. Pierce. 1985. "Race and Prosecutorial Discretion in Homicide Cases." Law & Society Review 19: 587–621.

Raeder, Myrna. 1993. "Gender and Sentencing: Single Moms, Battered Women, and Other Sex-Based Anomalies in the Gender Free World of the Federal Sentencing Guidelines." Pepperdine Law Review 20: 905–990.
Rafter, Nicole Hahn. 1985. Partial Justice: Women in State Prisons, 1800–1935. Boston: Northeastern University Press.
———. 1990. Partial Justice: Women, Prisons, and Social Control. 2nd edition, rev. New Brunswick, N.J.: Transaction.
———. 1992a. "Claims-Making and Socio-Cultural Context in the First U.S. Eugenics Campaign." Social Problems 39: 17–34.
———. 1992b. "Criminal Anthropology in the United States." Criminology 30:525–545.
Ramirez, Francisco O., and John Boli. 1987. "The Political Construction of Mass Schooling: European Origins and Worldwide Institutionalization." Sociology of Education 60: 2–17.
Raper, Arthur. 1933. The Tragedy of Lynching. Chapel Hill: University of North Carolina Press.
Rauma, David. 1981a. "Crime and Punishment Reconsidered: Some Comments on Blumstein's Stability of Punishment Hypothesis." Journal of Criminal Law and Criminology 72:1772–98.
———. 1981b. "A Concluding Note on the Stability of Punishment: Reply to Blumstein, Cohen, Moitra, and Nagin." Journal of Criminal Law and Criminology 72:1809–12.
Reed, John Shelton. 1972. "Percent Black and Lynching: A Test of Blalock's Theory." Social Forces 50: 356–60.
Reilly, Philip R. 1991. The Surgical Solution: A History of Involuntary Sterilization in the United States. Baltimore, Md.: The Johns Hopkins University Press.
Reiner, Robert. 1991. Chief Constables: Bobbies, Bosses or Bureaucrats? New York: Oxford University Press.
———. 1992. The Politics of Policing. 2nd edition. Brighton, Sussex: Wheatsheaf Press.
Reiss, Albert J., Jr. 1971. The Police and the Public. New Haven, Conn.: Yale University Press.
———. 1974. "Discretionary Justice," in Daniel Glaser, ed., Handbook of Criminology. Pp. 679–99. Chicago: Rand McNally.
———. 1992. "Police Organization in the Twentieth Century," in Michael H. Tonry and Norval Morris, eds., Modern Policing. Pp. 52–68. Chicago: University of Chicago Press.
Reinarman, Craig. 1988. "The Social Construction of an Alcohol Problem." Theory and Society 17: 91–120.
Remick, Helen. (ed.) 1984. Comparable Worth and Wage Discrimination. Philadelphia: Temple University Press.
Reynolds, Amos. 1879. "The Prevention of Pauperism." Conference of Charities, 6th Proceedings: 210–16.
Rice, Maria. 1990. "Challenging Orthodoxies in Feminist Theory: A Black Feminist Critique," in Loraine Gelsthorpe and Allison Morris, eds., Feminist Perspectives in Criminology. Pp. 59–69. Philadelphia: Open University Press.

Richardson, James F. 1970. The New York Police: Colonial Times to 1901. New York: Oxford University Press.
Richardson, Laurel. 1990. "Narrative and Sociology." Journal of Contemporary Ethnography 19: 116–35.
Rickett, Allyn and Adele Rickett. 1973. Prisoners of Liberation: Four Years in a Chinese Communist Prison. New York: Anchor.
Riley, Denise. 1988. Am I That Name?: Feminism and the Category of "Women" in History. Minneapolis: University of Minnesota Press.
Rodgers, Daniel T. 1982. "In Search of Progressivism." Reviews in American History 10:113–132.
Roediger, David. 1991. The Wages of Whiteness: Race and the Making of the American Working Class. London: Verso.
Rose, Nikolas. 1987. "Beyond the Public/Private Division: Law, Power and the Family." Journal of Law and Society 14: 61–76.
Rosenbaum, Marsha. 1981. Women on Heroin. New Brunswick, N.J.: Rutgers University Press.
Rosenberg, Gerald N. 1991. The Hollow Hope: Can Courts Bring About Social Change? Chicago: University of Chicago Press.
Ross, Dorothy. 1991. The Origins of American Social Science. New York: Cambridge University Press.
Ross, Edward A. 1901. Social Control: A Survey of the Foundations of Order. New York: Macmillan.
Ross, Harold. 1937. "Crime and the Native Born Sons of European Immigrants." Journal of Criminal Law and Criminology 28:202–09.
Rossi, Peter H., Jon E. Simpson, and JoAnn L. Miller. 1985. "Beyond Crime Seriousness: Fitting the Punishment to the Crime." Journal of Quantitative Criminology 1: 59–90.
Rossi, Peter H., Emily White, Christine E. Bose, and Richard E. Berk. 1974. "The Seriousness of Crimes: Normative Structure and Individual Differences." American Sociological Review 39: 224–37.
Rothman, David J. 1971. The Discovery of the Asylum. Boston: Little, Brown.
———. 1978. "The State as Parent: Social Policy in the Progressive Era," in Willard Gaylin, Ira Glasser, Steven Marcus, and David J. Rothman, eds., Doing Good: The Limits of Benevolence. Pp. 67–95. New York: Pantheon.
———. 1980. Conscience and Convenience. Boston: Little, Brown.
———. 1983. "Social Control: The Uses and Abuses of the Concept in the History of Incarceration," in Stanley Cohen and Andrew Scull, eds., Social Control and the State. Pp. 106–17. New York: St. Martin's Press.
Rubinstein, Jonathan. 1973. City Police. New York: Farrar,Straus and Giroux.
Rusche, Georg, and Otto Kirchheimer. 1939. Punishment and Social Structure. New York: Columbia University Press.
Russell, Diana. 1975. The Politics of Rape: The Victim's Perspective. New York: Stein and Day.
Russell, J. (ed.) 1985. A Feminist Review of Criminal Law. Canada: Minister of Supply and Services.
Rutherford, Andrew. 1984. Prisons and the Process of Justice: The Reductionist Challenge. London: Heinemann.

Ryan, Mary. 1990. Women in Public: Between Banners and Ballots, 1825–1880. Baltimore, Md.: The Johns Hopkins University Press.
Sampson, Robert, and John Laub. 1990. "Stability and Change in Crime and Deviance over the Life Course: The Salience of Adult Social Bonds." American Sociological Review 55: 609–27.
Samuel, Raphael. (ed.) 1989. Patriotism: The Making and Unmaking of British National Identity. Vols. 1–3. London: Routledge.
Sarason, Seymour B., and John Doris. 1969. Psychological Problems in Mental Deficiency. 4th edition. New York: Harper & Row.
Saussure, Ferdinand de. 1974. Course in General Linguistics. London: Peter Owen.
Saxton, Alexander. 1990. The Rise and Fall of the White Republic: Class Politics and Mass Culture in Nineteenth-Century America. London: Verso.
Scheff, Thomas J. 1984. Being Mentally Ill: A Sociological Theory. 2nd edition. New York: Aldine.
Schmid, Carol L. 1986. "Social Class, Race and the Extension of Citizenship: The English Working Class and the Southern Civil Rights Movements." Comparative Social Research 9:27–46.
Schmidt, Peter, and Ann D. Witte. 1984. An Economic Analysis of Crime and Justice. New York: Academic Press.
Schur, Edwin. 1971. Labeling Deviant Behavior: Its Sociological Implications. New York: Harper and Row.
———. 1983. Labeling Women Deviant: Gender, Stigma and Social Control. Philadelphia: Temple University Press.
Schutt, Russell K., and Dale Dannefer. 1988. "Detention Decisions in Juvenile Cases: Jins, JDs, and Gender." Law & Society Review 22: 509–20.
Scott, Robert A. 1976. "Deviance, Sanctions and Integration in Small Scale Societies." Social Forces 54:604–20.
Scruton, David L. 1986. Sociophobics: The Anthropology of Fear. Boulder, Colo.: Westview Press.
Scull, Andrew T. 1977. Decarceration: Community Treatment and the Deviant: A Radical View. Englewood Cliffs, N.J.: Prentice-Hall.
———. 1979. Museums of Madness: The Social Organization of Insanity in the Nineteenth Century. London: Allen Lane.
———. 1982. "Community Corrections: Panacea, Progress or Pretense?," in Richard Abel, ed., The Politics of Informal Justice. Volume 1. Pp. 99–118. New York: Academic Press.
Scully, Diana. 1990. Understanding Sexual Violence: A Study of Convicted Rapists. Boston: Unwin Hyman.
Sellin, Thorsten. 1928. "The Negro Criminal: A Statistical Note." Annals of the American Academy of Political and Social Science 140:52–64.
———. 1935. "Race Prejudice in the Administration of Justice." American Journal of Sociology 41:312–17.
———. 1938. Culture Conflict and Crime. New York: Social Science Research Council.
Sewell, William H., Jr. 1992. "A Theory of Structure: Duality, Agency, and Transformation. American Journal of Sociology 98: 1–29.

Shapiro, Susan P. 1985. The Road Not Taken: The Elusive Path To Criminal Prosecution for White-Collar Offenders." Law & Society Review 19: 179–217.
Shaw, Clifford R., and Henry D. McKay. 1969. Juvenile Delinquency and Urban Areas. Rev. edition. Chicago: University of Chicago Press.
Shearing, Clifford D. 1984. Dial-A-Cop. Toronto: Centre for Criminology, University of Toronto Press.
Shellow, Robert, Juliana Schamp, Elliot Liebow and Elizabeth Unger. 1972. "Suburban Runaways of the 1960's." Paper in the United States Senate Hearings on Runaway Youth before the Subcommittee to Investigate Juvenile Delinquency of the Committee on the Judiciary, 92 Congress, 1st Session. Pp. 210–32. Washington, D.C.: Government Printing Office.
Sherman, Lawrence W., and Richard A. Berk. 1984. "The Specific Deterrent Effects of Arrest for Domestic Assault." American Sociological Review 49: 261–72.
Sherman, Lawrence W., and Ellen G. Cohn. 1989. "The Impact of Research on Legal Policy: The Minneapolis Domestic Violence Experiment." Law & Society Review 23:117–44.
Sherman, Lawrence W., Janell D. Schmidt, Dennis P. Rogan, Patrick R. Gartin, Ellen G. Cohn, Dean J. Collins, Anthony R. Bacich. 1991. "From Initial Deterrence to Long Term Escalation: Short-Custody Arrest for Poverty Ghetto Domestic Violence." Criminology 29: 821–49.
Silbert, Mimi H., and Ayala M. Pines. 1982. "Entrance into Prostitution." Youth and Society 13: 471–500.
Simon, John. 1991. "Michel Foucault on Attica: An Interview." Social Justice 18: 26–34.
Simon, Rita. 1975. Women and Crime. Lexington, Mass.: Lexington Books.
Simpson, Sally S. 1989. "Feminist Theory, Crime and Justice." Criminology 27: 605–32.
Skocpol, Theda. 1985. "Bringing the State Back In: Strategies of Analysis in Current Research," in Peter B. Evans, Dietrich Rueschemeyer, and Theda Skocpol, eds., Bringing the State Back In. Pp. 3–43. Cambridge, Mass.: Harvard University Press.
———, and Edwin Amenta. 1986. "States and Social Policies." Annual Review of Sociology 12: 131–57.
Skolnick, Jerome. 1966. Justice Without Trial. New York: Wiley.
———, and James J. Fyfe. 1993. Above the Law: Police and the Excessive Use of Force. New York: The Free Press.
Skowronek, Stephen. 1982. Building a New American State: The Expansion of National Administrative Capacities, 1877–1920. New York: Cambridge University Press.
Slovak, Jeffrey S. 1986. Styles of Urban Policing: Organization, Environment and Police Styles in Selected American Cities. New York: New York University Press.
Smart, Carol. 1976. Women, Crime and Criminology: A Feminist Critique. London: Routledge & Kegan Paul.
———. 1984. The Ties that Bind: Law, Marriage, and the Reproduction of Patriarchal Relationships. London: Routledge & Kegan Paul.

———. 1989. Feminism and the Power of Law. New York: Routledge.
———. 1990. "Feminist Approaches to Criminology or Postmodern Woman Meets Atavistic Man," in Loraine Gelsthorpe and Allison Morris, eds., Feminist Perspectives in Criminology. Pp. 70–84. Philadelphia: Open University Press.
———. 1992. "The Woman of Legal Discourse." Social and Legal Studies 1: 29–44.
Smith, Tom W., and Glenn R. Dempsey. 1983. "The Polls: Ethnic Social Distance and Prejudice." Public Opinion Quarterly 47:584–600.
Social Justice. 1991. "The War on Drugs: Commentary and Critique." Social Justice 18: 1–178.
Soule, Sarah A. 1992. "Populism and Black Lynching in Georgia, 1890–1900." Social Forces 71: 431–49.
Sparrow, Malcolm, David M. Kennedy and Mark H. Moore. 1990. Beyond 911: A New Era for Policing. New York: Basic Books.
Spitzer, Steven. 1975. "Toward a Marxian Theory of Deviance." Social Problems 22: 638–51.
———. 1981. "Notes Toward a Theory of Punishment and Social Change," in Steven Spitzer and Rita Simon, eds., Research in Law and Sociology, Vol. 2. Pp. 207–29. Greenwich, Conn. :JAI Press.
Spohn, Cassia, and Jerry Cederblom. 1991. "Race and Disparities in Sentencing: A Test of the Liberation Hypothesis." Justice Quarterly 8: 305–27.
Spohn, Cassia, John Gruhl and Susan Welch. 1981–82. "The Effect of Race on Sentencing: A Re-Examination of an Unsettled Question." Law & Society Review 16: 72–88.
———. 1985. "Women Defendants in Court: The Interaction Between Sex and Race in Convicting and Sentencing." Social Science Quarterly 66:178–85.
———. 1987. "The Impact of the Ethnicity and Gender of Defendants on the Decision to Reject or Dismiss Felony Charges." Criminology 25: 175–91.
Stacey, Judith, and Barrie Thorne. 1985. "The Missing Feminist Revolution in Sociology." Social Problems 32:301–16.
Stark, Evan. 1993. "In Defense of Mandatory Arrest: A Reply to the Critics." American Behavioral Scientist 36:651–80.
Steffensmeier, Darrell J. 1978. "Crime and the Contemporary Woman: An Analysis of Changing Levels of Female Property Crime, 1960–1975." Social Forces 57: 566–84.
———. 1980. "Sex Differences in Patterns of Adult Crime, 1965–1977: A Review and Assessment." Social Forces 58: 1080–1108.
———, and John H. Kramer. 1982. "Sex-based Differences in the Sentencing of Adult Criminal Defendants: An Empirical Test and Theoretical Overview." Sociology and Social Research 66: 289–304.
Steinberg, Stephen. 1989. The Ethnic Myth: Race, Ethnicity and Class in America. Boston: Beacon Press.
Stiffman, Arlene Rubin. 1989. "Physical and Sexual Abuse in Runaway Youths." Child Abuse and Neglect 13: 417–26.
Straus, Murray, and Richard J. Gelles. 1986. "Social Change and Change in Family Violence in 1971–1985." Journal of Marriage and the Family 46: 465–79.

———, and Suzanne K. Steinmetz. 1980. Behind Closed Doors: Violence in the American Family. New York: Anchor.
Sudman, Seymour, and Norman M. Bradburn. 1983. Asking Questions. San Francisco: Jossey-Bass.
Sudnow, David. 1965. "Normal Crimes: Sociological Features of the Penal Code in a Public Defender Office." Social Problems 12: 255–75.
Sutherland, Edwin H. 1924. Criminology. Philadelphia: J.B. Lippincott.
———. 1934. Principles of Criminology. Chicago: J.B. Lippincott.
Sutton, John R. 1987. "Doing Time: Dynamics of Imprisonment in the Reformist State." American Sociological Review 52: 612–30.
———. 1988. Stubborn Children: Controlling Delinquency in the United States. Berkeley: University of California Press.
———. 1990. "Bureaucrats and Entrepreneurs: Institutional Responses to Deviant Children in the U.S., 1890–1920s." American Journal of Sociology 95: 1367–1400.
———. 1991. "The Political Economy of Madness: The Expansion of the Asylum in Progressive America." American Sociological Review 56: 665–78.
Sutton, L. Paul. 1978. Variations in Federal Criminal Sentences: A Statistical Assessment at the National Level. Albany, N.Y.: Criminal Justice Research Center.
Swidler, Ann. 1986. "Culture in Action: Symbols and Strategies." American Sociological Review 51: 273–86.
Swoboda, Joseph, Amiram Elwork, Bruce Sales and David Levine. 1979. "Knowledge of and Compliance with Privileged Communication and Child Abuse Reporting Laws." Professional Psychiatry 12:631–38.
Sykes, Gresham, and David Matza. 1957. "Techniques of Neutralization: A Theory of Delinquency." American Sociological Review 22: 664–70.
Symonds, Carolyn. 1971. "Sexual Mate-Swapping: Violation of Norms and Reconciliation of Guilt," in James M. Henslin, ed., Studies in the Sociology of Sex. Pp. 81–109. New York: Appleton-Century-Crofts.
Szasz, Thomas. 1965. Psychiatric Justice. New York: Macmillan.
Taft, Donald R. 1936. "Nationality and Crime." American Sociological Review 1:724–36.
Takaki, Ronald. 1979. Iron Cages: Race and Culture in Nineteenth-Century America. New York: Alfred A. Knopf.
———. 1982. "Reflections on Racial Patterns in America: An Historical Perspective," in Winston A. Van Horne, ed., Ethnicity and Public Policy. Pp. 1–23. Madison: University of Wisconsin Press.
Taylor, Ian, Paul Walton and Jock Young. 1973. The New Criminology. London: Routledge & Kegan Paul.
Terman, Lewis M. 1912. "The Binet-Simon Scale for Measuring Intelligence. Impressions Gained by its Application upon Four Hundred Non-Selected Children." Journal of Psycho-Asthenics 16: 103–12.
Therborn, Goern. 1977. "The Rule of Capital and the Rise of Democracy." New Left Review 103:3–41.
Thompson, E. P. 1975. Whigs and Hunters: The Origin of the Black Act. New York: Pantheon.
———. 1964. The Making of the English Working Class. New York: Pantheon.

Thompson, James D. 1967. Organizations in Action. New York: McGraw Hill.

Thornberry, Terence, and Richard Christenson. 1984. "Unemployment and Criminal Involvement: An Investigation of Reciprocal Causal Structures." American Sociological Review 49:398–411.

Tittle, Charles R. 1980. Sanctions and Social Deviance: The Question of Deterrence. New York: Praeger.

———. 1989. "Prospects for a Synthetic Theory: A Consideration of Macro-Level Criminological Activity," in Steven F. Messner, Marvin D. Krohn and Allen E. Liska, eds., Theoretical Integration in the Study of Deviance and Crime: Problems and Prospects. Pp. 161–178. Albany: State University of New York Press.

Tittle, Charles R., and Debra A. Curran. 1988. "Contingencies for Dispositional Disparities in Juvenile Justice." Social Forces 67: 23–58.

Tolnay, Stewart E., and E. M. Beck. 1992a. "Toward a Threat Model of Southern Black Lynchings," in Allen E. Liska, ed., Social Threat and Social Control. Pp. 33–52. Albany: State University of New York Press.

———. 1992b. "Racial Violence and Black Migration in the American South, 1910 to 1930." American Sociological Review 57: 103–16.

———. 1994. A Festival of Violence: An Analysis of the Lynching of African-Americans in the American South, 1882 to 1930. Urbana: University of Illinois Press.

Tolnay, Stewart E., E. M. Beck and James L. Massey. 1989. "Black Lynchings: The Power Threat Hypothesis Revisited." Social Forces 67: 605–23.

Tracey, Paul E., Marvin E. Wolfgang and Robert M. Figlio. 1990. Delinquency in Two Birth Cohorts. Boston: Plenum.

Trattner, Walter I. (ed.) 1986. Biographical Dictionary of Social Welfare in America. New York: Greenwood Press.

Trojanowicz, Robert, and Bonnie Bucqueroux. 1989. Community Policing: A Contemporary Perspective. Cincinnati, Ohio: Anderson.

Tremblay, Pierre. 1986. "The Stability of Punishment: A Follow-up of Blumstein's Hypothesis." Journal of Quantitative Criminology 2:157–80.

Tuan, Yi-Fu. 1979. Landscapes of Fear. New York: Pantheon.

Turk, Austin T. 1969a. Criminality and Legal Order. Chicago: Rand McNally.

———. 1969b. "Law as a Weapon in Social Conflict." Social Problems 23: 276–291.

———. 1982. Political Criminality: Social Control and Political Policing. Beverly Hills, Calif.: Sage Publications.

Tyor, Peter L. 1977. "'Denied the Power to Choose the Good:' Sexuality and Mental Defect in American Medical Practice, 1850–1920," Journal of Social History 10: 472–89.

———, and Leland V. Bell. 1984. Caring for the Retarded in America: A History. Westport, Conn.: Greenwood Press.

Ulmer, Gregory L.. 1985. "The Object of Post-Criticism," in Hal Foster, ed., Postmodern Culture. Pp. 83–110. London: Pluto.

U.S. Crime Commission. 1967. The Challenge of Crime in a Free Society. Washington, D.C.: Government Printing Office.

U.S. Department of the Interior, Census Office. 1883. Statistics of the Popula-

tion of the United States at the Tenth Census (June 1, 1880). Washington: Government Printing Office.
U.S. Immigration Commission. 1911. Immigration and Crime, Vol 36. Washington, D.C.: U.S. Government Printing Office.
van Maanen, John. 1974. "Working the Street," in Herbert Jacob, ed., The Potential for Reform of Criminal Justice. Pp.83–130. Beverly Hills, Calif.:Sage Publications.
———. 1990. Tales of the Field: On Writing Ethnography. Chicago: University of Chicago Press.
Vera Institute of Justice. 1977. Felony Arrests: Their Prosecution and Disposition in New York City's Courts. New York: Vera Institute of Justice.
von Hirsch, Andrew. 1985. Past or Future Crimes. New Brunswick, N.J.: Rutgers University Press.
Walker, Henry A., and Bernard P. Cohen. 1985. "Scope Statements: Imperatives for Evaluating Theory." American Sociological Review 50: 288–301.
Walkowitz, Daniel. 1990. "The Making of a Feminine Professional Identity: Social Workers in the 1920s." The American Historical Review 95: 1051–75.
Wallerstein, Immanuel. 1988. "The Ideological Tensions of Capitalism: Universalism versus Racism and Sexism," in Joan Smith, J. Collins, T. Hopkins and A. Muhammad, eds., Racism, Sexism, and the World-System. Pp. 3–9. New York: Greenwood Press.
———. 1991a. "The Concept of National Development, 1917–1989: Elegy and Requiem. Fernand Braudel Center, State University of New York, Binghamton, N.Y. Unpublished manuscript.
———. 1991b. Unthinking Social Science: The Limits of Nineteenth Century Paradigms. Cambridge, U.K.: Polity Press.
Walsh, Anthony. 1987. "The Sexual Stratification Hypothesis and Sexual Assault in Light of the Changing Conceptions of Race." Criminology 25: 153–73.
Walshok, Mary Lindenstein. 1971. "The Emergence of Middle-Class Deviant Subcultures: The Case of Swingers." Social Problems 18: 488–95.
Watt, David, and Michelle Fuerst. 1989. 1990 Tremeear's Criminal Code. Toronto: Carswell.
Wattenberg, Ben. 1987. The Birth Dearth. New York: Pharos Books/Ballantine Books.
Wauchope, Barbara, and Murray Straus. 1990. "Physical Punishment and Physical Abuse of American Children: Incidence Rates by Age, Gender, and Occupational Class," in Murray Straus and Richard J. Gelles, eds., Physical Violence in American Families. Pp. 133–48. New Brunswick, N.J.: Transaction.
Weber, Max. 1967. The Sociology of Law. New York: Scribners.
Weedon, Chris. 1987. Feminist Practice and Poststructuralist Theory. New York: Basil Blackwell.
Weeks, John R. 1981. Population. Belmont, Calif.: Wadsworth.
Weicher, John C. 1970. "Determinants of Central City Expenditure: Some Overlooked Factors and Problems." National Tax Journal 23:379–96.

Weick, Karl E. 1976. "Educational Organizations as Loosely-Coupled Systems." Administrative Science Quarterly 21: 1–19.
Weinberg, Julius. 1972. Edward Alsworth Ross and the Sociology of Progressivism. Madison: The State Historical Society of Wisconsin.
Weisburd, David, Elin Waring, and Stanton Wheeler. 1990. "Class, Status, and the Punishment of White-Collar Criminals." Law and Social Inquiry 15: 223–43.
Weisburd, David, Stanton Wheeler, Elin Waring, and Nancy Bode. 1991. Crimes of the Middle Classes: White-Collar Offenders in the Federal Courts. New Haven, Conn.: Yale University Press.
Westley, William. 1970. Violence and the Police. Cambridge, Mass.: MIT Press.
Wheaton, Blair, Bengt Muthen, Duane F. Alwin and Gene F. Summers. 1977. "Assessing Reliability and Stability in Panel Models," in David R. Heise, ed., Sociological Methodology. Pp. 84–136. San Francisco: Jossey-Bass.
Wheeler, Stanton, David Weisburd, and Nancy Bode. 1982. "Sentencing the White-Collar Offender: Rhetoric and Reality." American Sociological Review 47: 641–59.
Wheeler, Stanton, Kenneth Mann, and Austin Sarat. 1988. Sitting in Judgment: The Sentencing of White-Collar Offenders. New Haven, Conn.: Yale University Press.
Wheeler, Stanton, and Mitchell Lewis Rotham. 1982. "The Organization as Weapon in White-Collar Crime." Michigan Law Review 80: 1403–26.
Whitbeck, Les B., and Ronald S. Simons. 1990. "Life on the Streets—The Victimization of Runaway and Homeless Adolescents." Youth and Society 22: 108–25.
Widom, Cathy Spatz. 1989a. "Child Abuse, Neglect, and Adult Behavior: Research Design and Findings on Criminality, Violence, and Child Abuse." American Journal of Orthopsychiatry 59:355–67.
———. 1989b. "The Cycle of Violence." Science 244: 160–66.
Wiebe, Robert. 1967. The Search for Order 1877–1930. New York: Hill and Wang.
Wilbanks, William. 1987. The Myth of a Racist Criminal Justice System. Monterey, Calif: Brooks/Cole.
Williams, Kristen M. 1978. The Role of the Victim in the Prosecution of Violent Crimes. Washington, D.C.: Institute for Law and Social Research.
Williams, Robin, Jr. 1952. American Society: A Sociological Interpretation. New York: Alfred A. Knopf.
Wilson, David B. 1989. "The Narrow Basis of Roe vs Wade." The Boston Sunday Globe, January 22: A27.
Wilson, James Q. 1968. Varieties of Police Behavior. Cambridge, Mass.: Harvard University Press.
———, and Richard J. Herrnstein. 1985. Crime and Human Nature. New York: Simon and Schuster.
Wilson, Margo I., and Margo Daly. 1987. "Risk of Maltreatment of Children Living with Stepparents," in Richard J. Gelles and Jane B. Lancaster, eds.,

Child Abuse and Neglect: Biosocial Dimensions. Pp. 215–32. New York: Aldine de Gruyter.

Wilson, Margo I., Martin Daly and Suzanne J. Weghorst. 1980. "Household Composition and the Risk of Child Abuse and Neglect." Journal of Biosocial Science 12: 333–40.

Wilson, Stephen V., and A. Howard Matz. 1977. "Obtaining Evidence for Federal Economic Crime Prosecutions: An Overview and Analysis of Investigative Methods." American Criminal Law Review 14: 651–72.

Wilson, William J. 1978. The Declining Significance of Race. Chicago: University of Chicago Press.

Wisconsin Women's Law Journal. 1987. Special Issue on Equality, Vol. 3.

Wolff, Janet. 1991. "The Global and the Specific: Reconciling Conflicting Theories of Culture," in Anthony King, ed., Culture, Globalization and the World-System: Contemporary Conditions for the Representation of Identity. Pp. 161–73. Binghamton, N.Y.: Department of Art and Art History, State University of New York at Binghamton.

Wolfgang, Marvin E. 1958. Patterns of Criminal Homicide. Philadelphia: University of Pennsylvania Press.

Wolfgang, Marvin. 1974. "Racial Discrimination in the Death Sentence for Rape," in William J. Bowers, ed., Executions in America. Pp. 109–20. Lexington, Mass.: Lexington Books.

———, and Marc Riedel. 1973. "Race, Judicial Discretion and the Death Penalty." Annals of the American Academy of Political and Social Science 407: 119–33.

———, Robert M. Figlio, and Thorsten Sellin. 1972. Delinquency in a Birth Cohort. Chicago: University of Chicago Press.

———, Robert M. Figlio, Paul E. Tracy, and Simon I. Singer. 1985. The National Survey of Crime Severity. Washington, D.C.: U.S. Government Printing Office.

Worrall, Anne. 1990. Offending Women: Female Lawbreakers and the Criminal Justice System. London: Routledge & Kegan Paul.

Wright, George C. 1990. Racial Violence in Kentucky 1865–1940: Lynching, Mob Rule, and "Legal Lynchings." Baton Rouge: Louisiana State University Press.

Wuthnow, Robert. 1987. Meaning and Moral Order. Berkeley: University of California Press.

———, James Davison Hunter, Albert Bergesen, and Edith Kurtzweil. 1984. Cultural Analysis: The Work of Peter L. Berger, Mary Douglas, Michel Foucault, and Jürgen Habermas. Boston: Routledge & Kegan Paul.

Xie, Yu, and Charles F. Manski. 1989. "The Logit Model and Response-Based Samples." Sociological Methods and Research 17: 283–302.

Young, Alison. 1992. Untitled Manuscript on Feminism, Postmodernism, and Criminology. Department of Law, University of Lancaster, Lancaster, England. Unpublished manuscript.

Young, Iris Marion. 1990. Justice and the Politics of Difference. Princeton, N.J.: Princeton University Press.

Young, Peter. 1983. "Sociology, the State, and Penal Relations," in David Garland and Peter Young, eds., The Power to Punish: Contemporary Penality and Social Analysis. Pp. 84–100. London: Heineman Educational Books.

Zatz, Marjorie S. 1984. "Race, Ethnicity, and Determinate Sentencing: A New Dimension to an Old Controversy." Criminology 22: 147–71.

———. 1987. "The Changing Forms of Racial/Ethnic Biases in Sentencing." Journal of Research in Crime and Delinquency 24: 69–92.

Zellman, Gail, and Stephen Antler. 1990. "Mandated Reporters and CPS: A Study in Frustration." Public Welfare 48: 30–7.

Zimring, Franklin E., and Gordon Hawkins. 1986. Capital Punishment and the American Agenda. New York: Cambridge University Press.

———. 1991. The Scale of Imprisonment. Chicago: University of Chicago Press.

About the Book

This book brings together the most recent advances in theory and research on the relationship between social inequality and the control of criminal behavior. Noted sociologists and criminologists explore the ways in which social class, race, gender, and age shape societal and organizational responses to crime. They offer new directions for theoretical revision, innovation, and integration as well as new ways of conceptualizing the linkages between dimensions of inequality and a variety of social control mechanisms. The empirical research included here grapples with two questions that have become increasingly central to the study of law, crime, and social control: In what ways are social control mechanisms linked with one another? What role does human agency play in mediating the link between broader social forces and the social control of groups and individuals?

About the Editors and Contributors

Celesta A. Albonetti is professor of sociology at Texas A&M University. Her research focuses on those features of criminal justice organizations that dictate its social control responses.

E. M. Beck, professor of sociology at the University of Georgia, has completed a monograph on Southern lynchings and is continuing his interest in race and violence by examining racial violence in the twentieth century.

Gina Beretta is a research scientist at Battelle in Seattle, Washington. She is currently studying issues related to contraceptive choice among women in the United States.

George S. Bridges is professor of sociology at the University of Washington. His recent research examines race, gender, and the punishment of juveniles.

Pat Carlen is lecturer in criminology at the University of Keele in England. She has published extensively on the imprisonment of women, focusing on the role of gender in imprisonment decisions.

Kathleen Daly is professor of sociology at the University of Michigan. Her research documents the importance of gender, particularly gender-based roles, to prosecutorial and judicial decisions.

John Hagan is professor of law at the University of Toronto. His most recent work focuses on the importance of both class and gender to our understanding of historical changes in social control.

Darnell F. Hawkins, professor of criminal justice at the University of Illinois–Chicago, examines the link between race and social control over time and at the societal level.

James Inverarity is professor of sociology at Western Washington University. His research explores the link between changing economic conditions and incarceration rates.

Allen E. Liska is professor of sociology at the State University of New York. His most recent work explores the functions of crime, particularly the extent to which crime undermines or strengthens social solidarity.

Bill McCarthy is a professor in the Department of Sociology at the University of Victoria in British Columbia. He and John Hagan have written several articles on adolescent homelessness and crime.

Peter K. Manning is professor of criminal justice at Michigan State University. His particular interest is the organizational (as opposed to environmental) determinants of police behavior.

Martha A. Myers is professor of sociology at the University of Georgia. Her research examines the relationship between socioeconomic changes and trends in the criminal punishment of whites and blacks in the late nineteenth century.

Anthony M. Platt is professor at California State University–Sacramento. His work elaborates a distinctively Marxian perspective on social control.

Nicole Hahn Rafter is professor of sociology at Northeastern University. Her most recent work involves an exploration of the rise of the American eugenics movement.

Cassia Spohn is professor of criminal justice at the University of Nebraska–Omaha. Her interest centers on race and ethnicity, particularly the role each plays within the criminal justice system.

John R. Sutton is professor of sociology at the University of California at Santa Barbara. He is best known for a recent monograph that identifies the social sources of changing definitions of delinquency in the United States between 1640 and 1981.

Charles R. Tittle is professor of sociology at Washington State University. His current interest lies in the relationships among social class, crime, and criminal punishment.

Stewart E. Tolnay, professor of sociology at the State University of New York, is exploring the relationship between economic and demographic factors and levels of informal social control, namely, the lynching of blacks in the American South.

Index

Abuse. *See* Children; Family; Social control
African-Americans, 5, 44, 104–107, 111–114, 152, 168–193, 249–268. *See also* Crime; Ethnicity; Race; Social control
Asian-Americans, 104–105, 111–113, 115(n4)

Becker, Gary, 54, 148, 150
Becker, Howard, 73, 231
Black, Donald, 5–6, 36, 89–90, 100, 153–154, 162, 179, 195, 264
Blalock, Hubert M., 61–63, 109–110, 155, 190
Blumstein, Alfred, 3, 58, 123–124, 160
Bonger, Willem, 33–34, 102, 104
Border states in U.S. South, 185–191
Bourdieu, Pierre, 9–10, 80–85, 245
Bureaucratic theories, 22, 46–49, 51. *See also* Conflict theories; Consensus theories; Poststructural theories; Rational choice theories; Social-psychological theories; Theoretical integration

Career criminals. *See* Criminal careers
Chambliss, William, 30–34, 106, 208, 249. *See also* Conflict theories
Children
  abuse of, 195–196, 198–200, 228–229
  welfare, 7–8, 196–197, 200–226
  welfare reform, 7–8, 15, 227–248
  See also Family; Social control; Social welfare
Class
  and crime, 38, 99–100
  and gender, 163–164, 171
  and social control, 3–5, 10, 37–38, 74, 81–82, 88–94, 106–107, 269–282
Conflict theories, 3–4, 9–10, 14, 32–39, 50–51, 60–71, 73, 105–106, 108–109, 113–116, 159–161, 249–268. *See also* Bureaucratic theories; Consensus theories; Poststructural theories; Rational choice theories; Social-

psychological theories; Theoretical integration
Consensus theories, 3–4, 9, 22–32, 49–51, 56–60. *See also* Bureaucratic theories; Conflict theories; Poststructural theories; Rational choice theories; Social-psychological theories; Theoretical integration
Control theory, 137–138
Crime
  control of, 4–5, 21–52, 53–56, 58, 59–60, 84, 87–88, 90, 100–103, 107–117, 119–120, 123–125, 135–136, 158–160, 195–197
  and inequality, 4, 17, 25–26, 158–176
  and the life course, 244–246
  perceptions of, 18
  theories of, 4, 72–74, 101–103, 137–139, 176, 216–222, 232–233, 248(n4)
  violent, 25–26, 35–36, 81, 85–96, 136, 167–175, 176–193, 195, 198–210, 249–268
  white-collar, 269–282
  See also Class; Gender; Punishment; Race; Social control; Violence and violent crime
Criminal careers, 244–246
Criminality
  and gender, 11, 44, 134–139, 158, 170–171, 199
  and race, 11, 158–174, 249–266
  See also Ethnicity; Gender; Race
Criminal justice, administration of, 16, 23–24, 33–53, 161–175, 177, 208–209, 271
Criminal justice, outcomes
  class differences in, 134–135, 269–282
  gender differences in, 44, 117–133, 134–135, 169–175
  race differences in, 16, 161–175, 249–268
  See also Sentencing; Social control

Dahrendorf, Ralf, 33, 60–61, 66
Delinquency, 175–211, 216, 222, 227–248

327

Deviance, 227–234, 238–241
Disparity, 118, 131(n7), 251–253. *See also* Punishment
Durkheim, Emile, 3–4, 23, 56–57, 59, 73, 149–150, 156(n4), 160, 240–241, 243, 247

Economic explanations of punishment. *See* Conflict theories; Punishment
Elites, 33, 37–38, 63–66, 69
Erikson, Kai T., 54, 56–57, 243
Ethnicity
  and crime, 11, 100–105
  and social control, 5, 11, 13–14, 16–17, 77, 99–105, 131, 171–172, 247–268
Eugenics, 15, 215–226
Executions, 12–13, 151–152, 176–195. *See also* Social control

Family
  abuse and violence, 14, 195–211, 228
  domestic conflict and police, 86–94, 197, 209
  privacy, 196
  role in society, 25, 27, 71(n1), 137, 195–211
  role of women in, 164
Feminism, 10, 117, 125, 134–135, 142–143
Feminist theories, 10, 12, 71(n1), 117, 125–126, 129, 132(n18), 135–137, 142–143, 144(n1), 160–161. *See also* Bureaucratic theories; Conflict theories; Consensus theories; Poststructural theories; Rational choice theories; Social-psychological theories; Theoretical integration
Forms of social control, 6–8, 12–14, 147–175, 176–194, 195–211
Foucault, Michel, 73, 154, 220–221, 236

Garland, David, 72, 221, 280
Gender
  and class, 136, 138–139
  and crime, 14, 138–139, 158–165, 170–171, 209
  and race, 77, 118, 131(nn 6, 11), 132(n13), 137–138, 140–141, 170–173
  and social control, 5, 11–13, 17, 44, 75–76, 91, 93, 117–134, 140–144, 152–153, 158–175
  See also Crime; Social control
Gouldner, Alvin, 37, 46, 73

Heredity and crime, 215–218

Hispanic Americans, 104–105, 112, 115(n4)
Homelessness, 14, 199–211
Hospitalization of the mentally ill. *See* Social control
Human agency, 7–8, 10, 14–15, 75–76, 78, 143–144, 158–175, 215–282. *See also* Criminal justice, administration of; Criminal justice, outcomes
Human capital, 13, 148–152, 156

Ideology, 63, 75, 91–92, 135–137, 229, 238
Ignatieff, Michael, 230
Imprisonment
  and the labor force. *See* Labor force participation
  and race, 152, 158–175, 249–268
  research on, 13, 58–59, 66, 150–153, 160–166, 169–173, 261–262
  sex differences in, 13, 152–153, 158–175
Incarceration. *See* Imprisonment
Inequality, 4–5, 23–24, 30–32, 37, 45, 48, 137, 176–177, 217, 227
  and class, 164–165, 216–217
  and ethnicity, 11
  and gender, 11–12, 45, 117–144, 158–174
  and race, 11, 99, 158–174, 176–194
Informal social control, 179–194

Jim Crow laws, 192
Juvenile justice and juvenile court, 39–46, 227–248

Kirchheimer, Otto. *See* Rusche, Georg

Labeling theory (social reaction theory), 36–37, 73, 232–233, 245–246
Labor force participation
  and crime, 13–14
  and punishment, 147–157, 168–175
Labor markets, 13, 60, 147–157. *See also* Punishment
Law, 158, 161–162, 167–168, 174–175, 196, 208–209. *See also* Criminal justice, administration of
Lynchings. *See* Social control

Maltreatment of children. *See* Children
Marx, Karl, 10, 34, 60, 66. *See also* Marxism
Marxism, 62–63, 72–73
Marxist theories. *See* Conflict theories
Mental illness, 12–13, 53. *See also* Social control

Methodological issues, 11, 66–69, 118–123, 127–130, 140, 160–161, 181–182, 198–200, 204–205, 250–253
Minorities, 4–5, 40, 44, 61–64, 99–116, 155, 158–175, 249–268. *See also* African-Americans; Asian-Americans; Crime; Hispanic Americans; Imprisonment; Inequality; Native Americans; Punishment; Race
Moral individualism, 149–150

Native Americans, 104–105, 111

Parens Patriae, doctrine of, 218
Parole, 162, 167–168
Parsons, Talcott, 23, 229
Police, 9–10, 25, 33, 42, 53, 74, 80–96, 108–109, 113–114
Popular justice theories, 14, 177–179. *See also* Bureaucratic theories; Conflict theories; Consensus theories; Poststructural theories; Rational choice theories; Social-psychological theories; Theoretical integration
Poststructural theories, 10–12, 139–144. *See also* Bureaucratic theories; Conflict theories; Consensus theories; Rational choice theories; Social-psychological theories; Theoretical integration
Prior criminal record, 119, 121, 133(n27), 198, 259
Problem populations, 4, 62–64, 162–163
Progressives and the Progressive era, 219, 234
Psychiatric treatment. *See* Social control
Punishment, 53, 56–60, 269–282
  disparity, 13, 16, 117–134, 158–175, 251–253
  gender differences in, 117–137, 158–175
  and labor markets, 13–14, 147–157, 164, 168, 176
  role of victim and offender relationships, 251–253
  and the social context, 15–17, 175
  symbolic, 269–282
  of white-collar offenders, 16–17, 91–92, 269–282
  See also Social control

Quinney, Richard, 33–34, 62–64, 249, 252–253

Race
  and crime, 165–166, 176–177, 249–268
  discrimination and prejudice, 5, 8, 61–62, 77, 99–116, 127–128, 249–268
  and gender, 77, 118, 131(nn 6, 11), 132(n13), 137–138, 140–141, 170–173
  and social control, 11, 14, 16, 75, 99–115, 121, 127–128, 132(n19), 151–152, 165–166, 176–194, 249–268
Rational choice theories, 54–56. *See also* Bureaucratic theories; Conflict theories; Consensus theories; Poststructural theories; Social-psychological theories; Theoretical integration
Reforms, 7–8, 15–16, 215–226, 227–248
Rothman, David, 216, 225, 229, 230
Rusche, Georg, 3, 73, 147–151, 155–156

Sentencing, 13, 16–17, 118–119, 121, 161–162, 249–282. *See also* Criminal justice, outcomes; Punishment; Social control
Sexuality, 27, 75, 122
Social class. *See* Class
Social control. *See also* Class; Gender; Race
  of children and youth, 7–8, 14, 15, 75–76, 95(n7), 195–211, 227–248. *See also* Children; Delinquency; Family
  and courts, 25, 33, 39, 40, 42–43, 53, 122, 135. *See also* Criminal justice, outcomes; Sentencing
  of crime, 38, 54–56, 99–100, 117–144, 158–175, 215–218, 249–268, 270–282. *See also* Crime; Criminality; Violence and violent crime
  definition of, 53, 80, 83–84
  by execution and lynching, 14, 66–67, 151, 176–194. *See also* Executions
  and fear, 40–45, 50–51. *See also* Social-psychological theories; Theoretical integration
  and the historical context, 5–6, 14–16, 18, 28–29, 56–57, 175, 219
  hospitalization, 53, 66–67, 162–163, 165
  and identification, 40, 41–45, 50
  professionalization of, 15, 215–226. *See also* Eugenics
  sentencing, 16, 158–175, 249–282. *See also* Criminal justice, outcomes; Law; Punishment; Sentencing
  of status offenders, 228. *See* Delinquency
  sterilization, 217. *See also* Eugenics

and threat, 10, 14, 16, 23–30, 33–35, 42, 44, 49–50, 57, 61–66, 68–70, 86, 108–109, 114, 150–155, 162, 167–169, 176, 180, 193, 205, 216, 235, 243, 252, 265. *See also* Conflict theories; Problem populations; Threatening populations
and urbanization, 8, 169, 171. *See also* Urbanization and urban areas
of white-collar crime, 269–282. *See also* Sentencing
of women, 5, 11–13, 17, 44, 45, 91, 93, 117–133, 134–144, 152–153, 158–175
Social control, forms of. *See* Forms of social control
Social-psychological theories, 22, 39–46. *See also* Bureaucratic theories; Conflict theories; Consensus theories; Poststructural theories; Rational choice theories; Theoretical integration
Social standing. *See* Class
Social structure, 12, 13–14, 45, 53, 56, 59–60, 139–140, 147, 168, 218–220, 240
Social welfare, 220–226
Socioeconomic status. *See* Class
South, the American, 14, 151–152, 153, 176–194
Southern whites, 176–194
Spitzer, Steven, 3–4, 6, 62–65, 162–163. *See also* Conflict theories; Problem populations
Sterilization. *See* Social control
Structural functional theories. *See* Consensus theories
Symbolic capital, 9, 10, 81–83, 86, 90–91, 93. *See* Labor force participation; Labor markets; Punishment

Symbolic punishment. *See* Punishment

Theoretical elaboration, 4, 9–10, 53–72
Theoretical integration, 4–5, 32, 46, 49–52
Theories of inequality. *See* Bureaucratic theories; Conflict theories; Consensus theories; Poststructural theories; Rational choice theories; Social-psychological theories; Theoretical integration
Therapeutic state, 15, 227–248
Threat. *See also* Problem populations; Social control; Threatening populations
Threatening populations, 40–42, 61–62, 69–71, 150–151, 162. *See also* Conflict theories; Problem populations
Turk, Austin, 7, 33, 61, 63, 100, 252. *See also* Conflict theories

Urbanization and urban areas, 8, 110, 121, 154, 169, 171, 173, 218

Victim and offender relationships. *See* Punishment
Vigilantes, 179–194. *See* Social control
Violence and violent crime, 16, 25–26, 35–36, 81, 85–96, 136, 167–175, 176–193, 195, 198–210, 249–268. *See also* Crime; Criminality

Weber, Max, 95(n6), 229, 233
White-collar offenders. *See* Sentencing; Social control

CPSIA information can be obtained at www.ICGtesting.com
Printed in the USA
BVOW01s1257070716

454696BV00003B/37/P